THE
AMERICAN IRISH

◆

A HISTORY

STUDIES IN MODERN HISTORY

General editors: John Morrill and David Cannadine

This series, intended primarily for students, will tackle significant historical issues in concise volumes which are both stimulating and scholarly. The authors combine a broad approach, explaining the current state of our knowledge in the area, with their own research and judgements; and the topics chosen range widely in subject, period and place.

Titles already published

THE AMERICAN IRISH

◆

A HISTORY

Kevin Kenny

Associate Professor of History
Department of History
Boston College

Longman

An imprint of **Pearson Education**

Harlow, England · London · New York · Reading, Massachusetts · San Francisco
Toronto · Don Mills, Ontario · Sydney · Tokyo · Singapore · Hong Kong · Seoul
Taipei · Cape Town · Madrid · Mexico City · Amsterdam · Munich · Paris · Milan

Pearson Education Limited

Edinburgh Gate
Harlow
Essex CM20 2JE
United Kingdom

and Associated Companies throughout the world

Visit us on the World Wide Web at
www.pearsoneduc.com

Published in the United States of America
by Pearson Education Inc., New York

First published in Great Britain in 2000

ISBN 0 582–27817–1 PPR
ISBN 0 582–27818–X CSD

British Library Cataloguing in Publication Data
A CIP catalogue record for this book can be obtained from the British Library.

Library of Congress Cataloging-in-Publication Data
Kenny, Kevin, 1960–
    The American Irish / Kevin Kenny.
        p. cm.
    Includes bibliographical references (p.) and index.
    ISBN 0–582–27818–X — ISBN 0–582–27817–1 (pbk.)
    1. Irish Americans—History.   2. United States—Emigration and immigration—History.
3. Ireland—Emigration and immigration—History. I. Title.

E184.I6 K47 2000
973'.049162—dc21   00–021234

04 03 02 01

Set by 35 in 11.5/14 pt Garamond
Produced by Pearson Education Asia Pte Ltd.
Printed in Singapore

To Michael Crocitto Kenny

CONTENTS

——— ◆ ———

LIST OF ILLUSTRATIONS

◆

PREFACE

◆

As many as seven million Irish men, women and children have crossed the Atlantic for North America since the foundation of the first English colonies there in the early seventeenth century. Almost five million of them went to the United States between 1820 and 1920 alone. This vast movement of people was of great historical significance on both sides of the Atlantic. It played a fundamental role in the shaping of modern Ireland, and it determined in no small measure the economic, political and cultural development of the United States, where some 45 million people today (one-sixth of the population) claim some degree of Irish ancestry. The mass migration of the Irish has been the subject of intensive scholarly inquiry by historians on both sides of the Atlantic, resulting in a vast and varied literature on discrete aspects of the subject. But the last general histories of the American Irish were published in the 1960s, and there is a compelling need for a new synthesis. This book is designed to fill the gap.

The book is the product of a decade's reading, research and teaching in two very different fields, modern Irish history and the history of the United States. Studying the great Irish migration to North America has allowed me to bring these two fields together. As a work of synthesis, the book draws heavily on the scholarship of the historians mentioned in the bibliography and endnotes. Like every scholar working in the field today, I owe my biggest intellectual debt to Kerby Miller's monumental *Emigrants and Exiles: Ireland and the Irish Exodus to North America* (1985), which remains by far the best account of the causes, course and consequences of Irish emigration to North America. Building on the insights of a generation of scholars working on both sides of the Atlantic, the current volume attempts to reach a wider and less specialized audience of students and general readers.

Most of this book was written at the University of Texas at Austin, where I spent five very pleasant years as an assistant professor. I would like to acknowledge here the assistance, criticism and advice I received from my friends, students and colleagues in Austin, especially Marian Barber, Jason Bell, Dave Bowman, Theresa Case, Leilah Danielson, Alison Frazier, Michael Hall, Neil Kamil, Hal Langfur, Roger Louis, Martha Newman, Gunther Peck, Michael Stoff and Kim Wilson. Special thanks go to Bob Olwell, Jim

Sidbury and Mauricio Tenorio for reading several draft chapters and offering detailed criticism. The book was completed at Boston College, where Andy Bunie, Robin Fleming, Brian Liddy, Ruth-Ann Harris, Cynthia Lynn Lyerly, Prasannan Parthasarathi, Peg Preston, David Quigley, Rob Savage and the members of the Irish Studies Graduate Colloquium offered valuable criticism and comments. Kevin O'Neill, co-director of the Irish Studies Program, deserves particular thanks for his numerous helpful suggestions. Finally, special thanks are due to the Irish American Cultural Institute, which provided financial support for this project through the O'Shaughnessy family of St. Paul, Minnesota.

Rosanna Crocitto, Jennifer O'Connor, Edward O'Donnell, Peter Quinn and Patrick Walsh each read the entire manuscript and made innumerable suggestions for its improvement. The book is immeasurably better for their contribution. Daniel Noonan did an excellent job on the proofs.

The editorial team at Pearson Education – Heather McCallum, Emily Pillars, Pen Campbell and Louise Corless – did a splendid job, offering judicious and well-timed advice and bringing the book to publication with remarkable efficiency. I would also like to thank Andrew MacLennan and Hilary Shaw for their work on the initial stages of this project.

David Cannadine deserves a particular note of gratitude. My first attempt to combine the histories of Ireland and the United States took the form of a doctoral dissertation at Columbia University, in which I examined the Molly Maguire conflict in nineteenth-century Ireland and Pennsylvania. Shortly after that work was completed, Professor Cannadine invited me to apply the transatlantic approach I had adopted in my study of the Molly Maguires to the history of the American Irish more generally by contributing a volume to the Longman series 'Studies in Modern History'. The result is the current book.

My own intellectual biography made the opportunity to write a book of this sort quite compelling. Like most Irishmen of my generation, I come from a sizeable family of which several members have emigrated. Members of the family today are to be found not only in Ireland but also in England, Canada, New Zealand and the United States. My own emigrant itinerary has taken me from Dublin to London to Edinburgh to Philadelphia to New York City to Austin, Texas and, finally, to Boston. Most of my friends from early adulthood have also left Ireland, and live now in Australia, the United States or England. But, if my itinerary was not untypical of my generation, it was distinctive in at least one respect. Along the way I picked up a degree in modern history at Edinburgh University, spent a year studying American history as an undergraduate at the University of Pennsylvania, and then completed a doctorate in American history at Columbia. Throughout this educational journey, I tried to combine a knowledge of Irish history with an expertise in that of the United States. For both personal and intellectual reasons, then, this has been an ideal book for me to write.

The best thing that happened to me along my journey was meeting Rosanna Crocitto. New York City was the perfect place for immigrants from Italy and Ireland to meet, fall in love and get married. The book is dedicated to our son, Michelino, for reasons he will appreciate.

The next one will be for Owen, who has only recently joined us.

ACKNOWLEDGEMENTS

———— ◆ ————

We would like to thank the following for their permission to reproduce illustrations taken from their works within this title.

Frank Leslie's Illustrated Newspaper,
Harper's Weekly,
Museum of the City of New York,
National Gallery of Ireland,
National Library of Ireland,
Oxford University Press,
Perry-Castañeda Library, University of Texas at Austin,
State Historical Society of Wisconsin,
The Illustrated London News,
The Pictorial Times

Also, thanks goes to the *Crawford Municipal Art Gallery* for the use of their painting *Letter from America,* by James Brenan, which has been reproduced on the cover.

Ireland: county, provincial and political boundaries

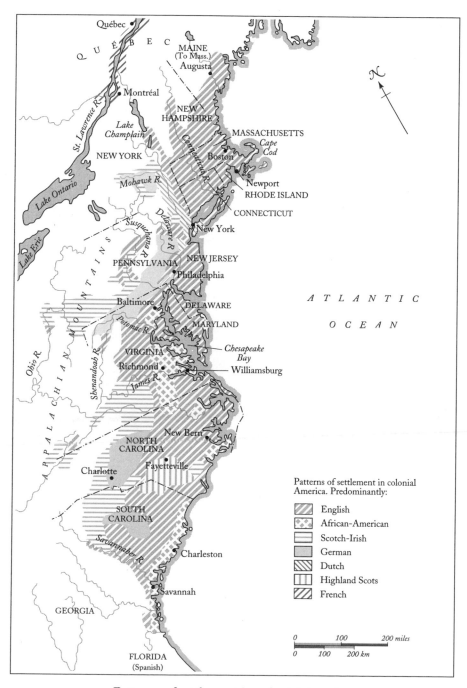

Patterns of settlement in colonial America

'Whether we may wish it or not, one half of Ireland is here.'
Thomas D'Arcy McGee, *A History of Irish Settlers in North America* (Boston, 1855), 195

INTRODUCTION

———— ◆ ————

History, in some fundamental sense, is about change over time. The best way to introduce a general subject to new readers is to write a narrative history that incorporates rigorous analysis into a clear chronological framework. In its initial conception, this book was arranged thematically, with each chapter examining a central topic in Irish-American history (migration, settlement, labour, religion, politics and nationalism) for the full period, 1700 to 2000. This approach was useful in providing an analytical framework to guide my research, but it quickly became clear that it would yield a book more suitable for experts and specialists than for students and general readers. The history of the great Irish migration to North America falls naturally into six sequential periods — colonial, pre-famine, famine, post-famine, early twentieth-century and late twentieth-century — and these six periods provide the chronological structure of this book.

While any account of the American Irish must place the period 1820 to 1920 at its heart, this is not to say that previous or subsequent periods were unimportant. Far from it. What will hopefully distinguish this book from previous histories, indeed, is the attention it pays to both the eighteenth and the twentieth century. The latter period, in particular, is only beginning to undergo the sustained historical investigation it deserves. Twentieth-century Irish-American political history has been studied in depth, but the social, cultural and even religious history of this period are still in their infancy compared to the rich body of historical literature that has been produced on the nineteenth century. One thing that is new about the current book is the sustained attention it gives to the period since 1900, where the object of study is not just immigration but the multi-generational ethnic group. A second principal innovation of the book is that it incorporates eighteenth-century emigrants from Ulster into the larger story of Irish transatlantic history. Before the arrival of Catholic Irish immigrants in massive numbers from the 1830s onward, Irish America was fundamentally Protestant in composition and character. Throughout the previous century, the typical Irish immigrant in America had been a Presbyterian from the northern province of Ulster, rather than a Catholic peasant from Munster or Connacht.

Nonetheless, most histories of the American Irish concentrate on the nineteenth-century migration at the expense of the Protestant migration from Ulster that preceded it. For most Americans today, the term 'Irish Americans' refers to descendants of Catholic refugees from the Great Famine of the 1840s, the one event from Irish history that almost everybody knows something about. The Great Famine, indeed, is part of American (and not just Irish-American) historical memory. In the 1990s several states mandated or recommended (not without controversy) that it be included on their high school history curricula, usually as one option in a required component called 'Holocaust Studies'. The contribution of the Catholic Irish to the labour movement is also quite well known, and Irish involvement in American politics from Tammany Hall to the Kennedys is justly celebrated. But what about the other Irish Americans, the Protestants who preceded the Catholic Irish by more than a century and who, mainly as a result of this priority, claim roughly the same number of descendants (some 22 million) in the United States today?

The great Presbyterian migration out of Ulster to North America between 1700 and 1850 has typically been segregated from the mainstream of both Irish and Irish-American history. Yet it cries out for understanding within an integrated context of transatlantic history. This book represents one modest step in that direction. Its starting point is geographical: it takes as its subject all Irish men and women who migrated from the island of Ireland to the present-day United States, rather than limiting the inquiry to particular groups of Irish people defined according to region, religion or culture. In broad transatlantic perspective, the Presbyterian emigrants of the eighteenth century and the Catholic Irish of the nineteenth have a great deal in common and are part of the same general story.

Why, then, is John F. Kennedy rather than Andrew Jackson considered the first Irish president of the United States? Jackson's parents emigrated from Carrickfergus, County Antrim in 1765, and settled in South Carolina, where he was born two years later; Kennedy's great-grandfather left County Wexford during the Great Famine, more than a century before the famous presidential election of 1960. Jackson was surely, in some basic sense, more directly Irish than that wealthy and urbane third-generation American, John F. Kennedy. But Jackson and the other Ulster-origin presidents of the United States have never been considered Irish in America, nor in Ireland (except perhaps in Ulster itself). The exclusion of these so-called 'Scotch-Irish' from authentic Irishness, and their consequent inclusion as true Americans, depended on definitions of national, ethnic and racial identity on both sides of the Atlantic, in which religion predictably occupied a central place. Not only did Catholic nationalists in both Ireland and America exclude Protestants from their definition of Irishness, Protestant Irish Americans from the 1830s onwards eagerly embraced the term 'Scotch-Irish' as a way of distinguishing themselves from the incoming waves of Catholic Irish immigrants. A further cause of the separation of 'Scotch-Irish' and Catholic Irish immigrants, of course, was the relative concentration of the former in the American South and the latter in the Northeast, Midwest, and West.

The 'Scotch-Irish' fade into the background of the story told in these pages after the early nineteenth century, having occupied center stage up to that point. Not only did Irish America cease to be Protestant and become predominantly Catholic in the early nineteenth century, as part of the same process the Ulster Irish began to fade from the historical record. To the extent that they became American they also became, if not quite invisible, increasingly difficult to distinguish from the native-born Protestant population. There is surely an important history of the post-1830s Ulster Irish in America to be written, and there is doubtless plenty of untapped source material available; but historians thus far have chosen not to pursue this subject. Hence the 'Scotch-Irish' make only an occasional appearance in this book after the opening chapters. Because the 'Scotch-Irish' ceased to be Irish (in their own estimation as well as that of others) in the early nineteenth century, the story of the American Irish thereafter is largely if not exclusively a Catholic one.

The term 'American Irish', as used here and throughout the book, refers to people of Irish origin, regardless of religion or regional background, living within the borders of the present-day United States. A comprehensive history of the Irish in North America as a whole would clearly require more attention to the Canadian Irish than is given in these pages. As a work of synthesis, this book depends heavily on the existing historiography, and as yet very little work has been done explicitly comparing the Irish in the United States and Canada. The need for sustained empirical research in this regard is manifest, a need extending beyond North America to the global Irish Diaspora. But for the present, the best that can be offered here is an account of the single most important site of Irish immigration, the United States. A note on usage might also be helpful at this point. In accordance with standard practice, the term 'Scotch-Irish' is hyphenated throughout this book; the terms 'Irish American' and 'American Irish', without a hyphen, are used as nouns (e.g., 'James Michael Curley was an Irish American' or 'the American Irish were concentrated in the Northeast and Midwest'); and the term 'Irish-American' is used as an adjective (e.g. 'Curley was an Irish-American politician' or 'Irish-American settlement patterns').

The story of the great Irish migration to America makes sense only if it is examined in terms of two intersecting national histories, Irish and American, overlapping in time but divided by the Atlantic Ocean. This book, therefore, is more than a history of a single American ethnic group; it tells the story of that group in terms of the simultaneous historical development of Ireland and the United States. Each chapter begins with a detailed account of the conditions in Ireland that were giving rise to mass transatlantic emigration and is followed by an account of the Irish in America arranged in terms of such key themes as labour, race, religion, politics and nationalism. Far from treating the ethnic group as somehow self-contained, the work that follows examines the history of the Irish in the United States in light of their inter-section and involvement with the dominant themes in American national development as a whole: mass transatlantic migration, ethnic and religious pluralism, racial and nativist ideologies, religious liberty and strife, the Civil War and its causes and effects, the labour movement and the industrial revolution, urban and party politics, and the social history of ordinary men and women.

It is axiomatic of recent American immigration history that national and ethnic identities are malleable, unstable and constructed, rather than fixed, essential and unchanging. They are contested rather than consensual, fought over rather than agreed upon in advance. Senses of collective identity change with history; they do not stand outside historical time. The case of the Irish on both sides of the Atlantic is no exception. A persistent theme throughout this work is the changing meaning of *Irishness*, in both Ireland and America. Who laid claim to being Irish at different times in history and why? Who was included and excluded from the fold? Which social classes had more power in determining the meaning and limits of ethnic and national identity, and how did they exercise this power?

The historiography on the American Irish, both Protestant and Catholic, is vast, varied, and uneven. I have incorporated into my narrative some of the principal current debates among historians working in the field. Thus, Chapter 1 takes a critical look at the so-called 'Celtic Thesis', a controversial theory on the ethnic origins of the US population in 1790, when the first federal census was taken. Chapter 2 examines the recent debate on the racial status of Irish Americans in the antebellum era, the story of 'how the Irish became white'. In Chapter 3, the controversial topic is how to interpret the origins and consequences of the Irish Famine. Chapter 4 takes a look at historians' debates on the position of women in the mass migration of the late nineteenth century, as well as examining various theories of Irish-American nationalism. Finally, Chapter 5 considers the arguments put forward by historians and political scientists on the uniquely Irish form of urban machine politics epitomized by Tammany Hall. No such controversy presents itself for consideration in Chapter 6, testifying to the relative underdevelopment of the historiography on the period since the Second World War.

After many years of teaching the history of the American Irish to undergraduates in the United States, I am convinced that they are attracted rather than repelled by these excursions into what scholars call historiography (the interpretation of history by historians). Readers are invited to pursue the various debates through the endnotes, but I have refrained from burdening the main body of the text with the names of specific authors, deciding instead simply to sketch the general positions in each debate. By the same token, I have kept demographic statistics to the liberal minimum inevitable in any undertaking such as this one, aware that a profusion of facts and figures might quickly make the text unreadable. For some readers, there will still be too many statistics, and for others too few; but, by the standards of the field, what is presented here is history with a fairly broad stroke.

While this book takes as its subject the history of the American Irish, it is intended not just for students of that topic but for anybody with an interest in American immigration and ethnicity. The principal themes of the book — migration and settlement, work and politics, gender and culture, race and ethnicity, religion and nationalism — are relevant not just to the American Irish but to the Germans, Chinese, Italians, Mexicans, and people of all other backgrounds who migrated to the United States. The history that unfolds in the following pages, in other words, is at once uniquely Irish and distinctively American. The story of the American Irish, like that of any ethnic group in America, is ultimately a story about the United States as a whole.

Chapter 1

◆

THE EIGHTEENTH CENTURY

While popular legend holds that mass emigration from Ireland commenced with the Great Famine of the 1840s, the Irish migration to America actually began in the seventeenth century and assumed the character of a mass movement as early as 1720. An estimated 50,000 to 100,000 people, three-quarters of them Catholics, left Ireland for the American colonies in the seventeenth century, and as many as 100,000 Catholic Irish may have come to America in the century after 1700. Virtually no evidence has survived on these Catholic settlers, however. Mainly young, single, rootless males, they seem to have blended into the general population rather than establishing themselves as a separate ethnic group in America. A great deal more is known about the remaining Irish immigrants of the eighteenth century, some 250,000 to 400,000 Protestants who crossed the Atlantic for the American colonies, about three-quarters of them Presbyterians from the northern province of Ulster.[1]

The volume of emigration in the eighteenth century may appear insignificant compared to the period 1820–1920, when almost five million people left Ireland for North America. But the population of Ulster in 1750 was only half a million, and the population of Ireland as a whole was just under 2.5 million (compared to 8.5 million on the eve of the Great Famine a century later). The demographic impact of the eighteenth-century migration was therefore considerable, with the 500,000 or so emigrants making up one-fifth of Ireland's population at mid-century, and the 250,000–300,000 Presbyterians accounting for half the total population of Ulster at this time.[2]

The impact of Irish migration on the history of the American colonies was also very important. People of Irish origin accounted for an estimated 14 to 17 per cent of the white population of the United States in 1790, the dominant presence being those of Ulster Presbyterian origin, who made up about 10 per cent. The verdict of one historian that 'emigration from Ulster was as much a feature of American history in the eighteenth century as Irish Catholic emigration in the next century and had a much greater effect on the development of the country', may be something of an exaggeration; but it underlines the need to expand the definition of 'Irish-American' history to include the distinctive migration of the eighteenth century. Over three-quarters of Ireland's transatlantic emigrants in the eighteenth century were Protestants, at a time when Protestants accounted for at most one-third of the Irish population. Irish America before the 1830s was decidedly Protestant in composition, and that must be the starting point for any history of the American Irish.[3]

ULSTER

Before turning to the Presbyterian migration of the eighteenth century, it is necessary to say a few words about the smaller but still significant emigration from Ireland to the American and Caribbean colonies in the seventeenth century. This emigration was sporadic and uncoordinated, consisting largely of young, single males. Very little is known about it. Most of the migrants were Catholics, and they came to the American colonies as soldiers, sailors, convicts and especially as indentured servants. Thousands of Irish political and military prisoners were sold into involuntary servitude in the West Indies after the British soldier and political leader, Oliver Cromwell, led a military conquest of Ireland in 1649–50. An estimated 12,000 Irish were living in the Caribbean by the 1660s. The white population of Barbados at that time was about one-fifth Irish, and as much as one-third of the free population of the neighbouring Leeward Islands was Irish a decade later. The Cromwellian deportees are sometimes referred to as 'slaves' in the historiography, but they were more properly prisoners or servants. To be classified as slaves in a sense recognizable to the modern reader, their status would have had to become hereditary. One reason why this never happened is that many, perhaps most, of these people died of disease or overwork within a few years of arrival, without wives or offspring. So, too, did most Africans, at least at first. But by the late seventeenth century African slaves were living longer and were less expensive than they had been, so that hereditary black slavery replaced servitude as the chief source of bound labour for the American colonies, especially on plantations producing staple crops.[4]

Bondage rather than freedom was the norm for most poor people, black or white, in the seventeenth-century Atlantic world. One form of servitude or another was the typical condition for members of the lower orders of society. Among the new inhabitants of the Americas in the seventeenth and eighteenth centuries, there were two principal categories of the 'unfree': slaves and servants. The first of these forms of bound labour never applied to the Irish; and by the late seventeenth century it had been defined in racially exclusive terms, applying only to people of African origin. While thousands of Irishmen came to the West Indies involuntarily as prisoners, most Irish settlers in the seventeenth-century Americas came as servants. In exchange for passage to America, these servants typically signed contracts (indentures) pledging their labour for a fixed term, usually three or four years. On arrival in the colonies, captains offered their cargoes of indentured servants for sale.[5]

Irish indentured servants in the seventeenth century included large numbers of artisans (skilled workers) with trades considered useful in the colonies. They did not come from the lowest ranks of the rural poor, who generally did not leave the country in this period. Irish servants began to move to Virginia and Maryland in significant numbers from the 1620s onward, on ships returning to the two Chesapeake colonies after delivering their cargoes of tobacco and West Indian sugar to Irish ports. By the end of the century, Virginia and Maryland (along with South Carolina) had passed laws restricting the entry of 'papists'. But these measures reflected the new availability of African labour and the general distrust of Catholics rather than a reaction against an inundation of Irish labour, for Irish Catholic emigration never reached a significant scale in the seventeenth century.[6]

While Protestant emigration had also been insignificant before 1700, for more than a century thereafter Presbyterians from the province of Ulster made up the great bulk of the transatlantic migration from Ireland. To grasp the nature of the Irish experience in colonial America, it is necessary first to understand how Ulster came to have such a large Presbyterian population, what life was like for the Presbyterians who settled there, and how and why they left Ireland for the American colonies in such large numbers.

Presbyterians had come to Ulster from Scotland throughout the seventeenth century as part of a concerted campaign of 'plantation' designed to secure British rule in Ireland. These 'Ulster Scots', as they are still sometimes called, were intended to form a loyal, Protestant bulwark between the native Irish and their English rulers. Scotland, of course, was much closer to Ulster than England was. The migrants came overwhelmingly from the Scottish Lowlands, where most of them paid their rent by performing a specified amount of labour and services for their landlord. Their goal in coming to Ulster was to secure land, ideally in the form of individual homesteads where they could set up as tenant farmers (i.e. renting their own farms from landlords, rather than working on landlords' estates).[7]

Religion was also of some importance in fuelling the migration from the Scottish Lowlands, though it was not nearly as significant as the desire for land. As Presbyterians, the lowland Scots stood on the extreme wing of the Protestant Reformation. They were alienated not just from the Roman Catholic Church, but from the established Anglican Church as well. They endured religious persecution several times in the seventeenth century, especially under Charles II (1660–83) and James II (1683–90), and must have hoped that emigration to Ulster would provide a haven in which they could practice their religion without interference. Because the migration took place when both Presbyterian zealotry and the persecution of dissenters were at their peak, religion would become a defining theme in the subsequent history of the Ulster Scots on both sides of the Atlantic.[8]

The Scottish plantations of Ulster began in 1608 and lasted, with some interruptions, until the end of the seventeenth century. Enticed by the availability of rental land confiscated from the native Catholic population, between 30,000 and 40,000 Scots, most of them Presbyterians, left lowland Scotland for Ulster between 1608 and 1618. By 1640 about 100,000 Scots had settled in Ulster. The migration from Scotland was disrupted by the outbreak of civil war in England in 1640, but resumed after the Cromwellian settlement in 1652, increased in volume after the accession of Charles II in 1660, and reached flood tide after William of Orange defeated the Catholic followers of James II at the Battle of the Boyne in 1690. An estimated 50,000 Scots settled in Ulster between 1690 and 1697 alone. By 1700, Scottish Presbyterians dominated the eastern half of Ulster (counties Ulster, Down and Antrim), and were present in substantial numbers in Derry, Tyrone and east Donegal. While Presbyterian tenant farmers were clearly better off than the dispossessed Catholic population below them, they were nonetheless subordinate to the Anglican (or 'Ascendancy') class above them, who owned the bulk of the land and belonged to the established Church.[9]

Just over two million people lived in Ireland in 1715, about 600,000 of them in the province of Ulster, where roughly one-third of the population were Anglicans, a little over one-third were Catholics and slightly under one-third were Presbyterians of Scottish origin. Thereafter, the number of Ulster Scots grew rapidly through natural increase, so that Presbyterians soon formed the largest Protestant denomination in Ulster. They remained sternly aloof from the surrounding population, in sharp distinction from British planters elsewhere in Ireland, such as the Cromwellian planters of Munster who quickly intermarried and were ultimately absorbed into the local population. In Ulster, the Scottish planters retained a separate group identity grounded in the religion they had taken with them from their homelands, a religion that remained largely immune from the transformations occurring in eighteenth-century Scotland, where Presbyterianism evolved into a hierarchical and often dogmatic established church. Ulster Presbyterianism, by contrast, remained more egalitarian in its structure and was dependent entirely for its financial support on individual congregations or presbyteries. This looser, more fluid structure arguably made the Ulster version of Presbyterianism more friendly to revivalist evangelical movements of the type that would characterize eighteenth-century America. Signs of evangelicalism and communal conversions were evident in Ulster itself as early as the seventeenth century, though American-style individualist evangelicalism, based on a conversion experience and personal salvation, does not seem to have become common in Ulster until the late eighteenth and early nineteenth centuries.[10]

The religious system developed by Ulster Presbyterians was highly organized and comprehensive. Each congregation governed its affairs through a body known as the kirk session, composed of the minister and the lay elders. Groups of congregations were arranged into presbyteries (composed again of ministers and elders), and from 1691 there was a General Synod. The individual kirks enforced a remarkable degree of religious and moral discipline. Elders inquired into and scrutinized the behaviour of their neighbours, and reported transgressions to the kirk sessions, which could summon the accused for examination and impose public penances, excommunication and ostracism. Moral offenses as well as theological ones were subject to punishment. To modern sensibilities, this system of church government may appear harsh and unattractive, but by prevailing standards it was also very democratic; ministers were chosen by their congregations (usually from the ranks of tenant farmers) and the laity played a very active role in church affairs. Precisely because the kirks expressed the will of the whole community, they were expected to investigate such matters as dishonesty in business, quarrelling with neighbours or outbidding a fellow Presbyterian who had a prior claim to a piece of land. In this way, Presbyterianism permeated every aspect of social existence, providing a considerable degree of communal cohesion. Not surprisingly, this communal character was also evident in the Presbyterian migration to America, with families, congregations and entire communities emigrating together whenever possible.[11]

One final, very important aspect of Ulster Scots society requires clarification before turning to examine their great migration to America: How did people make a living? The Ulster Scots were neither as rich as the Anglican elite nor as poor as the Catholic majority. Only a very small minority belonged to the landowning class, which was dominated by Anglicans, many of them absentees who rarely visited Ireland. The great majority of Ulster Presbyterians in the eighteenth century rented land and cultivated the soil. Only the largest of these tenant farmers were engaged exclusively in farming. The remainder practiced some combination of agriculture and linen production, whether as virtually landless labourers, as precarious small-holders, or (in the case of a prosperous minority) as farmer-craftsmen who purchased yarn from local merchants and employed poor farmers and journeymen (apprentices) to weave it. In the strongholds of Presbyterian settlement (especially counties Antrim, Derry and Down), these independent farmer-craftsmen lived on relatively large holdings, practicing a mixture of tillage (raising crops) and pasture (tending animals) and producing linen cloth for direct sale on the market. They were the bulwark of Ulster Scots society.[12]

At the opposite end of the social scale were the smallholders and cottier-weavers. Smallholders rented a few acres of land, drawing from it whatever sustenance they could, and meeting financial obligations like rents and tithes (dues owed to the established church) by spinning yarn or weaving linen. More precarious still than the smallholders were the cottier-weavers. In Irish history, the term *cottier* is roughly equivalent to the Scottish *cotter*, with the word *cottage* as the root in each case. Just as in Scotland, Irish cottiers were landless labourers who received a small plot of land and a cottage (more accurately a cabin), in return for a specified number of days' work performed for their landlord. Cottier tenancy was essentially a type of wage labour, the 'wage' taking the form of housing and access to land. Contracts were usually annual, and the plot of land in question might be two acres or less. In most parts of Catholic Ireland, cottiers subsisted by growing enough potatoes to feed their families, and in some cases raising a pig or a few chickens. While their landlords sold their products for profit, the cottiers themselves typically had little or no involvement in the wider capitalist marketplace. In Ulster, besides growing food for subsistence, they usually spun yarn or wove linen cloth as part of their labour contract, hence the term 'cottier-weaver'.[13]

There is also some evidence among the poorest of the Ulster Scots of joint rather than individual tenancies. In much of seventeenth and eighteenth-century Scotland and Catholic Ireland, communities held their land in common rather than in separate family plots. In Scotland and in Scottish

Ulster this system was known as *runrig*; in Catholic Ulster and elsewhere in Ireland it was known as *rundale*. Under this system, land held in common was typically divided into an area called the infield, used for crop cultivation; a larger area, called the outfield, used for pasture, cultivation or both; and a mountain or hillside, held in common for the grazing of animals. In the infield, each family held its land in numerous small strips, graded according to quality and arranged to give equal access to pasture and water. The essence of this system was the division of land in terms of the common good rather than individual profit. It had been widely practiced in lowland Scotland at the time of the Ulster plantation, and was still common in more isolated parts of Ireland in the late eighteenth century, despite concerted efforts by the British government to eradicate it. The Ulster Scots seem to have practiced rundale on only a very limited scale, however, settling on isolated family farms instead. But they did retain the traditional infield-outfield system, adapting it to the needs of individual farmers rather than the community as a whole. And the poorest of them seem to have practiced much the same forms of partible inheritance as the Catholic Irish, dividing the land equally among their children rather than consolidating it in the hands of a single heir.[14]

Women contributed as much as men to the maintenance of the domestic economy. They spun yarn, assisted in linen weaving, made clothing, cultivated, prepared and cooked food, managed most aspects of the household, and bore and raised children. They also worked in the fields, with the extent of their outdoor labour being closely related to the family's social standing. Yet women are virtually absent from the historiography on the Ulster Scots. They were not granted tracts of land or tenancies; they did not bring lawsuits, nor were suits brought against them; they did not attend school or university, and they could not become ministers. As a result, very little information about them has survived in the historical record. There is probably more information available about women than historians have yet exploited, especially in the records of kirk sessions and in deeds, wills and other public documents dealing with property and dower rights (property brought to the marriage by the bride). Archaeological work in both Ireland and Scotland may also yield important data. Pending this research, these women (whether in Scotland, Ireland or the American colonial backcountry) appear in the historiography as subordinate helpmates to men, playing an indispensable role in the household economy.[15]

This, then, was the world out of which the Ulster Presbyterian migration of the eighteenth century emerged. The migrants were descendants of Scots who had come to Ulster mainly in the seventeenth century, but what sort of identity did they ascribe to themselves on the eve of their departure to America? Did they see themselves as Irish or Scottish, or as something between or beyond these two? How important was regional identity, especially in terms of their lowland Scottish origins and Ulster settlement? As 'Ulster Scots', they were clearly both Scottish and Irish in some basic sense, but by the eighteenth century they appear to have identified themselves mainly as 'Irish'; they were born and lived in Ireland after all, and their culture and religion had diverged sharply from that of contemporary Scotland. For most of them, indeed, Scotland was an increasingly distant folk memory. But in claiming to be Irish, the Ulster Scots obviously did not regard themselves as identical to the Catholic majority; theirs was an alternative form of Irishness. Indeed, many of them spoke a Scots dialect, Lallans, which they would carry with them to America. They were both Irish and Scottish on the eve of their departure to the colonies in the early eighteenth century, and in this respect the term *Ulster Scots* is quite apposite. And, just as they had to some extent become Irish before they left for the American colonies, they would gradually become American once they crossed the Atlantic. Their distinctive history makes most sense in terms of a restless, hybrid, continuously evolving culture, always on the move in the seventeenth and eighteenth centuries, first from Scotland to Ireland, then from Ireland to America, and then throughout the American colonies from Maine to Georgia.[16]

EMIGRATION

The great migration from Ulster to America began in the late seventeenth century, and endured until the mid-nineteenth century. Emigration from Ulster was relatively insignificant before 1700, but it did not simply begin suddenly in 1717–19, the period of the first mass migration. Several cogregations seeking religious toleration had transplanted themselves from Ulster to the Chesapeake Bay in the seventeenth century, especially during the reign of Charles II (1660–85). There was a steady and increasing flow of emigrants out of Ulster from the 1680s onward. As many as 7,000 Ulster Scots are thought to have crossed the Atlantic for America between 1680 and the first big movement in 1717–19, which inaugurated the era of mass emigration from Ireland. The exodus continued, with varying levels of intensity, for the rest of the century, reaching its pre-revolutionary peaks in 1717–19, 1725–9, 1740–1, 1754–5, and 1771–5. Between 1717 and 1775 alone, an estimated 250,000 Ulster Scots left Ireland for the American colonies, with annual rates of almost 10,000 in the five years before the American Revolution.[17]

Why did the Ulster Scots leave for America? The causes of emigration in the colonial period, just as in the nineteenth century, were to be found in the interaction between those forces that were driving people out of Ireland and those that were enticing them to America, which were in practice often very closely related. While historians have typically described these forces separately under the headings of 'push' and 'pull' factors, they are better seen as part of a single process. They were certainly inseparable in the lives of actual emigrants, who would scarcely have made an analytical distinction between what was pushing them out of Ireland and what was pulling them to America. Most of them simply wanted to make a decent living for themselves or their families. For purposes of clarity, however, each phase of Irish emigration considered in this book will be discussed under three overlapping but distinct headings: the aspects of American life which attracted prospective emigrants; the developments within Ireland that forced or encouraged people to emigrate; and the various facilities, inducements and means of transportation that allowed emigrants to go to America once they had decided to do so.

Under the first heading, the most important influence was knowledge of potential economic opportunity and religious toleration in the American colonies. It was obtained, not through emigrant guidebooks or newspapers as would be the case in the nineteenth century, but through letters sent home by emigrants (also critically important for Irish Catholics in the nineteenth century) and, above all, through advertising by shipping agents and the promotional work of speculators who patented land, especially in border and frontier areas, and then imported settlers from Ulster. The bulk of the 33,000 emigrants who left Ulster for the colonies between 1760 and 1775, for example, came to America in schemes organized by land promoters and speculators. Among the more prominent Irish land promoters to bring settlers to America from Ulster was Arthur Dobbs, a native of County Antrim who became governor of North Carolina in 1753. From 1731 onwards, South Carolina offered generous programs of assisted passage, land bounties and other benefits to attract 'poor Protestants' specifically from Ireland. Irish land speculators were also very active in settling Georgia, though that colony's land inducement schemes (similar to those of South Carolina) were vetoed by the British government in 1766. Also important in attracting immigrants was the belief that the colonies might provide, if not religious liberty, at least a greater degree of tolerance than in Ulster. Compared to Ireland, where they faced threatening Catholics on one side and condescending Anglicans on the other, the Ulster Scots must have seen the American colonies as potentially a more conducive environment for their religion, and hence for their whole way of life.[18]

If the availability of land and the possibility of religious tolerance were the two most attractive aspects of the American colonies to prospective emigrants from Ulster, it was because both issues were so contentious at home. For the emigrants themselves, economic and religious 'pull factors' (opportunity and tolerance abroad) were inseparable from economic and religious 'push factors' (declining fortunes and intolerance at home). Thus, the manner in which the potential religious tolerance in the colonies attracted emigrants to America can be understood only if it is examined in tandem with the internal religious history of Ulster in the seventeenth and eighteenth centuries. And the reputed availability of land in the American colonies had as its counterpart in Ulster an ongoing crisis in the eighteenth-century countryside involving restricted land access and a number of related economic hardships for the tenantry.

Ulster Presbyterians had been subject to persecution in the seventeenth century and faced various restrictions and impositions in the eighteenth. Yet outright religious persecution was not among the causes of the eighteenth-century migration. The Ulster Scots clearly had no desire to emulate the English Puritans by founding a City-upon-a-Hill in the colonies; but they did want the freedom to practice their own distinctive faith as they saw fit. Above all, they wanted to be left alone. As dissenters from the established church, Ulster Presbyterians were subject to many of the same restrictions as the Catholic Irish, including (formally at least) some of the Penal Laws. A sacramental test Act passed in 1704, for example, effectively excluded them from office-holding by requiring them to be participating members of the Church of England. They had to pay tithes (a portion of their produce or its cash value, or a percentage of their annual rent) to support the Anglican Church. Their marriages could be challenged in ecclesiastical courts; and they were forbidden to teach in schools or enter universities.[19]

Like most of the Penal Laws, these restrictions were not rigidly enforced after the opening decades of the eighteenth century, especially against Protestant dissenters. Presbyterians were guaranteed religious toleration by an act passed in 1719, and they were already enrolling in Scottish universities in large numbers by that time. Freedom of worship, however, did not mean full civil or political equality. Ulster's Presbyterians now had the right to attend their own religious services without fear of prosecution, but their ministers could not legally officiate at marriages of Presbyterian couples until 1737, or at marriages where only one partner was a Presbyterian until 1844.

Moreover, they still faced the onerous and deeply offensive obligation of paying a tithe to the Anglican Church (ameliorated somewhat in 1838, but not abolished until 1870). And, as the great bulk of Ulster's Presbyterians rented their land rather than owning it, they could not become members of Parliament and were excluded from the political establishment generally. They therefore found themselves occupying a middle rung between a landowning Anglican elite and a dispossessed Catholic majority, precisely the place that had been intended for them by the British government in the plantation schemes of the seventeenth century.[20]

There was considerable doubt in the early eighteenth century about the future course and application of religious policies, and an understandable fear of renewed persecution. Nobody could foretell that an age of persecution was about to give way to one of relative tolerance. Fears of renewed intolerance helped inspire the first mass migration of Presbyterians from Ulster, which began two years before the legislation of 1719 was passed and was organized in large part by ministers. But problems in the linen and woollen industries, combined with poor harvests and rack-renting (the raising of rents on expired leases), were of at least equal importance in this first wave of emigration. Although religious issues shaped and encouraged the Presbyterian emigration throughout the eighteenth century, economic issues were clearly more important. At the heart of the matter was a dual crisis in the landholding system and the linen industry.[21]

For reasons that remain unclear, Ireland and much of Western Europe were afflicted in the years 1739–41 by probably the most sustained period of extreme cold in modern history. Due to the resulting crop failures, starvation and disease, somewhere between 310,000 and 480,000 people (12.5 to 20 per cent of the population) are thought to have perished in Ireland. The bad weather affected all crops, not just the potato (on which the bulk of the population was not yet dependent, in any case). In proportionate terms, mortality in 1740–1 was even greater than in 1845–51, when between 1.1 and 1.5 million out of a population of about 8.5 million would perish. Contemporaries remembered the disaster as *bliadhain an a'ir*, the Year of Slaughter, but it seems to have faded from popular and administrative memory very quickly, and this first 'great famine' remains largely unknown today, even in Ireland. This famine, combined with a serious drought over the following decade, was a principal cause of Irish emigration in the 1740s.[22]

If the famine was a single, relatively short-lived disaster, the most enduring problem in eighteenth-century rural Ireland concerned the nature of the landholding system. A tiny minority owned the land, while the great majority rented it in a variety of ways. While some landlords resided in Ulster, the biggest of them were absentees who rarely if ever visited Ireland and were interested primarily in draining as much revenue as they could out of Ulster. Nearly all the Ulster Scots were renters of land of one type or another, and questions of rent in particular lay behind most of the Presbyterian emigration.[23]

Tenants in the north of Ireland did benefit from the 'Ulster Custom', an informal but widely recognized tradition regulating relations between land-lords and their tenants. According to this custom, tenants were guaranteed security of tenure as long as rents were paid, and when they left they were compensated for improvements made to the property. But the first of these provisions, though it remained in practice until the nineteenth century, was thoroughly undermined by landlords who systematically reduced the length of leases and then raised rents in an arbitrary way ('rack-renting'), auctioned off leases to the highest bidder ('canting') or charged the tenants exorbitant fees, sometimes three or four times the annual rent, to renew their leases. Problems with rents and leases were further aggravated by high county taxes, and by the tithe owed to the established church, which was always an eco-nomic grievance as much as a purely religious one. When this wide variety of afflictions coincided with bad harvests, the people of Ulster left for America in their tens of thousands. The poorest left because they faced destitution, the marginal and relatively comfortable because their position was beginning to deteriorate. Ironically, it was the custom of compensating improvements (usually purchased from the sitting tenant as a right of occupancy by the incoming tenant, with the landlord taking a cut) which allowed many tenants to raise enough cash to pay the passage to North America.[24]

Matters were already reaching a crisis point when severe problems in the linen industry in the 1770s opened the floodgates of emigration. This rural-based industry had spread throughout Ulster in the eighteenth century and Presbyterian tenant farmers at various levels in society were usually involved in some combination of growing flax, spinning yarn and weaving linen into cloth, along with the cultivation of food crops. The level of involvement var-ied from the independent and prosperous craftsmen-farmers of east Ulster, who produced directly for the market; through the middling farmers and precarious smallholders, who spun yarn or wove cloth, whether for them-selves or others; to the penurious cottier-weavers, bound to the industry by their annual contracts. The various classes were affected differently, but with almost equal severity, by the recession and near collapse in the linen industry in the 1770s (caused in large measure by a sudden decline in foreign demand), which led to a mass exodus from Ulster on the eve of the American Revolution. Independent craftsmen found themselves on the brink of financial ruin, smallholders and cottier-weavers on the brink of starvation.[25]

Looking at the late eighteenth century generally, Ulster's rural poor responded to crisis in two ways, just as the poor elsewhere in Ireland would respond throughout the first half of the nineteenth century. The first response was to form secret societies and wage violent conflict against their oppressors, as in the Steelboy movement, composed mainly of smallholders and cottier tenants who rose up in protest against rent increases, evictions and high food prices in eastern Ulster in the early 1770s. The second response was to emigrate. A similar pattern is evident among more prosperous and independent Presbyterians in Ulster, especially the merchants, farmers and independent weavers of the eastern counties. On the one hand, they went to America in large numbers; on the other, they provided the backbone of a revolutionary republican movement in the 1790s called the United Irishmen. Some did both, coming to America as exiles after the failed insurrection of 1798.[26]

If emigrants were drawn to America by the promise of economic prosperity and religious tolerance, which were signally lacking in much of eighteenth-century Ulster, what means were available to them for getting there? Governments generally disapproved of emigration in the eighteenth century. But they actively opposed it only in certain cases, such as the departure of artisans (without much effect), or the bigger land colonization schemes. Adhering to the prevailing philosophy of 'mercantilism', the authorities in Dublin and London believed that a nation's wealth depended on the number of its inhabitants (in sharp contrast to the nineteenth-century British policy of encouraging mass migration from Catholic Ireland). Concern about Irish emigration reached near-panic proportions during the mass movement out of Ulster in the early 1770s. The government authorities and the landlords feared that both agriculture and industry might collapse, and that revenues from taxes and rents would be decimated. They also believed that an exodus of Presbyterians from Ulster would threaten the power of the Protestant Ascendancy, both regionally and in Ireland as a whole. Given the scale of the Presbyterian migration to America in the eighteenth century, these fears were understandable. But they were to prove groundless over the long term, because Ireland's population, unbeknown to contemporaries, had already commenced a period of momentous growth (for reasons disputed by historians). The population of Ireland doubled from 1 million to 2 million between 1672 and 1732, from 2 million to 4 million by 1788 and from 4 million to 8 million by 1841. Ulster's population, which stood at about half a million in 1740, increased fivefold by 1840, despite the departure of almost one million emigrants to North America.[27]

The first prerequisite for mass emigration was the availability of vessels to transport those who wanted to leave. Ships travelling to Ulster from the colonies with items like flaxseed and potash (both needed in the manufacture of linen) were used to carry linen cloth and emigrants back to the colonies.[28] Merchants and ship captains engaged in extensive recruiting activities. Deception and misrepresentation about the terms of passage were common, and shipowners regularly took on more passengers than could be comfortably or safely carried. The principal port of embarkation was Belfast, with other departures from Newry, Derry and Larne, and occasionally from southern Irish ports like Dublin, Waterford and Cork. It took six to eight weeks to cross the Atlantic, longer in rough weather. Contagious diseases often broke out on board, as in the case of an overcrowded ship bound from Belfast to Charleston in 1767, on which 100 of the 450 passengers perished of fever. On longer, delayed Atlantic crossings, hunger and even starvation were common. On one voyage from Belfast to Philadelphia in 1741, for example, forty-one passengers died and the remaining sixty reportedly survived only by resorting to cannibalism.[29]

Perhaps the most important means of mass migration from Ulster was the system of indentured servitude, which provided the primary means of emigration for the poor. The lower classes could not afford to pay the fare to America, or to emigrate in family groups. The Atlantic passage, including provisions, cost between £3 5s and £9 in the period 1720–70. Those who intended to become farmers in the colonies needed at least £10 more to pay for inland transportation, land grants, tools and seed, and to survive until the first harvest. This latter sum represented more than a year's wages for weavers and labourers. Hence, increasing numbers of the rural poor came to America as servants.[30]

Bound servitude in the eighteenth century was undoubtedly a harsh way of life. But it was by no means as brutal as it had been in the seventeenth century. With slavery providing a cheap source of unskilled labour in the American colonies after 1700, the ranks of indentured servants generally included a much higher proportion of artisans than in the seventeenth century, and conditions for servants were correspondingly better. Servants emigrating from Ulster included a large number of artisans (carpenters, tailors, shoemakers, smiths, weavers, cabinetmakers, coopers and many more) among their ranks, despite the ban on their emigration. For those emigrants with some resources, the signing of indentures appears to have been a calculated economic decision rather than a blunt necessity. Understandably wary of spending everything on the transatlantic passage and then arriving penniless in a land that was frighteningly unknown, some servants decided to hold on to their limited resources, trading temporary servitude for structure and certainty, and hoping to attain freedom (with freedom dues) and independence within a few years of arrival. Still, servitude was less a choice than a necessity for the poor, the only way of getting to America. Moreover, at least 10,000 of the indentured servants who left Ireland for the American colonies between 1700 and 1775 did so as convicts. Vagrants and petty thieves, they were sentenced to long terms of involuntary servitude and transported to America.[31]

Throughout the eighteenth century, Ireland was the single most important source of bound labour for the American colonies. This form of emigration was apparently more common for Anglicans and Catholics, even if they left Ireland in much smaller numbers than Presbyterians. It was the poorer (though not the poorest) of the Anglican and Catholic groups who tended to emigrate, and they were therefore more likely to come as individual servants than in communal or family groups. Religious dissenters, by contrast, preferred to leave in familial or congregational networks whenever possible, and could afford to do so more often than Catholics or the Anglican poor. Nonetheless, the Ulster Scots found themselves in increasingly straitened circumstances as the eighteenth century progressed. According to one estimate, more than 100,000 Scotch-Irish came to America under indentures in the eighteenth century. This figure accounts for about one-third of the total migration from Ulster to America in that century. Between 1730 and 1770, it is estimated that half of all Presbyterian emigrants from Ulster went to America as indentured servants or 'redemptioners'. Into this category fell poor smallholders, artisans, cottier-weavers and labourers, as distinct from more prosperous tenant farmers. Freedom dues, paid at the end of servitude, included clothing, tools, seed and provisions. But land grants, which had been used to entice servants in the seventeenth century, were rarely offered by the mid-eighteenth century, except in the newer southern colonies. Hence, most freed servants did not become independent yeomen. Instead, they became wage-labourers on farms or plantations, drifted into the towns or settled as squatters or pioneers on the frontier. A few returned to Ireland.[32]

Irish emigration to America fell sharply during the turmoil of the American Revolution, but resumed after 1783 and continued in ever-increasing numbers until the end of the century. An average of about 5,000 people a year left the north of Ireland for America in the 1780s and 1790s, bringing at least 100,000 new Irish immigrants to the United States. The great majority were substantial or small farmers, artisans (weavers, millwrights, coopers, tanners), small businessmen (merchants, shopkeepers and clerks), or petty professionals (especially schoolmasters or general physicians). Nearly all were fare-paying passengers; conspicuously absent, especially when compared to the period 1730–70, were indentured servants. The taking of indentures in Ulster was already beginning to decline before the American Revolution, and it quickly fell into disfavour in the new republic. Though bound servants continued to come to the United States from some countries well into the nineteenth century, the practice had all but ceased for Irish immigrants by 1800.[33]

Thus concluded the great Presbyterian migration of the eighteenth century. Why, over the course of this century, had Protestants left Ireland on such a remarkable scale, while Catholics departed in relatively insignificant numbers? Catholics outnumbered Protestants by almost three to one in Ireland, after all, yet Protestant emigration to America in the eighteenth century was three times greater than Catholic emigration. The various economic and religious considerations already examined explain why so many Protestants emigrated from Ireland; but, given the poverty of the Irish masses and the availability of indentures, it is remarkable how few Catholics decided to leave in the colonial period. According to the most influential interpretation, most Catholics still lived in a culture that was relatively isolated from external commercial and market forces, in which emigration had yet to become either a necessity or a possibility for the poor. To the extent that attitudes towards emigration are discernible, it seems to have been frowned upon, feared or condemned by Catholics rather than applauded and encouraged. Even though the population was growing rapidly, it was only after 1800 that pressure on land, combined with the commercialization of agriculture, ushered in the era of mass Catholic emigration. Before that, emigration is likely to have been seen by all but the most prosperous Catholic Irish as a form of exile and banishment rather than self-improvement.[34]

Ulster Protestants, by contrast, were more likely to see emigration to America as a form of escape and opportunity than as involuntary exile. This is not to say that they saw emigration in solely individualistic or selfish terms. Opportunity could be collective as well as individual, and the great Presbyterian migration was often more communal than individual in form, especially among those who could afford to travel in family groups or congregations. Unlike the Catholic population, the Ulster Scots had relatively shallow roots in Ireland, and many had never felt very welcome there. Whatever dreams they or their ancestors might have had when they moved from Scotland had long since faded in the face of land shortage, famine, economic recessions, taxes and tithes, and religious discrimination. And so they came to America.

ARRIVAL AND SETTLEMENT

The Ulster Scots who emigrated from Ireland in the eighteenth century, and their descendants, became known in America as the 'Scotch-Irish'. [35] One of the first places in the American colonies that immigrants from Ulster settled in the eighteenth century was New England. Several thousand settlers arrived there from Ulster in the first three decades of the century. But if the Ulster Presbyterians expected a warm welcome from their fellow religious dissenters, the Puritans, they were to be sorely disappointed. The Puritan divine, Cotton Mather, alarmed at what he saw coming, denounced proposals to bring in Irish colonists in 1700 as 'formidable attempts of Satan and his Sons to Unsettle us'. The Scotch-Irish, indeed, quickly became almost as unpopular among New Englanders as their Catholic counterparts would be in the nineteenth century.[36]

The principal sources of conflict were religion and the manners, lifestyles and frequent poverty of the new arrivals. Practicing an austere brand of Protestantism, early Scotch-Irish settlers immediately clashed with the Puritans, attacking them on matters concerning baptism in particular. Even if the Puritans no longer practiced their religion with the same rigour as they once had, they must have found attacks of this sort quite galling. Compounding the tensions provoked by religious disagreements were perceived deficiencies in the manners and morals of the newcomers, whose growing reputation for drunkenness, blasphemy and violence earned them the sobriquet 'Wild Irish' almost a century before it was inherited by Catholic Irish immigrants. Moreover, many of the newcomers were poor and some were indigent. Between 1729 and 1742, for example, two-thirds of the inmates of the Boston almshouse were Irish.[37]

Unwelcome in Boston, the Scotch-Irish migrated northward to other parts of New England, or westward to more remote parts of Massachusetts. They settled in Maine, New Hampshire and present-day Vermont, where traces of their history survive today in the names of towns like Londonderry, Antrim, Belfast and Bangor. And they moved to western Massachusetts, filling for the first time the role of a buffer between the zone of British settlement and the areas populated by American Indians. It was a role they would play over and over again in the eighteenth century, in a line descending southward from Pennsylvania through the southern backcountry all the way down to Georgia.[38]

Pennsylvania was the next zone of settlement for the Scotch-Irish. The shift in settlement patterns away from New England to the middle colonies took place in part because of the hostility of the Puritans, in part because Ulster's transatlantic trade was oriented primarily toward the ports of the Delaware River in the middle colonies, and in part because Pennsylvania was about the most religiously tolerant place in America. The colony had been founded in 1681 by William Penn, an egalitarian Quaker, and was dominated by Quakers until the Revolution. The Scotch-Irish began to settle southeastern Pennsylvania in the 1720s, initially receiving a warm welcome from the colony's proprietary government, which provided land on attractive terms. Very soon, however, they came to be regarded as a troublesome and turbulent people, in constant friction with neighbouring German settlers and the local Indian populations.[39]

At the heart of the problem in Pennsylvania was the Scotch-Irish propensity for squatting on land to which they did not have legal title. Many of them could not afford to pay even the modest prices asked by the colony's proprietors. The Quaker government, though often unscrupulous in its land dealings with Indians, was more equitable than most of the colonial governments in this respect. The Scotch-Irish, however, generally settled wherever they chose, without permission or title. 'Empty' land, they insisted, should not be left idle when it was needed by hungry Christians. In search of land, the Scotch-Irish soon began to migrate out of southeastern Pennsylvania, moving west from the Delaware River and then westward across the Susquehanna River to the Cumberland Valley, which by 1750 was overwhelmingly Scotch-Irish.[40]

About 100,000 people of Ulster origin or descent lived in Pennsylvania in 1790, comprising just over one-quarter of the estimated total Scotch-Irish population in America. Moreover, about half the Scotch-Irish population of Pennsylvania in that year lived in the eastern counties of the state, and an estimated 28 per cent of the citizens of Philadelphia were of Scotch-Irish origin. Among their ranks were some of the wealthiest and most influential of the city's merchants, including John Maxwell Nesbit. Wealthy Irish immigrants apparently drew few distinctions among themselves along religious lines at this time. For example, the Friendly Sons of St Patrick, a fraternal organization founded in Philadelphia in 1771, had as its first president the

Catholic merchant Stephen Moylan (the brother of a bishop) and as its second the Protestant merchant, Nesbit.

While Pennsylvania was an important center of settlement, it is the southern backcountry that has been most intensively studied by historians of the Scotch-Irish. This emphasis is quite understandable, for it is in the Appalachian backcountry, from Pennsylvania southward to Georgia and westward to Kentucky and Tennessee, that most of the Scotch-Irish settled and questions of cultural continuity and adaptation take on their sharpest focus. By 1790 an estimated 50 per cent of white settlers on the trans-Appalachian frontier were of Ulster origin. In North Carolina, they accounted for between 39 and 48 per cent of the white population in counties near the eastern seaboard, and from 60 to almost 100 per cent in the remotest western regions of the state. In western Virginia an estimated 80 per cent of the white population was of Ulster origin in 1790, and in western Pennsylvania in the same year as many as three-quarters of the residents in some counties were Scotch-Irish.[41]

The internal migration of the Scotch-Irish is a remarkable story. From Pennsylvania's Cumberland Valley they crossed the Allegheny Mountains, settling in the area where Pittsburgh stands today and, in even greater numbers, in southwestern Pennsylvania. By the time these settlers had penetrated beyond the Alleghenies at mid-century, several other waves of land-hungry Scotch-Irish migrants had already moved southwest across the Potomac River and down into western Maryland and the Shenandoah Valley (or 'Great Valley') of western Virginia, between the Blue Ridge and Appalachian Mountains, which was first settled by Irish and German migrants in the 1730s. By the 1740s the Irish had penetrated to the southern reaches of the valley. From there they pressed on either southward through the Fancy Gap into the Carolinas, as far south eventually as Georgia and West Florida; or westward through the Cumberland Gap into the territory that would eventually become the states of Kentucky (1789) and Tennessee (1790). By the eve of the Revolution, the Scotch-Irish had settled all the way along the southern backcountry, from Pennsylvania to Georgia. 'A map of their main settlements,' as one historian has remarked, 'is almost a map of the pre-Revolutionary frontier.'[42]

The forebears of Andrew Jackson (1767–1845) and John C. Calhoun (1782–1850), two of the dominant figures in nineteenth-century American politics, offer exemplary illustrations of this Scotch-Irish backcountry migration. Despite later myths of humble origins, Jackson's Irish forebears were well-to-do. His grandfather, a substantial weaver and merchant in

Carrickfergus, County Antrim, left him a legacy of between £300 and £400, and his father was a prosperous farmer who led a party of emigrants to America in 1765. They settled in Waxhaw, South Carolina, where Andrew was born two years later. As a boy he fought during the Revolutionary War and was captured by the British; he lost all but one of his family during the conflict, but went on to a successful career as a lawyer, soldier and politician. Elected the seventh president of the United States in 1828, he has since been taken by historians as the icon of his age, the era of Jacksonian Democracy, with all its strengths and shortcomings. But this most directly Irish of American presidents, the son of immigrants from Ulster, did not apparently regard himself as Irish in any meaningful sense, and neither did his country-men. His considerable antipathy to the British can be traced to his experi-ences in the Revolutionary War and the War of 1812, rather than any spirit of Ulster dissent. Jackson became president just as Catholics were beginning to dominate emigration from Ireland and Americans of Ulster descent were rapidly attaining, through the twin vehicles of race and religion, their bona fides as authentic Americans.[43]

The case of the Calhoun family presents an equally fine illustration of both the ongoing migration of the eighteenth-century Ulster Scots and their even-tual assimilation into American life. Patrick Calhoun, father of the southern politician John C. Calhoun, was born to an Ulster Scots family in County Donegal in 1727 and emigrated to America with his parents in 1733. The family settled first in Pennsylvania, then moved south to Virginia, where Patrick's father accumulated 3,000 acres in Augusta County before his death. He left his family quite prosperous but, concerned perhaps about Indian attacks, the family soon relocated to South Carolina, attracted no doubt by the colony's offer of a free fifty-acre grant (or 'headright') for each house-hold. They appear to have been one of countless Virginia families who sold their property at a profit to migrants coming down from the North, and then relocated further down the southern backcountry in search of greater wealth. Trained as a surveyor, Calhoun knew what sort of land to look for. He settled on an offshoot of the Savannah River called Long Canes Creek, where the Calhouns were soon joined by the Anderson, Pickens and Noble families (with whom they had intermarried in both Ireland and America), who had also made the trek southward from Augusta County. Long Canes became one of the flashpoints of the Cherokee War of 1760–1, and Patrick's mother, Catherine Montgomery Calhoun, was among fourteen settlers killed there in an ambush by Creek Indians in 1763. Patrick went on to a career in South Carolina politics, as one of the leaders of an emerging backcountry planter elite. His son, John Caldwell Calhoun, far surpassed him in prominence, becoming a major player in national politics and an uncompromising spokesman for the slave South in the antebellum era. John C. Calhoun, however, seems to have been no more consciously Irish than his sometime ally and political enemy, Andrew Jackson.[44]

Why did these two scions of Ulster Irish families regard themselves not as Irish but as impeccably American? The answer lies in the evolving identity of Ulster immigrants in America, who have been known since the early nineteenth century as the *Scotch-Irish*. The term is quite a useful one, as it succinctly describes people of Scottish origin who left Ireland for America. It is not intended to signify intermarriage between Ulster Scots and Catholic Irish, as rates of marriage between these two groups were always very low in both Ireland and America. The name 'Scotch-Irish' is largely an Americanism; it is known, but not used, in the north of Ireland, where 'Ulster Scots' is preferred. The Ulster Scots became 'Scotch-Irish' in America rather than Ireland, and in so doing they conformed to one of the classic patterns of American immigration history, whereby ethnicity is discovered or invented in the new homeland, rather than being carried across the ocean from the old. Having an ethnic identity, far from being an impediment to assimilation, has been for most immigrants a defining characteristic of becoming American.[45]

The appropriation of the term 'Scotch-Irish' by Americans of Ulster Scots origin is a case study in this process. Scattered use of the term 'Scotch-Irish' is evident from the late sixteenth century in Britain, and from the late seventeenth century in the American colonies, where it was widely employed by the 1750s. But by far the most common label for immigrants from Ulster in the colonial period was simply 'Irish' (sometimes 'Wild Irish'), because there was as yet no substantial Catholic Irish population against whom to compare them. Then, from about the 1830s onwards, the Ulster Scots in America eagerly appropriated the term 'Scotch-Irish' in order to mark themselves off as different from the incoming waves of Catholic immigrants. The term 'Irish' would henceforth be reserved for the latter group in America, with Scotch-Irishmen often at the vanguard of nativist movements against them. By asserting their Protestant 'Scotch-Irish' identity, the descendants of the Ulster Scots distanced themselves from other, less respectable Irishmen, thereby staking a successful claim to being bona fide Americans. Established as a separate ethnic group by the early nineteenth century, they further pressed their case for inclusion by trumpeting their allegedly central role in the American revolution.[46]

If the nineteenth-century Scotch-Irish routinely exaggerated the role played by their forebears in founding the American nation, one area where they do seem to have had a considerable influence is on American speech patterns and popular music. Recent linguists have detected signs of the Scotch-Irish legacy from western Pennsylvania southward through the Appalachian backcountry. In Scotland and Ulster, the Scotch-Irish had spoken a dialect of English called Lallans (or Broad Scots), and they continued to do so in America. Blended with local forms of English in the colonies, this dialect produced distinctive patterns of speech in areas of heavy Scotch-Irish settlement. One historian, for example, has identified thirty-six different aspects of grammar, pronunciation and vocabulary in Pennsylvania that can convincingly be traced to Ulster. Another has traced forty similar features of Appalachian speech to their Scotch-Irish, southern British or general British sources, of which seventeen clearly appear to be Scotch-Irish. In Pennsylvania, such words included the nouns fireboard (for mantelpiece), diamond (for town square), poke (for bag) and *bonny-clabber* or *cruddled* milk (both meaning curdled sour milk), along with verbs like hull (to shell) and *driv* or *druv* (as the past tense of drive). In southern Appalachia, they included pronouns like *y'all* or *you-all* (along with similar combinations like *we-all*, *where-all*, and *what-all*); prepositions and conjunctions like *fornent* (next to); and verb usages like 'I used to could' (I was able), 'I might should' (I ought to), or 'I *done* landed in jail again'. It should be noted that these findings, while based on thorough research, are by their nature quite tentative. Some of the speech patterns identified as Scotch-Irish are also associated with African Americans in the South, and an intriguing if very difficult line of inquiry would be to investigate the borrowings and interactions between these two groups. Likewise, the southern Scotch-Irish are thought to have had a considerable if often intangible influence on American folk music, with their styles and practices interacting in turn with those of other ethnic groups.[47]

The primary motivation of the great internal migration by the Scotch-Irish was hunger for land, just as it had been in both the Scottish migration to Ulster and the transatlantic movement out of Ulster. The lack of affordable and accessible land in Pennsylvania in the 1730s first drove the Scotch-Irish south to Virginia. By the 1740s, the same problem in the Shenandoah Valley led them to migrate to the Carolinas. South Carolina was by this time offering prospective immigrants free transportation from Ireland and grants of land with provisions and tools, so that Scotch-Irish people coming southward from Virginia were joined by fellow-countrymen arriving directly from

Ulster. Both sets of migrants, of course, had come to the South for the same reason – access to land they could call their own.[48]

Access to land, however, remained a highly contentious issue in the South, just as it had been in Pennsylvania. Because so many Scotch-Irish settled on land over which they had no proper legal title, they quickly developed a reputation for lawlessness. Those who set up as squatters were regarded as a turbulent and contentious people and were constantly in conflict with German settlers, from Pennsylvania to the Carolinas. Their aggressive attitude toward the land often placed the Scotch-Irish at odds with the American Indians they encountered, whose land they evidently regarded as theirs for the taking. Once again, this pattern is evident all the way from Massachusetts to Georgia. Wherever they settled, the Scotch-Irish soon uprooted themselves and moved westward, as though it were the natural thing to do. This remarkable pattern of settlement demands explanation.[49]

The Scotch-Irish tended to come into conflict with the established British culture in most parts of the eastern seaboard where they settled. They moved westward and southward through the backcountry in part because of this sentiment, in part because they needed land, and in part because they wanted an isolated environment in which they could practice their religion and culture, and simply be themselves. Frontier life certainly gave the Ulster Scots the isolation and freedom from interference that they and their ancestors had for so long been seeking. But it was also a very spartan, harsh and dangerous existence. The Scotch-Irish were encouraged to settle the frontier by the colonial authorities, however, in the hope that they would serve as a buffer against Indian attacks. In South Carolina, for instance, the authorities offered substantial land inducements to those Irish who would settle on the frontier, especially after the Yamassee War of 1715 and the Cherokee uprising of 1759–61. Life in Ulster had prepared the Scotch-Irish for this role of a human buffer between so-called 'civilization' and 'savagery'. They were no strangers to the appropriation of land once held by a 'heathen', indigenous people, whether Catholics in Ulster or Indians in America. In the north of Ireland, they had occupied an intermediate role between the Anglican elite and the native dispossessed, and in the southern backcountry their role was in some ways very similar.[50]

It was, of course, a very dangerous role. The Scotch-Irish quickly established a reputation as aggressive and ruthless Indian fighters, slaughtering and being slaughtered in gruesome numbers. They had come into conflict with Indians in eastern Pennsylvania almost as soon as they settled there, and this conflict intensified as they commenced their westward movement in the colony. Immigrant incursions on Indian territory in Pennsylvania led to severe tensions between the western Scotch-Irish and the Quaker proprietary government in Philadelphia. Relations between Europeans and Indians in both Pennsylvania and Virginia had been quite peaceful in the early eighteenth century, but this period of relative harmony was rudely disrupted by the arrival of the Scotch-Irish with their often cavalier disregard of legal claims to land, especially those held by Indians. The conflict in both colonies reached a peak in 1754–63 with the outbreak of the French and Indian War, known in Europe as the Seven Years' War.[51]

In this protracted struggle for mastery over North America, British regulars did most of the fighting against the French, but it was the Scotch-Irish who fended off most of the border raids by Indians and bore the brunt of the civilian casualties. Allied with the French, a variety of Indian peoples from Ohio to Virginia fought a war against further westward expansion by the British. Their nearest target was the Scotch-Irish settlements along the frontier of Pennsylvania and Virginia, whose residents in turn saw the war as an opportunity to wrest full control of their land from the Indians. In Pennsylvania and the Shenandoah Valley of Virginia, the Shawnee and Tuscarora Indians launched devastating attacks on the Ulster immigrant frontiersmen. The killing by both sides was brutal and extensive, with each resorting to arson, butchering women and children, and engaging in wholesale destruction. As for more formal military engagements, Scotch-Irishmen composed the majority of the Pennsylvania militia who assisted British Regulars in the capture of Fort Dusquesne, the key to French defenses in the Ohio Valley, in 1763, helping to bring the conflict to an end. No sooner had the war ended, however, than Pontiac, the Ottawa leader, formed an alliance of tribes against the British colonists, killing hundreds of settlers in Pennsylvania and Virginia. The Scotch-Irish provided the only effective defense against Pontiac, and again suffered most of the casualties. In one notorious incident in 1763, which seems to have been inspired in part by gratuitous revenge and in part by hunger for land, Scotch-Irish settlers massacred twenty of Pennsylvania's peaceful Conestoga Indians.[52]

Scotch-Irish frontiersmen, of course, were not engaged exclusively or even primarily in fighting Indians. They were, of necessity, cultivators of the soil, and their particular style of agriculture is worthy of close attention. Scotch-Irish settlement patterns in the colonial backcountry were in several respects strikingly similar to those in contemporary Ulster. The forms of agricultural settlement to which the Scotch-Irish had already been accustomed in Ulster were well suited for adaptation to the new American environment. In both places, individual homesteads were widely dispersed, rather than being clustered in villages. This pattern of scattered homesteads, rather than English-style farm villages, became the norm in the backcountry. On their isolated backcountry farms, Scotch-Irish immigrants continued to practice their traditional grain-and-livestock agriculture, a mixture of tillage and pasture that was oriented toward subsistence rather than monetary profit. In addition, many of them grew flax, spun yarn and wove fine linen cloth, just as they had in Ireland. One other domestic-based tradition that crossed the Atlantic was the distilling of whiskey and its consumption in prodigious quantities.[53]

Similar patterns of cultural continuity, along with adaptation and borrowing, can be seen in the various techniques the Scotch-Irish used to farm the land. The farming of joint tenancies by rundale did not survive the Atlantic crossing, but the practice of infield-outfield farming did. In the colonial backcountry, as in Ulster, landholdings were divided into an infield used for purposes of tillage, an outfield used for a mixture of grazing and tillage, and a mountain or forest used for grazing. This system was well suited to the rugged and hilly terrain of southern Appalachia. As in Ireland, the Ulster Scots tended to opt for well-drained hillsides over more fertile but wetter bottomlands. They had little experience farming heavily wooded areas, but quickly adopted a form of 'slash and burn' agriculture, burning a temporary clearing, cutting back excess vegetation, girdling the trees (i.e. stripping their bark so they would eventually die rather than uprooting them at once), growing some crops and then allowing the forest to grow back after a couple of seasons. Though sometimes lamented by their Euro-American contemporaries, this practice was actually a highly efficient form of agriculture in heavily wooded areas where labour was very scarce. Indeed, much the same technique was used in forest agriculture in both Britain and New England, under the name *swidden*. The backcountry Scotch-Irish, therefore, adopted farming techniques that were widespread in wooded terrain throughout the Atlantic world.[54]

Contemporary critics insisted, nonetheless, that the Scotch-Irish were slovenly and wasteful, especially when compared to their fellow immigrants from Germany. German homesteads were routinely described as neat and well-tended, with their trees felled and uprooted and clearings laboriously converted to ploughed fields. The Scotch-Irish, by contrast, girdled rather than uprooted their trees, often abandoning the land after a season or two. In contrast to the tidy German homesteads, contemporary observers often found Scotch-Irish holdings dirty and chaotic, the landscape scarred by dead and dying trees. The French observer of the newly-formed United States, de Crèvecouer, noted that the Scotch-Irish did 'not prosper so well' as the Germans or the Scottish, attributing their failure in part to 'their ignorance in husbandry' and in part to their love of quarrelling and cheap whiskey. Examined more closely, however, it appears that the rough-and-ready farming practices of the Scotch-Irish involved both a logical strategy for a people accustomed to being on the move, and an adaptation to American conditions of farming techniques traditionally followed in Ulster. Deliberately situating themselves on hillsides for better drainage, the Scotch-Irish settlers rarely ploughed entire clearings into neatly tilled land.[55]

While Scotch-Irish agricultural practice apparently differed substantially from German, the differences should not be overestimated. After all, the Germans were no more able than any other settler group to move onto forest land and plough it straight away. Settlement took time, and this was one thing the highly mobile Scotch-Irish did not have at their disposal. The difference between them and their German backcountry counterparts was typically that they had much less intention of settling permanently where they were, and hence were concerned primarily with quick, rough exploitation of the land over the short term rather than more durable settlement. It is not that the Scotch-Irish were poor farmers, or slovenly by nature; instead they were accustomed to movement and often settled briefly in three or four different parts of the backcountry before finally putting down more permanent roots. The Calhouns, even if they were better off than most, are one good example of this pattern of southward migration.

A similar distinction between permanence and transience is evident when Scotch-Irish and German backcountry housing is compared. The mark of the Scotch-Irish backwoodsman was the single, isolated homestead, vulnerable to attack but embodying the desire for independence and mobility so evident among the Ulster Scots on both sides of the Atlantic. The loghouses in which the Scotch-Irish lived were borrowed from a German model, adapted so that their design (internal dimensions, placement of doors and windows, width of hearth) reproduced the space-relations of the single-roomed cabin, with gable chimney and walls of mud or stone, found throughout eighteenth-century Ulster. On both sides of the Atlantic, these dwellings were rudimentary. While German cabins were generally waterproof and permanent, the Irish-American versions often lacked floors and watertight roofs, and were clearly designed for temporary rather than life-long shelter.[56]

The extent to which the material culture of the Scotch-Irish was influenced by the Indians they encountered is unclear. Certainly they killed a lot of Indians, but they also traded with them extensively. Some historians have argued that they learned from the Indians as well, borrowing cures, herbs, crops and cultivation methods; techniques for deadening or 'girdling' wood, for hunting and for using the forest; and styles of dress that included moccasin shoes, deerskin shirts and long hair dressed with bear grease and tied with eel-skin. It is difficult to document this cultural borrowing and important not to exaggerate its extent. In the first place, it is very hard to reconcile the idea of cultural borrowing with the justified reputation of the Scotch-Irish as Indian killers. This would not, of course, have prevented the settlers from imitating much of what they saw. But it is by no means clear how 'Indian' these borrowings were. The Indians they encountered were not nomadic. The Scotch-Irish practice of slash-and-burn agriculture had plenty of antecedents elsewhere in Britain and British America, and may not have owed much to the Indians.[57]

Just as in Scotland and Ireland, females were the mainstay of the domestic economy. Women and girls cooked, washed and sewed, milked the cows and churned the butter. They ground corn into flour, prepared cures and home remedies, tended the garden and searched the forest for herbs, nuts and wild fruit. They picked, dyed and carded wool; broke and carded flax; spun and wove cloth; cut out garments; and made clothing. They also assisted with the harvest, preserved foodstuffs and laid in supplies for the winter. And they raised the children, taught them to read and write, and instructed them in religious matters. The extent to which a woman worked outdoors was a fair measure of the status of the family to which she belonged. The poorest women joined their menfolk in the fields, but families aspiring to some degree of respectability restricted outdoor female labour to the harvest rush and to tasks in the immediate vicinity of the household that were traditionally considered 'women's work'. The better-off the household, the more likely it was to employ a small number of slaves (from one to five) to do the heavy work. Scotch-Irish women married young, and endured considerable drudgery and isolation on the frontier. As in Ireland, the roles assigned to them were those of homemaker and child rearer, always subordinate to the dictates of adult males.[58]

Further research by historians would presumably reveal a lot more about the lives of these women. Absent from the historiography, they may not be entirely absent from the historical record. Examining church records, wills, deeds and other public documents may reveal a higher degree of agency on the part of women than is suggested by the standard account of Scotch-Irish history. Historians of colonial America have recently begun to demonstrate, for example, how some women refused to sign away their dower rights, retaining control over the future disposal of the property they brought with them to their marriages. The extent to which Scotch-Irish women did similar things is unknown, as questions of this type have yet to be asked of the sources.[59]

It has often been said that the Scotch-Irish assimilated easily into American life because they fitted the bill so closely, conforming to the national stereotype of rugged individualism. This formulation is not especially helpful for the eighteenth century, however. Colonial frontier life may have been based on scattered, individual homesteads, but Scotch-Irish communities had a strong communal emphasis, not only in their religion but also in collective barn-raisings and harvest-gatherings, festivals like weddings and not least in Indian fighting. American-style individualism, as one historian has remarked, better characterizes the Scotch-Irish of late nineteenth-century Pittsburgh than their southern backcountry predecessors a century before. To the extent that the colonial Scotch-Irish were ruggedly individual pioneers, it was not so much that they conformed to an existing ideal as that they helped create one which would become dominant in the nineteenth century.[60]

RELIGION AND POLITICS

By the mid-eighteenth century, the Ulster Scots had a well-established presence in colonial America. As well as dominating much of the backcountry South, they settled in large numbers in Pennsylvania. The settlers in these two areas played important, and often rather different, roles in four central aspects of Scotch-Irish history in the latter half of the eighteenth century: religion, education, politics and the American Revolution.[61]

Protestantism, if not always Presbyterianism, remained central to the identity of the Scotch-Irish in America. Immigrants from Ulster played a major role in the establishment of Presbyterianism in the American colonies. As early as 1698, the Ulster-born 'father of American Presbyterianism', Francis Makemie, had settled in Virginia. He was not the first minister of his denomination to preach in the colonies, but he was the first to found churches. In 1706 Makemie convened a group of ministers from Maryland, Delaware and Pennsylvania (all but one of them from Ireland or Scotland) at Philadelphia to form the first presbytery in America. Thereafter, the Scotch-Irish established churches wherever they settled, in deliberate opposition to the Anglican Church. There was a strong religious component to the conflicts between backcountry Presbyterians and eastern Anglican elites, at times almost indistinguishable from economic and political issues. But, if the kirk had been the center of community life in Ulster, it rarely acquired the same power and prestige in the colonial backcountry, especially in South Carolina, where neither the religious nor the secular authorities appear to have been able to impose much by way of law and order. Throughout the southern backcountry, the religious court often predated or took precedence over civil authority. But, while religious authority did sometimes substitute for civil authority on questions of property, social justice and community morality, it was more often the case that both forms of authority were lacking. Government officials often turned to the Presbyterian clergy for help in times of violence and disorder, but without notable success. Many farmsteads were at least a day's ride not only from the nearest courthouse but also from the nearest minister.[62]

Presbyterianism in the backcountry therefore faced serious obstacles to its survival. Congregations were small, isolated and widely scattered. Transport and communications in the backcountry were rudimentary, and qualified clergy were in very short supply. Presbyterians demanded high standards of their ministers, who had to be familiar with Greek, Latin and Hebrew as well as theology. Not nearly enough ministers came from Ireland with their congregations, and few of those trained in America could hope to satisfy the standards of the ministry. Many frontier settlements lacked not only ministers but churches. Congregations held themselves together on an informal basis, sustained by occasional visits by itinerant preachers who rode the circuit from one settlement to the next. Under these circumstances, it is not surprising that many of the Scotch-Irish drifted away from religion altogether, or that many more converted to Baptism or Methodism.[63]

In the 1740s American religion underwent a mass religious revival that scholars have termed the 'Great Awakening'. The revival divided the Protestant churches, including Presbyterianism, with some members of each church enthusiastically endorsing evangelical fervour and personal salvation, and others sternly condemning it. Presbyterian clergymen split into an 'Old Side' and a 'New Side', with the latter favouring the revival. The Scotch-Irish clergy appear to have been divided in roughly equal numbers for and against the Great Awakening.[64] The Scotch-Irish laity, by contrast, overwhelmingly supported the revival. They responded enthusiastically to the optimistic and often highly emotive nature of evangelical revivalism, with its emphasis on personal salvation through conversion. This message must have appeared very attractive when compared to the austere discipline and predestinarian pessimism of orthodox Presbyterianism. The idea of exercising some control over one's destiny also fitted better with the experience of men and women who had voluntarily made the transatlantic crossing from Ireland to America. As Ulster Presbyterianism tended to be looser and more democratic in structure than the Scottish variety (on both sides of the Atlantic), the Scotch-Irish were often more predisposed to religious revivalism than their Scottish co-religionists. Moreover, the Great Awakening has been linked by some historians to a growing antipathy to the British, and hence to some sense of an emerging American national identity. Some Ulster Irish immigrants, therefore, may have seen siding with the revivalists as a means of assimilation into the mainstream of American culture. At the same time, Baptists and Methodists required much lower educational standards of their preachers than Presbyterians did. Unable to provide adequate numbers of trained clergy, 'Old Side' Presbyterians could do little to prevent the evangelical sects from converting huge numbers of Scotch-Irish in the three decades before the American Revolution.[65]

The Great Awakening eventually transformed the character of American Presbyterianism as well. It became more evangelical in tone, placing greater emphasis on the idea of a personal relationship with God, and less emphasis on the doctrine of election (or predestination) which had been the hallmark of its original Calvinist theology. As part of the same process, the traditional communal emphasis of Scotch-Irish Presbyterianism also declined. Similar developments, interestingly enough, would mark the history of the denomination in Ulster in the late eighteenth and early nineteenth centuries. In both cases, Presbyterianism was moving decisively away from its origins in the early modern world to confront instead a new world of unfettered individualism, social and geographical mobility, and (in urban centers) commercial and industrial capitalism. But the losses incurred by Presbyterianism to the evangelical sects in the mid-eighteenth century were irreversible. If Presbyterianism was still the most popular religion among the Scotch-Irish as the eighteenth century drew to a close, Baptism and Methodism had made major incursions, especially in the South, and would continue to increase in popularity thereafter.[66]

Closely bound up with the history of religion was the question of education. In Pennsylvania and the middle colonies, the Scotch-Irish had an important impact on the development of American schools and colleges. Education had been a central ingredient of the Scottish reformation: Presbyterian ministers received intensive training in theology, classics and other subjects, and basic literacy at least was a necessity for the bible-reading laity. The primary focus of Scotch-Irish education was the training of ministers, and it was for this purpose that the Reverend William Tennent founded his celebrated Log College at Neshaminy, near Philadelphia, in 1726 or 1727. A graduate of the University of Edinburgh, Tennent placed a heavy emphasis on the classics as well as theology. The Log College, which survived until 1742, inspired the foundation of similar schools in Pennsylvania, as well as the College of New Jersey (later known as Princeton University, founded in 1746 by Scottish Presbyterians). Graduates of the Log College were among the most vociferous Presbyterian supporters of the Great Awakening. Another prominent Scotch-Irish educator was the classical scholar, Francis Alison (1705–79), a graduate of Edinburgh who emigrated to Pennsylvania in 1735, and became Professor of Moral Philosophy and Vice Provost at the College of Philadelphia.[67]

If Protestantism of one sort or another remained integral to the identity of the Scotch-Irish, another arena that was critical to their self-definition was politics, broadly defined here in terms of the contestation of power. So determined were the Scotch-Irish to assert their rights and demands, indeed, that they found themselves in frequent conflict with the eastern authorities, wherever they settled. As a result, the Scotch-Irish played an important, if ambiguous, role in the politics of colonial America. Much has been written about their heroic contribution to the American Revolution but, with the possible exception of Pennsylvania, that contribution has been greatly exaggerated. Considerably more important in understanding Scotch-Irish political consciousness are the various conflicts that erupted in the backcountry and along the frontier from the mid-eighteenth century onward.

Trouble arose first in Pennsylvania. Scotch-Irish frontiersmen bitterly resented the colony's Quaker oligarchy for denying them the vote and adequate representation in the assembly, for overtaxing them and above all for failing to pursue more aggressive policies to provide them with protection against Indians. Tensions reached a peak during the French and Indian War (1754–63) and Pontiac's Rebellion (1764). Lurking behind the notorious Conestoga massacre of December 1763, when the Scotch-Irish slaughtered twenty peaceful Indians, was a group called the 'Paxton Boys'. This shadowy group, active during both Pontiac's War and the French and Indian War, is best known for its march on Philadelphia in 1764.[68]

Five or six hundred armed 'Paxton Boys' set out from the Pennsylvania backcountry for the colonial capital in February of that year. The authorities, fearful of a general massacre of Indians and the possible overthrow of the Quaker government, enlisted a volunteer army and called on British regulars for assistance. The Paxton Boys were eventually stalled at Germantown, six miles outside Philadelphia. There they presented *A Declaration and Remonstrance*, justifying their actions at Conestoga on the grounds that Quaker policy provided them no protection, calling for aggressive tactics against Indians, more equitable taxes and greater representation for the counties of western Pennsylvania in the colonial assembly. Benjamin Franklin, at this time an advocate of the proprietary Quaker government, replied to the *Declaration and Remonstrance* with a pamphlet stridently attacking the Scotch-Irish for their massacres of Indians. An exchange of pamphlets followed, but the protest by the 'Paxton Boys' ended without further violence.[69]

In North Carolina a similar, but more violent, struggle was evident between the residents of the eastern low country and the western backcountry. The eastern political elite, which denied political rights to the Presbyterian backcountrymen, was largely Anglican in composition. Presbyterians, indeed, had to pay tithes to the established Anglican Church, and their marriages were not recognized in North Carolina until 1766. How bitter a disappointment it must have been for the Scotch-Irish to have faced in America precisely the forms of religious discrimination that had plagued them in Ireland. To protest political and religious oppression, along with what they regarded as outright extortion by tax-hungry tidewater officials, the Scotch-Irish of western North Carolina joined a movement called the Regulators in the mid-1760s. They controlled much of the backcountry until 1771, when they suffered military defeat at the 'battle' of Alamance (more of a skirmish than a major engagement) and several of their leaders were hanged by the authorities. The Regulators adapted to American conditions the tactics of intimidation and violence (though not the secrecy) characteristic of agrarian protest movements in contemporary Ulster, notably those of the Oakboys in the 1760s and the Steelboys in the 1770s. A similar pattern of violence would be evident in the Whiskey Rebellion of 1794, when settlers in western Pennsylvania, with the Scotch-Irish at the forefront, rose up in protest at the hated excise tax.[70]

The ongoing conflict between backcountry and tidewater also raises the critical question of slavery. While early settlers of the backcountry, isolated from commercial centers, may have farmed the land more for subsistence than profit, recent historians have questioned the traditional distinction between a backcountry characterized by self-sufficiency, freedom and egalitarian democracy, and a tidewater marked by the pursuit of profit, the institution of slavery and abuses of power and privilege. Such distinctions are too clear-cut to capture the complexities of life in the backcountry. Even if many smallholders were of necessity isolated from markets and slavery until the expansion of cotton production in the 1790s, a class of aspiring backcountry planters had arisen long before that. In South Carolina this class was led by men like Patrick Calhoun, whose resentment of eastern power and privilege was based not on a rejection of the way of life in the eastern part of the colony but on a desire to be incorporated into that culture through the accumulation of slaves and property, the opening up of markets and the establishment of a judicial system in the backcountry. This was the central issue when South Carolina produced its own Regulator movement in the late 1760s.[71]

In other words, while the backcountry leaders demanded the imposition of social order, what they really wanted was a type of order compatible with their own economic and political aspirations. They were slave-owning planters on the make, rather than frontier democrats. The invention of the cotton gin in 1793, then, did not so much bring slavery to the backcountry as consolidate a form of social power already held by the elite, while spreading it more widely among the lower orders of society (most of whom typically went on to own a slave or two, rather than large numbers). The greater the stake of the Scotch-Irish in slavery the more they came to be regarded as the equals of other white Americans in the South. Race and slavery, even more than religion, were their primary vehicles of assimilation. While the story of how the nineteenth-century Catholic Irish in the North 'became white' has been the subject of intensive recent inquiry, a story in some ways similar but in others strikingly different remains to be told of the Scotch-Irish in the South. Among other things, this story of Scotch-Irish racial formation would need to be told in terms of interactions with native Americans as well as African Americans.[72]

Conflicts between backcountry settlers and eastern elites, rather than urbane acts of statesmanship, lay behind much of the Scotch-Irish involvement in the American Revolution. Contrary to popular mythology, not all the Scotch-Irish rallied to the patriot cause. They did support the revolution overwhelmingly in Pennsylvania, in part out of a genuine democratic impulse and in part because the revolution offered an opportunity to help replace the proprietary Quaker government they so disliked. Even in Pennsylvania, however, the British succeeded in raising a loyalist regiment, consisting of Scotch-Irish and Catholic Irish from the Philadelphia region. Several individual Scotch-Irishmen played important roles in the high politics of the revolution in Pennsylvania, among them Thomas McKean and Joseph Reed. But there was considerable regional variation, determined in large measure by long-standing tensions between eastern elites and western settlers and between Anglicans and Presbyterians. New Jersey, for example, was riven by sectarian and political conflict, as was North Carolina, where the issues behind the Regulator movement survived well into the revolutionary period.[73]

In the North Carolina backcountry, where the fight for independence was led by the eastern elite, the Scotch-Irish were understandably hostile to the revolution. Hostility to the local Anglican elite overrode traditional Scotch-Irish antipathy to the British, and fugitive members of the Steelboys who had fled Ulster for North Carolina joined their Scotch-Irish brethren in forming a loyalist regiment. In the Waxhaws region of the Carolinas, on the other hand, the Scotch-Irish were resolutely anti-British. In parts of the southern backcountry, especially in South Carolina, the revolution degenerated into a bloody civil war, with the emerging planter elite of ex-Regulators continuing its fight for security, property and order.[74]

The Scotch-Irish role in the American Revolution, in short, was complex and ambiguous rather than unequivocal. Even where they supported the patriot cause, as they clearly did in Pennsylvania, they showed little enthusiasm for its egalitarian aspects, remaining staunchly anti-Catholic and opposing the abolition of slavery. Here, once again, the history of Irish attitudes to race and slavery could profitably be extended back from the antebellum period to the Protestant Irish America of the eighteenth century.[75]

The Scotch-Irish played a significant role in the emergence of an American political system in the years directly after the Revolution. While southern frontier life continued to define the experience of most Scotch-Irish people in the 1790s, it should be recalled that about one-quarter of them lived in Pennsylvania. Of this latter group, approximately half lived in the eastern portion of that state, and they included among their number some highly urbane and politically radical individuals. These were a far cry from the 'wild' backcountry settlers of South Carolina, memorably described in the disparaging words of the Anglican minister Charles Woodmason as 'a Sett of the most lowest vilest Crew breathing', 'a Tribe of Presbyterians', 'firing hooping, and hallowing like Indians'. While the Scotch-Irish of the southern backcountry formed the great majority of settlers from Ulster, and have duly received most scrutiny from historians, the urban dwellers of eastern Pennsylvania also deserve close attention.[76]

In both Ireland and eastern Pennsylvania, Ulster Presbyterians were heavily involved in republican politics in the 1790s. At the heart of their movement was an organization called the Society of United Irishmen. Inspired by the republicanism of both the American and the French Revolution, the international societies of United Irishmen included members in Ireland, France and the United States and have been aptly described as 'an important catalyst for the radicalism of the contemporary Atlantic world'. Out of the American Society of United Irishmen (founded in 1797) and similar Irish republican clubs in the United States emerged strong Irish support for Thomas Jefferson and his Republican faction, combined with an equally strong antipathy toward the then-dominant Federalist party.[77]

Fearful of Jeffersonian links with French and Irish radicals, the Federalists secured passage of the Alien and Sedition Acts in 1798. The first manifestation of anti-radical nativism in United States history, these laws required the registration of all resident aliens, extended the naturalization period for citizenship from five to fourteen years, and outlawed publications considered defamatory of the government or subversive of its laws (including, by implication, those too laudatory of France). That same year, the anticipated insurrection in Ireland came and went, with massive loss of life and eventual military destruction, followed by the Act of Union of 1800 which abolished Ireland's Parliament and introduced direct rule from London. Many of the rebellion's leaders made their way to America as political exiles, though the more prominent had to wait until the election of Jefferson in 1800. Among the exiles were Thomas Addis Emmett, William Sampson and William McNeven, each of whom would achieve prominence in American life while at the same time perpetuating a tradition of Irish republican radicalism that was well established in the United States by the 1790s.[78]

Among the more prominent Americans of Ulster Protestant heritage since the American Revolution have been the Confederate general, Thomas J. 'Stonewall' Jackson; the pedagogue, William H. McGuffey; the inventor of the mechanical reaper, Cyrus H. McCormick; the pro-slavery politician, John C. Calhoun; the frontiersman, Davy Crockett; and the outlaws, Frank and Jesse James. The Ulster Irish and their descendants have also exerted an influence on American politics quite out of proportion to their numbers, especially in the nineteenth century. Fifteen American presidents, from John Adams through Bill Clinton, have traced their lineage in part to Irish Protestant forebears. Three were the sons of Ulster Presbyterian immigrants: Andrew Jackson (1829–37), James Buchanan (1857–61) and Chester A. Arthur (1881–5). Three others were directly descended from Presbyterians who had come to America from Ulster: James K. Polk (1845–9), William McKinley (1897–1901) and Woodrow Wilson (1913–21). Of course, the extent to which these men regarded themselves as 'Scotch-Irish', let alone 'Irish', is quite another matter.

THE SCOTCH-IRISH IN 1790 AND AFTER

When the first federal census was taken in the United States in 1790, there were an estimated 3.17 million Americans of European origin and between 500,000 and 600,000 of African origin. It is generally agreed that somewhere between 440,000 and 517,000 Americans in 1790 were of Irish origin, accounting for between 14 and 17 per cent of the white population. More than three-quarters of the American Irish (over 350,000 of them) had either emigrated from Ulster or were descended from emigrants from that part of Ireland, and the great majority of the Ulster Irish were Presbyterians of Scottish origin. In 1790, Irish Presbyterians and their offspring accounted for about 10 per cent of the Euro-American population in the United States, with other Protestants (Methodists, Quakers and especially Anglicans) accounting for perhaps another 2 per cent. About 4 per cent of the population, or one-quarter of the American Irish, is thought to have been of Catholic Irish origin. In Pennsylvania, North Carolina and Georgia, Ulster Presbyterians accounted for more than 20 per cent of the population. And in the United States as a whole, the Scotch-Irish were second in numbers only to the English, with the Germans third.[79]

The ethnic origins of the American population in 1790 have been the subject of a heated, yet ultimately barren, historiographical controversy in recent years, with the cultural heritage of the Scotch-Irish at the heart of the matter. Just as Irish-American nationalist historians in the early twentieth century tried to subsume the Scotch-Irish into the general category of Irishness, a group of American historians has more recently tried to subsume them into the even more general category of 'Celticness'. Into this category are placed not only the Catholic Irish, the Welsh and Cornish, and the upland Scots, as one might expect, but also the lowland Scots, the Ulster Scots and even the northernmost and westernmost English. All are taken to be Celts, sharing similar languages and a common set of cultural characteristics. An extraordinary vision of American history then emerges. The Celts dominate the United States south of Philadelphia, while the Anglo-Saxons predominate north of that city. American sectionalism becomes a matter of Celt versus Anglo-Saxon. The American Civil War, a latter-day struggle between Cavaliers and Roundheads, features patterns of warfare (fierce, reckless and foolhardy) that were seen also at the battle of Culloden in 1746 and even among those fearsome Celts who resisted Roman incursions into Gaul. The famous 'rebel yell' of the Confederacy, in short, was more than a primordial echo; it was a living manifestation of Celticness in the nineteenth-century American South.[80]

It is not difficult to see the flaws in this Celtic thesis. It defines the word 'Celt' in a way that conforms to no previously accepted usage, lumping together the most disparate of peoples into an ostensibly common heritage and culture. The upland Scots, for example, referred to lowlanders as *sassenachs* (Englishmen), such was their sense of cultural difference between their own Gaelic-speaking culture and the heavily Anglicized polyglot culture to the South. The Lallans dialect spoken in the Lowlands, far from being authentically 'Scottish', was derived from Northumbrian Anglo-Saxon, with Norman French, Scots Gaelic, Flemish and Scandinavian influences. If the Scots differed so substantially among themselves, it is even more difficult to see how a western Englishman, a Welsh speaker, a lowland Scot and a peasant from southern Ireland might be said to share a common Celtic culture and attributes. If that were really so, the entrenched conflict in Northern Ireland could presumably have been solved quite easily many years ago. The pan-ethnic claims of the Celtic thesis, then, are easily refuted. More disturbing is its claim that the Celtic peoples (granting their existence, for the sake of argument) share common attributes that transcend historical time and space. Most historians, by virtue of the historical method itself, would reject this claim. While cultural continuity is certainly as important as cultural change, historians by definition tend to avoid the ahistorical, especially when it shades into racial mysticism, as it so clearly does in this case. A new theory of racial essentialism is surely the last thing the American South needs at this point in its history. The Celtic thesis, as one historian aptly concludes, merely serves to envelop the South in clouds of 'Celtic mist'.[81]

Nor did the Celtic thesis represent the first attempt by historians to incorporate the Scotch-Irish into an ethnic narrative ill-designed to accommodate them. In the late nineteenth and early twentieth centuries, Irish-American nationalist historians had insisted that the 'Scotch-Irish' assimilated into Irish culture after the plantations of the seventeenth century, and hence were neither Scottish nor half-Scottish but thoroughly Irish. In this way, they could be included in a single glorious chronicle of the 'Irish contribution' to the American past. Protestant Irish-Americans, however, had strenuously resisted this forced assimilation, employing the term 'Ulster Scots' as well as 'Scotch-Irish' to make their point. The Scotch-Irish, they insisted, were ineffably different from the Irish, despite their temporary sojourn in Ireland. This sensibility is perhaps most vividly captured in a rhetorical and doubtless apocryphal question, attributed to an 'old Ulster Scot' by one chauvinistic historian as late as 1944: ' "If a man is born in a stable, does that make him a horse?" ' Put another way (in the words of the same historian): 'The mere fact of a temporary residence of Scots in Ireland before emigrating to America does not transform them into people of a different race.' According to this interpretation, Scots who happened to reside in Ulster were and always would be pure-blooded Scots (whatever that might mean). Ethnic chauvinism of this kind, which stood as the counterpart of an often equally chauvinistic Irish Catholic nationalism, was for long a staple of Scotch-Irish history. That history was told largely in terms of a regrettable but largely unimportant Scottish detour through Ireland en route to America.[82]

The time is now surely ripe to move beyond all three of these outmoded narratives, Celtic, pan-Irish and ethnic chauvinist. What is needed instead is the incorporation of the Ulster Scots and their various migrations into the mainstream of Irish, British, and Atlantic historiography, and especially into the rich new vein of social and cultural historical writing opened up in both the United States and Ireland since the 1960s. Remarkably little has been written on the Scotch-Irish in the last generation. Compared to the recent historiography of Ireland, of the United States, and of the American Irish in the nineteenth century, theirs is a restricted and impoverished one. A good book on the eighteenth-century Scotch-Irish, taking the story from Scotland via Ulster to America, is badly needed. Such a book, doubtless somewhere in the making, would tell the history of the Scotch-Irish as the first great migration out of Ireland, a movement of people that had decisive consequences for the development of American history.[83]

In the year 1800, and for most of the preceding century, Irish America was a fundamentally Protestant place. To be Irish in America meant, in effect, to be Protestant and probably Presbyterian, a resident of Pennsylvania or the southern backcountry. This predominantly Protestant Irish America has as much claim to inclusion in the history of the American Irish as the predominantly Catholic versions that would follow, even if the Scotch-Irish deliberately sought to exclude themselves from the fold of Irishness in the nineteenth century. They did so in the face of a massive Catholic migration from Ireland, aware that the nature of Irish America, and of America itself, was about to change beyond recognition.

W hile Irish emigrants to America in the eighteenth century had been mainly Protestant, the emigrants of the nineteenth century were overwhelmingly Catholic. By the 1830s, Catholics exceeded Protestants in the transatlantic migration from Ireland for the first time since 1700. As mass emigration from Catholic Ireland got underway in the pre-famine era (1800–44), Irish Americans of Protestant descent loudly proclaimed their difference from the newcomers, calling themselves Scotch-Irish rather than Irish and assimilating rapidly into the mainstream of Protestant America. Irish-American history thereafter has a two-fold interest. It is the story, firstly, of the ongoing formation of ethnic identity among the predominantly Catholic Irish immigrants in the United States; but this story can be told only in terms of the repeated intersection of the Irish presence with the principal themes in American history, especially regarding urban life, labour, race, religion and politics.

ECONOMY AND SOCIETY IN RURAL IRELAND

Protestants continued to emigrate from Ulster in large numbers throughout the first half of the nineteenth century, dominating the transatlantic migration out of Ireland until about 1830. In the thirty-year period from the end of the American war for independence to the end of the Napoleonic wars (1783 to 1815), between 100,000 and 150,000 Irish crossed the Atlantic for North America. At least two-thirds of them were Presbyterians, with substantial farmers, weavers and artisans predominating. Then, between 1815 and 1845, another 800,000 to 1 million left Ireland for North America, twice as many as in the preceding two centuries combined. The rate as well as the volume of emigration accelerated sharply during this period; half the emigrants left Ireland in the twenty years from 1815 to 1834, the other half in the single decade from 1835 to 1844. Annual rates of transatlantic emigration from Ireland exceeded 20,000 for the first time in 1819–20, 50,000 in 1830–2, and 70,000 in 1840–2, reaching a peak of 90,000 in 1842. By 1840 only about 10 per cent of Irish emigrants to North America were Protestant, a figure that remained fairly constant for the remainder of the century. The age of mass Catholic emigration had begun.[1]

Why did this exodus take place? The overriding causes were population growth, lack of diversification in the economy and consequent pressure on land. The population of Ireland, which stood at 1.1 million in 1672, had doubled by 1732, doubled again by 1788 (4 million) and again by 1841 (8.2 million). Ulster, too, participated in this population explosion. Only about half a million people lived there in the mid-eighteenth century, but this number had increased almost five-fold to 2.4 million by the 1840s, despite more than a century of heavy emigration. The critical period in Ireland's population boom was about 1780 to 1820 when, for reasons that remain disputed by historians, the population of the country rose by 75 per cent. The most likely causes were earlier marriages and increased marital fertility, facilitated by greater ease of acquiring land and the expansion of potato cultivation. From 1820 onward, the rate of growth slowed significantly, due to later marriages and a consequent fall in the birthrate. But the massive expansion of population since the mid-eighteenth century had set the stage for the mass Catholic exodus that followed.[2]

While overpopulation is the most commonly cited explanation for nineteenth-century Irish emigration, it is not strictly speaking the case that there were too many people and too little land; the problem for the great bulk of the Irish population lay instead in how to get access to that land. The critical issues concerning land in Irish history have to do with tenure rather than ownership. The land was owned by a very small number of people; it was then leased, sublet and further sublet to rural dwellers ranging from graziers and strong farmers to penurious labourers. Most poor people in this period thought only of getting and retaining access to land as tenants, rather than actually owning their holdings themselves. Outright ownership would come only with the passage of various land reform acts in the late nineteenth and early twentieth centuries.

The rural poor in early nineteenth-century Ireland, just as in late eighteenth-century Protestant Ulster, responded to the unavailability of land in two principal ways. First, they banded together in secret societies, wreaking vengeance on those who enclosed common land with fences, restricted common rights of pasture, converted tillage land to grazing, reduced the amount of land available for rent in small patches for potato cultivation or took a lease on land from which another tenant had recently been evicted. From the Whiteboys of the 1760s to the Molly Maguires of the 1840s and 1850s, these societies sought to enforce their own moral code in response to violations and transgressions of customary practices of land usage by landlords, agents and tenants. Pre-famine Ireland had perhaps the most widespread and concerted pattern of agrarian violence anywhere in early nineteenth-century Europe. If this violence was one of the two principal responses to Ireland's land crisis, the other was emigration.[3]

Both the violence and the emigration were taking place within the context of British colonial control over Ireland. Within that colonial setting, the aspect of Irish society that demands most explanation in any account of emigration is the nature of the landholding system. Ireland is a small country, but in the nineteenth century it was one of remarkable diversity along regional lines and in terms of its social structure. Where in Ireland one lived, and what niche in the social structure one occupied, determined in large measure one's occupation, culture, religion and likelihood to emigrate.

Economically and socially, there were three distinct regions in nineteenth-century Ireland. The Northeast was the only part of the country with a diversified economy, the thriving industrial sector in and around Belfast being surrounded by relatively prosperous farming country. The rest of Ireland can be divided into two regions, lying on either side of 'an imaginary line, drawn from Dundalk in County Louth southward to the cities of Limerick and Cork'. East of this line stood most of the commercialized farming districts of Ireland, where strong and middling farmers made an often comfortable living, landless labourers were common and intensive pasture farming was widely practiced. West of the line lay a very different Ireland, where the land was generally poor and unsuited to grazing, populated by hundreds of thousands of small subsistence cultivators, often on joint tenancies, who were generally isolated from the wider market economy. Historians have pointed out that Ireland at this time contained not just a dual economy (commercial and subsistence farming), but several different economies, varying according to region and social class. In general, pre-famine Ireland can be characterized as 'a peasant society similar to that which existed in many parts of Europe, which was being penetrated, progressively but unevenly, by a money economy', such that different parts of the country stood at different levels of commercialization.[4]

There were just over eight million people in Ireland in 1841 (the last census before the Great Famine), of whom less than 14 per cent lived in towns of 2,000 or more inhabitants. Seventy-five per cent of all occupied males worked the land. Just over half of all rural dwellers (an estimated 900,000 families) held less than two acres of land on a temporary basis and on very precarious terms, usually paying their rent in labour rather than cash. Among those holding more than two acres, the agrarian social structure took the following form. At the very top of the pyramid were those who actually owned the land, including the Crown and a small number of wealthy landlords (about 10,000), many of them absentees. Some absentee landlords managed their estates through British or Irish agents, who were among the more frequent targets of agrarian violence. Most land in Ireland, however, was not managed by or for its immediate owners; instead it was leased to middlemen, who sublet to 'strong' and 'middling' farmers, who in turn often sublet to the rural poor, sometimes in parcels of less than one acre. Outside the Northeast, Dublin and a handful of other Irish cities and towns, the vast majority of the Irish population attempted to make a living cultivating land leased from others. This Irish farming population, measured by the occupation of heads of households, fell into four principal classes in 1841: 128,000 'strong farmers', 253,000 'middling farmers', 310,000 'smallholders' and 100,000 holders of joint tenancies, along with the 900,000 landless or virtually landless labourers who formed the base of the pyramid. Together with their families, these four groups accounted for the great bulk of the Irish population.[5]

A closer look at each category will help explain the nature of the rural class structure in pre-famine Ireland. The strong farmers accounted for only about 15 per cent of those rural dwellers holding two acres or more, yet they leased the great majority of Ireland's land and served as landlords to the vast classes of subletting farmers and tenant labourers below them. Strong farmers held a minimum of thirty acres in densely populated areas where tillage (or crop cultivation) predominated. In grazing areas they might own hundreds of acres, with herds of cattle or flocks of sheep in commensurate numbers. Except in Ulster, most of the strong farmers were Catholics. They employed large numbers of landless labourers, typically on a daily wage, and produced crops or animals for commercial sale. Both the farmers and the labourers who worked for them were caught up in the workings of a wider capitalist economy, the former producing commodities for sale and the latter selling their labour power in order to live. Below the strong farmers was a heterogeneous group of 253,000 families, falling into the category of 'middling farmers' by virtue of owning between ten and thirty acres. In 1841 they accounted for 30 per cent of Ireland's farmers.[6]

Close to the bottom of the rural pyramid were some 310,000 smallholders and their families, holding between two and nine acres of land, along with about 100,000 families holding land in common with others on joint tenancies (of which there were 30,000 in Ireland at this time). Nearly all the smallholders and joint tenants were Catholic (except in some parts of Ulster). The smallholders lived a very precarious existence, drawing what sustenance they could from the soil to pay their rent, tithes and taxes. Five acres of relatively good land was perhaps the bare minimum necessary for a family to survive; yet tens of thousands of smallholders held considerably less than this, and the prevailing custom of partible inheritance (dividing the land among all the children) meant that their children faced the prospect of even tinier holdings.[7]

The 100,000 or so joint tenants practiced forms of agriculture that stood in sharp contrast to the commercialized farming of the East. Under the *rundale* system, the tenants of a village (or, in Irish, a *clachan*) held the land in common, dividing it into an infield for cultivation and an outfield and mountain or wasteland for pasture. In the infield, each family held a series of small, widely scattered strips, graded according to quality and giving equal access to pasture land and, where appropriate, to water. Land in these communities was measured by quality rather than quantity; hence, a 'cow's grass', the amount of pasture land needed to graze a cow for a year plus the amount of arable land required to grow fodder for the winter, varied considerably in size according to the quality of the land allotted. Other, smaller measures included a cow's foot, a cow's toe and a sheep's foot, and there were reports of animals being held in common as well as land. This system of community landholding, found most commonly in the west of Ireland in the early nineteenth century, differed starkly from the commercial and individualistic ethos pervading agriculture in much of the rest of Ireland by that time.[8]

These, then, were the three principal categories of farmers or cultivators who held two acres or more: strong farmers, middling farmers and, at the bottom, precarious smallholders and joint tenants. Forming the base of the pyramid, below the ranks of the farmers proper, was by far the biggest single class in Ireland, the 900,000 families who either held no land or held less than two acres on a temporary basis. These were the labourers, who in areas of intensive pasture farming like Limerick and parts of Cork, often outnumbered farmers (defined as those with relatively secure access to two acres or more) by three or four to one. They accounted for 56 per cent of the Irish rural population as a whole in 1841, the remainder being composed of the three categories holding two or more acres. Many labourers held no land at all; at least 100,000 of them were farm servants, usually young men and women between sixteen and twenty-five years old, who lived with their employers. For them, labouring was often a phase in adolescence and early adulthood rather than a permanent occupation. Those who worked permanently as labourers desperately needed access to land for potato cultivation to feed their families, and could attain it by working as *cottiers* or as *conacre* tenants.

Cottiers were bound labourers who received a cabin and a plot of land, from two acres to as a little as a quarter-acre or less, on which to grow potatoes and perhaps raise a cow or pig. In return, the tenants performed a stated number of days' labour in the fields of their landlord, who was typically a strong or middling farmer rather than a big Anglo-Irish or British landowner. If an animal or two were raised, they might be sold to help pay the rent or to meet other expenses. Beyond these occasional cash transactions and the annual labour contract, however, cottiers rarely had much contact with the capitalist marketplace, especially in isolated areas. Even more precarious than the cottier was the *conacre* tenant, who grew his year's supply of potatoes by renting access to a plot of land, but not the right to live on it, again in return for his labour. Strong and middling farmers, once again, were the typical landlords in these cases. The piece of land rented might be as small as one-quarter of an acre.[9]

Which of these social groups was least and most likely to emigrate from Ireland? The least likely to leave in the pre-famine period were the richest and the poorest: landlords and strong farmers on the one hand, and joint tenants, landless labourers and cottier or conacre tenants on the other. Large numbers of middling farmers and smallholders left, but it was not until the Great Famine that the poorest rural dwellers would begin to emigrate to America. Before the famine they could not afford to go, and their culture may have constrained them from leaving even when it was possible. Those poor Irish who did leave generally went only as far as England or Scotland. This migration was a sizeable one, with 419,256 Irish having permanent residence in Britain by 1841, mainly in London, Liverpool, Manchester, Glasgow and a host of smaller industrial cities.[10]

Those who crossed the Atlantic in the pre-famine period were certainly very poor by American standards, but they were not usually as poor as those who stayed behind. If sheer poverty was the main impediment to overseas migration in the pre-famine era, historians have also pointed to cultural taboos, especially among the Irish-speaking peasantry of the West of Ireland. Conceptions of America varied according to class and region, with strong farmers from eastern Ireland and Protestants from Ulster much more likely to see emigration as opportunity than Irish-speaking peasants from the West, who composed only a very small minority of the overseas migration before the Famine. Prosperous middling and strong farmers among the Catholic emigrants, along with most Protestant farmers, were more likely to visualize their home-to-be in terms of individual liberation, family welfare and economic prosperity. Irish speakers from more remote regions of Ireland, by contrast, still tended to see emigration in terms of tragedy and alienation, a conception they appear to have retained until the catastrophe of the 1840s and in many cases beyond.[11]

While ever-increasing pressure on land was the essential precondition for the mass Catholic emigration of the early nineteenth century, matters were exacerbated by a variety of ailments besetting the Irish economy. Historians have pointed to the year 1815 as a major turning point in Irish history in this respect. High agricultural prices during the long Napoleonic wars between Britain and France had rewarded labour-intensive tillage rather than pasture farming, encouraging the subdivision of holdings and providing regular employment to labourers and cottiers. The end of the wars in 1815, however, triggered a chain of economic events with disastrous consequences for Ireland. As war-inflated grain prices fell by as much as 50 per cent, landlords began to shift from tillage to grazing (from 'corn' to 'horn'), raising rents, evicting tenants and enclosing common land. Just as the rate of population growth was reaching its peak, therefore, the amount of land available for rent, conacre and potato cultivation was contracting. Pushed out from the best land, some smallholders and cottiers began to settle the bog-lands and mountainsides if they could, a move made possible by the ubiquitous but precarious potato. Countless others emigrated.[12]

The collapse of the agricultural economy was accompanied by a drastic decline in rural-based domestic industry. Until 1815, the domestic spinning and weaving industries were widely diffused, not only throughout Ulster but also in east Connacht, north Leinster and even parts of Munster, providing an important supplementary income for many families. But in the grip of the economic depression after 1815, the woollen and cotton industries collapsed, and the linen industry was transformed. Under the traditional system of linen production, the farmer-weaver had generally grown his own flax, his wife and children had spun it into yarn, and he and his elder sons had woven the cloth and taken it to market. In poorer areas, mainly in northwest

Ireland, farmers supplemented their income by growing flax and providing yarn to weavers in the cloth-producing counties of south Ulster and north Leinster. Prosperous weavers in these counties often rented potato ground to cottiers who paid the rent by piecework in linen. The depression of the post-1815 era, followed by the mechanization of spinning after 1828 and of weaving after 1845, led to the rapid contraction of the linen industry in and around Belfast, causing severe economic dislocation in north Leinster and south Ulster, stretches of which were transformed into what one historian has aptly termed 'rural slums'.[13]

Those areas of Ireland that had contained a thriving domestic textile 'proto-industry' at the turn of the nineteenth century, indeed, underwent a process of de-industrialization, resulting in widespread unemployment, poverty and emigration. North-central Ireland, the region worst hit by the contraction of the linen industry, produced more emigrants, both numerically and as a proportion of its population, than any other region in both the pre-famine and the famine periods. The remainder of the country, outside the Northeast, did not industrialize during the nineteenth century, in large measure because Ireland could not hope to compete with cheap goods imported from Britain. Without industrial centers and thriving cities, nineteenth-century Ireland lacked the principal obstacle which might have prevented mass emigration from the countryside.[14]

By the 1830s, women made up about 35 per cent of all Irish emigrants to the United States. Most rural women in pre-famine Ireland played a critical role in the domestic economy, through some combination of household work, farm labour and (before its decline) cottage industry. Almost regardless of their social status, they were expected to be subservient to their fathers, husbands and brothers, and to appear in public only in strictly limited and controlled circumstances. Those women who emigrated left behind an authoritarian and patriarchal family structure which they must at times have been very glad to escape. In north-central Ireland, the devastation of the rural textile industry robbed tens of thousands of women of their livelihood, leading to substantial emigration in the 1830s and 1840s, so that by the latter decade the region already had an excess of males over females, a pattern found elsewhere in Ireland only in the late nineteenth century.[15]

In return for their inheritance or dowry (property given to daughters to assist them in marriage), children helped their parents in farm work or cottage industry, and were customarily obliged to look after them when they grew too old to support themselves. Family practices on inheritance and landholding varied widely across regions, with subdivision of the land between all the children, and consequent earlier marriages, most common in more remote western regions, where wasteland and cottage industry prevailed and where agricultural output for the market was limited. Travellers in west Kerry and Mayo reported that men were marrying in their early twenties and women as young as thirteen or fourteen. The daughters of these remote smallholders often brought a small portion of the family patrimony with them to their marriage. As a result, they were often able to marry landless labourers. Partible inheritance and early marriages were also quite widespread among middling and strong farmers, but the daughters of more prosperous farmers were granted cash dowries with increasing frequency. They usually married later than those further down the social scale, taking the inheriting sons of substantial farmers as their grooms if possible. Usually arranged by the bride's father through the mechanism of the 'match', these economically driven marriages paved the way toward impartible inheritance and primogeniture (whereby only one sibling, usually the eldest son, inherited the land), anticipating the dominant form of matrimony in post-famine Ireland. One of the peculiarities of the Irish land system is that what was being handed down through impartible inheritance was not actually a legal title to landed property but a customary right of tenant occupancy. Likewise, in partible inheritance, the parents subdivided land which they held as tenants, passing on and indeed proliferating a right to occupancy rather than outright ownership.[16]

How poor was Ireland in the first half of the nineteenth century? Visitors to Ireland often went home shocked by the degree of deprivation and suffering they had encountered. Among the most prominent of these visitors was the young French aristocrat, Alexis de Tocqueville, who toured the country with his friend Gustave de Beaumont in July and August 1835. Four years earlier, these two men had made a famous tour of the United States, one result of which was Tocqueville's classic text, *Democracy in America*. But where Tocqueville had detected considerable equality and opportunity in the United States, in Ireland he saw mostly poverty, squalor, and rapacious landlords. 'You cannot imagine', he wrote to his father, 'what a complexity of miseries five centuries of oppression, civil disorders and religious hostility have piled up on this poor people.' And to a cousin he wrote: 'I defy you . . . whatever efforts of the imagination you may make, to picture the misery of the population of this country. Every day we enter mud houses, covered with thatch, which do not contain a single piece of furniture, except a pot to cook potatoes.' The presence of pigs and other animals in these houses was a particular source of consternation to Tocqueville. Historical research has tended to confirm Tocqueville's gloomy picture. One historian has estimated that Irish per capita income before the famine was only two-fifths that in the United Kingdom as a whole (though it should be remembered that England was the richest country in Europe at this time). Still, even by more general European standards, much of Ireland was desperately poor, and the Irish poor were getting poorer as the famine approached.[17]

This, then, was the Ireland the pre-famine emigrants left behind. It was a country marked by a rapidly expanding population competing for ever-scarcer supplies of land, an ongoing crisis in the economy, pervasive poverty and considerable violence. The potato blight of the late 1840s, when it came, was unprecedented; nobody knew what it was and nobody could have predicted the scale of the catastrophe to come. But it was clear by the 1830s to anybody who cared to look that the bulk of the population was now dependent on a single, precarious crop; that the Irish peasantry lived in conditions of increasing squalor and degradation; that repeated subdivision of landholding, facilitated by potato cultivation, was making the problem worse; and that Ireland lacked the urban infrastructure or industrial base to absorb the impoverished, overflowing population of the countryside. One measure of the mounting crisis is that there was widespread destitution and even local starvation in the generation before the Great Famine, with the potato crop failing on a local or national basis in 1822, 1825–9, 1831–2, 1835–7, 1839 and three times again between 1840 and 1844. Counting emigration to Britain as well as North America, well over 1 million Irish men, women and children left Ireland between 1815 and 1845, out of a population that stood at only 5.5 million at the beginning of this period. Long before the Great Famine, which nobody knew was coming, the great Irish migration of the nineteenth century was well underway.[18]

EMIGRATION, ARRIVAL AND SETTLEMENT

While the fundamental causes of emigration in nineteenth-century Ireland lay in questions of landholding and economic structure, any comprehensive account of the subject also needs to consider the inducements that attracted Irish people to America and the means available to them to leave the country. The principal forces attracting emigrants to the United States were letters from Irish people already there, along with publicity and promotional material published by shipping companies and emigrant assistant societies. Alongside these enticements were a number of mechanisms of emigration that served to expedite the overseas passage from Ireland, chief among them assistance by landlords and the government, and a burgeoning transatlantic shipping industry.

Letters sent home by emigrants were a ready source of information about America, and the money they contained was critical to financing emigration out of Ireland. While much of the money was used for the upkeep of families and farms in Ireland, remittances came increasingly in the form of prepaid passage tickets. Already by the 1820s and 1830s, signs of a 'chain migration' out of Ireland are evident. Under this system, a single sibling went to America and, once established, did everything possible to bring out other relatives, including parents and the entire family if possible. 'This strongly marked sense of duty to family and kin', as one historian has remarked, 'meant that Irish emigration was peculiarly cumulative in its effects.'[19] The same historian has found that between one-third and one-half of Irish transatlantic emigrants in the period 1830 to 1845 had their passages financed by cash remittances or tickets sent by relatives from the United States. Along with letters, a second source of information for prospective emigrants was provided by the often propagandistic material on the United States circulated by brokers and agents of shipping companies. A third source was the emigrant guides published by emigrant assistance groups in the United States, of the sort founded by distinguished Catholic and Protestant Irishmen like Matthew Carey in Philadelphia and William J. MacNeven, William Sampson and Thomas Addis Emmet in New York City. On arrival in the seaports of the American Northeast, many of the immigrants were provided with work by these societies, along with information on wages and routes to inland destinations.[20]

One way the Irish poor could get to America in the pre-famine period was through assistance by the British government or by landlords. When the government placed some 2,500 impoverished Munster emigrants on farms in Canada in 1823–5, thousands of petitions arrived in London from Irish families asking for similar assistance. But the precedent was not followed and the government played only a very minor role in assisting emigration in the pre-famine era. Individual landlords played a more important role, though assisted emigration never accounted for more than a very small percentage of the total number of departures. Earl Fitzwilliam, for example, began to clear his congested Wicklow estates through eviction and assisted emigration in the early 1830s. Landlord assistance accelerated after 1838 when a new Poor Law made workhouse paupers chargeable to the estates from which they had been evicted and made possible their emigration through a combination of tax revenue and landlord assessments. The Wandesford family of

County Kilkenny sent over 2,000 people to Upper Canada and the mines of eastern Pennsylvania and southwestern Wisconsin between 1840 and 1844. Several other landlords launched smaller schemes of assisted emigration in the early 1840s. The great majority of emigrants in the pre-famine period, however, left not on assisted schemes but through their own devices. This circumstance explains why most of them came from the ranks of strong and middling farmers and the better-off smallholders, rather than the most vulnerable and impoverished elements of society.[21]

If, by 1830 or so, large numbers of these potential emigrants had decided to leave the Irish countryside and seek a better life in America, what means were available for their migration across the Atlantic? Ireland by the eve of the Famine had a communications and transportation network that had improved greatly since the turn of the century. It was, as yet, too early for railroads to have an impact on the emigrant flow, but the network of roads was much more extensive and efficient than it had been, and there were more boats and ships available to take the emigrants on the first leg of their journey, to the Irish or British port cities from which they would embark for America. For most of the early nineteenth century, the majority of Irish emigrants sailed to British North America, rather than the United States, travelling mainly on empty lumber ships returning to Québec or the Maritime Provinces after delivering their cargoes. The journey to the United States was about twice as expensive as that to Canada until the mid-1830s, due to carriage restrictions imposed by the British government on American-bound vessels, which forced shipping companies to raise prices. Complementing the cheap fares, the Canadian government enticed substantial numbers of immigrants to present-day Ontario by offering 50-acre land grants after 1819. For two decades after the end of the Napoleonic wars, then, most Irish emigrants came to British North America and sailed direct from Irish ports.[22]

Irish Protestants who emigrated to British North America typically settled there, especially from the 1820s onward as the Irish community in the United States became predominantly Catholic. Even after 1835, when most Irish transatlantic emigration was diverted to New York City, the Scotch-Irish continued to favour Canada. Coming from an Ireland in which Catholic nationalism was on the rise, they preferred Canada to the United States because it was British, mainly Protestant and relatively lacking in Irish Catholics. Two-thirds of the estimated 120,000 to 134,000 Irish-born and their offspring in Ontario in 1842, for example, were Protestants, most of them from Ulster. As many as 450,000 emigrants from Ulster came to North America between 1800 and 1845 alone, compared to only about 300,000 over the entire previous century. While most of these settled in British North America, immigration from Ulster to the cities of the United States had by no means ceased. Indeed, cities like New York, Philadelphia, Baltimore and New Orleans included Scotch-Irishmen among their most substantial merchants, lawyers and public figures throughout the antebellum era.[23]

In sharp contrast to the Irish Protestants, the majority of Irish Catholics who landed in British North America quickly made their way south to settle in the towns and cities of the United States. Some vessels simply touched port very briefly in Nova Scotia or New Brunswick before sailing on to New York with their passengers. Most of the United States-bound emigrants, however, disembarked in Canada before making their way south across the Canadian border. Québec was the most important port of arrival. From there the emigrants went by steamboat up the St Lawrence to Montreal, crossed by land and boat to New England, and then trekked down to Troy, Albany and New York City. A second route led from Montreal to Kingston, across Lake Ontario to Buffalo, Cleveland, Toledo and the West. In Cleveland, the emigrants could make connections for Cincinnati, Pittsburgh, Louisville and other Midwestern cities. Other Irish emigrants moved westward across Canada before turning south to settle in Michigan, Illinois, Wisconsin, Iowa and Minnesota.[24]

From the mid-1830s onward the British port of Liverpool emerged as the primary point of departure for Irish transatlantic emigrants, with New York City rather than Canada as the primary destination. The average sailing to both Canada and the United States was six weeks. Passage from Liverpool to New York was generally safer and faster than from Ireland to Canada, but it was still more expensive; getting across the Irish Sea was an additional expense, so many of the poorer emigrants continued to go to British North America direct from Ireland and made their way from there to the United States. The relaxation of British passenger regulations, combined with ever-increasing trade between Liverpool and New York, however, continued to drive prices down, so that by the mid-1830s the fare of £3 10s from Liverpool did not greatly exceed that of £2 15s from the Irish ports. Departures from Ireland to the United States equalled those to Canada by this time, and would quickly exceed them. The Canadian trade, though it remained very important in the 1830s and 1840s, was increasingly overshadowed by the Liverpool-New York route.[25]

Conditions in Liverpool prior to the transatlantic crossing left a great deal to be desired in terms of safety, hygiene and basic human decency. On arrival in the city, the Irish were preyed upon by a variety of hucksters, confidence tricksters and small-time entrepreneurs who populated the fringes of the emigrant trade. Many of these people were themselves Irish, and used their Irishness to good advantage in preying upon the new arrivals. In the worst cases, gullible emigrants were tricked into buying worthless passage tickets, and having lost their savings they often ended up staying in Liverpool permanently, in conditions of great poverty. More often the emigrants arrived with, or purchased on arrival, tickets on vessels whose departure was weeks later than advertised. Sometimes there was no vessel at all. 'Runners' were sent out from the numerous boardinghouses along the waterfront to defraud these emigrants of what little money they might have. For short-term accommodation, the boardinghouses were able to charge highly exorbitant rates. Or a family might rent attractive-sounding accommodations at more reasonable rates, only to end up sharing a cellar or a windowless room with several other families, in damp and pestilent surroundings. While some Irish emigrants had certainly come to Liverpool with the intention of staying there at least until they could earn enough to finance a transatlantic passage, many others had hoped to pass through quickly but ended up staying for months or years. [26]

When the time finally came for departure, conditions on board the old and leaky vessels often bore scant resemblance to what had been promised by the ticket brokers at the time of sale. Irish ships that crossed the Atlantic were engaged primarily in the timber, potash and grain trades, carrying these goods into Ireland and emigrants on the return voyage. Ships from Canada brought timber to Liverpool and filled their holds with emigrants for the return leg; those travelling between Liverpool and the United States carried emigrants, chemicals and iron, across the Atlantic to New York and often continued their journey with manufactured goods bound for southern ports like Charleston, Mobile or New Orleans, before travelling back to Liverpool with a cargo of cotton. The primary function of these vessels was trade in commodities rather than the transport of human cargo. They were built to carry goods, not emigrants, and they adapted to the latter purpose only gradually and crudely. Passengers travelled in the steerage holds, which were empty of cargo on one leg of the voyage. The first ships exclusively for the emigrant trade were equipped in the 1830s, but even these were usually hastily converted cargo ships on which passengers were typically allotted only a few square feet apiece, not enough room for adults to stand up in. Passengers were usually allowed on deck during the day but slept below decks. Ventilation was poor, and the steerage quarters were highly conducive to the spread of contagious diseases such as smallpox, dysentery, cholera and typhus. Shipboard mortality rates were high during the cholera years of 1832 and 1834, but remarkably low (2 per cent or less) in normal years, given the conditions. During the frequent Atlantic storms, the hatches were battened down, so that passengers endured chaos and panic in total darkness. This must have been all the more terrifying to a rural people whose folklore about the sea included fearful tales of shipwreck, death and the horrors of the unknown.[27]

As well as the mass immigration to Canada and the Northeast, there was a smaller but still significant migration, both directly and indirectly, from Ireland to the American South. Seaboard cities like Baltimore, Charleston and New Orleans sent out products like tobacco, flax and cotton to the leading Irish ports, and brought back Irish emigrants as ballast on the return voyage. The Irish-born population in Charleston in the late 1840s helped to tip the balance of the city's population, for the first time in its history, toward a brief-lived white majority. Immigration direct from Ireland to Charleston had declined after about 1800, so that the majority of the city's Irish-born population in the 1820s, 1830s and 1840s came to the city from New York, usually to fill positions of menial labour. New Orleans, the largest (and in many ways the most distinctive) city in the South, was the most significant southern port of arrival for Irish and German immigrants. By 1850, one in every five members of the city's white population had been born in Ireland (and many more, usually of Ulster Protestant extraction, were second-generation or beyond). The 'old Irish' of New Orleans, in the period up to 1830, included some very wealthy and prominent merchants of Ulster origin, as well as many artisans, coffeehouse owners and managers of dry good stores. St Patrick's Day was celebrated by these Protestant Irish in New Orleans as early as 1809. From the 1830s onward, however, there was a steadily increasing flow of Catholic Irish, shifting the racial balance of the city, as in Charleston, to a white majority. Most of these new immigrants arrived on cotton ships direct from Liverpool and, being generally quite poor, settled in New Orleans as manual labourers.[28]

One of the more colourful episodes in the story of Irish emigration to the American South took place in Texas in the 1820s and 1830s. After its war of independence in 1821, the new republic of Mexico took over from imperial Spain a vast expanse of land extending from Guatemala to Oregon, including the state of *Coahuila y Tejas*, which served as a buffer against the expansionist United States. Seeking to populate this northern state, the Mexican government provided huge land grants to agents called *empresarios*, whose task was to colonize the land with settlers in return. Among these *empresarios* were two Irishmen, John McMullen and James McGloin, who established a colony named *San Patricio de Hibernia* in the Nueces River Valley, just south of San Antonio. A second colony, *Refugio*, was founded in 1834 on the Gulf of Mexico by two more Irish *empresarios*, James Power and James Heweston. Power had distributed handbills and posters in the Wexford area of Ireland in 1833 and led a party of colonists on the ship *Prudence* from Liverpool at the end of that year. In all, about 150 Irish families were settled in this way in *Coahuila y Tejas* between 1829 and 1834, and many emigrants died from cholera or shipwreck en route. The Irish colonists in Texas were clearly among the better-off Irish emigrants of the pre-famine period, paying up to £60 (roughly four times the annual wages of a labourer) for their passage from Ireland to Liverpool, stopover in Liverpool, transatlantic fare to New Orleans and passage from there to Texas. Most arrived in family groups, bringing with them farming implements, provisions, furniture and textile looms, and enough capital to survive until the first harvest. Clearly, they did not come from the more impoverished ranks of the Irish social hierarchy.[29]

The Irish colonists of Texas in the 1830s were but one small stream feeding into what had by then become a great river of Irish Catholic emigration. The Irish accounted for a remarkably high proportion of total immigration to the United States in the antebellum era. The 54,338 immigrants who arrived from Ireland between 1821 and 1830 made up 36 per cent of the total number of arrivals, while the 207,381 of the period 1831–40 made up 35 per cent. This percentage would reach 45.6 per cent during the 1840s, before dropping to 35 per cent again in the 1850s. For the remainder of the nineteenth century, while the aggregate numbers never dropped far below 400,000, the Irish percentage of total immigration hovered between 10 and 20 per cent. In proportional terms, then, Irish immigration had its greatest impact on the United States between 1820 and 1860. Long before the Great Famine of the 1840s, the Irish had a considerable impact on American social life, especially in towns and cities. Just as in contemporary Britain, Irish immigrants displayed a very strong preference for settling in urban centers.[30]

As might be expected given social conditions in Ireland, poverty and disease were among the distinguishing characteristics of the Irish in virtually every American city where they settled. The Irish-born share of the inmates of Boston's House of Industry, for example, rose from 28 to 37 per cent between 1834 and 1845, at a time when the Irish still made up only 2 per cent of that city's population. In the almshouses of Philadelphia and New York City almost half the foreign-born inmates were Irish-born in 1834. Given their poverty, the Irish were susceptible to a wide range of infectious diseases as well. In New Orleans, to cite one of the starker examples, they were the chief victims of cholera, malaria and yellow fever. The 6,000 residents of the city who died in the cholera outbreak of 1832 were mainly Irish. Malaria was especially common among the city's ditchers and canal diggers, occupations in which the Irish were heavily concentrated. And the mortality rate of the Irish in New Orleans during the great yellow fever epidemic of 1853 is estimated at one in every five, with the Irish accounting for one-third of all fatalities.[31]

Alongside poverty and disease, contemporaries reported widespread criminality and violence, though the accounts are often so distorted by nativism and snobbery that it is difficult to disentangle fact from fantasy. Perhaps the most notorious center of Irish settlement anywhere in the United States in the antebellum era was Five Points, in the heart of New York City's Sixth Ward. Populated by African Americans and the poorest Irish immigrants in the 1820s and 1830s, the area lay at the intersection of five streets in lower Manhattan, situated next to the filled-in Collect Pond, which soon became a major health hazard. In the middle of Five Points was the Old Brewery, which was transformed into a dwelling in 1837 that housed several hundred men, women and children, divided about equally between Irish and African Americans. Clustered around it were other crowded, dangerous tenements, with individual buildings housing as many as one hundred residents. By 1830, Five Points had become notorious as a center of crime, prostitution, bawdy entertainment, alcoholism and violence. Irish gangs like the Kerryonians and the Dead Rabbits, based in Five Points and the neighbouring Bowery, gave the area a colourful and dangerous reputation. Recent archaeological research, however, has revealed details of the family lives, work habits and material culture of the Five Points Irish, calling into question the nativist perception of the area as a den of Irish iniquity.[32]

LABOUR AND RACE

Measured by the indices of almshouse admissions, disease, housing and criminality, it is abundantly clear that the Irish in antebellum America were very poor. By all accounts they were the poorest social group in the country other than African Americans and Native Americans. The obvious question is why? Part of the answer lies in the desperate conditions that were enveloping the Irish countryside in the pre-famine period, and part in the nativist discrimination they encountered on arrival in America, which will be considered presently. Before turning to nativism, however, it will be useful to get some sense of the types of work available to Irish immigrants and how this affected their position in their new society. The Irish were consigned to particular jobs in part because of prejudice and in part because they arrived in the United States with few skills or resources compared to the native-born or to other immigrants. The more substantial of the Irish Catholic immigrants arrived in the United States in a position to do well and usually fulfilled their expectations; but the majority lacked the resources to leave the cities where they landed and soon settled into lifetimes of menial labour. German immigrants, by contrast, tended to arrive with greater skills and resources and were more likely to come in family groups; they were much more likely than the Irish to move on from their port of arrival, whether New York or New Orleans, and settle in the rural interior. Cities like Boston, New York, Philadelphia, Baltimore, Charleston and New Orleans all developed substantial populations of impoverished and indigent Irish immigrants long before the great influx of Irish refugees from the famine of the late 1840s.[33]

The history of the American Irish in the workplace during this period can be summed up in two words: menial labour. As Ralph Waldo Emerson put it: 'The poor Irishman, the wheelbarrow is his country.' Not every Irish immigrant was consigned to manual work, of course; but the great majority, both men and women, were. In the cities and towns of the North, Irish men worked predominantly at manual jobs, digging, demolishing and building. They worked also as carters, draymen (haulers of goods), teamsters, stage drivers, stablemen, boatmen, hucksters and peddlers. The Irish displaced free blacks from many unskilled positions, especially from work as waiters, servants, coachmen, white-washers, carpet shakers, chimney sweeps and boot-blacks. The more skilled Irish immigrants (artisans) included carpenters, masons, plasterers and bricklayers. But many of these Irish skilled workers were concentrated in crafts that were declining under the pressure of mechanization and factory labour, most notably tailoring, shoemaking and weaving. They were often employed as temporary out-workers and pieceworkers, rather than being employed in a factory or a craftsman's shop. And those Irish apprentices who did serve time in these trades under craftsmen found, like many other American workers at this time, that their own path to independence as a full-fledged artisan was blocked by the erosion of their craft in the face of industrialization.[34]

Irish women in the North came to dominate domestic service and the so-called 'needle trades'. They held three-quarters (about 8,000) of the domestic service jobs in New York City by mid-century. While domestic work was by definition servile, most historians have argued that Irish women were better off in the homes of rich New Yorkers or Bostonians, which offered a regular income, food and a roof above their heads, than in the world of factory work with its irregular employment, low wages and long hours. Still, second only to domestic service as a source of employment for Irish women in early and mid-nineteenth-century America was industry. From the late 1830s and early 1840s onward, Irish women worked increasingly in the 'needle trades', as seamstresses, milliners, dressmakers, shirt and collar makers, embroiderers and makers of lace fringe, tassel and artificial flowers. While much of this work had traditionally been done at home, now it was being concentrated in sweatshops and factories. Taking in laundry or lodgers provided an alternative for many women, but in general the options beyond service or sewing were rather limited in the antebellum period. Many immigrant women turned to the streets, so that by the 1840s Irish women comprised the largest group of prostitutes in most northern cities.[35]

In the South, the Irish were so associated with servile labour that they were consistently used as substitutes for slaves in more dangerous tasks like draining plantations, building levees and digging ditches and canals in malaria-infested land. Compared to the valuable investment of a slave, an Irish labourer was cheap and expendable. As one Virginia planter told Frederick Law Olmsted, the northern observer of slavery, 'It's dangerous work . . . and a Negro's life is too valuable to risk at it. If a Negro dies it's a considerable loss you know.' In southern ports like Charleston and New Orleans, the Irish were used in place of slaves to perform the dangerous task of catching and stacking the huge bales of cotton thrown down onto ocean-going vessels from the levees. In the words of another southerner quoted by Olmsted: 'niggers are worth too much to be risked here; if the Paddies are knocked overboard . . . nobody loses anything'. The Irish in southern cities also tended to displace hired-out slaves and free blacks from positions as waiters, servants, cabmen and, to a lesser extent, female domestic servants. They also joined volunteer fire companies and the police force in large numbers, a pattern that had already come to mark the history of the Irish in northern cities.[36]

From Canada to the Old Northwest and from the Northeast to the deep South, the Irish provided a cheap, expendable labour force for the construction of North America's emerging industrial and urban infrastructure. Chief among the types of work they did in this respect was canal construction. The more skilled work on these projects was typically done by English or Welsh miners and masons, but the Irish provided most of the muscle and brawn. 'Who else would dig, and delve, and drudge, and do domestic work, and make canals and roads, and execute great lines of Internal Improvement?' asked Charles Dickens after visiting the United States in 1842. Living in tents and shanty towns, Irish labourers in the 1810s and 1820s built the Erie Canal in New York, the Blackstone Canal to Worcester, Massachusetts, the Enfield Canal near Hartford, Connecticut and the Farmington Canal to New Haven, Connecticut. In the 1820s and 1830s, Irishmen built the canals leading into the Pennsylvania anthracite region, often staying there to work as labourers in the mines when their job was done. In the South, too, the Irish played a dominant role in canal construction, often working on the same projects as slave labourers. On the 147-mile canal to Lynchburg, Virginia in the 1830s, for example, two-thirds of the labourers were Irish. And the New Basin Canal from New Orleans to Lake Ponchatrain was manned by Irish labourers specially recruited from Philadelphia along with others imported direct from Ireland. The thousands who died in the course of building the canal were commemorated in a popular song, which doubtless exaggerated the scale of the casualties: 'Ten thousand Micks, they swung their picks,/To dig the New Canal/But the cholera was stronger "n thay,/An" twice it killed them awl.'[37]

Irish canal culture in the United States has been intensively studied by historians. The most recent accounts have emphasized the destructive impact of immigration and canal work on an already disintegrating peasantry that was abruptly removed from Ireland and transplanted into the industrial United States. The 'rough culture' of the Irish canallers in America, according to this interpretation, was marked by transience, appalling living conditions, a highly dangerous work environment, self-destructive expressions of masculinity (including alcoholism and faction-fighting) and general social degradation. This emphasis on the destructive impact of early industrial capitalism on human lives stands in sharp contrast to the emphasis on human agency and cultural autonomy at the heart of most historiography on nineteenth-century American labour. Unlike native-born artisans, whose skilled positions were gradually eroded by industrialization and who therefore suffered a decline in status and a gradual descent into wage labour, most Irish immigrants had few if any skills and did not fill a privileged social position from which to fall. Impoverished peasants in Ireland, they became in America a mobile army of cheap, unskilled labour for the industrial revolution. Their story therefore has to be told differently from that of the native-born artisans who responded to the erosion of their skilled positions and privilege by becoming the leaders of the antebellum labour movement in the United States. The Irish canallers and diggers and haulers belonged to a largely forgotten narrative of American history, that of the unskilled immigrant worker.[38]

Despite the severity of their exploitation, it should not be thought that these Irish canallers belonged to a dysfunctional culture, devoid of resources with which to fight back. The point is that they fought back with different resources from those of the native-born skilled workers who founded and led powerful trade union movements as early as the 1830s. The unskilled Irish, by contrast, had available to them a rich tradition of violent resistance in rural Ireland, which they deployed to dramatic effect along the canals, public works and railroads of early industrial America. At first this violence took the form of faction-fighting, with workers from one part of Ireland doing battle with those from another. The most commonly reported antagonists were the Corkonians (evidently from County Cork) and the Fardowners (apparently from County Longford), who clashed frequently on canal and railroad construction projects from Canada to New Orleans. Hundreds of Longford men and Corkonians fought along the banks of the Chesapeake & Ohio Canal in Maryland in 1834. When five men were killed and countless others wounded in a pitched battle between the two sides near Willamsport, Maryland in November of that year, the local militia was assisted by US Army troops in restoring order. This was the first time in American history that the federal government intervened to stop a labour dispute. The troops, ironically enough, were sent in by President Andrew Jackson, the son of immigrants from northern Ireland.[39]

It needs to be emphasized that there was more to this violence than faction-fighting. Irish labourers were not feuding for the sake of it; the Corkonians and Fardowners fought each other for access to employment, each side attempting to drive the other off the works and take its place. Irish labourers often retaliated against bosses who were late in paying them by destroying the work they had done. Clearly this was not mindless violence but deliberate sabotage, reminiscent of how fences were destroyed and pasture land dug up to render it fit for conacre tillage (i.e. potato cultivation) in contemporary Ireland. Even more reminiscent of the Irish context was the presence of secret societies in Irish-American canal communities. Organizations of the Whiteboy and Ribbonmen type – complete with handgrips, passwords, recognition signs, oaths of secrecy and coffin notices – were widely reported as being active among canallers in the Northeast and mid-Atlantic states. When more than one hundred Irish labourers, armed with 'guns, clubs and other deadly weapons', descended on the parts of the Chesapeake & Ohio operated by German contractors and labourers, destroying their living quarters and attempting to drive them off the canal on 11 August 1839, for example, their uprising was crushed by the local militia and blamed on the machinations of a secret society.[40]

If faction-fighting and secret society violence represented a form of labour activism with its roots in the pre-industrial Irish countryside, the form of organizing most suited to the prevailing conditions in industrial America was the trade union, with its standard weapons of collective bargaining and strikes. Already by the 1840s, Irish canal workers throughout North America were substituting strikes for violence, and more formal labour organizations for secret societies. But it was in industry and the urban trades, rather than on the canals, that the antebellum Irish made their most significant contribution to trade unionism. Irish coal heavers, shoemakers, carpenters, construction workers and boatmen played a central role in the massive strike that began in Philadelphia in 1835 and spread up the Schuylkill River to the anthracite region of northeastern Pennsylvania, making common cause with the leaders of Philadelphia's General Trades Union. While the leaders of this organization were largely British and native-born, two of the more prominent leaders, John Ferrall and John Ryan, were born in Ireland. Inspired by this spirit of inter-ethnic and inter-religious solidarity pervading many labour movements in the Northeast in the mid-1830s, Irish Catholic and Protestant handloom weavers in the suburb of Kensington banded together to win better wages from their employers. This short-lived unity quickly crumbled, however, with the onset of economic depression in 1837, and the labour movement of Philadelphia disintegrated into anti-immigrant violence. Similarly in New York City, the inter-ethnic cooperation of the 1830s did not survive the downturn in the economy and consequent upsurge in nativism.[41]

While nativists tended to regard the Irish as a source of cheap, 'scab' labour, the Irish regarded African Americans in strikingly similar terms. The extent to which the Irish were in direct competition for jobs with blacks in the pre-famine period is open to debate. African Americans and Irish immigrants did vie with each other for jobs as personal and domestic servants, as labourers and waiters, and on the waterfront. And black workers were often used as strikebreakers to end strikes by Irish labourers. Yet the Irish typically succeeded in displacing black labour quickly, so that some historians have suggested that their chief source of labour competition thereafter was actually new Irish immigrants rather than African Americans. While the Irish did sometimes fight each other over work, and fought white immigrants like the Germans as well, most of their animus on this matter was directed against black workers, often in the form of riots and other outbreaks of violence.[42]

The degree of racial conflict between the Irish and African Americans in the antebellum United States raises the question of the racial status of the Irish themselves. What does their fear and dislike of African Americans say about their own insecurity in racial terms in their adopted homeland? Irish immigrants in the nineteenth century, as is well-known, were depicted both textually and visually in racially inferior terms. The images are stark and at first sight shocking: swarthy, low-browed, simian Irishmen, standing only a level or two above the animal kingdom, and apparently sharing the same degree of racial degradation attributed by contemporaries to African Americans. And yet, by the end of the nineteenth century (even sooner, according to some historians), Irish immigrants or their American-born children had achieved not only occupational parity but rough social and cultural equality with other native-born Americans. African Americans, on the other hand, had been liberated from slavery but were still subject to a pernicious variety of racial controls.[43]

To what extent was the racism of the Irish, and specifically their self-conscious adoption of a 'white' racial identity, a means to their assimilation into American life? The Irish in Ireland presumably shared to some extent the general European propensity to attach negative connotations to 'blackness', even if they had not yet encountered racial oppression in its distinctively American form. When Irish immigrants came to the United States, they soon discovered that all sorts of actions – from the acceptance of certain types of work to the putting on of 'black face' by working-class minstrels (practiced also by secret society members in Ireland, though with a very different meaning) – were fraught with racial significance. But to argue, as some historians do, that the Irish 'opted for' or 'chose' whiteness, deliberately distancing themselves from African Americans in order to advance themselves socially, seems unnecessarily abstract and tends also to overestimate the degree of conscious agency involved in the process. The Irish, we seem to be told, *ought* to have adopted a more egalitarian sense of racial identity in America. That they did not is explained by most historians in terms of the failings of individual immigrants, which cumulatively had disastrous effects for the history of American race relations. But explaining the formation of racial ideologies too heavily in terms of individuals' actions, rather than the structure that determined those actions, runs the risk of blaming one victim (the Irish) for the greater misfortunes of another (African Americans).[44]

Picture the case of an impoverished Irishman living with his family in an infested cellar in Manhattan's Sixth Ward. If he took a job on the docks once held by an African American, so that he could move his family up to a tiny, windowless room on the floor above, had he really 'opted for whiteness' in any meaningful sense? Or had he taken an action, which, because of the racial structure of the United States, had important racial consequences?

Those Irishmen who drove black workers from the docks and excluded them from labour organizations knew what they were doing, and they doubtless advanced their assimilation by doing so. But the American Irish did not create the social and racial hierarchy into which they came, and to expect them to have overturned this hierarchy in the course of putting food on their tables is surely unrealistic. It goes without saying that the argument here is intended not to downplay the extent of Irish-American racism in the nineteenth century, which was undeniably considerable, but simply to call for a better historical explanation of that racism – one that shifts at least part of the focus away from individual agency and toward the wider social and cultural structure in which both Irish immigrants and African Americans operated. Nor, of course, was assimilation through racism the only course followed by Irish immigrants in America; throughout the nineteenth century many Irish men and women rejected this course of action and did what they could to promote racial justice and social reform generally. To explain why the majority did not, the actions and decisions of individual immigrants need to be put in a broader economic, political and cultural context, both American and Irish, than they have been so far.[45]

One potential source of Irish-American racism was that Irish immigrants were themselves 'racialized' as an inferior people on arrival in the United States, which may have made them all the more outspoken and militant in their claims to 'whiteness'. Yet the extent of Irish racial subjugation in America is open to considerable exaggeration. At the level of popular stereotype, the Irish were widely portrayed in racially inferior terms, though this does not mean that everybody saw them in this way or, more importantly, that they saw themselves in such terms. At the level of employment, the Irish were undoubtedly confined to manual labour in the period before 1870, filling positions (canal workers and domestic servants, for example) that the native-born and even other immigrants would not touch. Very often, as in the case of dock-workers, cartmen, waiters and servants, they took jobs that had previously been reserved for the most subordinate group in northern society, 'free Negroes'. Working in these occupations inevitably carried certain racial connotations, reinforcing and indeed generating the popular imagery of the Irish as inferior. At the level of political, civil and legal rights, however, the Irish faced few restrictions. Irish immigrants were eligible for citizenship after a five-year waiting period and, when they became citizens (even before, once Tammany Hall perfected its technique), male Irishmen could vote.

In this respect, an important distinction needs to be drawn between the nineteenth-century Irish, on the one hand, and racially subordinate groups like

African Americans and the Chinese, on the other. Neither of the latter two groups was considered eligible for citizenship for long stretches of American history. While free African Americans in the antebellum North had some degree of abridged citizenship, they were denied the right to vote in most states. Indeed, the removal of property qualifications for white males was accompanied in states like New York by the enactment of racial barriers, so that the minority of African Americans who had passed the property test before the 1820s were now disenfranchised along with all black males. The infamous Dred Scott decision of 1857 excluded black Americans altogether from protection under the Constitution. In the states of the Old Northwest, moreover, blacks were excluded not only from citizenship but from the right to settle at all; no such restrictions, of course, were placed on the internal migration of the Irish. As for the naturalization of immigrants, American statute law dating from 1790 held that only 'free white' people could become citizens, thereby excluding the Chinese from naturalization when they began to arrive in large numbers from the mid-nineteenth century onward. During Reconstruction, black Americans were deemed eligible for citizenship through naturalization or birth, but racial barriers against Asian citizenship remained in place until the 1950s. The closest that Irish immigrants came to suffering similar disabilities was the nativist proposal, repeatedly made in the nineteenth century but never passed, to extend the waiting period for naturalization from five to twenty-one years. And Irish voting rights, despite widespread accusations of fraudulent naturalization and bloc voting, were never abridged.[46]

Judged by the criteria of naturalization and citizenship rights, then, it is clear that the Irish were never consigned to the same inferior position as African Americans and Asian Americans. The law, however, is a tricky subject to interpret. Formally speaking, the Irish were in one sense better off than other subordinate groups; but in social practice and popular stereotype the antebellum Irish faced abundant discrimination, much of it frankly racial in character. If this racial subordination was less severe than that faced by others, it was racial nonetheless. In distinguishing between degrees of racial subordination, the point is not to downplay the extent of popular hostility, labour discrimination and general social degradation faced by the Irish in nineteenth-century America. It is simply to insist that there are degrees of racial discrimination, and that racism cannot be understood at the level of cultural stereotype alone; the perspectives of labour, politics and citizenship laws must also be added to the picture.

The great unanswered question in the debate over 'whiteness', however, is surely the most important one: How did the Irish regard themselves? It might be noted, first, that the debate as it stands deals almost exclusively with the public actions of male Irish workers and their male, native-born critics. Yet no theory on Irish racial identity could claim to be complete or valid unless it incorporated the missing half of the Irish-American population. What becomes of the debate on whiteness if we incorporate into it the female half of the Irish population, so many of whom worked not in factories or other places outside the home, but as domestic servants? How did Irish-American women, and hence the Irish-American community as a whole, 'become white'? This question has scarcely been asked by historians let alone answered. As for the male and public realm to which the debate confines itself, the existing historiography says a great deal more about how hostile observers viewed the Irish than about how they saw themselves, relying largely on sources (political and cultural texts) left by people other than the working-class immigrants.[47]

How, then, did the (male) Irish regard themselves racially? Preliterate peasant immigrants, by definition, tend to leave less accessible forms of evidence for historians to use. But by the same token, most of them would have known little or nothing of the political cartoons and other forms of iconography in which Americans portrayed them as racially inferior and even subhuman. These images were intended for elite and middle-class rather than Irish consumption. Most Irish people, of course, were painfully aware of their subordinate status in the eyes of their British and American detractors; but it does not follow that they experienced this oppression in racial terms, even if their oppressors did. To have asked the immigrants themselves how they 'became white' would surely have been to ask a nonsensical question. If the immigrants had to attach a racial label to themselves, in order to conform to the peculiar conventions of their new homeland, there was never much question what that label would be. That they were 'white' was self-evident, if such odd terminology were required; in the meantime, they might continue to fraternize with their black friends in Five Points and other neighbourhoods. But to adopt the label 'white' in America was to automatically define oneself as non-black, and so it quickly became clear that the best route to acceptance as fully 'white' was at the expense of those defined as black.[48]

Perhaps the most pressing task is to begin to investigate the Irish origins of immigrant attitudes and behaviour. While some historians have examined the history of racial oppression in Ireland, considerable work on this question remains to be done. The dynamics of Irish society in the eighteenth and nineteenth centuries, with its religious sectarianism and segregation, provide an important background to the American story. Accustomed to religious and status group identity and conflict in Ireland, the immigrants arrived in America with a notion of group survival and militant force that translated easily into racism and violence. They may have had no experience of American-style racism before coming to New York and Boston and San Francisco, but they had plenty of experience of a society riven by prejudice and conflict. Assailed by nativists and racists once they arrived in New York, the Irish found themselves fighting battles over identity that were not, after all, that dissimilar from the ones they and their ancestors had long been fighting in Ireland. Many of them must therefore have turned to racial politics and even violence in America as though it were the natural state of affairs.[49]

RELIGION

Any proper understanding of the question of race in Irish-American history, in terms of both anti-Irish racial prejudice and Irish racial attitudes, requires due attention to the history of religion, especially the Catholic Church. The Catholic Church was arguably the single most important institution in the lives of Irish immigrants in the nineteenth-century United States. It was at least as important as the neighbourhood tavern, the Democratic party and the labour movement; and in its cultural authority the Church often exceeded the power of these three, exerting a determinative influence on the emergence of Irish-American ethnic identity, just as it played a central role in molding national identity in Ireland. The equation of Catholicism with Irishness on both sides of the Atlantic should not be taken for granted, however. It was part of a cultural process that reached fruition only in the mid- and late nineteenth century, when the general social transformation wrought by the Great Famine was accompanied by a 'devotional revolution' in Irish and Irish-American Catholicism. Before that, the hold of the Catholic Church over the Irish people was often surprisingly tenuous. Moreover, the Catholic Church in America was anything but Irish in tone and leadership before the 1830s. These two characteristics, the relative laxity of devotion among the Irish immigrants and the non-Irish origins of the American Church, are central to understanding Irish-American history in the antebellum period.

To grasp the distinctive nature of the Catholic Church in the antebellum United States, it is first necessary to trace briefly the history of American Catholicism back to its colonial origins. Catholicism had a long and difficult history in America before the nineteenth century. The colony of Maryland was founded in 1632 as a refuge for Catholics, but this early tolerance did not last. A series of penal laws were passed in Maryland between 1690 and 1720, just as in contemporary Ireland. The Catholic mass was outlawed, Jesuits were driven from the colony and Catholics were prohibited from voting and from practicing law. Anti-popery festivals and demonstrations were common elsewhere in the colonies, often in conjunction with commemorations each 5 November of Guy Fawkes's alleged plot to blow up parliament in 1605. Catholics were subject to a variety of disabilities and impositions, ranging from the payment of tithes to restrictions on office-holding. Catholics continued to suffer various disabilities and restrictions throughout the colonies until the American Revolution, although they faced little prospect of outright persecution after the relaxation of the penal laws in the 1720s.[50]

Just like their Presbyterian brethren, Irish Catholics in America appear to have converted to Baptism and Methodism in large numbers in the eighteenth century. Among the probable reasons for this were the debilitating effect of the Irish penal laws on religious observance, a shortage of clergy in both Ireland and America, and the tendency of Irish males in America to intermarry with other groups in the relative absence of Irish women. Attendance at mass and other sacraments in late eighteenth- and early nineteenth-century Ireland was very low by later standards (especially the century after the Great Famine) and the Catholic peasantry mixed elements of orthodox practice with folk beliefs and what might today be called popular 'magic'. The Church itself was by no means as central to people's faith as it would later become; and Catholic priests, to the extent that they did exert influence over the laity, were even scarcer than Presbyterian ministers in colonial America. Irish Catholic immigrants seem to have lapsed easily from formal adherence to Catholicism, attending other churches or, in isolated areas, not attending church at all. According to one estimate, there were only 25,000 Catholics in the United States in 1783, even though three or four times that number had arrived from Ireland alone since 1700.[51]

Very little is known about these early Irish Catholics in America. Most of them probably converted to other faiths or abandoned formal religious practice entirely; but as part of the same process they faded imperceptibly from the historical record. Most of them appear to have been young single males, without bonds of community on either side of the Atlantic. Many were indentured servants. Lacking women from their own background to marry, they never coalesced into a distinct ethnic community in colonial America. Nor did they establish networks to bring out immigrants from Ireland and help them settle in America. The contrast with the contemporary Scotch-Irish, and with Catholic Irish immigrants in nineteenth-century America, could not be starker.[52]

The standing of Catholics improved noticeably during the American Revolution, in part because of the revolutionary emphasis on religious toleration, and in part because the great majority of Catholics supported the patriot cause. The most prominent Catholic revolutionary was Charles Carroll, scion of an old and respected Maryland family. A leading proponent of independence and the doctrine of natural rights, Carroll was a member of the Continental Congress and a signatory of the Declaration of Independence. When he was elected to the Maryland constitutional convention in 1774, he became the first Catholic to hold office there since the seventeenth century. His relative, John Carroll, was another enthusiastic supporter of the American Revolution. Ordained as the first Catholic bishop in the United States at Baltimore in 1790, he initially endorsed the use of the vernacular over Latin, the involvement of lay parishioners in parish management and the election rather than appointment of bishops (thereby guaranteeing American autonomy from Rome). In supporting these practices, Carroll was clearly trying to mold American Catholicism along the lines of democratic republicanism. In the American context, such a move clearly entailed the borrowing by Catholicism of styles of church government and lay participation that were distinctively Protestant in nature.[53]

But Carroll's republican fervour, born of the 1770s and 1780s, did not long survive his ascendancy to the episcopate. Like many Americans, the Catholic clergy turned away from radicalism in the wake of the French Revolution. Antipathy to the French Revolution among American Catholics was heightened by the ethnic origins of the clergy, a majority of whom were French-born at this time. Many of these priests had experienced the revolution in France directly, equated republicanism with its excesses, and were strong supporters of monarchy and papal authority. At the same time, while Rome had acquiesced in the election rather than appointment of Carroll in 1790, it was not likely to tolerate this practice indefinitely. As for the vernacular, its use was widely opposed by the American clergy, and a hierarchical ruling in 1810 that Latin be used in all but the most inessential prayers of the sacraments merely formalized what was by then already existing practice. By 1815, when Carroll died, the Church had lost the republican fervour of the 1780s and was noticeably more authoritarian in its style.[54]

The American Catholic Church in the year 1800 was emphatically not an Irish institution, in either its clergy or its laity. Its one bishop, John Carroll, may have been of Irish ancestry, but he viewed himself as an American.

Small, genteel and conservative, the Church was dominated by Englishmen and Frenchmen and was based mainly in the South, especially Maryland. But even if the emerging tension within the Church between republicanism and hierarchical authority did not directly involve or affect the mainly Protestant American Irish in the late eighteenth century, it would be a central theme in the century that followed, when Catholics came to dominate Irish immigration to America and the Irish, in turn, came to dominate the American Catholic Church. The ongoing debate on the proper place in a democratic republic of what many Americans saw as a foreign, hierarchical and authoritarian church would decisively shape not only the internal history of the American Church, but also the position of Irish immigrants in American society, the nature of nativist politics and the meaning of both Irish-American and American identity.

Republicanism and hierarchy clashed most directly in the early nineteenth century in the controversy over the lay trustee system, which was eventually resolved decisively in favour of the Church. The trustee system was distinctively American in origin. Whereas lay Catholics in Europe generally played a minimal role in parish affairs, the American laity adopted elements of the Protestant 'congregational' style by providing money to build churches, electing committees (exclusively male) from among themselves to exercise control over church property and finances, and sometimes even staking a claim to some control over clerical appointments as well. The Church was prepared to accept some degree of lay control over secular matters, at least in the short term. Cork-born John England, Bishop of Charleston, approved of lay involvement as distinctively American, allowing the laity greater involvement than ever in supervising parish expenditures; but, at the same time, he asserted his own authority unequivocally on questions of property and clerical appointments. It was the threat of lay interference in the appointment and dismissal of priests, most noticeably in New York City, Philadelphia, New Orleans and Norfolk, Virginia that led to most conflict between hierarchy and laity. Lay involvement in clerical matters, as distinct from financial or administrative matters, was antithetical to the basic structure and authority of the Catholic Church in general. Gradually but firmly, between the first and third provincial councils held at Baltimore in 1829 and 1848, the American Church moved from a congregational to a more clerical model. By the 1850s the practice of lay involvement, in finances as well as property issues and appointments, was all but at an end. The Irish takeover of the American Catholic Church in the nineteenth century, therefore, reversed an earlier trend of congregationalism (referred to more bluntly as 'Protestantization' in some quarters).[55]

The American Catholic Church grew rapidly in the first half of the nineteenth century. In 1815, it consisted of a single archdiocese, Baltimore and four recently created dioceses, Bardstown, Boston, New York and Philadelphia, serving some 90,000 Catholics. By 1850, fuelled by Irish and German immigration, the number of Catholics in America had risen to about 1.6 million. With the recognizable structure of a church building located at the center of immigrant, working-class neighbourhoods, Catholic parishes (both Irish and German) became the basis for the 'ethnic villages' throughout the cities of the Northeast. The Church became a means of preserving and creating cultural and ethnic identities for both groups. The Germans generally favoured more lay initiative than the Irish, emphasized their Catholicism to distinguish themselves from Protestant Germans, and sought to retain their language through vernacular services and the appointment of German priests. The Irish, by contrast, tended to be much more accepting of clerical authority, while at the same time emphasizing their Catholicism as a distinguishing sign from Irish Protestants and a marker of their emerging identity as Irish-American. Because the Irish considerably outnumbered the Germans until the 1850s (by as much as six to one in New York City) they soon came to dominate the hierarchy, imposing their distinctive and often authoritarian style on American Catholicism as a whole.[56]

This authoritarian Irish style was perhaps best embodied by the dominant character in the American Church in the mid-nineteenth century, John Hughes of New York City. Born in County Tyrone in 1797, Hughes retained throughout his life the combative style of an Ulster Catholic. After emigrating to the United States in 1818, he spent seven years at the seminary of Mount Saint Mary's, near Baltimore, before being ordained in Philadelphia in 1826. Hughes quickly established a reputation as a polemicist, attacking anti-Catholic nativism in the newspapers and writing a propagandistic novel. In a famous hoax, he published a series of absurdly anti-Catholic letters in a newspaper called *The Protestant* under the pen-name 'Cranmer', to extravagant praise from the editor, before revealing the joke in a final letter. In 1833 he debated with a Presbyterian minister, John Breckinridge, in a series of letters that were published in *The Presbyterian* and Philadelphia's *Catholic Herald*. This debate spread Hughes's reputation as America's foremost Catholic apologist as far as the Vatican. Partly as a result, he was appointed as an assistant (co-adjutor) bishop to the ailing Bishop DuBois of New York in 1838 and bishop of that city in 1842, going on to become its first archbishop in 1850. While Hughes was quite tolerant of German parishes in New York City, he did more than anyone in the antebellum era to build the American

Catholic church along Irish lines. Part of this transformation involved the elimination of the lay trustee system, which Hughes saw as a 'Protestant' innovation in American Catholicism.[57]

At the heart of John Hughes's Irish-dominated Catholic Church was an emphasis on hierarchy and authority, anchored in a revived form of the Tridentine faith (an orthodox and conservative faith first laid down at the Council of Trent, 1545–63). By mid-century, the hierarchy had effectively imposed its authority over the trustees, asserting traditional Church practice in the face of republican innovations. This emphasis on authority and hierarchy was also central to the distinctive style of faith and devotion propagated by the Church in the United States, which emphasized the necessity of taking sacraments, attending Sunday Mass, receiving communion and confessing one's sins at least once a year. Taking the Catholic catechism as its handbook, this was an active and even militant, rather than contemplative, style of religion. It sought to bind the Catholics of various different backgrounds in the United States in a single, coherent and powerful faith, not simply by preserving the faith of immigrants, but in most cases by educating them on basic doctrines and enforcing regular worship for the first time.[58]

This emphasis on authority and regular devotional practices, which emanated ultimately from Rome as well as Dublin and New York, was directed not simply at German immigrants, who had had their own distinct traditions of piety, but even more so at Irish immigrants, whose understanding of Church doctrines and rates of attendance at the sacraments left a great deal to be desired from the point of view of the hierarchy. Many Irish Catholic immigrants, for example, arrived in America unable to make the sign of the cross, which today might be considered emblematic of Catholicism in general. Attendance at Sunday Mass in western Irish-speaking counties was often as low as 20 to 40 per cent, and it was often about the same in New York City. The numbers of clergy relative to parishioners, grossly inadequate in Ireland, were even lower in cities like New York before the 1840s. Popular Catholicism in pre-famine Ireland, partly as a result, was a mix of orthodox doctrine and popular 'magic', with widespread belief in the efficacy of holy wells and fairy rings, boisterous celebrations of saint's days (often, like St Brigid's Day or St John's Eve, imposed over Celtic holidays), and wakes featuring heavy drinking, sacrilegious games and sometimes even overt sexuality and nudity. There was also a prolonged tradition of hostility, including violence, between Irish secret societies and the Catholic clergy. 'The task of the church,' as one historian of the Catholic Irish in antebellum New York City aptly puts it, 'was not only to preserve the faith of the immigrants; in many instances it was to change nominal Catholics into practicing believers.' This task began, on both sides of the Atlantic, in the 1830s and 1840s. It reached fruition in the 'devotional revolution' of the mid-nineteenth century and culminated in an austere, distinctively Irish and widely popular form of Catholicism.[59]

The American Catholic Church, with its heavy Irish inflection from the 1830s onward, adopted a distinctive and controversial position on questions of social reform. Like other Christian denominations, the Church was deeply involved in dispensing charity to the needy, most of whom were Irish immigrants. By the 1820s the Catholic immigrant poor of New York City were being served by a Roman Catholic Benevolent Society, a Roman Catholic Orphan Asylum and St Patrick's Asylum for Girls. The Society of St Vincent de Paul was founded in the city in 1846, and many individual churches had their own benevolent societies. Most important of all was the work of nuns, including the Sisters of Charity, who provided vital services during New York City's cholera epidemics of 1832 and 1849, and the Sisters of Mercy, who were brought to the city by Bishop Hughes in 1846 to open a home for destitute immigrant girls. Extensive though its efforts were, the Catholic Church was interested only in dispensing charity, not in eradicating poverty through social change. Poverty was a given of human society; the goal of religious charity was to alleviate the worst suffering and, in so doing, to save individual souls rather than reforming society as a whole.[60]

This teaching apparently fitted well with the social perceptions of most Irish immigrants, who came from a rigidly hierarchical peasant society in which poverty was endemic and social position was typically fixed for life. The experience of emigrating doubtless liberated many of the Irish from the stultifying constraints they had suffered in Ireland, but they nonetheless came from a society that was in many respects the antithesis of the socially fluid, rapidly expanding, democratic republic of the United States. And they happened to arrive at a time when the United States was undergoing one of its periodic bursts of progressive social reform. They were, to say the least, ill-suited for the role of social reformers, and quickly found themselves opposed to the major crusades of the day – public education, temperance, sabbatarianism, women's rights and, above all, abolitionism. These movements, moreover, were deeply infused with a spirit of evangelical Protestantism, adding a critical religious and nativist dimension to the problem. In many cases (though not abolitionism), the language of reform was inevitably also that of nativism. As a result, the Irish generally, and the Catholic Church in particular, quickly developed a reputation as one of the chief anti-reform and pro-slavery constituencies in the country.[61]

The question of educational reform is a case in point. The expansion of public schooling in the late 1830s and 1840s was viewed by most native-born Americans as a triumph of democracy. But the Irish, alarmed by the domination of school administrations by Protestants and the use of the King James version of the bible, set up their own parochial school system, staffed in part by nuns brought over from Ireland. The number of parochial schools was never sufficient, accommodating only about one-third of New York City's Catholic children in 1840; but the existence of this alternative school system was enough to draw the ire of Protestant nativists. Why, the nativists wanted to know, were public schools not good enough for Irish immigrants? This question, among others, lay behind the great anti-Catholic riots that broke out in Philadelphia and its suburb, Kensington, in 1844.[62]

In New York, Bishop Hughes waged a campaign on the question of schooling that revealed both the strengths and the limitations of his militant and combative religious style. The schools in that city were controlled by a fervently Protestant Public School Society. To protect Catholic children from indoctrination, Hughes requested a share of the city's common school fund for his parochial schools. When this request was turned down in January 1841, and the state legislature postponed a decision on the matter until after a forthcoming election, Hughes decided to run his own candidates on an independent ticket. None of his candidates was elected to office, but they won enough votes to decide the results in several cases. The outcome of this peculiar incident was that the legislature passed a school bill removing the powers of the Public School Society and incorporating the city's schools into the state-wide education system, but without providing funding for parochial schools. Hughes's victory, therefore, was limited and destructive. Convinced that the United States generally was a hostile climate for the Catholic Church, Hughes typically responded to Protestant militancy with an equally militant style of his own; in this case, however, it is difficult to avoid the conclusion of one historian that the net effect of the episode was greatly to stoke the fires of nativism.[63]

A second question on which Irish immigrants clashed sharply with native-born reformers was that of temperance. Protestant evangelicals made the cause of temperance and even outright prohibition a virtual crusade in the 1840s and 1850s. But Irish immigrants liked to drink, as did Germans. As a result, the temperance crusade soon became indistinguishable from the general nativist critique of Irish immigration. Large numbers of Irish people on both sides of the Atlantic, led by Father Theobald Mathew in the late 1830s and 1840s, did ultimately embrace temperance, but they insisted on doing so on their own terms. They certainly did not want outsiders telling them how, when and where they would be allowed to drink. Closely related to temperance reform was the question of sabbatarianism. Evangelical reformers wanted to make the Sabbath holy by greatly restricting what people could do in public on that day, inevitably including alcohol-related activities. Irish and German immigrants, by contrast, wanted to drink and carouse, among other things, on Sundays – the one day a week they had off from work. However puritanical the Irish Catholic hierarchy may have been in certain respects, this puritanism did not extend to taking the fun out of Sundays.

Finally, many Irish Americans were outspokenly opposed to the greatest moral crusade of the day, the campaign to abolish slavery. While there were various reasons for this opposition, it should be noted here that the teachings of the Catholic Church dovetailed with the position of most Irish immigrants on slavery. If the hold of the Church over the Irish was, by later standards, rather weak in the pre-famine era, Irish people were nonetheless likely to obey their priests when they were preaching what they already believed. And, to the extent that the Irish were predisposed to defend slavery against the abolitionists, they could certainly turn to the Church for powerful moral sanction. Mindful of the splits over slavery that were occurring in the major Protestant churches, the Catholic Church deliberately avoided stating an absolute official position on the question. But members of the hierarchy implicitly defended slavery and explicitly attacked abolitionism on several occasions.

According to a Catholic tradition that stretched back to antiquity, slavery itself was not inherently sinful, only the abuse of slaves and the slave trade. In other words, there was no sin in slavery so long as the master did not mistreat or sell his slaves. Hence, Catholic plantation owners, including Jesuit priests, had held slaves in Maryland since the seventeenth century, and their successors continued to do so in the nineteenth century. Under Catholic doctrine, masters had a moral obligation to treat their slaves well, and to see that they received religious instruction; manumission was encouraged in favourable circumstances, but not morally required. Of course, from the abolitionist point of view this concept of 'humane slavery' was a contradiction in terms, at best a piece of sophistry and at worst a heartless defense of the status quo. When leading theologians like Bishop Kenrick of Philadelphia or Bishop England of Charleston published their personal positions on the question in the early 1840s, they reiterated the Catholic position, explained the moral obligations of masters to treat their slaves well, and urged Americans to not do anything about slavery that would break the law. In practice this amounted to an implicit defense of slavery and a repudiation of abolitionism. Archbishop Hughes of New York, a practical man rather than a theologian, put the matter more bluntly: the slaves, he declared after visiting the South, were well-treated and were clearly better off than they would have been in Africa. Sympathetic to the cause of abolitionism as a young man, Hughes by the time of the Civil War had emerged as an embattled ethnic chieftain, championing the cause of the Irish at the expense of all others. Clearly, he had been hardened by the realities of American life, and especially by the treatment of Irish immigrants, defending his own 'tribe' in a society whose promise of universal liberty and equality he now regarded as little more than a pious lie.[64]

NATIVISM AND ABOLITIONISM

Irish and Catholic hierarchical opposition to Protestant reform crusades was one of the principal grievances of the native-born Americans who launched the nativist (anti-immigrant) crusade of the 1830s and 1840s. This nativist crusade was specifically anti-Irish and anti-Catholic in character. Its principal flashpoints are well known. In 1834 the Ursuline convent in Charlestown, Massachusetts, was burned to the ground. A year later, Samuel F.B. Morse, better-known to history as the inventor of the Morse Code, published his *Foreign Conspiracy Against the Liberties of the United States*, in which he revealed the machinations of the so-called St Leopold Foundation, a fantastic international conspiracy emanating from Catholic Austria and featuring a fifth column of Jesuit fathers plotting the downfall of democracy from their base deep in the American interior. In 1836, in an even more sensational case, a disturbed young woman named Maria Monk, assisted by leading Protestant nativists, published her *Awful Disclosures*, purporting to tell of her time in a Montreal nunnery, complete with intercourse between priests and nuns, infanticide and other diabolical goings-on. Anti-Catholic literature of this type, as has often been noted by historians, was a form of nineteenth-century pornography. Though the Monk hoax was fairly quickly exposed, the book went through twenty printings and sold 300,000 copies before the Civil War, becoming the second-best-selling work of literary fiction in nineteenth-century America after *Uncle Tom's Cabin*. It resurfaced during several subsequent nativist campaigns, including the presidential election of 1960, when John F. Kennedy finally laid to rest much of the American anti-Catholic tradition by being elected president.[65]

Irish Americans of Ulster origin played a central role in the nativist crusades of the antebellum era. So long as they had made up the majority of immigrants from Ireland, they had been happy enough to be known as 'Irish', often collaborating with wealthy Catholic Irishmen in business, civic and ethnic institutions, and the organization of annual St Patrick's Day parades. But the influx of masses of poorer Catholics from Ireland soon led these Americans of Ulster origin to distinguish themselves sharply from their countrymen as 'Scotch-Irish' and to assert their Americanness in often strident tones. Branches of the Orange Order, a militant Protestant organization founded in Ulster in 1795, were established in Canada and the United States in the early nineteenth century. In the 1820s, Irish-American Protestants began to parade on 12 July, the anniversary of the victory by William of Orange over James II at the Battle of the Boyne in 1690, which is still celebrated in Protestant Ulster today. Orangemen and Irish Catholic immigrants clashed repeatedly in New York City and Philadelphia from the 1820s onward, culminating in the riots and church-burnings of 1844. The Scotch-Irish used their Orange societies for nativist purposes and joined organizations like the American Protestant Association (which they dominated) in large numbers. That Ulster-born Protestants were allowed to join this and other nativist societies clearly illustrates the religious character of ostensibly anti-immigrant sentiment. What better way for Scotch-Irish immigrants to assert their own Americanism than by condemning Catholic Irish newcomers as unfit for assimilation?[66]

Tensions between Irish Protestants and Catholics, operating in the wider context of anti-immigrant sentiment by American-born workers during the severe depression of 1837–44, were at the heart of the bloody nativist riots that broke out in Philadelphia and its suburbs of Kensington and Southwark in 1844. Throughout American history, especially in periods of economic depression, organized labour has been one of the principal sources of nativism. Perhaps inevitably, Irish immigrants during the pre-famine era were accused of working for wages that would never have been accepted by the native-born. Skilled American workmen also blamed the erosion of their apprenticeship system in many crafts on cheap Irish labour. Artisans, therefore, were among the leaders of the nativist crusade, as is evident in the name of prominent anti-immigrant organizations like the Order of the United American Mechanics. The Irish bore the brunt of the blame when wages plummeted during the great depression that began in 1837. Emerging ethnic and religious divisions among workers were readily exploited by nativists, evangelical preachers and employers. In this context, the efforts of Bishop Francis P. Kenrick of Philadelphia to prevent public schools from requiring Catholic children to use the King James version of the Bible were widely denounced. The tensions that had mounted gradually through the depression years finally exploded in May 1844, when mobs of native-born workers, in conjunction with local Orangemen, invaded the Catholic sections of the suburb of Kensington. Two churches, St Michael's and St Augustine's, were burned as nativist mobs battled Irish workers for four days. In July of the same year, a third church was burned by nativists in the nearby suburb of Southwark. With Catholic Philadelphia in ruins, Bishop Hughes pre-empted any such attacks by nativists in his own city by publicly warning that, if a single Catholic Church were burned in New York, the city would become 'another Moscow'.[67]

In subsequent generations, Irish Americans were to use the labour movement as one of their principal bases of power. Before the Civil War, however, virtually the only two national organizations that welcomed them wholeheartedly were the Catholic Church and the Democratic Party. Among the more colourful themes in the history of the Irish in America is their conquest of Tammany Hall and the political machines of other American cities. That story, too, belongs mainly to the period after the Civil War, but the foundations for subsequent triumphs were laid in the antebellum period and deserve some consideration here. The abolition of the property qualification for voting in New York and other states in the 1820s placed the incoming masses of Irish immigrants, by virtue of their sheer numbers, in the position of eventually becoming power brokers. Tammany Hall, the Democratic political organization in New York City that had been founded in 1789, was transformed from a nativist but largely non-political fraternal society, closed to foreigners, into one that courted the Irish vote. In pursuit of Irish support, Tammany built a city-wide system, with the neighbourhood saloon as its cornerstone. Irish immigrants, who dominated the city's saloon business by mid-century, thereby became important cogs in the Tammany machine. It was in the saloons that politicians met, favours were dispensed and advice was given; it was there, also, that neighbourhood gangs were based. So powerful did this base prove to be, that by the 1870s the Irish had used it to take over Tammany for themselves, along with the political machines of several other cities.[68]

At least in retrospect, the Democratic party and the nineteenth-century Irish appear to have been made for each other. The Democrats gave the Irish access to political power, something that had always been denied them in Ireland. Whereas the Whig party was closely associated with Protestantism and nativism, the Democrats actively courted the Irish, with such success that the American Irish voted overwhelmingly Democrat in most elections until the

1960s. Irish opposition to reform movements, especially abolitionism, found a natural home in the Democratic party. With its antebellum power base among southern slaveholders and Catholic immigrant workers, the Democratic party was the chief bastion of white supremacy and pro-slavery sentiment in the United States. It offered, in the words of its leading historian, 'political democracy and an inclusive patriotism to white male Americans'.[69]

If the Irish in America generally opposed abolitionism, this was not necessarily true of the Irish in Ireland. Not only did the Irish at home have no reason to oppose the abolition of slavery, they possessed in the revered figure of Daniel O'Connell (1775–1847) one of the heroes of the world anti-slavery movement. Known as 'The Liberator' for his contribution to Catholic Emancipation in 1829, O'Connell spent the remainder of his political career agitating for repeal of the Act of Union of 1800. The Repeal movement failed, but it consolidated O'Connell's position as the towering figure in Irish constitutional nationalism in the first half of the nineteenth century. The nationalist movement he led spanned the Atlantic Ocean, intersecting in America with issues of race and slavery in ways that are critically important to any understanding of Irish-American history in the antebellum era.

Daniel O'Connell was an inspiration to the American abolitionist movement. William Lloyd Garrison (1805–79), the leader of the abolitionists, chose *The Liberator* as the name of the movement's newspaper. The first issue of that paper (1831), and many subsequent issues, were filled with quotations from O'Connell's speeches about the hypocrisy inherent in any republic that held slaves. O'Connell was an active member of the British and Foreign Anti-slavery Society, and a key figure in the parliamentary debates that led to the abolition of slavery in the British Caribbean in 1838. Garrison met O'Connell in London in 1833, and again in 1840 at the World Antislavery Convention. So popular did the abolitionist O'Connell become in the United States that in 1833 African Americans in New York City held a special meeting in the Abyssinian Baptist church in his honour, praising him as the 'uncompromising advocate of universal emancipation, the friend of oppressed Africans and their descendants, and of the unadulterated rights of man'. African Americans in the other major northern cities repeated this acclaim on various other occasions. The notion of 'universal emancipation' pointed to by his American admirers is critical in any understanding of Daniel O'Connell. Irish national subjugation and black slavery, he insisted, were twin examples of a single form of injustice that would eventually yield to the same techniques of mass agitation, moral suasion and legal redress. This was a compelling moral vision, but it would eventually be shattered by the grim realities of Irish-American life.[70]

Another abolitionist who made extensive contacts with Daniel O'Connell and the Irish abolitionist movement was the African American Charles Lenox Remond. A great admirer of O'Connell's oratory as well as his principles, Remond toured Ireland after the World Anti-slavery Conference of 1840 and delivered rousing speeches against slavery in Dublin, Waterford, Wexford, Cork, Belfast, Limerick and elsewhere. How, he demanded to know, could America continue to act as an asylum for the oppressed of Ireland and a prison for slaves and free blacks? Remond helped compose 'An Address of the People of Ireland to Their Countrymen in America'. Members of the Hibernian Anti-Slavery Society and other volunteers collected 70,000 signatures, with those of O'Connell and Father Theobald Mathew, the famous temperance reformer, at the top of the list. The 'Address' opened with an expression of Ireland's admiration for the United States, but quickly moved on to condemn slavery as undermining all that was attractive about America. Slavery was an egregious violation of the doctrine of natural rights on which the United States had been founded, and a sin against God. For both reasons, Americans of Irish origin should do everything within their power to win the abolition of slavery through peaceful means. It was sent across the Atlantic and ceremoniously rolled in to a huge meeting of the Massachusetts Anti-Slavery Society at Fanueil Hall, Boston, on 28 January 1842. Consciously modelled on the 'Monster Meetings' O'Connell had convened to agitate for Repeal, the meeting was addressed by leading abolitionists, including Frederick Douglass.[71]

This high-point of transatlantic Irish abolitionism, however, was to be one of the last moments of international solidarity tying together what were, after all, two very different movements. Abolition of American slavery and national freedom for Ireland were compatible only up to a point. They may have complemented each other quite nicely in the universalist mind of Daniel O'Connell. But the majority of Irish immigrants in America, while they supported the cause of Repeal to some extent at least, not only failed to support abolitionism but found it threatening. The reasons for this are not hard to find.[72]

The abolitionists were a radical minority in American political life. Seeing slavery as a sin, they embarked on a moral crusade designed to uproot it from American soil, even at the price of disrupting the Union. Unlike the anti-slavery and free soil forces that coalesced to form the Republican party in 1854, designed to contain rather than immediately eradicate slavery, the abolitionists were extremists. The original flag-burners, they publicly tore to shreds the US constitution, because it gave sanction to slavery. Only a small number of committed individuals in any society can be expected to join movements of this sort. Immigrants sometimes join these groups; but they are less likely to do so when, like the Irish, their status as potential Americans is highly suspect to begin with. How then, historians have asked, could the Irish realistically be expected to have supported a movement that subverted the constitution and was prepared to split the Union if necessary?[73]

Yet nativism alone cannot explain the Irish antipathy to abolitionism. While immigrants certainly feared being tarred with the brush of disloyalty, Garrison and his followers were themselves staunch opponents of nativism and religious bigotry, extending a welcoming hand to the Irish. Indeed, it was the more moderate anti-slavery forces, which would merge to form the Republican party in the 1850s, that exhibited the more virulent forms of nativism. The anti-slavery movement, like most other crusades for reform in the antebellum era, was shot through with the language of Protestant evangelical reform, rendering it highly suspicious to Irish immigrants. For this reason, as well as their racist hostility to slaves, the Irish opposed mainstream antislavery almost as strenuously as they opposed abolitionism.[74]

A third reason for Irish antipathy toward the abolitionist movement was its British and Protestant associations. The British had led the way with emancipation in the Caribbean, and it was in Britain that the world movement against slavery was based. It was all too easy for opponents of the abolitionists to convince wavering Irishmen that the campaign against slavery was a British movement, that Irish people should therefore shun it and that abolitionism was simply a distraction from more worthy goals like repeal of the Act of Union. Its British associations also made abolitionism vulnerable to charges of foreign involvement in American affairs, making Irish Americans even more susceptible to nativist charges of divided loyalty.[75]

The influence of the Roman Catholic Church was critically important in providing moral guidance to Irish immigrants on the question of slavery. The American hierarchy was not only opposed to abolitionism but openly supported the status quo on slavery. Much to O'Connell's embarrassment, his friend, Bishop England of Charleston, published a series of letters repudiating O'Connell's condemnation of American slavery and reiterating the Catholic distinction between slavery, the slave trade and cruel rather than humane masters. The contrast with the abolitionists, for whom slavery was by definition a grave sin, could not have been starker. O'Connell's discomfort grew all the more acute when the bishop published his letters in book form in 1844, with a dedication to 'The Liberator' himself. With friends like

Bishop England, O'Connell needed no enemies. Bishop Hughes of New York denounced the 'Address' by the Hibernian Anti-Slavery society as foreign interference in American politics. The *Boston Pilot* praised Irish Americans for rejecting it and thereby asserting their loyalty to American institutions. How, the newspaper demanded, could O'Connell preach peaceful moral suasion in Ireland while throwing his support to abolitionists who were seeking to foment bloody slave revolts in America? Given the pacifism and belief in moral suasion of the Garrisonians, this charge was rather implausible; but the radical rhetoric of abolitionism made it vulnerable to such distorted indictments.[76]

This is the unfavourable background against which Daniel O'Connell attempted to unite Irish-American nationalism with abolitionism. The Repeal movement of the 1840s was the first major Irish nationalist movement in America. Local associations of the movement came together in national meetings held in Philadelphia, Boston and New York in the early 1840s. The first national gathering of the American Irish in support of an Irish cause convened in Philadelphia on 22 February 1842, when twenty-seven delegates from twenty-six cities or towns (all but four in the Northeast) met at the National Repeal Convention. Matters came to a head in 1843, when the Pennsylvania Repeal Association called on its members to uphold the slaveholding Union. The Pennsylvania Anti-Slavery Society responded by accusing the Irish-American Repeal movement of being pro-slavery, insisting that Irish Americans would not violate their constitutional duties by supporting abolition.[77]

Faced with this dilemma, O'Connell came down firmly on the side of abolitionism, stridently denouncing Irish-American racism. A consummate politician, O'Connell was aware that taking a moral stand on slavery might wreck the Repeal movement in America. On occasion, therefore, he had been outspokenly critical of Garrison, condemning his anti-clericalism and some of his tactics. This political maneuvering aside, O'Connell clung fast to his anti-slavery principles in 1843, repudiating all Irish Americans who supported the 'aristocracy of skin', and rebuking those 'who had taken the wrong side with regard to the liberties of the human race'. He concluded with a characteristic plea to those Irish Americans who would countenance human bondage: 'The man who will do so belongs not to my kind. Over the broad Atlantic I pour forth my voice, saying – Come out of such a land, you Irishmen, or if you remain, and dare countenance the system of slavery ... we will recognize you as Irishmen no longer.'[78]

O'Connell's position, while morally laudable, had a disastrous impact on the American Repeal movement. In reaction to O'Connell's statements on slavery, the branches of the Repeal movement in Charleston, Natchez and New Orleans dissolved by the end of 1843. Faced with the ultimatum delivered by their leader in Ireland, they repudiated O'Connell and opted to support slavery over nationalism. The movement lasted a few years longer in the cities of the North, but the Repealers there also rejected O'Connell eventually, choosing to support nationalism over anti-slavery. Divorced from the Irish leadership and divested of its southern portion, this movement could scarcely hope to survive for long. By 1845 it had ceased to exist. In the summer of that same year, as Ireland's farmers went to harvest their first potato crop, they noticed that it had been afflicted by a strange new disease. About one-third of the crop was lost. As the year drew to a close, the poor throughout Ireland wondered how they would make it through the winter. But nobody suspected the scale of the catastrophe that was underway.

Chapter 3

◆

THE FAMINE GENERATION

In 1845 the people of Ireland were suddenly afflicted with an ecological catastrophe. The potato blight, a fungal infestation called *phytophthora infestans*, was a new disease, unknown in Europe before the 1840s. It attacked the leaves of the potato plant first, then the stalk and then the tuber. The potatoes, when not already reduced to a pestilent pulp before the harvest, often turned out to contain the blight within their apparently healthy exterior. The disease was carried through the air by spores, devastating the crop throughout the country. Nobody at the time knew what the blight was, or where it came from. The rural poor were apt to see it as a visitation from God, perhaps in punishment for their wastefulness in previous seasons when potatoes were so abundant that not all of them could be consumed. They referred to it as *an gorta mór*, 'the great hunger'. Botanists at first thought the blight was a form of wet-rot caused by an even damper Irish summer than usual; it took almost thirty years to find an antidote, based on the realization that it was a fungus. It is now known that the blight reached Europe from the eastern United States, having probably originated in Peru. In Europe, the blight affected Flanders, southern France, Switzerland, eastern Germany, southern Scandinavia and Scotland, as well as Ireland. But it spread most rapidly in damp conditions, such as those in Ireland. Only in Ireland did the population depend so overwhelmingly on the potato, and only there did the blight lead to demographic disaster.[1]

The blight struck repeatedly in Ireland in the late 1840s, devastating the potato crop on which the bulk of the population depended. Between 1.1 and 1.5 million Irish people died of starvation and famine-related diseases in the famine decade, 1846–55, out of a population that stood at about 8.5 million at the beginning of the catastrophe. Another 2.1 million fled the country,

1.8 million of them to North America (all but 300,000 of these to the United States). Not surprisingly, the Irish during the Famine accounted for a higher proportion of American immigrants than ever before or since. The 780,719 immigrants from Ireland accounted for 45.6 per cent of total immigration to the United States in the 1840s, while the 914,119 in the 1850s accounted for 35.2 per cent (German immigration having increased in size by this time to exceed Irish). As the most intensive period of Irish immigration to the United States, the famine era was central to the development of Irish-American history. The tragic drama at the heart of this period throws into stark relief some of the central themes in the history of the American Irish, including patterns of urban settlement and labour history, the expansion of the Catholic Church, the power of American nativism, the rise of the Irish in municipal politics and the emergence of powerful Irish nationalist movements on American soil.[2]

AN GORTA MÓR

By the 1840s, Ireland was considerably more vulnerable to demographic disaster than it had been at any time in its history, even during the first great famine a century before.[3] The population explosion of the late eighteenth century, combined with restricted access to land and repeated subdivision by smallholders, meant that the bulk of the population found its search for subsistence increasingly difficult. Hundreds of thousands were already landless, desperately seeking access to the soil as cottiers or conacre tenants (see Chapter 2). Smallholders, basing their precarious stability on the retention of less than ten acres of often very poor land, faced the daily prospect of joining the ranks of the landless poor. Insufficient funds to pay the rent, or arbitrary evictions (most tenants did not have fixed leases), might reduce them overnight to the position of conacre tenants or landless itinerants. Strong and middling farmers, as well as larger landlords, had every incentive to evict the poor, converting their various rental properties into undivided tracts of grazing land. And even if the smallholders managed to retain their farms, they were more likely than not to subdivide their holding among their heirs.

This system of partible inheritance (dividing the land among all the children) was equitable compared to primogeniture (giving the land to the eldest son only). It allowed the great bulk of the population to stay in the countryside, rather than emigrating as they would have to in the post-famine period. But its very fair-mindedness contributed, in the context of the prevailing landholding system, to a crisis of over-population. Add to this the remarkable dependence of most of the population on a single crop, and the stage was set for demographic catastrophe should nature intervene adversely. Out of a population of just over eight million in the early 1840s, at least one and a half million (the poorest rural dwellers) had no significant sources of food other than the potato, and three and a half million more were very largely dependent on it. Regionally, the greatest dependence was in the South and West, the provinces of Connacht and Munster, which would be hardest hit by the famine.[4]

A word of clarification is needed about the potato. It should not be concluded that reliance on the potato was a sufficient cause of the Great Famine, even if such a conclusion is difficult to avoid in hindsight. The potato is highly nutritious, and three servings daily (amounting to as much as 14 pounds in weight per day for a male labourer, 11 for women, and 5 for younger children) provided more than adequate sustenance. It is generally agreed that the pre-famine Irish were quite healthy, even if they were poor. Although the potato crop failed frequently due to bad weather or disease (in 1816–18, 1821, 1829, eight times in the 1830s and three times in 1840–4), these failures were usually local and short-lived. Given the damp Irish climate, the potato was a more reliable staple crop than any grain. The masses of Irish poor by the 1830s (especially, again, in the South and West) were certainly in a precarious position, subsisting on a more prolific but less nutritious and less durable variety of potato (the 'lumper'). Deprivation was widespread in the 'hungry months' of summer, between the consumption or deterioration of the previous year's potatoes and the harvest of the next crop. But the calamity that began in 1845, when the potato blight first struck, was unprecedented and largely unforeseeable.[5]

The blight first hit the Irish potato crop in the autumn of 1845, then again more heavily in 1846, 1848, 1849 and 1850. It destroyed 30 to 40 per cent of the potato crop in 1845, and almost the entire crop in 1846, when the harvest dropped to only 20 per cent of its pre-famine level and the entire country was affected. The following year, known as 'Black '47', is remembered as the worst year of the ordeal, as most of the crop had failed the previous autumn. Ironically, the blight did not strike strongly in 1847 itself; but a starving and demoralized population had planted very few potatoes, so that the harvest was only 10 per cent of its 1844 level. To compound the misery, the healthy harvest in 1847 encouraged a heavy planting in 1848, only for the blight to return in full force and wipe out most of the crop. The blight abated in the 1850s, but the harvest remained below half the pre-famine level until the middle of that decade.[6]

The impact of the famine on Irish history, and the degree of British responsibility, have been the subject of heated debate by historians. Popular memory on both sides of the Atlantic (especially in America) has long held the famine to be a catastrophe which dramatically altered the course of Irish history, with deliberate British negligence turning crop failure into mass starvation or even genocide. Historians, on the other hand, have typically seen the story as considerably more complicated and ambiguous. As far back as the 1950s, the standard academic work on the Great Famine was notably circumspect and even-handed in its account of the famine's impact and the degree of British responsibility. It was not so much in universities as in elementary schools and popular memory, from Cork and Limerick to Boston and San Francisco, that the idea of the Great Famine as Britain's greatest sin against Ireland survived in potent form.

In the 1970s and 1980s a new generation of 'revisionist' historians, working to overturn one-dimensional nationalist explanations of the Irish past, tilted the balance even more sharply away from the popular consensus that a British-inspired famine had transformed the course of Irish history. Irish population growth, the revisionists pointed out, had already slowed considerably in the generation before the famine struck. Impartible inheritance (passing the land on to a single heir instead of dividing it among the children) was already on the rise, at least among the more prosperous, leading to later marriages and slowing the rate of population growth. The National School system, introduced by the British in 1831 with English as the sole language of instruction, had already seriously undermined the Irish language. And emigration, of course, was already very substantial for a generation (in the case of Ulster for more than a century) before 1845. The Great Famine, these revisionists argue, cannot therefore be seen as a watershed event that reversed the trend of Irish demographic history, transformed the landholding system and the structure of Irish families, threw open the gates of emigration and all but eradicated Gaelic language and culture. Instead, it merely accelerated social trends that were already long underway. As for the vexed question of government responsibility, the standard revisionist answer is that the British government, trapped by the laissez-faire economic logic of its times, could not realistically be expected to have done more. To assume otherwise is to abandon historical inquiry in the name of romantic nationalism. Even if Ireland had been self-governing, the revisionists suggest, the outcome of the potato blight would have been much the same.[7]

While revisionism offered a much-needed debunking of various mythologies pervading Irish historical memory, especially unexamined notions of systematic genocide during the famine, it clearly went too far in the opposite direction at times. It added new levels of complexity to our understanding of the Irish past, at its best opening the way for examination of the internal dynamics of Irish society, for example in terms of new questions to do with class and gender. Yet, in its more extreme versions, revisionism sometimes threatened to sanitize the nineteenth-century Irish past beyond recognition. Certainly the British cannot be held responsible for every form of injustice to be found in nineteenth-century Ireland; one cannot begin to appreciate the complexity of Irish history without conceding this point. But if, as is both necessary and laudable, one departs from the unilinear direction of Irish nationalist history, an alternative explanation for social injustice and political struggle is needed. Faced with this dilemma, the revisionists sometimes gave the impression that the injustice and struggle were not all that important to begin with. In the case of the Great Famine, the burden of revisionism was to diminish its impact and largely exonerate the British government. But in a series of works published to coincide with the sesquecentenary (150th anniversary) of the famine, a new group of Irish historians began to challenge the revisionist consensus. Arguing with considerable sophistication and persuasiveness, these 'post-revisionists' (for want of a better term) insisted that the famine was indeed the central event of nineteenth-century Irish history, and that the British government seized the opportunity to expedite a long-anticipated social and moral transformation in Ireland. They agreed with the revisionists in debunking nationalist ideas of genocide; but they disagreed with them in their estimation of British responsibility for the famine and the impact of the catastrophe on Irish history.[8]

One thing that reemerged quite forcefully from this new historiography on the famine is the extent to which Ireland was a colony in an empire rather than a genuinely equal and integrated part of the United Kingdom. British bureaucrats, visitors and journalists repeatedly emphasized the inherent strangeness and foreignness of the Irish, along with their need for moral reformation according to British standards. Most Irish people, on both sides of the Atlantic, have always found it difficult to believe that the British government would have responded to famine in England the way it did in Ireland. It was one thing to stick rigidly to laissez-faire liberal ideas in starving Ireland; it would surely have been quite another thing in a starving England. In constitutional terms, Ireland may have been an equal and integrated part of the United Kingdom; in actual practice, the country was a colony in an empire. Ireland's colonial dependence, and the low regard in which British administrators held its inhabitants, should be the starting point for any analysis of British policy on the Great Famine.[9]

The revisionist argument that British officials could not move beyond the laissez-faire ideology of their times does not stand up to serious scrutiny. Vast amounts of state spending were certainly condoned on some matters, if not on others: on the compensation of Caribbean slaveholders in the 1830s, for example, or on the Crimean War in the 1850s. Liberal governments elsewhere in Europe in the late 1840s, most notably Belgium and France (not to mention Scotland) were considerably more effective in dispensing famine relief than the British were in Ireland. The Irish depended much more heavily on the potato, of course, but this might have been interpreted as a reason for more state assistance, not less. Extensive assistance clearly was possible, not only in continental Europe but also in the United Kingdom, provided that governments were sufficiently interested and committed. In the Irish case, evidently they were not. British soup kitchens in Ireland were feeding almost three million people in the summer of 1847, illustrating the extent of relief that could be granted by a mobilized British state. Yet these soup kitchens were abruptly closed in the autumn of 1847 under the pressure of politics in England; they had been introduced strictly as a temporary measure and could not be allowed to interfere with the longer-term workings of an ostensibly laissez-faire economy. Encouraged by a healthy potato crop in 1847, British administrators discontinued the soup kitchens and the starving poor were forced to fall back on the ineffectual device of the Poor Law. Ireland, the country that needed government assistance most, was in this respect unique among the European countries affected by the blight.[10]

Under the Poor Law Extension Act passed by the British Parliament in June 1847, local Irish communities (divided into Poor Law unions) were made responsible for relieving all local destitution. The boards of guardians who administered the Poor Law unions were obliged to collect taxes sufficient to relieve distress. This new principle of 'local responsibility' and 'local chargeability' was explicitly designed to shift the burden of famine relief away from central government to individual Poor Law unions. Because of the extent of the destitution during the famine, 'outdoor' as well as 'indoor' relief was permitted. In other words, as well as being incarcerated in workhouses, the poor could continue to occupy their homes and be granted relief in return for work on public projects. These projects, still strewn across the Irish landscape today, included walls and bridges, roads leading nowhere, jetties where no boats could land and various make-work 'follies', meaningless and vaguely monstrous structures erected solely that the starving poor should not be morally compromised by receiving food or money for free.[11]

To finance this new system of poor relief, a rate (i.e. a tax) was levied on everybody holding property with a rateable value of £4 or more. Rates on properties valued at less than this sum were chargeable to the landlord leasing the holding. As a result of the new rates, smallholders whose farms were just above the taxable limit often emigrated rather than pay the tax, while larger landholders (many of whom were unable to collect rents and stood on the verge of bankruptcy) complained with some justification that they could not afford to pay poor law rates for themselves and their smaller tenants. The exemption from rates granted to the poor and the assumption of that burden by their landlords, indeed, gave landlords a very strong incentive to evict their tenants, level their cabins and consolidate their holdings. As a result, the rate of evictions was drastically higher in and after 1847 than at any time during the pre-famine era.[12]

This massive increase in evictions was attributable, in part, to a second aspect of the Poor Law reform legislation of 1847. The notorious Gregory Clause of the amended Poor Law Act denied public relief assistance to any head of household renting more than a quarter-acre of land who refused to relinquish the land to its proprietor. Some starved to death rather than do so; hundreds of thousands abandoned their holdings, accepted relief and, faced with homelessness and destitution, emigrated while they still could. An estimated half a million people were evicted from their homes in the famine decade alone, often under the cruelest circumstances.[13]

In the face of compelling evidence presented by the post-revisionists, it can no longer be denied that large segments of British public, journalistic and government opinion regarded the famine as a heaven-sent opportunity to stamp out Irish laziness, ingratitude, violence and ignorance, and to remake Ireland in the image of industrious, efficient, orderly England. Historians have documented in abundant and harrowing detail the degree to which this providentialist thinking pervaded the opinion of officials concerned with Ireland, most notably Charles Edward Trevelyan (the man in charge of famine relief). Trevelyan's *The Irish Crisis*, published in 1848, depicted the Famine as a form of divine intervention designed to solve the problem of Irish overpopulation through natural disaster, setting the stage for the subsequent moral and social regeneration of the country. As the leading recent historian of the subject puts it: 'The policy that followed [from autumn 1847 onward] was not pure *laissez-faire* but the use of a penal mechanism – the poor law – to forcibly transform Irish behaviour and to proletarianize the cottier.' Or, in the words of a contemporary newspaper, the *Illustrated London News*, the Irish poor law 'will ultimately turn the small, potato-feeding, near-naked farmers, into the meat-eating, well-clad labourers of [*sic*] men of capital, skill and energy'.[14]

This rehabilitation of Ireland during the Great Famine was conceived in both moral and social terms. British newspapers spoke repeatedly of a 'moral plague' afflicting Ireland, a plague of indolence and indiscipline epitomized by the cultivation of the potato and the subdivision of landholdings facilitated thereby. The potato itself came to symbolize laziness and lack of discipline in nineteenth-century British culture, standing for everything that was allegedly wrong with the Irish. The 'potato people' of Ireland appeared to British observers not simply to lack those virtues held to be characteristically English – prudence, frugality and a strong work ethic – but to regard as virtues what 'civilized' people considered vices, especially laziness and violence. Ireland, in short, was in need of moral regeneration; and, to many British observers, the collapse of the potato economy in the late 1840s was a golden opportunity. As early as October 1846, for example, the *Times* of London predicted that 'an island, a social state, a race is to be changed . . . all are to be created anew'.[15]

Ireland's moral regeneration, as conceived by the British, was to be social and economic as well as moral. The ideal means of regeneration would be the elimination of cottier, conacre and joint tenancies in favour of the classically English tripartite division of agrarian society into landlords, tenants and landless labourers. Primogeniture would replace partible inheritance as part of the same process. Cottiers and conacre tenants were accused by British government administrators of working on their potato plots for only about sixty days a year, spending the remainder of their time in idleness and vice, and it was believed that this transformation would eliminate the prime source of laziness and violence in Ireland. At the same time, consolidation of small-holdings and the rise of primogeniture would stabilize the landholding system in favour of middling and prosperous farmers. In this ideal new Ireland there would be no room for either the rural poor or profligate landlords; those of the poor who had not perished of famine and disease would emigrate, while those who remained in Ireland would either prosper as tenants or work industriously as labourers. In other words, capitalist Irish farmers would employ honest, content and hard-working labourers on the English model and the transformation of Ireland would be complete.[16]

Emigration and mortality aside, the most important impact of the famine lay in its remaking of Irish agrarian society at least partly along these lines.

As a result of evictions, emigration and disproportionately high fatalities among the poor, the rural class structure shifted decisively in favour of middling and strong farmers during the famine. Holdings of less than five acres, which had accounted for 44.9 per cent of total landholdings in 1841, made up only 15.5 per cent a decade later. Holdings of between 15 and 30 acres more than doubled in the same period, from 11.5 per cent to 24.8 per cent of all holdings. And holdings above 50 acres almost quadrupled, from 7 per cent to 26.1 per cent. This trend continued after the famine, decimating the landless labourers and the more precarious smallholders. Post-famine Ireland would be a land dominated by strong farmers who, by the close of the century, were well on the way to owning (rather than simply renting) their own land.[17]

Departures and fatalities in the famine decade together accounted for over one-third of the pre-famine population of 8.5 million, with 2.1 million emigrating in addition to over 1 million dead of starvation or disease. About 1.5 million of the emigrants went to the United States, 340,000 to British North America, 200,000 to 300,000 (often the poorest of those who could afford to leave) to Great Britain and tens of thousands more (usually the better-off) to Australia and New Zealand. By 1861, 700,000 Irish-born people were living in Great Britain, compared to just over 400,000 twenty years earlier. The number of people leaving Ireland for North America reached 200,000 a year in 1849 and 1850, and almost a quarter of a million at its peak in 1851. The population of Ireland had fallen to 6.6 million by 1851, and 5.7 million by 1855. Spurred by mass emigration, this downward spiral continued inexorably for the rest of the century so that by 1901 the population had fallen to 4.4 million, slightly over half the figure in 1845. Bucking the trend of contemporary European and American history, Ireland was drastically depopulated at a time when populations elsewhere were rapidly expanding. In terms of fatalities and emigration, British policy and the social transformation of the countryside, it is difficult to avoid the conclusion that the Great Famine of the 1840s was the single most important event in modern Irish history.[18]

EXODUS

The famine had only a small impact on emigration in 1845, but thereafter the outflow increased to levels unheard of before or since in Irish history. Most emigration at this time occurred in spring or early summer, and the blight did not appear until late July. Nonetheless, about 75,000 people emigrated to North America that year, more than in any previous year in Irish history. An estimated 106,000 left Ireland for North America in 1846, two-thirds of them bound for the United States. The crop failed almost entirely in 1846, leading to 214,000 departures for North America in 1847, of whom 117,000 sailed directly to the United States. Of the remaining 97,000, who went to Canada, as many as 40,000 of those who survived the voyage then travelled by boat or overland (often on foot) to the American republic. The number of transatlantic departures from Ireland fell to 177,000 in 1848, following the healthy if very limited harvest the previous summer. But, with the return of the blight thereafter, departures rose steadily, reaching an all-time peak of 245,000 in 1851. By 1855 the exodus was trailing off, the figure of 63,000 for that year closely resembling pre-famine levels. This vast movement of people between 1846 and 1855 was largely involuntary and by its very nature collective and anonymous. Although it was composed of an aggregate of distinct individuals, its story is best told in terms of a mass exodus.[19]

What types of people left Ireland during the famine years, where did they live and why did they leave? The lowest rates of emigration during the famine, predictably enough, were from the most heavily Protestant areas, especially Belfast and the Lagan Valley in Ulster, and the Dublin area. Protestants made up an estimated 25 per cent of the Irish population, but only 10 per cent of those who emigrated during the famine. The highest rates of emigration were from north-central Ireland (counties Sligo, Roscommon, Longford, Cavan, Monaghan and Fermanagh) and the south-central plains (Queens, Tipperary and Kilkenny) where emigration reached levels of more than 26 per cent of the pre-famine population. Rates of emigration elsewhere in Ireland varied between 20 and 26 per cent, with the exception of Dublin, Wexford, the four counties of northeast Ulster and, somewhat anomalously, Donegal (where landlords and religious charities dispensed considerable relief).[20]

There was usually an inverse proportion between famine mortalities and emigration. Where famine mortalities were high, rates of emigration were typically low, and vice versa. In Ulster, rates of both were uncharacteristically low, while County Mayo (with its proliferation of holdings under five acres and relatively few labourers) was one of the few places to suffer high rates of emigration as well as mortality. Elsewhere, the inverse proportion usually held true, with very high emigration but relatively low mortality in north-central and south-central Ireland, and very high fatalities but relatively few emigrants in the poorest and most gaelicized regions of the country, especially along the Atlantic seaboard. Perhaps half to three-quarters of the rural population simply could not afford the fare to North America, which varied between £3 and £5 in this period. Along the Atlantic seaboard in particular, people were unable (and sometimes unwilling) to leave. Those who did emigrate often made it only as far as Great Britain. Irish speakers, being heavily concentrated in the West and among the poor, were less likely than most to have the resources to cross the Atlantic. Nonetheless, it is estimated that somewhere between one-quarter and one-third of American-bound emigrants during the famine were Irish speakers. Half of all the famine emigrants came from the two provinces of Connacht and Munster, where at least half the population still spoke Irish as late as 1851.[21]

The exodus to America was dominated not by the landless poor or conacre tenants, but by cottiers, smallholders and middling farmers. The counties of north-central and south-central Ireland produced the heaviest volume of emigration, measured as a proportion of pre-famine population. If emigration was disproportionately low among the destitute, it was disproportionately high among those holding five to fifteen acres, and very substantial among middling and strong farmers (especially in 1847 and 1849–50). Even if the very poorest did not leave Ireland for America at this time, the famine emigrants were still noticeably poorer and less skilled than those who had crossed the Atlantic in the previous fifty years. Poverty, of course, is a relative term: smallholders may have been better off than cottier and conacre tenants in Ireland, but as urban immigrants in the United States they vied only with African Americans as the most impoverished members of society, a status that was aggravated by starvation, disease and the great haste with which they had uprooted themselves from Ireland. Hundreds of thousands of famine refugees were penniless, diseased and dressed in rags on arrival in the United States. Nearly all the emigrants in this period (80 to 90 per cent) identified themselves to the emigration authorities as labourers or servants, with only 10 per cent or so in the category of craftsman or artisan.[22]

From these findings it is possible to draw a profile of the famine emigrants. The great majority were rural dwellers, Catholics, lacking in capital beyond their passage money, usually English-speaking and able to read and write to some extent, and wherever possible they left Ireland in family groups rather than alone. It is estimated that 60 per cent or more of the famine emigrants were aged between 20 and 45, famine mortalities being highest on either side of this age range. While men had outnumbered women by two-to-one in the emigration of the 1830s, this gap appears to have narrowed somewhat in the late 1840s. By the same token, pre-famine emigration had been characterized mainly by single males, while the late 1840s saw entire families (presumably the better-off or those who received assistance) emigrating in large numbers.[23]

Given the scale of the catastrophe, remarkably little assistance was offered to potential emigrants. Evictions were frequent, but only rarely were they accompanied by financial assistance to leave the country. Perhaps 50,000 people received monetary aid from their landlords between 1846 and 1855, usually in some combination of eviction and compulsory emigration (the option being to become homeless and starve). Two thousand tenants were sent out from the Sligo estate of Lord Palmerston in this way, 3,500 from the Kerry estate of the Marquess of Landsdowne and 1,000 from the Roscommon estate of Denis Mahon. The British crown also took the opportunity to clear some of its estates, notably those at Ballykilcline, County Roscommon, where all the tenants were evicted and those willing to emigrate to America were offered free passage. The only state-assisted migration in this period took place under the revised Poor Law of 1847, which allowed the use of poor law taxes to help destitute emigrants. If the landlord of holdings below a certain value paid two-thirds of his tenants' passage money, then the local Poor Law union would furnish the remainder. The unwillingness or inability of most landlords to participate, combined with the financial collapse or bankruptcy of most Poor Law unions under the pressure of the late 1840s, meant that only about 5,000 emigrants received assistance in this way. In addition, some 15,000 inmates of poorhouses and orphanages, mostly young women and children, were removed to America between 1851 and 1855. The vast majority of famine emigrants, however, had to make their own way out of Ireland to America. The chief form of assistance available to them came not from landlords or the state, but from their own relatives in America. Remarkably, it was calculated in 1867 that more than $120 million had been sent from the United States by Irish immigrants over the preceding twenty years.[24]

By the time the Great Famine struck, Ireland was already well-equipped for the emigrant trade. There was a relatively efficient network of communications and transport within Ireland and between Ireland and the British port of Liverpool. Already by the late 1830s and early 1840s, two out of every three Irish emigrants who crossed the Atlantic did so via Liverpool. For a fare of 5s to 10s, the emigrants made their way from Ireland to Liverpool by steam or, more arduously, in a variety of fishing boats, coal barges and channel packets. In a bitter irony that cannot have escaped the starving emigrants' attention, many of them travelled alongside livestock and grain being exported from Ireland as they starved. Conditions were abysmal. Ships carrying emigrants across the Irish sea, unlike those crossing the Atlantic, were not required to provide provisions, basic hygiene or a minimum space per passenger. They did not even have to report on the numbers they carried.[25]

Ships leaving western Ireland for Liverpool were the most dangerous. Not only were they equipped to carry fish, coal, wool, livestock and other goods rather than a human cargo, they also had to navigate the perilous Atlantic waters of Ireland's west coast. It was on these ships that some of the worst disasters and shipwrecks of the famine years occurred. The steamer *Londonderry*, for example, left Sligo on 1 December 1849, carrying 178 emigrants, divided between the deck and steerage, which also carried cattle. When it arrived in the Irish port of Derry two days later, there were only 102 survivors. When a storm had blown up, the passengers had been forced below deck by the crew; each passenger had only two square feet and, after the steerage lights went out, seventy-six men, women and children were killed in the crush.[26]

As many as a million Irish arrived in Liverpool as transients or settlers between 1847 and 1853. Most of the Irish moved on from Liverpool as fast as possible, continuing their journey across the Atlantic if they could, settling in the industrial towns of Lancashire and other parts of Britain if they could not. Those hoping to cross the Atlantic often had to wait weeks for the next sailing, even though they had typically been promised a swift connection when they had purchased their tickets in Ireland. Hundreds of thousands of them lived temporarily on the Liverpool waterfront, suffering from malnutrition and a variety of contagious diseases. 'The people are as numerous as maggots in cheese,' American novelist Nathaniel Hawthorne noted of the scene in Liverpool, 'you behold them, disgusting, and all moving about, as when you raise a plank or log that has lain on the ground, and find many vivacious bugs and insects beneath it.' The emigrants camped out while they waited, or took refuge in squalid boardinghouses or putrid cellars rented out to them at exorbitant rates. Succumbing already to starvation and disease, they now fell prey to criminals, conmen and the ubiquitous 'runners' and 'agents', eager to make what profit they could off the defenseless. As Herman Melville put it in *Redburn* (1849): '. . . of all seaports in the world, Liverpool, perhaps, most abounds in all the variety of land-sharks, land-rats and other vermin, which make the hapless mariner their prey. In the shape of landlords, barkeepers, clothiers, crimps and boarding-house loungers, the land-sharks devour him, limb by limb; while the land rats and mice constantly nibble at his purse.' Some of the emigrants killed themselves; others committed mercy killings and many went mad. The corpses of entire families were later found in the unlit cellars and basements on which they had spent the last of their money.[27]

During the famine decade, 1846–55, the number of Irish emigrants to North America who left from Liverpool was four to five times greater than the number leaving from all Irish ports combined. In his novel *Redburn*, Melville described the Irish emigrants from Liverpool 'as the most simple people I had ever seen. They seemed to have no adequate idea of distances; and to them America must have seemed as a place just over a river.' They had a six-week journey to endure on rough seas and often under the most diseased and unsanitary conditions. Their primary destination was New York City, but there was also a huge passage of emigrants between Liverpool and Canada, especially in 1847. When a new Passenger Act was passed in the United States that year, imposing stricter regulations on emigrant shipping and raising transatlantic fares steeply, many emigrants opted for the cheaper, less-regulated Canadian route. The same year, New York levied a tax on immigrants to cover the cost of those who became public charges, further diverting passengers to Canada. The New York-Liverpool trade recovered the following year, but 1847 became the single most notorious year of the famine, with some of the most heart-wrenching scenes of death and devastation occurring on Canadian rather than American shores.[28]

'Black '47' has remained preeminent in popular memory of the famine among the Irish on both sides of the Atlantic. Emigration that year was marked by panic and hysteria. The majority of the emigrants appear to have been middling and strong farmers getting out of Ireland while they still could. Thirty per cent of those bound for British North America in 1847, and 9 per cent of those sailing to the United States, perished on board ship or shortly after their arrival. Swarming with disease and 'fever', the vessels they sailed on became known as 'coffin ships'. In *Redburn*, Melville wrote with heartfelt outrage of an outbreak of 'fever' among Irish emigrants bound from Liverpool to New York: 'The sight that greeted us, upon entering [the steerage], was wretched indeed. It was like entering a crowded jail. From the rows of rude bunks, hundreds of meagre, begrimed faces were turned upon us; while seated upon the chests, were scores of unshaven men, smoking tea-leaves, and creating a suffocating vapour.' Women, children and the elderly lay huddled together, starving and dying. As the contagion spread, panic ensued; but there was no possibility of escape, the ship being like a hospital and prison at once.[29]

The Irish immigrants to Canada in 1847 were certainly the most impoverished and diseased that country ever received. About 40,000 of them came via Liverpool, the remainder of them from the Irish ports. Faced with this vast influx of impoverished, diseased refugees, the Canadian authorities used an old quarantine center on the island of Grosse Île as their clearing center. Located on the St Lawrence River about thirty miles downstream from Québec City, the Grosse Île quarantine center had opened during the cholera epidemic of 1832. Its hospital could house only 150 patients and it was utterly overwhelmed in 1847; by the end of May some 12,500 Irish immigrants were waiting in ships off the island, the healthy and sick and dead crammed together for weeks in overcrowded quarters, with barely any food or water.[30]

It was in this context that some of the most shocking scenes of the Irish famine occurred. The *Agnes* arrived at Grosse Île with 427 passengers; after a quarantine of fifteen days, only 150 survived. The *Larch*, which sailed from Sligo with 440 passengers, arrived at Grosse Île with 108 passengers dead and 150 sick with fever. Of the 477 passengers on the *Lord Ashburton*, most of them tenants evicted by Lord Palmerston, 107 died at sea and 60 were ill on arrival. Of the 3,006 tenants evicted by Denis Mahon from his estate in Strokestown, County Roscommon in 1847, about 1,000 received assistance to emigrate to Canada; 158 of them died on board *The Virginius* out of Liverpool, 19 died waiting in quarantine off Grosse Île, and at least 90 more died in the hospital sheds on the island. On vessels leaving Cork in 1847, one passenger in every nine died; on vessels from Liverpool, one in fourteen. Shipboard mortality was never again so high as in Black '47, though it rose sharply in 1849 and 1851 when cholera struck.[31]

By June 1847, some 21,000 Irish immigrants were housed on Grosse Île, most in sheds and military tents but thousands out in the open; as many as 150 died every day. It is estimated that at least 12,000 Irish famine victims are buried on the island. Altogether, about 30,000 (32 per cent) of the 97,000 Irish emigrants who sailed to British North America in 1847, and 20 per cent of the total number of Irish transatlantic emigrants who crossed the Atlantic from Ireland that year, died either at sea or shortly after arrival. Thousands more died when struck with fever on their way up the St Lawrence river to Québec, or after they arrived in the cities of Montreal, Kingston and Toronto. In general, the reaction of the Canadian authorities and people seems to have been remarkably generous, though there was understandable fear of disease and in some places citizens' committees were formed to keep the immigrants moving on. Those who survived the sea voyage and their early days in Canada often set out overland or by lake and river for the United States.[32]

Choosing between starvation and flight, the famine Irish emigrated to North America in their hundreds of thousands. The two million men, women and children who crossed the Atlantic from Ireland in the decade after 1845 represented one-quarter of the pre-famine population and accounted for the largest European mass migration, in proportional terms, in nineteenth-century history. Once settled in America, they tended to see themselves as exiles rather than voluntary emigrants, looking back on their exodus from Ireland as banishment. Herein lay a potent source of support for Irish nationalism in the United States. For the American Irish had little doubt who was responsible for the catastrophe. In the words of one of their leaders, the political exile John Mitchel: 'The almighty indeed sent the potato blight, but the English created the Famine.'[33]

ARRIVAL, SETTLEMENT AND LABOUR

Never before or since did the Irish account for so high a proportion of American immigration as during the famine era. In the 1840s, the Irish made up 45.6 per cent of all immigrants to the United States, and 35.2 per cent in the 1850s. Two-fifths of all foreign-born Americans in the decade of the 1850s were Irish. Moreover, for every Irish-born person in the United States in 1860, only five remained at home; the corresponding ratio for Germany was one to thirty-three. The famine migration, in short, transformed the character of Irish history and had a major impact on American history as well.[34]

With the rise of Liverpool in the 1830s, New York City had become the principal port of arrival for Irish immigrants, a status it retained permanently thereafter. Fuelled by a mass influx of Irish and German immigrants, the population of the city rose from 371,000 in 1825 to 630,000 by 1845. What was it was like for an Irish immigrant to arrive in New York City in this period? The words that spring immediately to mind are fear, uncertainty, chaos, excitement and deception. Before the establishment of Ellis Island as a clearing center for immigrants in 1892, the federal government did not play an active role in regulating immigration. Instead, immigration was the responsibility of individual states and cities. Immigration into New York City was almost entirely unregulated until the establishment of Castle Garden as a clearing center in 1855. Immigrants simply arrived off the boat onto the streets of Manhattan, with no sense of where they were, where they might go or how they might get there. As a result, many were descended upon by a variety of entrepreneurs, hucksters and conmen, eager to take advantage of them. 'Agents' were sent out by the numerous boardinghouses clustered on the waterfront, promising comfortable quarters in what often turned out to be rat-infested cellars, roach-infested basements or single windowless rooms in which one or, more often, several families would be housed. 'Runners' were sent out by transportation companies, offering to take the immigrants elsewhere in the city, state or country. Like the boardinghouse agents, they took full advantage of the immigrants' ignorance of local prices, charging exorbitant fees and offering services far inferior to what they had promised, or even selling counterfeit tickets.[35]

On arrival in New York, in short, immigrants faced much the same forms of deception and abuse they had endured during their weeks in Liverpool and other ports, waiting for the ship to finally depart. On both sides of the Atlantic, and especially in New York, their deceivers and abusers were very often their fellow-Irishmen, who exploited putative bonds of nationality to take the immigrants into their confidence and then rob them blind. Germans preyed on Germans in similar ways, it might be noted, and English on English. The impoverished Irish, of course, were the most vulnerable to this sort of exploitation and, for the same reason, perhaps the most likely to engage in it.

The American Irish in the mid-nineteenth century have aptly been described as 'urban pioneers'. Whereas the Irish who stayed in Canada, especially Ontario, appear to have settled in rural areas as often as in urban centers, the Irish in the United States showed a marked preference for towns and cities. Thirty-seven per cent of the Irish-born population in the United States in 1850, for example, lived in cities of 25,000 or more, compared to just under 9 per cent of the American-born population as a whole. Fully 44.5 per cent of the Irish-born lived in the fifty largest cities in the United States in 1870, and well over half of the remainder lived in small towns, mill villages, mining areas and in labour camps along rivers, canals and railroads. Combining the population of these smaller industrial and urban areas with that of the large cities, one historian has estimated that three-quarters of the American-born Irish lived in urban-industrial areas in 1870. The Irish were easily the most urbanized people in the United States, for three-quarters of the American population as a whole was rural at this time. The five American cities with the largest Irish-born populations in 1860 and 1870 were New York, Philadelphia, Boston, Chicago and San Francisco. New York City (including Brooklyn as well as Manhattan) had 275,984 Irish-born residents in 1870, Philadelphia 96,698, Boston 56,900, Chicago 39,988 and San Francisco 25,864. These five cities were followed by St Louis (23,329), Jersey City (17,665), Pittsburgh (13,119), Providence (12,085) and Cleveland (9,964).[36]

The famine Irish settled most heavily in the states of the Northeast and Mid-Atlantic, then in the Midwest, the West and, least heavily, in the South. Since 1850, some 60 per cent or more of the American Irish have resided in the four states of New York, Massachusetts, Pennsylvania and Illinois. In 1860, fully one-quarter of the populations of both New York City and Boston were Irish-born, along with 16 per cent of the population of Philadelphia. In the Midwest, there were about 150,000 Irish-born residents as early as 1850; the Irish-born populations of cities like St Louis, Cincinnati and Detroit in that year stood at between 12 and 15 per cent. Chicago had 40,000 Irish-born residents by 1870, giving it the fourth largest Irish population in the United States.[37]

The Irish also settled in the West and South in significant numbers. Settlement in the western interior was encouraged by immigrant leaders in the East, who were shocked by the degree of urban poverty the immigrants faced there, but opposed by conservative clerics like Bishop John Hughes of New York, who feared that the Catholic Church lacked the clergy and resources to cater to new Irish settlements in the Protestant interior. Moreover, the Irish Emigrant Aid Convention which met in 1856 to discuss plans to create western colonies for Irish immigrants was presided over by the anti-clerical political exile Thomas D'Arcy McGee. Nothing came of McGee's plan, mainly because of Bishop Hughes's staunch opposition. But General James Shields, an Irish-born veteran of the Mexican-American War and the Civil War, set up several successful colonies for Irish immigrants in Minnesota, as did General John O'Neil in Nebraska. In the Far West, 54,000 Irish were living in California by 1870, with San Francisco (25,864 Irish-born residents) as the major center of settlement. The South attracted the fewest immigrants, with only 84,000 Irish-born inhabitants in 1860; but even there the Irish were predominantly urban, an estimated 70 per cent of them settling in cities, towns and urban counties in a culture that was overwhelmingly rural. The main centers of Irish settlement were the ports of New Orleans, Charleston and Baltimore, along with smaller cities like Richmond, Savannah and Memphis.[38]

New York City was the principal location of Irish settlement during the famine era, just as it had been in the early nineteenth century and would remain in the post-famine period. The Irish-born residents of New York City in 1860 made up the largest Irish enclave in the United States, 13 per cent of all Irish-born people in the country. About half the city's population was foreign-born in the mid-nineteenth century, and half of these foreigners were Irish. One in every four residents of Manhattan in 1860 had been born in Ireland, one in every six in Germany. Combining the populations of Manhattan and the neighbouring city of Brooklyn, there were 133,730 Irish-born in 1850 and 275,984 in 1870. The poorest of the New York Irish lived in shanty towns on the outermost rim of the city's development, in the areas soon to be occupied by Central Park and St Patrick's Cathedral. From the Irish settlements in the Seneca Village area of today's Central Park would emerge two of New York City's pre-eminent political leaders of the late nineteenth century, George Washington Plunkitt and 'Boss' Richard Croker of Tammany Hall. In the 1850s, as many as 30,000 Irish men, women and children, could be found living in cellars in New York City, without light or drainage. The heaviest Irish concentrations were in the First, Fourth and Sixth Wards, all in lower Manhattan. The Sixth Ward included the notorious Five Points district, with its immigrant boardinghouses, grog shops, brothels, gambling dens and gangs. Most of the African-American residents of this district had been driven out by the Irish influx from 1840 onward; only 200 remained in 1870, compared to an estimated 2,000 in 1830.[39]

Living in poverty and squalor wherever they settled, the poorer famine immigrants fell victim to a variety of infectious diseases. The highest death rate in New York City in the 1850s was to be found in the Sixth Ward, or the 'Bloody Ould Sixth' as it had become known since the Irish takeover. The leading causes of death among the non-elderly were pulmonary afflictions such as tuberculosis, pleurisy, pneumonia and hemorrhage of the lungs. Children died in their thousands from malnutrition, convulsions, suffocation and neglect. Living in dark basements and cellars flooded with sewage and devoid of natural light (electric light not yet being an option), the Irish-born fell prey to yellow fever, cholera and other diseases. In New York City in the 1850s they accounted for an estimated 70 per cent of the recipients of charity and over 60 per cent of the population of almshouses (where the indigent poor were housed). While natives of Ireland made up 54 per cent of the city's immigrants in 1855, they accounted for 85 per cent of all foreign-born admissions to the city's public hospital, Bellevue. Ravaged by illness, disease and psychological trauma, Irish immigrants in the famine era also suffered from alarmingly high rates of mental illness. Three-quarters of the admissions to New York City's Bellevue asylum were foreign-born in the period 1849 to 1859, for example, and two-thirds of these were Irish.[40]

To an even greater extent than in the pre-famine era, Irish immigrants in the mid-nineteenth century were the worst off of all Euro-Americans. Those Irish immigrants who settled in the interior or on the West Coast typically did better than those who stayed in the East, in part because they arrived with greater resources and could afford to move west on arrival. But outside the far West, many of the famine-era Irish were as poor and disadvantaged as African Americans (even if their citizenship rights and voting and legal rights were more secure). This pattern held true not just in cities like New York and Boston but wherever the Irish settled in the East, the Midwest and the South. In Buffalo, for example, the Irish-born constituted 63 per cent of the poor-house population at the height of the famine in 1849, and an average of 51 per cent in the 1850s. In New Orleans, the Irish were ravaged by cholera, malaria and yellow fever, which spread rapidly through their overcrowded tenements and boardinghouses. About 4,000 of the 12,000 who died during the city's great yellow fever epidemic of 1853 were Irish-born. More than half the patients in Charity Hospital were Irish in 1850 though, as defenders of the Irish in New Orleans liked to point out, many of the Sisters of Charity who ran the hospital were also natives of Ireland.[41]

Irish immigrants in the famine era developed an enduring reputation for violence and criminality in the United States. This reputation was in many ways unjust, stemming as it did from nativist discrimination; but it also reflected to some degree the poverty faced by the immigrants, the continuation in the United States of traditions of protest rooted in the Irish country-side, and the emergence of a rich tradition of gang life well-suited to the American urban environment. The Irish proportion of inmates in jails from Buffalo to New Orleans was always much higher than their share of the population as a whole. In New York City in 1859, to cite one example, 55 per cent of all people arrested were Irish, as compared with 23 per cent for native-born Americans, 10 per cent for Germans and 7 per cent for British. The number of Irish convicted of crimes in New York was five times that of the native-born. Arrests for drunkenness and for disorderly behaviour were especially common. Among the more infamous gangs active in Five Points and the neighbouring Bowery were the Dead Rabbits, the Kerryonians, the Forty Thieves, the Chichesters, the Roach Guards, the Plug Uglies and the Shirt Tails. Gangs of this sort predated the arrival of the Catholic Irish in American cities, but the Irish variety contributed to a growing reputation for violence among the American Irish, as did the Astor Place Riot of 10–11 May 1849, when Irish labourers (among others) favourable to the American actor Edwin Forrest battled supporters of his English rival, William C. Macready. Police and militia fired into the crowd, killing twenty-two and wounding forty-eight; the crowd then retaliated against the police, wounding seventy. The Irish also began their conquest of American prize fighting in the famine era, with John 'Old Smoke' Morrissey, a native of Tipperary who had come to Troy, New York, as a child, winning the national heavyweight championship in 1853 after a bare-knuckle fight that lasted thirty-seven rounds. But violence as pathology rather than entertainment had a more enduring and negative impact on the Irish image in America in this period, most notably in the cases of the Draft Riots of 1863, the Orange and Green Riots of 1870 and 1871 and the Molly Maguire affair of the 1860s and 1870s.[42]

The rough culture of Irish immigrants in mid-nineteenth century America makes sense only against the backdrop of the social and working conditions they faced. Just as in the pre-famine period, common labour and domestic service were the dominant forms of work reserved for the Irish. Arriving without marketable skills, the majority of the Irish had to take whatever positions were available; they could not afford to be too choosy, given that most of them were virtually penniless and many were hungry, diseased or dying. In Philadelphia, 30 per cent of the Irish-born worked in day labour (with another 11 per cent working as hand-loom weavers), faring poorly compared to the Germans (11 per cent day labourers) and all other groups in the city. In New York City in 1855, 46 per cent of the Irish-born worked as unskilled labourers or service workers (53 per cent in the Sixth Ward). In Jersey City, 56 per cent of Irish-born men worked in unskilled jobs in 1860. As late as 1870, four out of every ten Irish-born men and women gainfully employed in the United States worked as unskilled labourers or domestic servants, compared to only 16 per cent of the total labour force. Three-quarters of New York City's labourers and half its domestics in that year were Irish-born. Those who avoided menial labour typically worked in skilled or semiskilled jobs, rather than in the professions or as self-employed businessmen. Although the Irish tended to fare better the further west they moved (so that in Detroit or Denver or San Francisco, where they still worked as labourers more than any other white ethnic group, they did so to a lesser extent than in New York or Boston), it is clear that the immigrants of the famine generation were close to the bottom of the American social scale. There were many individual exceptions, of course, but the American Irish in the period 1845 to 1870 were clearly the least successful and most exploited of all European Americans.[43]

Common labourers in the mid-nineteenth century performed a wide variety of tasks. They worked as longshoremen on the docks, as cartmen and teamsters hauling goods throughout the cities, as coal heavers, lumberyard men, quarrymen, pipe layers, street pavers, ditch diggers, boatmen, bricklayers and plasterers. The Irish erected the buildings, paved the streets, quarried the stones and laid out the parks in cities from New York to New Orleans,

Boston to Buffalo, Jersey City to Waltham, Massachusetts and Detroit to San Francisco. Half of the teamsters in Buffalo in 1855 were Irish-born and four-fifths of the teamsters and carters in New York City. Employment for casual labourers was sporadic, with payment often on a daily rather than weekly basis. They were often laid off for the winter, especially from construction projects. They followed work to wherever it was available, leaving their families to fend for themselves until they returned (if indeed they ever did). Underpaid and miserably housed, they were not only despised by native-born workers but exploited by contractors and foremen who were more often than not Irish themselves.[44]

As well as labouring and hauling, Irishmen were employed in a variety of other jobs in the mid-nineteenth century, most of them menial. They worked, for example, as stablemen, waiters, bartenders, inn-keepers and tailors. In 1855, 27 per cent of New York City's police force was Irish (slightly more than the Irish proportion of the city's population). Practically all the shoemakers in New York City in 1855 in the same year were foreign-born, and one-third of them were Irish. About 17,000 Irish immigrants were working in shoe-making in the United States in 1870. The semi-skilled trades were also open to the Irish, most notably as tavern-keepers and grocers. The Irish worked as well in the emerging factories of the United States, especially in the textile industry and metal production. And they worked throughout the country in railroad construction and mining, again typically filling manual rather than skilled positions.[45]

Irish women were also concentrated in menial, unskilled jobs. Domestic service was the single biggest form of employment for Irish women in America between 1850 and 1900. In New York City as early as 1855, 74 per cent of all domestics were Irish and 45 per cent of all Irish-born women aged under fifty were employed in this line of work. Servants worked extremely long hours, typically from 4 or 5 in the morning until 9 or 10 at night; in houses with young children at least one servant was on call round the clock. They did the cooking, cleaning, washing, housekeeping, sewing and mending, and a host of other household tasks. Within the ranks of female servants there were important gradations from cooks and waitresses to personal servants, chambermaids and scullions (the lowest rank of female servant, employed to wash dishes and perform menial tasks in the kitchen). Although domestic service was clearly onerous, many young Irish women evidently found it preferable to the alternatives. Room and board were free, and employment was relatively secure; domestics could be fired at will, but they did not face the same pattern of sporadic, uncertain employment endured by women who took work into their home and by many factory workers. Domestic servants were usually able to save money for use as dowries or to finance the emigration of family members from Ireland.[46]

Irish women who did not work as domestic servants found a variety of other jobs. Many took washing or textile work into their homes, did temporary housework for others, or provided lodging to boarders to supplement their income. Those who worked outside the home were often employed as bookbinders, peddlers, storekeepers, makers of umbrellas and paper boxes, or in the needle trades, which became their second major source of employment after domestic service. While needlework was often done at home on a piecework basis in the early nineteenth century, it was increasingly concentrated in factories thereafter, under conditions often resembling the modern 'sweatshop'. One-third of Irish women under the age of thirty worked in the needle trades in New York City in 1855. Those who could not get work in service or sewing often made a living as prostitutes. One-third of 2,000 prostitutes questioned by an investigator in New York City in 1855, for example, were born in Ireland. Overall, a disproportionately high number of Irish women in the famine period seem to have fended for themselves, often with the support of working children, but with no able-bodied male present in the household. Explanations for the absence of males vary; some of them may have been away seeking work but most, it appears, had either abandoned their wives, died in industrial accidents or succumbed to famine and disease.[47]

As in the pre-famine period, there are intriguing signs during the famine period of transplanted traditions of Irish peasant violence merging in the United States with newer forms of industrial organization. The evidence is scanty, but in Buffalo, for example, gangs of 'Corkonians' and 'Fardowners' did battle in a manner typical of the pre-famine period, and Irish workers drove black longshoremen from the docks. The Irish of Buffalo also organized crowd protests against unemployment and high food prices, reminiscent of pre-industrial protest in Europe. At the same time, they began to organize spontaneous strikes against contractors (many of them Irish) and employers, moving towards forms of protest and organization better-suited to their new industrial conditions. A similar pattern is evident on the canals in the 1840s and 1850s, with faction fighting and interethnic feuding giving way to Irish participation in concerted strike activity for better wages and conditions. The Molly Maguires in the anthracite region of Pennsylvania represented a hybrid form between traditions of Irish agrarian protest and American-style trade unionism. A secret society of Irish mine workers, they emerged in the early

1860s to protest against low wages, poor conditions and the military draft, adapting to industrial Pennsylvania a mode of protest that had its roots in the Irish countryside.[48]

As the secret society tradition faded, the American Irish became leading players in the American trade union movement. This was particularly true in the post-famine era, but the seeds were sown in the period 1845–70. The largest unions in New York City in the 1850s were those of the labourers, with the Irish making up the highest proportion of members. Nearly all the officers of New York's Tailors' Trade Association were Irish in 1855. The textile spinners' union in Fall River, Massachusetts was also under Irish leadership at this time. In 1859 Irish immigrant spinners in Lowell, Massachusetts who had replaced a largely female textile workforce over the previous decade, launched their first strike. The Irish also dominated long-shoremen's work on the waterfront of New York City by this time, having driven out black labour and formed a powerful but racially exclusive trade union, the Longshoremen's and Laborers' United Benevolent Society. Among its leaders were two recent Irish immigrants, Thomas Masterson, a Fenian shoemaker and Robert Blissert, a tailor and organizer for the International Workingmen's Association. Irish immigrants played a prominent role in the foundation and leadership of the American Miners' Union in 1861, and Irish-born miner John Siney was a founder and the first leader of the largest union in the country in this period, the Workingmen's Benevolent Association, which mobilized some 35,000 anthracite mine workers in Pennsylvania after its founding in 1868. The second largest union at this time, the Knights of St Crispin, had its home among the largely Irish shoe-makers, and out of it would emerge the Knights of Labor, a nationwide organization that attracted a remarkable 750,000 members in the mid-1880s. That the Knights of Labor were led by Terence Powderly, the son of Irish immigrants, signified that the American Irish had moved from the margins to the mainstream of the American labour movement, a position they would retain for most of the century to come.[49]

RELIGION, NATIVISM AND POLITICS

The history of religion, nativism and politics in the famine era represents a continuation and intensification of the themes that had arisen during the pre-famine period. The Irish consolidated their control of the Catholic Church, which in turn emerged as the largest and most powerful Christian denomination in the United States. Partly in response, nativist hostility to the Irish grew to fever pitch, especially in the 1850s. At the same time, the Irish began to discover in politics not only a means of protection from nativist attack but a potential path to power for themselves, a path that would reach its terminus in the late nineteenth and early twentieth centuries.

The American Catholic Church grew enormously in the mid-nineteenth century, in line with mass immigration from Ireland and Germany. Between 1840 and 1860, the period when immigrants accounted for the highest percentage of the total population in American history, the number of Catholics in the United States increased from 663,000 to 3,103,000. By 1870 it had reached 4.5 million. The Church was at first ill-equipped to deal with this enormous and rapid expansion. The number of Catholic priests in the United States jumped from 480 in 1840 to 1,500 in 1850. At least one-third of these priests were Irish, with many of them coming from the College of All Hallows in Dublin, which sent 1,500 priests to the Americas in the sixty years after it was founded in 1842. Nonetheless, the ratio of priests to parishioners was remarkably low at mid-century, standing at 1:4,500 in New York City compared to 1:3,000 in Ireland. In the American interior at this time, the ratio was as high as 1:7,000.[50]

Aware that the Irish in both Ireland and the United States often had only the most cursory understanding of Catholic doctrine, observed the sacraments only rarely and lacked adequate numbers of clergy, the hierarchy in both countries embarked in the mid-nineteenth century on an ambitious plan of growth and renewal known to historians as the 'devotional revolution'. Rates of attendance at Sunday Mass in New York City in the 1840s rarely exceeded 40 per cent, while in the more remote parts of western Ireland the rate was as low as half that figure. The laity's grasp of Catholic doctrine was for the most part superficial, and their vibrant tradition of folk religion and popular magic rested uneasily with orthodox teaching. The 'devotional revolution', presided over by Cardinal Paul Cullen in Dublin and Archbishop John Hughes in New York, encouraged attendance at mass and confession, introduced a series of devotional practices and institutions – novenas, blessed altars, *via crucis* ('stations of the cross'), pilgrimages, shrines, retreats, benedictions, rosary beads, scapulars, missals, catechisms, holy images and devotion to the Sacred Heart, the Virgin Mary and the Immaculate Conception – thereby imposing orthodoxy on the heterodox religious practices of the peasantry in rural Ireland and, by the same token, in industrial and urban Irish America. The boisterous and sometimes sexual and sacrilegious games played at wakes were discouraged and frowned upon; peasant festivals with only the loosest associations with Catholicism were more closely tied to the Church; attendance at Sunday mass and confession in particular were actively encouraged. The impact of the 'devotional revolution' was greatly heightened by the devastation of the famine, which undermined the efficacy and predictive power of popular magic and folk religion, reinforcing the position of the Catholic Church among the Irish on both sides of the Atlantic.[51]

As part of this expansion of the power and influence of the Church, Irishness in the nineteenth century came to be almost synonymous with Catholicism on both sides of the Atlantic. So central a role did the Catholic Church play in defining Irish nationality in Ireland and Irish-American ethnicity in the United States that it has been virtually impossible since the mid-nineteenth century to think of Irishness in either country without simultaneously thinking of Catholicism. As the Irish came to dominate the American Catholic Church, the Church in turn became one of the critical institutions in Irish America, along with the Democratic party and the labour movement, wielding enormous cultural power and determining in no small measure how the emerging Irish-American ethnic community defined itself. The Church was the one genuinely transatlantic institution in Irish life, the one institution that Irish immigrants could unhesitatingly recognize in America. Herein lay a classically American dilemma. The credentials of the Catholic Church as an authentically American institution were fiercely challenged by nineteenth-century nativists, so that the Irish-American community, to the extent that it was defined by Catholicism, was consequently vulnerable to charges of disloyalty and un-Americanism.

The Catholic clergy fought these accusations in several ways, and with some success. The Church, they argued, was perfectly compatible with American ways, and Catholics pledged their secular allegiance unequivocally to the United States. At the same time, to the extent that immigrants were indeed violent or drunken, the clergy preached against these vices and in favour of material self-improvement and individual effort and success. This message closely complemented an emerging ideology of middle-class Irish-American respectability that would assume its most powerful form in the late nineteenth and early twentieth centuries. Finally, the Church responded to nativist attacks by arguing that Irish Catholics made ideal Americans because they had fled Ireland in search of religious and political toleration, the same cause that had brought the Puritans to America. Whether the Puritans or the Irish famine refugees of the mid-nineteenth century had actually come to America in search of toleration is irrelevant here; the point is that the Catholic Irish, by establishing the connection, could fit themselves neatly into a quintessentially American story.[52]

Running counter to this emphasis on the Americanism of Catholics, in the eyes of nativists at least, was the parish (parochial) school system. The extent of that system differed from city to city. Archbishop Hughes of New York City, the foremost champion of parochial schools, saw them as the best foundation on which to build a durable Church in a hostile environment. Bishop John Fitzpatrick (1846–66) of Boston and his successor John Williams (1866–1907), by contrast, concentrated on building the Church first and the schools second. Even in New York, there were never enough parochial schools to educate a majority of the city's Catholic children. Many of the schools were staffed by nuns imported from Ireland, among them the Ursuline Sisters in Charleston and the Sisters of Mercy and Sisters of Charity in New York, who also did valuable relief work in New York's cholera epidemics of 1832, 1849 and 1866. Through the efforts of these nuns and members of the clergy, the parochial school system became an integral part of the Catholic mission in the United States and was strongly endorsed by the Second Provincial Council of the Church at Baltimore in 1852, after which many Catholic pastors began to deny the sacraments to parents who refused to send their children to the schools. But, while the system of parish schools undoubtedly strengthened the position of the Church in the immigrant community, it also exposed the immigrants to accusations of rejecting not just Protestantism but America itself. If the Irish rejected the common school system, the nativists argued, it was clear that they had no intention of assimilating. In other words, the Irish could be seen as antithetical to God, government and nation as defined by American nativists.[53]

The expansion of the Catholic Church in the 1840s and 1850s, therefore, was matched by an intensification of the religious nativism that had been mounting since the early nineteenth century. Matters began to come to a head when mobs of nativists and workers attacked Irish Catholics in Philadelphia, Richmond and Charleston in 1844 and 1845. When Archbishop Gaetano Bedini was sent to the United States as a papal delegate in 1853, in part to settle lingering disputes over trusteeism (lay control of parish affairs) in New York and Philadelphia, he was mobbed by nativists. Ironically, the nativists acted in concert with radical German immigrants and a handful of Italians who were upset at Bedini's alleged role in suppressing the Revolution of 1848. This form of cooperation underscores the point that most nativists at this time were opposed not to immigration generally, but to Irish Catholic immigrants in particular. Anti-Irish Catholic sentiment was also enflamed by the Scotch-Irish, especially through their Orange Lodges and their domination of the American Protestant Association. Founded in

1844 by Protestant ministers with the initial aim of advocating retention of the King James version of the Bible in the schools, the Association was open to foreign as well as native-born Protestants.[54]

Nativist labour organizations, by contrast, were often closed to all immigrants, not just the Irish. Fraternal societies like the Order of the United American Mechanics restricted their membership to American-born workingmen, whom they attempted to unite in opposition to immigrant competition for jobs. Rhetorically at least, they were opposed equally to German, British, Scotch-Irish and Catholic Irish immigrants, but in practice it was the unskilled status of the last which caused them greatest concern. The Catholic Irish, they believed, provided employers with an inexhaustible reservoir of cheap labour with which they could break strikes and drive down wages. The willingness of Irish workers to work for low wages was a particular grievance, though that 'willingness' was of course a necessity for most famine refugees, who were often excluded from even the most menial occupations. As an advertisement in the New York *Daily Sun* put it on 11 May 1853: 'Woman wanted – To do general housework . . . English, Scotch, Welsh, German, or any other country or color except Irish.'[55]

The high point of nativism in the famine period was the Know Nothing movement of the 1850s, when anti-immigrant sentiment assumed a more powerful *political* form than ever before or since in American history. The Know Nothings emerged out of a series of smaller nativist organizations founded in the 1840s, such as the Order of United Americans and the Order of the Star Spangled Banner. They became a national political party because the mass immigration from famine-stricken Ireland coincided with an escalating national crisis over the question of slavery. That crisis wrecked the Whig party in 1852–54, and before the foundation of the Republican party in 1854 the nativists briefly and unexpectedly held the balance of power. After a series of electoral victories in Massachusetts, Pennsylvania, New Jersey, Delaware, Maryland, Kentucky and California in 1854, it looked as though the Know Nothings rather than the Republicans might provide the major opposition to the Democrats by 1856. But, after reaching their peak in 1855, the Know Nothings fell from power even more rapidly than they had ascended, split asunder by slavery, the inescapable political question of the day. Know Nothingism had been strong in the South, especially in New Orleans, as well as in the North; but the two sides parted company over the question of slavery in 1855, allowing the new Republican party to emerge as the principal opposition to the Democrats in 1856 and, even more remarkably, to capture the presidency in 1860. The Republicans inherited much of the old Whig and Know Nothing opposition to immigrants, but their anti-slavery position took precedence and some, like Abraham Lincoln, explicitly rejected nativism.[56]

For northern nativists in the 1850s, anti-immigrant and anti-slavery sentiment were often opposite sides of the same coin. The two causes were complementary parts of a single, coherent ideology of republican society based on the conviction that honest, productive work would reap its just rewards, and that a virtuous citizenry was impossible without social mobility and potential economic independence for all. At the heart of this vision was the notion of free labour. Labour was free in the sense that it was dignified, independent and self-sustaining; every labourer was potentially a small, independent entrepreneur. But how could all labourers become entrepreneurs, given that the existence of the latter was based, to a large extent, on the existence of the former? The answer was that labouring was a temporary rather than a permanent position, a way-station on the road to economic self-sufficiency. If slaves represented the antithesis of free labour in this sense, Irish immigrants came a close second. Native-born American workers and certain immigrants may have hoped realistically for some degree of social success, but the Irish had little hope of completing the process of occupational mobility in question. Increasingly aware of this fact, the nativists lashed out at them, complaining about their religion, their culture, their work habits and their drinking practices. Their preference for the pro-slavery Democratic party made them even more objectionable. While it would be an oversimplification to see anti-Irish nativism as involving only economic concerns, the targets the nativists chose – drunkenness, ignorance, laziness, moral laxity, idolatry, political indoctrination – were clearly seen as obstacles to the emergence of a self-sufficient work force as well as a virtuous citizenry.[57]

Nativism was based largely on concrete issues that had to do with religion and labour, but there was also a less tangible and more disturbing quality to the attacks on the Irish. The genre of nativist 'convent literature' in the early and mid-nineteenth century, which claimed to expose the gruesome goings-on in Catholic nunneries and hospitals, spread its message of hate through an appeal to voyeurism and lust. It was in some ways the pornography of its day, titillating as well as outraging its largely middle-class audience. At the same time, the language of patrician nativists like George Templeton Strong, describing the Irish in America in the wake of the great draft riots of July 1863, betrayed an extreme racial sentiment that defies easy explanation: the immigrants, he wrote in his diary, are 'brutal, base, cruel, cowards, and as insolent as base'; they came from a land populated by 'creatures that crawl and eat dirt and poison every community they infest'. Likewise, the violence directed against the Irish displayed a terrifying element of the irrational, especially the burning of convents and churches and the pogrom against the Irish unleashed by the Committee of Vigilance in San Francisco in 1856, in which four men were hanged and perhaps a hundred more driven out.[58]

Hounded and harassed by nativists, the Irish turned to the Democratic party for refuge. The pre-famine Irish had gravitated to the Democratic party as a matter of course, in part because the other prinicipal political party, the Whigs, embodied the earlier Federalist tradition of hostility to foreigners. Only in the 1840s, when it was already too late, did Whig politicians like William Seward and Thurlow Weed of New York and the Whig editor, Horace Greeley, of the New York *Tribune*, begin to make overtures to the Irish. By that time, the great mass of Irish Americans were already voting Democrat, and they would retain this affiliation for more than a century. Sensing an opportunity in the 1820s, when the abolition of property qualifications in northern states greatly broadened the electorate, the Democrats had perfected the arts of mass popular politics, cementing a durable alliance with immigrants, especially those from Ireland. Street fighting, election-day riots, political parades and huge outdoor meetings became the order of the day. No strangers to faction-fighting, popular demonstrations and the 'monster' meetings of O'Connellism, the Irish proved adept at this new form of popular politics, and none more so than the remarkable figure of Mike Walsh, the first of a long line of colourful Irish politicians produced by New York City.[59]

Born in Ireland in 1815 and brought to the United States as a child by his parents, Walsh was apprenticed to a lithographer and went on to a career in journalism and politics. He excelled in the rough and ready style of politics that characterized New York after the broadening of the suffrage in 1821, organizing a gang known as the Spartan Band to support and protect him at mass meetings and demonstrations. In 1843 he founded *The Subterranean*, a political newspaper he ran for the next several years, with the motto 'Independent in Everything – Neutral in Nothing'. *The Subterranean* blended radical politics with lively gossip and twice brought Walsh to jail on charges of libel. Walsh was the first Irish politician to break through the edifice of Tammany Hall, winning its nomination for a state Assembly seat in 1846. Four years later, he was elected to the US Congress, holding his seat until his death in 1859. Walsh's populist radicalism did not prevent him from adopting a reactionary position on the question of slavery. He was a great admirer of the racist southern pro-slavery politician John C. Calhoun; and, like the majority of his Irish supporters, a sworn enemy of the abolitionists. During the critical debate over the future of slavery in the territories in 1854, he outspokenly defended the institution of slavery and its extension into both Kansas and Nebraska. Although he attacked what he called 'white slavery' (the subjection of northern workers to their employers), he did so only to argue that white workers were in a worse position than black chattel slaves, whose bondage he apparently regarded as part of the natural order of things and vociferously defended. Not for the first time in Irish-American history, or in American history more generally, populist radicalism was combined with ugly racism.[60]

The American Irish of the mid-nineteenth century were opposed not simply to the extreme position of abolitionism but also to more moderate forms of anti-slavery. While the abolitionists were by definition 'anti-slavery', the wider anti-slavery movement did not favour the immediate, outright abolition of slavery. Embodied in the newly formed Republican party from 1854 onward, the anti-slavery movement instead opposed the further expansion of slavery into the unorganized territories of the West, from Texas to California. In the future of these territories lay the fate of the United States as a whole. Would the West, and hence the country, be predominantly slave or free? While they opposed the expansion of slavery, however, the anti-slavery men did not demand the abolition of slavery in the South. Many of them, indeed, were outspoken racists who cared nothing for the slaves, so long as the country as a whole did not come under the domination of the slave South.[61]

The American Irish tended to oppose not just the radical position of abolitionism but the anti-slavery cause in general, and the Catholic Church to which most of them belonged was among the most outspoken defenders of slavery. In the 1850s, as sentiment against slavery mounted, Archbishop John Hughes became increasingly outspoken on the subject. Abolitionism, for Hughes, was an abomination, a form of treason and violent extremism, emanating logically from the antebellum reform impulse. It could only have disastrous consequences for those Irish immigrants who became associated with it. Catholic clergymen reiterated the teaching of the Church that slavery, as distinct from the slave trade or the abuse of slaves, was not itself inherently wrong. They insisted that Africa was a continent of savagery, warfare and murder, so that people of African descent were much better off as slaves in America than as free people in their ancestral homeland. This point of view fit perfectly with the ideology of the Democratic party, further cementing the alliance between Democrats and Irish Catholics.[62]

It was through the Democratic party that the American Irish rose to political power, and at the heart of that story was Tammany Hall, an organization that long pre-dated the arrival of the Catholic Irish but which they turned into a fabled political machine from the 1870s onward. Tammany's endorsement allowed Mike Walsh to rise to power in the 1840s, just as control of the machine would guarantee Irish control of the city as a whole from the 1870s until the 1930s. The roots of this eventual conquest were laid in the pre-famine and famine periods, when sheer force of numbers was the key to Irish power. With one of every four New Yorkers born in Ireland by mid-century, Tammany leaders realized that their future depended on controlling the Irish vote. As early as 1840, Tammany had opened its infamous Naturalization Bureau to help immigrants file for citizenship, often earlier than the law permitted. The immigrants were also given jobs or were assisted in finding employment. In return for these favours they delivered their vote to the machine at election time. Mayor Fernando Wood secured his hold on power in New York City by doubling the number of naturalized voters between 1855 and 1865, while the number of native-born voters remained almost constant. David Broderick, a veteran of New York City politics, built a short-lived machine along similar lines in San Francisco in the 1850s, before going on to serve in the US Senate from 1857 until his death in 1859. The heyday of Irish machine politics was yet to come, but the techniques that would be perfected in the late nineteenth century were already in place in New York by 1850, the difference being that the Irish did not yet control the machine itself. However, the machine was increasingly dependent on them, and it was only a matter of time before the Irish translated their power into a conquest of municipal politics.[63]

The most infamous of the early Tammany bosses, William Tweed, was Scottish rather than Irish. But, like all New York politicians by mid-century, he depended heavily on the Irish vote. Moreover, he rose to power by using the springboard of an Irish volunteer fire company. By 1859 he had ousted Mayor Fernando Wood and taken control of Tammany Hall. Under Boss Tweed's rule, Tammany paid the New York Printing Company, owned by none other than Tweed himself, to produce 105,000 blank naturalization applications and 69,000 certificates of naturalization. The machine then paid the required court fees and provided false witnesses to testify that the immigrants had been in the United States for the required period of five years. During Tweed's tenure, the city's electorate almost doubled. In 1868 alone, Tammany naturalized 41,112 immigrants in a successful effort to win the gubernatorial election of that year. At its height, the Tweed machine provided as many as 15,000 jobs to its supporters. When Tweed was jailed in 1872, following a massive corruption scandal involving public construction projects, he was succeeded by the aptly-named 'Honest John' Kelly, the first of three great Irish bosses (the others being Richard Croker and Charlie Murphy) who would dominate Tammany Hall for the next half-century.[64]

BEING IRISH IN AMERICA

Most of the more than two million people transplanted from Ireland to the United States between 1840 and 1870 are long since forgotten. Anonymous and powerless even at the time, they left little or no mark on the historical record. But, even if details of individuals' lives are necessarily scarce, one can detect in Irish-American history during the famine era a persistent theme of evolving ethnic identity. What did it mean to be Irish in America? This question was clearly central to the development of the Catholic Church in the United States, and to the emergence of a distinctively Irish form of politics in American cities. It was at the heart, also, of four fascinating and revealing episodes from the famine period: the San Patricio affair of the late 1840s, the Irish experience of the American Civil War, the emergence of Irish-American nationalist movements and the bloody Orange and Green Riots of 1870 and 1871. Each of these episodes, some tragic and others heroic, raised important questions about who the American Irish were. And each of them, significantly, involved violence, the crucible from which so much of Irish and Irish-American identity historically emerged.

About half of the troops recruited to fight for the United States in the Mexican-American War of 1846–48 were foreign-born. One-quarter of the troops were from Ireland. Between 100 and 150 of these foreign soldiers deserted the US Army and fought on the Mexican side. At least forty of these men were Irish; the remainder came from eleven different countries, most from the United States, Britain and Germany. Led by an Irishman named John Riley, the deserters joined a Mexican battalion that came to be known as the San Patricios. Its flag of green silk featured a crudely drawn figure of St Patrick, a shamrock and a harp. The San Patricios saw action at Monterrey, Buena Vista (a few miles south of present-day Saltillo) and in the final defense of Mexico City against the army of General Winfield Scott. Many were killed in battle, and they gained a reputation for valour that survives in Mexico to the present day.[65]

At the end of the war, 85 San Patricios were captured, 72 were court martialled, and 50 were sentenced to death. Sixteen of them were executed in the town of San Angel, just outside Mexico City, where a plaque today commemorates 'the Irish soldiers of the heroic San Patricio Battalion, martyrs who gave their lives for the cause of Mexico during the unjust American invasion'. Four were executed at Mixcoac, and the remaining thirty, in one of the most gruesome incidents of the war, were taken to witness the final Mexican defeat at the battle of Chapultepec, sitting for several hours on the gallows with nooses around their necks until the battle was over, when they were executed. Fifteen San Patricios, including Riley, were sentenced to be whipped and branded on each cheek with the letter D, rather than executed, as they had deserted before the war was actually declared. Riley stayed in the Mexican army until 1850, when he was discharged; thereafter the trail vanishes, but it is possible that he returned to his native Galway.[66]

Why did the San Patricios do what they did? And what do their actions suggest about Irish ethnic and national identity in the mid-nineteenth century? The answers to these questions are limited by the paucity of surviving evidence. Still, a number of motivating issues emerge from the sources, some quite concrete and specific, others more abstract and intangible. Contemporary accounts talk of the contempt and racism displayed by Anglo-American officers to enlisted immigrant soldiers, especially Irishmen, along with harsh discipline and punishments in the US Army and arduous living conditions on the plains of south Texas. Aware of dissatisfaction among the enlisted men, the Mexican government astutely offered enticements, including higher pay and land grants of as much as 320 acres. The Mexicans also knew that some 50 per cent of the US troops were Catholics, many of them Irish, and it had been little more than a decade since the Mexican government had actively recruited Irish settlers to colonize *Coahuila y Tejas*. One can hypothesize that Catholic Irishmen would have had a certain affinity for Catholic Mexico, if only through a common antipathy toward Anglos and Protestants. The idea of a trans-national Catholic identity uniting Mexicans and Irish against the United States is quite plausible, especially at the level of practical decision-making by disgruntled soldiers. Given the extent of nativist prejudice the Irish were encountering in the United States at this time, it is hardly surprising that some soldiers cast their lot with Mexico, despite the enormous risk involved in doing so.[67]

If Irish involvement in the Mexican-American War raised questions of ambivalence and disloyalty, the Irish military contribution to the American Civil War was in some respects a major step forward in their assimilation. One proviso needs to be added at the outset: like most Americans, the Irish were loyal primarily to their region rather than the nation as a whole, so that they fought in significant numbers on both sides in the Civil War. Ireland provided five Confederate generals, Cleburne, Finnegan, Hagan, Lane and Moore. General Patrick Cleburne, an Irish-born Episcopalian based in Arkansas, and commander of the 5th Confederate regiment, was the outstanding Irish-born leader of the Confederate Army. The Irish also provided the largest number of foreign-born troops in the South. If first and second-generation Scotch-Irish were added, the numbers would rise dramatically; but by this time the Scotch-Irish (even recent arrivals) were regarded, and usually saw themselves, not as Irish but as American. Irish units of the Confederate Army were raised in Alabama, Georgia, Missouri, North Carolina, South Carolina, Texas, Tennessee and Virginia. New Orleans had its own Irish Brigade, and most Louisiana regiments had a number of companies with a significant or majority Irish presence. In one of those twists of fate that only war can bring, Irish immigrants fought directly against each other at several battles, most notably Fredericksburg.[68]

The involvement of Irish Catholics in the Union Army was considerably greater than in the Confederacy. Regiments throughout New England and the Middle Atlantic region had heavy Irish contingents. New York provided the predominantly Irish 'Fighting 69th', led by Colonel Michael Corcoran, who was reinstated in 1861 after being relieved of his command the year before for refusing to participate in a parade honouring the visiting Prince of Wales. The 69th suffered heavy losses at first Bull Run, before being incorporated into the famous Irish Brigade, led by the veteran nationalist leader Thomas Francis Meagher, which saw action at Gettysburg, second Bull Run, Antietam (where it lost 196 out of 317 men on the front lines), Fredericksburg (128 out of 238 men killed leading the Union charge) and Chancellorsville. Pennsylvania's 69th, which fought at Gettysburg, was also Irish, while the Pennsylvania 48th, which fought at Petersburg and several other major battles, included many Irish as well. High-ranking Irish-born officers of the Union Army included Meagher, Corcoran and James Shields; the most prominent second-generation Irish general was Philip Sheridan. Fully thirty-eight Union regiments had the word 'Irish' in their names, and at least 144,221 (possibly as many as 170,000) Irish-born men served in the Union Army, along with countless others from the second generation. Through this contribution to the war effort, especially in the North, many Irish immigrants were incorporated into the mainstream of American society as never before, and at least some of the nativist doubts on whether the Irish could assimilate were laid to rest.[69]

If the military participation of the Irish in the Civil War worked in favour of their acceptance and assimilation, however, their involvement in aspects of its wider politics had the opposite effect. While the embrace of a 'white' racial identity by working-class Irish immigrants has been seen by several recent historians as a primary means of their assimilation, the vehemence of Irish opposition to emancipation and military conscription in the era of the Civil War can also be seen to have alienated them even further in the eyes of many Americans. The Irish were by no means unique in their pro-slavery sentiment; but what distinguished them from other pro-slavery northerners during the Civil War was their violence. During the Draft Riots of July 1863 in New York City, Irish mobs systematically attacked innocent African Americans and went so far as to burn down the city's Colored Orphan Asylum. In so doing, they consolidated a reputation for violence that cannot be reduced to a figment of the nativist imagination and exhibited a virulent form of racism that was too extreme even for a northern society that was riven by divisions over the Civil War and contained a substantial pro-slavery contingent other than the Irish. Elite northerners responded to the Irish racial violence of 1863 with a racism of their own, producing some of the most sustained and virulent anti-Irish sentiment in American history. Denouncing the 'barbarism' of the rioters, the *New York Times* went on to condemn the Irish as 'brutish' and 'animal', while the *New York Tribune* called the rioters a 'savage mob', a 'pack of savages', and a mob of 'incarnate devils'. In this way, the racist Irish were themselves racially reduced to the level of the animal kingdom.[70]

As ever, the Catholic Church stood at the forefront of Irish opinion on slavery. Once the Civil War broke out, Archbishop Hughes adopted a firmly pro-Union stance, and he was even sent by President Abraham Lincoln and Secretary of State William Seward to Ireland, France and Rome to rally support for the Union cause. This does not mean, however, that Hughes had changed his position on slavery. Bishops like John Purcell of Cincinnati, who strongly favoured emancipation, were in a small minority within the hierarchy. Hughes, the ever-more-combative chieftain of Irish America, represented the majority position. When he debated with the Catholic convert and intellectual, Orestes Brownson, on the matter in the fall and winter of 1861–2, Hughes responded to Brownson's defense of emancipation as a necessary war measure by insisting that Catholics would fight only for the preservation of the Union, that the abolitionists were dangerous and insane and that the slaves were in any case better off in the United States than they would have been in Africa. This line was supported by the *Metropolitan Record*, one of the more racist and virulently Copperhead (i.e. anti-war Democrat) papers in the country, and by James McMaster's *Freeman's Journal*, the official organ of the Catholic hierarchy in New York City. So outspoken were McMaster's denunciations of a war against slavery, indeed, that he was briefly imprisoned by the government in August 1861 and publication of his paper was temporarily suspended. The dominant Catholic line on slavery was challenged in print by Patrick Donohoe, editor of the *Boston Pilot*, Fr. Edward Purcell (brother of the bishop) of the Cincinnati *Telegraph*, and the editors of the Pittsburgh *Catholic* and the New York *Tablet*. It was the views of Hughes, McMaster and their followers, however, that continued to define the Catholic position in the early 1860s.[71]

Irish opposition to the emancipation of slaves was rooted not just in theology but, more importantly, in social and labour conditions in the cities of the North. The Irish believed themselves to be in competition for jobs with African Americans, and they feared (without justification, as it turned out) that the abolition of slavery would lead to a great inpouring of cheap black labour from the South. The Irish regarded southern blacks, in other words, much as nativists regarded the Irish. Tensions of these kinds lay behind the ongoing conflicts between Irish workers and African Americans in the 1850s and early 1860s, which culminated in the draft riots of 1863. Ever since the 1830s, Irishmen in northern (and some southern) cities had been driving black men out of jobs as white-washers, coachmen, stablemen, porters and bootblacks, while Irish women took jobs as laundresses, seamstresses, cooks, domestic maids and scullions that had once been reserved for black women. By the 1850s, one of the few areas where blacks and Irish were still competing for work was on the docks. The Irish dominated the ranks of longshoremen by this time, founding a union called the Longshoremen's and Laborers' Benevolent Society in New York City in 1852. When the Irish longshoremen went on strike in 1855 and 1863, the employers brought in black strike-breakers, causing the Irish to retaliate in subsequent years with even greater racial exclusivism.[72]

These deep-rooted tensions between Irish and black workers, aggravated by the Emancipation Proclamation and the Conscription Act, both passed early in 1863, exploded in violence during July of that year in the great New York City draft riot. Despite the Irish reputation for valour in the Union Army, Irish immigrants were the most under-represented group in the army compared to the population as a whole. Because of this under-representation, the draft of 1863 fell more heavily on the Irish than on other groups, and could therefore be conceived as a punishment for prior resistance to joining the military effort. At the same time, the war had become since 1 January 1863 a crusade to abolish slavery, something the majority of Irish Americans

vehemently opposed. And, as a final insult from the Irish immigrant perspective, exemptions from the draft were offered to those who could furnish
a substitute or pay a commutation fee of $300, a sum equal to the annual
wage for a labourer at that time.[73]

The great New York City draft riot began on Monday, 13 July when Irish
workers systematically attacked symbols of power and privilege in the city,
especially those connected with conscription and the anti-slavery Republican
party. The authorities could scarcely have chosen a more inflammatory day
for the Irish Catholics who would bear the brunt of conscription: 12 July,
which fell on the eve of the draft, was the anniversary of William of Orange's
victory over James II at the Battle of the Boyne in 1690, a day that had been
celebrated by Ulster Protestants and lamented by Irish Catholics on both
sides of the Atlantic ever since (as it continues to be in Northern Ireland
today). Although the most infamous of America's Orange Riots would occur
in 1870 and 1871, the day had been the occasion of sectarian violence for
several decades before the Civil War. It was in this context, among others,
that the great Draft Riots of July 1863 broke out. For four days, mobs of
Irish workers, with longshoremen at the vanguard, roamed the waterfront
in search of black workers, beating, lynching and driving them out. The
city's Colored Orphan Asylum was burned to the ground. Contemporaries
estimated the number killed in the riots at between 1,200 and 1,500, most of
them shot by police and troops called in from the recent battle of Gettysburg.
While these figures, produced by nativists like George Templeton Strong,
are doubtless too high, the official police figure of 119 dead is probably
too low. A second major center of Irish resistance to the draft was the
anthracite region of northeastern Pennsylvania, where mine workers pro-
testing against conscription, low wages and dangerous working conditions
banded together in secret labour organizations known variously as 'Buckshots',
'Committeemen', and 'Molly Maguires'. In both New York and Pennsylvania,
Irish opposition to the war effort and to emancipation led to charges of
treason and disloyalty, offsetting the positive impact of heavy Irish enlist-
ment in the Union army.[74]

The era of the Civil War was also one in which a new Irish-American
nationalism took root, starting with the Young Ireland movement of the late
1840s and culminating in the Fenian movement of the 1860s. Young Ireland
represented a break with the constitutional nationalism of Daniel O'Connell
(1775–1847) and, ultimately, a return to the tradition of physical force republicanism that had been pioneered by Wolfe Tone (1763–98) in the United
Irishmen movement of 1790s. Whereas the United Irishmen had wanted

nothing less than an Irish republic and were prepared to fight for that cause, O'Connell's goal was autonomy within the Union of Great Britain and Ireland, rather than full independence. His methods were always peaceful, never violent; moral persuasion through mass political agitation, he believed, could be used to force the British to give Ireland greater autonomy. Impatient with this slow and peaceful strategy, a group of young O'Connellites broke away in the early 1840s to found the Young Ireland movement. Among the leaders of this breakaway group were Thomas Davis (1814–45), John Blake Dillon (1816–66), Charles Gavan Duffy (1816–1903), John Mitchel (1815–75), Thomas Francis Meagher (1823–67), James Fintan Lalor (1807–49) and William Smith O'Brien (1803–64). Not all the Young Irelanders favoured republicanism or violence. But many did, and an increasingly desperate leadership eventually launched a rebellion in 1848. The rebellion, led by Smith O'Brien, failed miserably, and many of its leaders made their way to America as exiles. Like many Irish immigrants of this era, they brought with them an abiding memory of the Great Famine as the most egregious in a long line of English offenses against Ireland.[75]

Of the many exiles of '48 who came to the United States, the two most influential were John Mitchel and Thomas Francis Meagher. Mitchel, born in County Derry, was the son of a Presbyterian minister. Educated at Trinity College, Dublin, he practiced law before joining the Repeal Association and the Young Ireland movement. Among the most militant of the Young Irelanders, he edited the *United Irishman*, calling for a 'holy war' to sweep English influence from Ireland. Sentenced to fourteen years' transportation to Australia, he escaped in 1853 and made his way to New York City, where he briefly published the *Citizen*, alienating Bishop John Hughes with his vehemence and radicalism. He also became the most influential proponent of the idea that the British had deliberately allowed the famine to proceed, an idea that struck a receptive chord among Irish immigrants in the United States, reinforcing their self-conception as exiles banished from their native land. A prolific author, Mitchel published his best-known work, *Jail Journal*, in 1854. The following year he left New York for Tennessee, where he worked for a while as a farmer, published a newspaper, the *Southern Citizen*, and emerged as a prominent defender of slavery and a critic of what he saw as the crass materialism and utilitarianism of northern society. Thereafter he lived the restless life of a political exile, settling in Paris in 1856 but returning to the American South in 1862, where he outspokenly defended the Confederacy, for which two of his sons were fighting. Briefly imprisoned at the end of the war, he sailed for Paris in 1865, where he was peripherally involved in the emerging Fenian movement. Mitchel returned to New York in 1867 after breaking with the Fenians and took evident pleasure in mocking their grandiose ambitions in his latest newspaper, the *Irish Citizen* (1867–72). Elected MP for County Tipperary in his absence in February 1875, he returned to Ireland, where he died the following month. During his time in the United States, Mitchel had never really tried to assimilate; America, for him, was but a base from which to further nationalist revolution in Ireland.[76]

The case of Thomas Francis Meagher stands in sharp contrast to that of Mitchel. A graduate of the elite colleges of Clongowes (Ireland) and Stonyhurst (England), Meagher was arrested after the insurrection of 1848 and sentenced to penal servitude for life. But he escaped to America in 1852, where he joined the New York bar, helped John Mitchel found the *Citizen*, and established his own newspaper, the *Irish News*, in 1856. During the Civil War he founded the famous Irish Brigade of the Union Army and was appointed to the rank of Brigadier-General. In New Orleans, an Irish militia company that had named itself the Meagher Rifles after the nationalist hero, renamed itself the Mitchel Rifles once the war broke out; the Meagher Rifles in Charleston similarly dropped the name of their erstwhile hero. Appointed temporary governor of the state of Montana after the Civil War, Meagher accidentally drowned in 1867. Through his service on the Union side in the war, he had taken steps towards assimilation that were neither possible nor desirable for the intractable John Mitchel, his co-conspirator from 1848. The question of whether Irish revolutionaries should assimilate as Americans or retain their separate identity in the name of Irish freedom would return to haunt the Irish-American nationalist movements of the late nineteenth century.[77]

The chief importance of the Young Irelanders lay not so much in their impact on Irish-American history in the late 1840s as in their legacy to the later Fenian movement. The Fenian Brotherhood was founded in 1858 in New York City by John O'Mahony (1816–77), another veteran of 1848, as a sister organization to the more prosaically named Irish Revolutionary Brotherhood (IRB), organized in Dublin by James Stephens (1825–1901) in the same year. The aim of the Fenians and IRB was to rid Ireland of English rule by providing American money and manpower to encourage insurrection. By 1865 the Fenians had attracted 250,000 followers, many of them Civil War veterans, and an Irish Republican government on the American model had been set up in Philadelphia.[78]

Fenianism, however, also spawned dissident factions hoping to benefit from Anglo-American conflict by attacking Canada. On 12 April 1866, an attempt to seize the Canadian island of Campobello in the Bay of Fundy was thwarted at Eastport, Maine. The British and American navies cooperated in intercepting a shipment of arms, and US troops under Major General George Meade forced the Fenians gathered at Eastport to disperse. On 1 June, Colonel John O'Neill crossed the border and defeated a Canadian militia company before retreating to Buffalo. O'Neill's second foray into Canada, on 25 May 1870, was easily repelled. Meanwhile, James Stephens, fleeing from the threat of arrest in Ireland, had arrived in New York on 10 May 1866. Denouncing the attacks on Canada, he ousted O'Mahony from the leadership of the movement and reasserted the goal of insurrection on Irish soil alone. Betrayed by police informants, this goal ended in sporadic rural skirmishes on 5–6 March 1867. The Fenians survived in the United States but were superseded in the 1870s by a new organization of an altogether more serious and determined character, Clan na Gael.[79]

By 1870 the famine generation of Irish immigrants had established a foothold in the United States. Their social position was still precarious, with 40 per cent working as labourers, and anti-Irish racism and nativism far from dissipated. One final episode of violence, the Orange and Green riots of 1870 and 1871, illustrates the distinctive nature of Irish America at this time, raising once again the insistent question of national and ethnic identity. The episode pitted Irish people of Catholic and Protestant background against each other in bloody combat on the streets of New York City. Orangemen in New York had been parading on 12 July, the anniversary of the Battle of the Boyne (1690), since the early nineteenth century, and there had been limited violence between Protestants and Catholics during several such celebrations. In 1870 and 1871, the violence spilled out of control. By the late 1860s the Scotch-Irish of New York City were formally organized into Orange Lodges under the auspices of the Grand Orange Lodge of Ireland. When 4,500 Orangemen and their families, marching under the banner of the nativist American Protestant Association, convened for a picnic in the Elm Park district of the city on 12 July 1870, they were attacked with sticks and stones by Irish Catholic labourers. In the ensuing gunfire at least nine men were killed and as many as 150 injured. The following year, Mayor A. Oakey Hall, controlled by Boss Tweed's Tammany Hall, initially revoked the Orangemen's permit to march, but he was overruled on 12 July by Governor John T. Hoffman. When the parade was attacked with stones, missiles and gunfire, troops brought in to protect the Orangemen from a repeat of the previous year's violence opened fire. At least 60 people died, most of them Irish Catholics, and about 100 were injured.[80]

Ultimately at stake in this bloody sectarian violence were two competing visions of the place of the Irish in the American republic. For the Orangemen, the presence of violent, permanently impoverished, bloc-voting, Catholic Irish immigrants threatened the very basis of republican government. For the Catholic Irish, conversely, nativist and Orange prejudice violated the spirit of republican democracy by erecting old-world barriers of religious bigotry to prevent them from advancing socially and politically to take their rightful place as full-fledged Americans. These questions would be central to Irish-American history in the fifty years that followed. During the post-famine era (1855–1921) almost 3 million individual Irish men, women and children would cross the Atlantic to settle in the United States. As the Irish community in the United States expanded across the country, and came to embrace not one generation but two or three, the face of Irish America was dramatically altered once again.[81]

O f the four principal waves of Irish emigration to America – colonial,
pre-famine, famine and post-famine (1855–1921) – the last was by far
the largest, accounting for almost half of all the Irish emigrants to North
America since 1700, and for 60 per cent of the emigration to the United
States in the century after 1820. The Irish-born population of the United
States reached its historical peak in 1890 at 1,871,509, in which year there
were also 2,924,172 second-generation Irish Americans (native-born with
one or both parents born in Ireland), for a total of 4.8 million. The second
generation reached its highest level in 1900 at 3,375,546, though the Irish-
born population had fallen to 1,615,459 by this time, for a total of just under
5 million. These five million first and second generation Irish Americans in
1900 exceeded the entire population of Ireland by more than 500,000. Irish-
America by the late nineteenth century had assumed the form of a large,
diverse and durable ethnic community. Its chief characteristics emerge, once
again, through an examination of patterns of migration and settlement,
labour and social mobility, politics, religion and nationalism.[1]

ECONOMY AND SOCIETY IN RURAL IRELAND

About 3.5 million people left Ireland for overseas destinations between
1856 (the end of the famine decade) and 1921 (the last year of British rule
over most of Ireland). Just over 3 million of these emigrants went to the
United States, 209,000 to Canada, 289,000 to Australia and New Zealand,
and 60,000 to South Africa, Argentina and elsewhere. In addition, between
500,000 and 1 million people left Ireland for Great Britain, for a total departure level of between 4 and 4.5 million people, roughly the same as the

population of Ireland itself at the turn of the twentieth century. The average annual rate of overseas emigration from Ireland was 19 per 1,000 in the 1850s, 16 per 1,000 in the 1880s, and 9.7 per 1,000 in the 1890s. The only other European country to attain an emigration rate of over 10 per 1,000 between 1850 and 1913 was Norway. One final measure of sheer scale of Irish post-famine migration is that while Germany sent three times as many emigrants to the United States in this period its population was nine times that of Ireland.[2]

In the post-famine era emigration was numerically and proportionately heaviest in the provinces of Munster and Connacht, but emigrants in this period continued to leave all parts of Ireland. Indeed, 30 per cent of the post-famine emigrants, or 1,073,000 people (both Catholic and Protestant), came from Ulster, compared to 16 per cent from Leinster (577,000), 33 per cent from Munster (1.1 million), and 18 per cent from Connacht (637,000). The last two provinces, which provided 51 per cent of the emigrants in the post-famine era, contained only 41.5 per cent of Ireland's mean population in the period 1856–1910, while Ulster (33.3 per cent) and Leinster (25.2 per cent) contained 58.5 per cent of the country's population but provided only 49 per cent of the emigrants. Both Munster and Connacht lost a minimum of 10 per cent of their populations to emigration in each decade between 1861 and 1910, and in the 1880s and 1890s they each lost at least 15 per cent. Ulster, by contrast, lost only 5 per cent of its population to emigration in the 1890s, and Leinster only 4 per cent. And, while emigration from Ireland as a whole declined by 15 per cent in 1881–1910 compared to 1856–80, it declined by only 13 per cent in Munster and increased by fully 53 per cent in Connacht. In proportional terms, then, the two most western provinces were most affected by emigration in the post-famine era.[3]

From the late 1870s onward more than half of Ireland's transatlantic emigrants came from the most impoverished, often Gaelic-speaking, regions along the Atlantic seaboard of Munster and, especially, Connacht. They were driven out by a combination of poor harvests, evictions and a collapse in farm prices. As many as half of these western emigrants were Irish speakers. The remote areas where they lived had often retained the basic structure of the pre-famine economy, with subdivided small-holdings, potato cultivation, self-sufficiency and isolation from the marketplace, until the end of the 1870s. In the following decade, their fragile economy collapsed, leading to the emigration of 400,000 people from western Ireland to the United States (half the total exodus from Ireland to America in the 1880s). By the last two decades of the nineteenth century, nearly all of the counties with the heaviest emigration were on the western seaboard – Cork, Kerry, Clare, Galway, Mayo and Donegal – though emigration remained heavy as well from north-central Ireland, as it had throughout the nineteenth century. Much of the impoverished West of Ireland was designated as 'congested districts' (i.e. areas that were very densely populated and wretchedly poor) by the British government, and emigration was encouraged as one major solution to poverty. Irish-speakers from these areas were probably the most likely in the late nineteenth century to see trans-oceanic emigration as a form of involuntary exile.[4]

Nineteenth-century Ireland, especially in the post-famine era, was a distinctive country, bucking several of the major trends of European and North American social history. Just how distinctive Ireland was in these respects is a matter for disagreement among historians. It used to be thought that post-famine Ireland was unique (some said pathological) in its social and cultural practices. But, in a forceful new interpretation of Ireland's demographic and economic history, one recent historian has pointed out that none of Ireland's demographic peculiarities was in fact unique in the context of European history. Rural depopulation, high emigration rates, low rates of marriage and high rates of permanent celibacy (i.e. non-marriage) were found in other regions and countries in Europe besides Ireland. Nonetheless, these patterns developed in specific ways in Ireland and their particular combination in the Irish case was distinctive. Thus, while Ireland did not stand outside the mainstream of European history, it was still in many ways quite atypical.[5]

Ireland's distinctiveness is clearly evident in terms of population growth, industrialization and urbanization. The country's population was cut in half between 1845 and 1900, even as the populations of Europe and the United States were expanding more rapidly than ever before (though rural depopulation, it should be emphasized, was common throughout the western world at this time, and Ireland was predominantly a rural country). Ireland lost most of its proto-industrial base in a century when the Industrial Revolution was transforming much of western Europe and the United States. There was more industry in many parts of the country in 1800 than in 1900, and more people were employed in industry both proportionately and in absolute numbers at the beginning of the nineteenth century than at the end. The great bulk of the population remained dependent on agriculture in an economy that could not provide an adequate supply of either land or employment. In the absence of industry, Ireland's rate of urban growth lagged significantly behind that of Europe and America. The populations of most

Irish cities stagnated or declined, by more than twenty per cent in the cases of Kilkenny and Galway. Without urban or industrial employment, the displaced rural masses had few options other than emigration. In this respect, the allure of higher-paid jobs in America (a 'pull factor' for those who emigrated) was inseparable from economic developments in Ireland (the principal 'push factor'), reflecting the reality that, whether the emigrants realized it or not, they were actors in a single capitalist economy that spanned the Atlantic ocean.[6]

The lack of industry and vibrant cities in Ireland might not have been a problem if the Irish countryside had remained more or less unchanged after 1855. But the famine had accelerated major changes in the agrarian class structure that continued throughout the second half of the nineteenth century. Between 1861 and 1911 the number of cottier subtenants (landless labourers renting two acres or less in return for their labour) fell by 60 per cent. By 1911 labourers and cottiers constituted less than one-third of adult males working in agriculture, while farmers accounted for 39 per cent and farmers' sons and assisting relatives for another 20 per cent. Hand-in-hand with this shift in class composition went the ongoing commercialization of agriculture, which finally penetrated the remote West of Ireland in the late nineteenth century. This transformation of agriculture was typically marked by the breaking up of joint tenancies and rundale farming; a general shift from tillage to pasture; the resulting eviction of smallholders; the consolidation of holdings and the enclosure of common lands; the rise of impartible inheritance and primogeniture; and the consequent emergence of the 'strong farmer' as the backbone of the Irish economy.[7]

These strong farmers, it should be mentioned, were Irish rather than British. They consolidated their position following the land reform legislation in the 1870s and 1880s, so that by the early twentieth century they were well on the way to owning their own land, through schemes engineered by the British government (in what might best be described as the great 'quiet revolution' of Anglo-Irish history). The majority of the new 'improving' landlords of the post-famine period were also Irish, having acquired their estates from bankrupt members of the British and Anglo-Irish ascendancy during and after the Great Famine. It was typically they who sought to impose rationalized, commercial farming on the Irish peasantry, especially in the West.[8]

The contrast between the cultures, economies and social structures of pre-famine and post-famine Ireland is of critical importance in understanding the history of emigration. The social structure of pre-famine Ireland had been bottom-heavy with smallholders and the landless poor. Outside the ranks of the wealthy, people tended to marry young. Potato cultivation facilitated the subdivision of land among all the heirs into ever-smaller holdings. Poverty was endemic, but emigration was relatively low. Post-famine Ireland was in many respects the opposite: a land top-heavy with middling and strong farmers, in which people married late (or often did not marry at all), and land was typically passed on to a single heir (impartible inheritance), though not always to the eldest son (primogeniture). As the majority of Irish farmers were tenants rather than owners, it should be noted that what they were passing on to their children was a right of occupancy rather than a legal title to the land. Prospects for the remaining siblings were few, especially among poorer families. In the aftermath of the Great Famine, early marriage came to be regarded as reckless; marriage became almost strictly an economic calculation, to be delayed or even avoided as circumstances dictated. While between 7 and 8 people per 1,000 of the population had married annually in pre-famine Ireland (about the European average) the rate of matrimony dropped to only 4 per 1,000, the lowest rate in Europe, in the period 1881–1900. Ages at first marriage and rates of permanent non-marriage rose accordingly, becoming the highest in Europe by the end of the nineteenth century.[9]

Questions of demography, landholding and marriage have been among the most fruitful and contentious in recent Irish historiography. Until quite recently, historians generally described the household structure in post-famine Ireland as a 'stem family' with impartible inheritance. These 'stem' families, it was argued, typically included three generations under one roof; but only one child, almost always a son (usually the eldest), inherited the land. His parents often held onto the land until they were very old, and the son had to delay marrying until he received his inheritance. He would then marry a woman much younger than himself, if one were available with a suitable dowry (in the form of land or money), or he would not marry at all. If the dowry took the form of land, the match between a male heir and his spouse often became a convenient way of consolidating two landholdings, allowing middling farmers to become strong farmers, or strong farmers to further secure their social standing. Given the family structure and inheritance practices in post-famine Ireland, the rise of these strong farmers can be seen as the triumph of a particular form of patriarchy in the countryside.[10]

According to this standard picture, the outlook for the non-inheriting siblings was bleak. One daughter might get married, if the family could provide a dowry. But most of the remaining siblings, male and female, often had few prospects in Ireland. In better-off families, some younger siblings did receive small parcels of land from their parents; others inherited cash from their parents, though it was often used to emigrate rather than to set up a life in Ireland. If they chose not to emigrate, young people of both sexes might join a religious order (which could involve an overseas posting). Young men who stayed in Ireland could expect to work as labourers without securing land (and hence being referred to as 'boys' rather than men). Young women might get work as farm servants. Non-inheriting sons spent much of their non-working hours drinking in all-male groups. With little apparent outlet for heterosexual sex outside marriage, both males and females faced lives of either 'permanent celibacy' (i.e. non-marriage and, in the Irish context, probable sexual inactivity) or covert homosexuality (though little evidence other than innuendo has survived on the latter). Young single men apparently sublimated much of their sexual desire in relentlessly heavy drinking with their peers; among women, and many men, even the discussion of sex was often taboo. The repressive view of sexuality and the body distinctive to modern Irish Catholicism stems in large measure from the systems of marriage, family and inheritance that arose in response to the Great Famine. The teaching of the Catholic Church surely reflected the existence of these social practices more than it created them.[11]

Much of this interpretation of rural Irish history remains valid, especially in terms of the transformation of the class structure. But more recent historians have questioned what they see as an unnecessarily pessimistic and gloomy portrayal of Irish society and culture. Taking their cue from the 'revisionist' school, these historians have pointed out that Ireland's rural social structure was considerably more complex than scholars have tended to believe. Ages at marriage, rates of permanent celibacy and rates of marital fertility were indeed extraordinarily high in Ireland, these historians concede, but they offer a different explanation of why this was so. Most Irish households, they find, were not strictly speaking of the 'stem family' variety, in that they did not typically contain two married couples at once. Instead, post-famine Ireland contained a wide variety of households (a considerably wider variety than England) ranging from solitary occupants through simple or nuclear households to the most common type, complex extended households. Both the inheriting males and their younger siblings, male and female, appear to have had greater freedom than the standard interpretation implies, especially because they could escape Ireland and go to America if they wished. In better-off families, moreover, some younger siblings received small parcels of land from their parents. Others inherited cash, which was often used to emigrate rather than to set up a life in Ireland. Emigration in this scheme of things was voluntary and enterprising, in sharp contrast to the dominant thesis of emigration as involuntary exile. Nor was the Church, despite the devotional revolution, sufficiently powerful to impose its views on the Irish people, who appear to have followed its teachings most closely only when they accorded with existing beliefs and practices. Contraception, on the basis of withdrawal (regarded by the Church as sinful) and abstinence (not sinful) appear to have been widely practiced by the early twentieth century. Overall, this new approach offers a salutary corrective to the exaggerations and over-simplifications of the old interpretation, even if its tendency to interpret Irish history in terms of the profit-maximizing actions of rational individuals can itself be a rather limiting perspective.[12]

This historical revisionism notwithstanding, post-famine Ireland remains truly distinctive in its massive rate of emigration. The rise of a strong farming class and the accompanying commercialization of agriculture might best be described as both cause and effect of this emigration. The strong farmer class was part of a triumvirate dominating modern Ireland by the end of the nineteenth century, the other two components being the nationalist movement and the Catholic Church. The farmers, the nationalists and the Church, as one historian has convincingly demonstrated, loudly protested the exodus from Ireland; yet none of them could have attained the power they did without emigration. The rise of a strong farmer class depended on the eviction and clearance of the rural poor; nationalists, who drew the bulk of their support from this class, blamed the evictions and emigration on the British. The Church, in turn, drew much of its support from these strong farmers, and these farmers' sons frequently attended seminaries where they were trained as priests. At the same time, the nineteenth-century devotional revolution in Irish Catholicism was predicated on the removal of the rural poor and their heterodox religious practices. Thus, while mass emigration resulted primarily from competition over access to land in a colonized country that lacked both industry and prosperous cities, the strong farmers, nationalists and churchmen who dominated late nineteenth-century Ireland found it expedient to explain emigration almost exclusively as a matter of British-imposed exile.[13]

The social profile of emigrants in the post-famine era was quite distinctive in the context of both previous Irish history and European emigration more generally. Irish emigrants were overwhelmingly Catholic, better-off than during the famine period, more likely to speak Irish than the population as a whole, typically young and single, and as often female as male. Roughly 750,000 Protestants left Ireland in the post-famine period, some 560,000 of them from Ulster; but the remaining 80 per cent of emigrants were Catholic.

The post-famine emigrants were not as poor as those who had fled the famine; they were poorer, less skilled, but more literate than those who had left Ireland in the pre-famine period. In 1875, over 75 per cent of the emigrants were classified as labourers and servants, and in 1900, 91 per cent. The most prosperous Irish emigrants in the late nineteenth century went to Australia and New Zealand, which were more expensive to get to than America; the least prosperous went to Britain, and the vast majority went to the United States. It is estimated that between one-quarter and one-third of the post-famine emigrants to America were Irish-speakers, and perhaps another one-quarter were the children of Irish-speakers. The greatest preponderance of Irish-speakers came later in the nineteenth century rather than earlier; between 1881 and 1910 almost one-quarter of all transatlantic emigrants left counties where between 41 and 59 per cent of the inhabitants spoke Irish in 1891. The post-famine emigration therefore contributed significantly to the continuing decline of the Irish language while, as part of the same process, it made the language more common in many Irish-American neighbourhoods than it had been earlier in the nineteenth century, often provoking cultural conflict between the newcomers and the established community.[14]

In the post-famine era, Irish transatlantic emigrants were younger and more likely to be single and female than in previous periods. In the pre-famine era the median age of Irish emigrants arriving in New York was 24; between 1852 and 1891 the median age of Irish emigrants to the United States was 22.5 for males and 21.2 for females. Fewer than 16 per cent of the post-famine emigrants left Ireland in family groups; the great majority were single. Virtually alone among the European emigrants to America, Irish women emigrated in the same numbers as men, even slightly outnumbering them in several of the post-famine decades. Before the famine, male emigrants had outnumbered females by two-to-one. Already fluent in English, and often having gained extensive experience as farm servants or household servants in Ireland, young Irish females were in considerable demand for domestic work in the United States.[15]

In this respect, Irish emigrants in the post-famine era differed starkly from most other Europeans who emigrated to the United States. Only Swedish women resembled the Irish, with large numbers of single female immigrants entering domestic service in America. The sex ratios of Jewish immigrants were comparable to those of the Irish, but most Jewish women were married when they arrived whereas the great majority of Irish women arrived alone, young and single. About 40 per cent of German immigrants in the late nineteenth century were female, and only about 20 per cent of southern

Italians. Italian immigration to the United States was dominated by men, so-called 'birds of passage', who eventually returned to their homeland. Young women in Italy were discouraged from appearing alone in public without a chaperone, let alone crossing the Atlantic as unattached emigrants.[16]

For young women in rural Ireland, by contrast, grappling with the decision whether or not to emigrate became an expected part of the life cycle. They worked at farm labour and at household tasks, such as cooking, cleaning and child-rearing; the most important paid occupation for Irish women was farm servant, which usually involved single women living in the homes of their employers. But, without industry or dynamic cities, earnings opportunities for women were generally poor. The majority of young Irish women, lacking a dowry, had very little to look forward to if they stayed in Ireland; making the best of a bad lot, they often saw in America a land of opportunity rather than exile or banishment. Even those who did have a dowry often fled Ireland rather than marry a man twice their age and move in with him and his mother. Emigration could therefore become a form of escape, a means of throwing off the shackles of an authoritarian, patriarchal society in which women's status was distinctly subordinate. Offsetting this potential new freedom, however, was the necessity imposed on many young women to send money back to their families. In this respect, the new patriarchal bonds of post-famine Irish society had a transatlantic reach.[17]

Virtually every young man and woman who grew up in Ireland in the late nineteenth century had to consider emigration as a serious option. Favourable reports of American conditions reached Ireland via promotional pamphlets, the press (increasingly), and above all from emigrant letters. An estimated £52 million ($260 million) in emigrant remittances was sent to Ireland from North America between 1848 and 1900, 90 per cent of it from the United States. Forty per cent came in the form of prepaid passage tickets. Public assistance was more readily available than in any previous period, especially from Poor Law boards, which sent an estimated 80,000 Irish paupers to the United States in the late nineteenth century. Private assistance was also provided by landlords, charitable and friendly societies, and philanthropists. Two such philanthropists, Vere Foster and James Hack Tuke, financed 30,000 departures from the West of Ireland to the United States in the 1880s alone.[18]

The development of steam-powered ships transformed the nature of emigration in the post-famine period. Steamships began to replace sailing ships on the transatllantic voyage in the 1850s. By the mid-1860s, 80 per cent of Irish emigrants were travelling to America by steam, and after 1870 nearly 100 per cent. The ocean liners introduced by the Cunard company in the

1850s and 1860s were small, made of wood, propelled by paddles and capable of only eight to twelve knots. By the 1880s, steamships were 500 feet long; built largely of iron and steel, they were driven by screw propellers and were capable of twice the speed of ships in the 1860s. As a result, the length of the transatlantic crossing was greatly reduced. In the eighteenth century, it had taken six to eight weeks to cross the Atlantic, and in the first half of the nineteenth century it still took five to six weeks. The advent of steam reduced the voyage to two to three weeks, and by 1900 it took only ten to twelve days. Emigration out of Ireland was further facilitated by the opening up of Irish ports to steam shipping. During the famine the primary ports of departure had been Liverpool and Glasgow, by way of a short but rough sail from Ireland. From the late 1850s onward, the major British companies called at Queenstown (in Cork harbour) and Moville (near Derry) to pick up Irish passengers before crossing the Atlantic. Fares for transatlantic passage varied between £2 and £6 in the late nineteenth and early twentieth centuries, depending on season. In the 1890s, one could travel from Ireland to America for as little as £1 16s (about $8.75, or a week's wages for an unskilled labourer in the United States). Put another way, a small farmer in County Mayo could travel across the Atlantic for about the cost of a heifer or the annual rent on his farm. Moreover, a series of government regulations had greatly improved the conditions in steerage compared to the pre-famine and famine eras.[19]

What was the impact of emigration on post-famine Ireland? Some historians have argued that a social hemorrhage of the scale that occurred in the late nineteenth century can only have damaged the country. It has been suggested, for example, that emigration carried away many of the most talented of each generation, thereby robbing the country of initiative and enterprise. It is difficult, however, to assess the impact of something so intangible; and the idea of a 'brain drain' is, in any case, surely more applicable to the Irish emigration of the 1980s than that of the 1880s. Nonetheless, mass emigration may well have discouraged those farmers who stayed behind from modernizing their farming techniques or generally acting in too enterprising a way. Be that as it may, the consensus among historians is that those who remained in Ireland gained much more than they lost as a result of emigration. For one thing, they were the recipients of tens of millions of dollars in emigrant remittances, perhaps half of which was used for upkeep of farms and households rather than to finance emigration. More fundamentally, mass emigration was a social safety-valve, serving to defuse tensions between the landless poor and prosperous farmers and landlords. From the Great Famine onwards, mass emigration simply removed the poor and land-hungry from the picture. Post-famine Ireland, as a result, lacked the pervasive tradition of secret society violence that had pitted Irish against Irish in the century before the famine. The single most important cause of this transformation was an emigration so massive that by 1890 two-fifths of all people born in Ireland lived abroad. Viewed from the perspective of the United Kingdom of Great Britain and Ireland as a whole, the combined results of Irish depopulation and British population growth are equally striking: the Irish, who had represented about one-third of the UK population in 1841, represented less than one-tenth in 1911.[20]

There was a grim finality about Irish transoceanic emigration, even at the end of the nineteenth century. While more than half of all Italian and East European immigrants in this era came to the United States as 'birds of passage', returning to their homelands after only a few years, at most 10 per cent of Irish emigrants went back home. It is not necessarily that they were too poor to do so, especially after working a few years, for they sent millions of dollars back to their families in emigrant remittances. Instead, there was usually little or nothing for them to go back to in Ireland. When they left, they left for good. Their departure was often marked by a custom known as the 'American wake'. Common throughout the nineteenth century, it was especially popular in Irish-speaking communities in the West of Ireland toward the end of the post-famine period. The 'American wake' was modelled on the traditional Irish wake for the dead, only in this case it was the living dead who received the send-off, in the knowledge that they would not be seen in Ireland again. Like regular wakes, these occasions were marked by charades, all-night drinking and the emotional lamentations known as 'keening'. In the morning, the emigrant was often accompanied by his family and neighbours in a solemn parade to the crossroads, harbour or train station from which he or she would leave for America. In the midst of this mourning, however, there was often room for some optimism: the emigrants might never return to Ireland, but they had high hopes of bringing their friends or siblings out to the United States after them.[21]

ARRIVAL AND SETTLEMENT

Between 1870 and 1900, even as the number of Irish immigrants arriving in the United States continued to represent a remarkably high proportion of the population of Ireland, the Irish percentage of total immigrant arrivals in the United States declined sharply. German immigration surpassed Irish after the famine decade, and by the 1880s the so-called 'new immigrants' were coming in from eastern and southern Europe. The 436,871 immigrants from Ireland in the 1870s made up 15.5 per cent of all arrivals in the United States (compared to 35 per cent in the 1850s), the 655,482 in the 1880s made up 12.5 per cent, and the 388,416 in the 1890s accounted for 10.5 per cent. While the Irish-born had made up 5 per cent of the American population and almost 40 per cent of the foreign-born population in 1860, they accounted for only 2.2 per cent of the national population and 16 per cent of all foreign-born in 1900. The first and second generations combined that year made up 6.6 per cent of the US population.[22]

The regional distribution of the American Irish in the late nineteenth century continued to display a strong bias toward the Northeast, Mid-Atlantic and Midwest. Two-thirds of Irish-born Americans in every decade from 1860 to 1900 lived in the Northeast and Mid-Atlantic regions, and over 20 per cent in the Midwest. Only 5 per cent settled in the South and 7 per cent in the West. Contrary to a commonly held belief, the greatest concentration of Irish immigrants was not in New England but in the Mid-Atlantic region; the two states of New York and Pennsylvania alone contained 35 per cent of America's Irish-born in 1900. As well as settling predominantly in the Northeast and Mid-Atlantic, the Irish continued to show a strong preference for settling in cities. In all the major American cities, the Irish-born population increased numerically but declined proportionately in the late nineteenth century. The five cities with the largest Irish-born populations in 1890 were, in order, New York-Brookyln (275,156, or 12 per cent of the two cities' combined population), Philadelphia (110,935, 11 per cent), Boston (71,441, 16 per cent), Chicago (70,028, 6 per cent) and San Francisco (30,718, 10 per cent). The next five were Pittsburgh, St Louis, Jersey City, Providence and Cleveland. If the American-born offspring are added, the Irish percentage of the population in America's major cities climbs substantially, to resemble the figures of the first generation at mid-century. New York City-Brooklyn, for example, had 600,000 Irish-stock residents (born in Ireland or America of an Irish-born mother) in 1890, in addition to its 275,000 Irish-born residents; together the immigrants and their offspring accounted for 26 per cent of the population. New York, indeed, was the largest Irish settlement in the world in 1890 and 1900. Its immigrant Irish population alone exceeded the entire population of Belfast (223,092 in 1891) and of Dublin (245,001), while the figure for the immigrants and their American-born offspring dwarfed the populations of these two Irish cities put together.[23]

Beyond the Northeast, Mid-Atlantic and Midwest, there was a small number of first and second-generation Catholic Irish in the South and a significant number in the West. The Irish in the closing decades of the nineteenth century were among the three largest immigrant groups in all western territories or states (with the exception of Utah). Substantial numbers of American-born Irish also made their way west. In general, this movement of first and second-generation Irish Americans away from the East Coast 'was selective of the young, skilled, literate and generally more resourceful newcomers'.[24] Not surprisingly, therefore, the Irish tended to do much better in the West than in the East; so too did most white Americans, whether immigrant or native-born. The westward migration of the Irish was overwhelmingly male, with men outnumbering women by as many as ten to one. One obvious result was greater intermarriage by Irish men in the West than in established Irish Catholic communities back east. California was the favoured western destination, with 60 per cent of that state's Irish population living in San Francisco in the period 1870–90. Towards the end of the nineteenth century, Denver, Colorado was also an important center of Irish settlement, as was Butte, Montana.[25]

While most Irish people who migrated west made their own way, the idea of assisted Irish colonization was at its most popular in the post-famine period. The Irish-dominated Catholic Church, which had tended to oppose previous schemes for fear of apostasy among the migrants, became an important sponsor of internal 'colonization' schemes for Irish immigrants from the 1870s onward, though not without some continuing opposition from conservative bishops (especially Michael Corrigan of New York City) on the East Coast. The first important colonization plan was launched by the Irish Catholic Benevolent Union (established in 1869), which formed stock companies in Philadelphia and St Louis during the economic depression of the 1870s in hopes of settling urban Irish Catholics in the interior. The Philadelphia company purchased 7,000 acres near Roanoke, Virginia and founded the town of Kerrville, while the St Louis company bought land in Pottawotamie County, Kansas and founded Butler City. Due to inadequate fund-raising and internal dissension, however, these schemes were short-lived and unsuccessful.[26]

The most ambitious attempt at colonization was that of Bishops John Ireland and John Lancaster Spalding, who founded the Irish Catholic Colonization Association of the United States in 1879. Spalding, the Bishop of Peoria, was its president, and the board of directors included Archbishops Gibbons of Baltimore and Williams of Boston, Bishops Ireland of St Paul and Ryan of Buffalo, and prominent laymen like John Boyle O'Reilly of the *Boston Pilot*. The association was incorporated with a proposed capital stock of $100,000 (of which only $83,000 was ever raised), and with this money several small communities were founded in Nebraska, Minnesota and Arkansas. Within five years of its foundation, however, the Association had dissolved. It had succeeded in the narrow sense that its small colonies flourished and its stockholders were paid off with full interest; but in terms of its goal of transferring large numbers of the Catholic poor from eastern cities it had failed utterly, in large measure because the urban Irish poor showed little interest in being transplanted to the West.[27]

This disparity between the goals of the colonizers and the aspirations of the potential colonists was particularly evident in Minnesota, where the colonies established by Bishop Ireland in the late 1870s represented the largest and most successful attempt to settle Irish Catholic immigrants and migrants from the East Coast. In one of Bishop Ireland's schemes, 319 destitute, unskilled immigrants were transplanted to Minnesota from Connemara, in the remote West of Ireland, the idea being to transform them into self-sufficient farmers in America. Eighty of these so-called 'Connemaras' (45 young men and 35 young women) found work in the city of St Paul; the remainder were sent to Graceville colony, where they were to be housed by established colonists until homes were built for them. Each family was given a supply of clothing, house furnishings, farming implements, a year's worth of seed and credit for a year's supply of food.[28]

But how would these poor, Irish-speaking fishermen and small farmers adjust to farming on the plains of Minnesota? The settled colonists soon began to complain about their speech, manners and morals; the 'Connemaras', in turn, shunned the idea of setting up as self-sufficient farmers, preferring to perform day labour at wages for other members of the farming community. Without developing their own farms, they could never attain the status and security required of successful colonists, let alone pay off the money they owed for their farm and the supplies advanced to them. The 'Connemaras' neglected to follow instructions to sod the exterior foundations of their frame houses to protect against cold, suffering greatly in the winter as a result. Eventually, it was agreed that they would give up their farms, and most of the men found labouring jobs on the railroads. 'At least in this instance,' as one historian puts it, 'cheap and fertile lands, with their promises of good harvest to come, did not remake all comers into sturdy western yeomen.' Bishop John Sweetman had a very similar experience in the colony of Currie, Minnesota in 1881, when he brought out forty-one families from County Meath who once again evinced a strong preference for wage labour, preferably urban, over independent farming.[29]

It is not entirely clear why the American Irish so strongly favoured urban life in the post-famine period. Partly it was because their predecessors in the pre-famine and famine periods had established ethnic communities in cities, into which the newcomers could settle when they arrived in the United States. More difficult to document, but perhaps equally important, the Irish experience of rural life in the nineteenth century, marked by starvation, evictions and general immiseration, must have predisposed many Irish immigrants against settling on the land in America, even when they had the resources. Most Irish immigrants, in any case – including the great majority of those who originated in the underdeveloped West of Ireland – still lacked the money to move beyond the American port cities where they landed. Italians, East Europeans and other 'new immigrant' groups, it should be noted, also settled predominantly in cities in the late nineteenth century, and native-born Americans were moving from the countryside to urban centers in the same period. Nonetheless, the American Irish at the turn of the twentieth century were about twice as likely as the population as a whole to live in cities, and were by far the most urbanized of the 'old' immigrant groups from Northwest Europe.[30]

In their new urban locations, Irish immigrants continued to suffer from disproportionately high levels of poverty, alcoholism and insanity. Between 1867 and 1890, for example, the percentage of almshouse inmates in New York City who were Irish-born varied from 58 to 73 per cent. Irish women, especially widows and the abandoned, often bore the brunt of the poverty. Even in San Francisco, where the Irish did better than in most American cities, one historian has found that 35 per cent of the residents of almshouses, 31 per cent of those examined for insanity and 24 per cent of those incarcerated in the House of Correction were Irish-born between 1870 and 1890, whereas the population of the city as a whole was only about 13 per cent Irish-born. Figures for the second generation were closer to, but still above, the average. The Irish, both male and female, immigrant and native-born, also had the highest rates of alcoholism and alcohol-related deaths and insanities among all ethnic groups in the United States in the late nineteenth century. Heavy drinking appears to have been an integral element of Irish identity, even more so in the United States than in Ireland. 'The more one drank,' as one historian puts it, 'the more Irish one became.' But the physical and psychological costs were clearly considerable.[31]

In the dispensing of charity and relief to assist the sick and indigent, Irish nuns played a central role. Although there were only eighty-two nuns in New York City in 1848, there were 300 by 1855 and 1,000 by 1875, most of them members of the Irish-dominated Sisters of Charity and Sisters of Mercy. Their work in the late nineteenth century helped transform American practices of charity and welfare. The prevailing, Protestant-dominated model in the second half of the nineteenth century involved giving alms only to the 'deserving poor', in other words to those whose poverty was deemed not to be their own fault. The deserving poor included the elderly, the chronically ill and the helpless, along with able-bodied industrious workers who were temporarily out of work through bad luck or economic recession. The non-deserving poor, by contrast, were regarded as lazy, usually drunken and indigent through their own fault. It is not difficult to see that the latter characteristics were the same ones typically used by nativists to describe the Irish character in general. To be Irish was, by definition, to fall into the ranks of the undeserving poor. Emphasizing the hereditary nature of social pathology, reformers pointed to the racially inferior Irish as the source of expanding poverty and vice in American cities. At the same time, advocates of so-called 'scientific charity' insisted that able-bodied recipients of relief should always receive less than the poorest workers made.[32]

This debate over charity and welfare became particularly important to the history of the American Irish when it came to alleviating the plight of poor children. In the standard Protestant model of charity and relief, a poor woman who worked was seen as neglectful of her children. The most vulnerable children were those of single, destitute mothers; yet, whether single or married, most Irish immigrant women had no choice but to work. There was therefore an enormous gulf between Irish immigrant families, in which women worked of necessity, and middle-class Protestant reformers, who denounced women's work as contributing to the neglect of already disadvantaged children. The Catholicism of the immigrants was itself seen as a major cause of their poverty and alcoholism. The reformers' solution, whenever possible, was to take poor Catholic children away from their families and place them with 'Christian' families, typically in Protestant homes far removed from the vices of the city. In order to be redeemed, Catholic children needed to be removed from their homes, their mothers and their religion. By the 1870s, some 10,000 children a year were being placed out from New York City alone, transported on 'orphan trains' to the interior for reformation and redemption. The ostensible redemption of the 'orphans' often took the form of years of drudgery and hard labour in the homes of their redeemers.[33]

Irish Catholic charities fought back with considerable success in the late nineteenth century. When Protestant reformers secured the passage of a law in New York state in 1875, making the sheltering of children in poorhouses illegal, a group called the Catholic Union successfully lobbied the state legislature for the addition of a 'religion clause' stipulating that any institutions into which children were henceforth placed would be controlled by people of the same religion as the children's parents. The 'Children's Law' therefore backfired on its proponents, creating the legal and financial basis for taking care of Catholic children in state-funded institutions run by nuns. American nuns, most of them Irish in origin, began to take in hundreds and then thousands of children, transforming the Protestant welfare system by overturning its central device, the placing out of indigent children in 'respectable' homes. The number of nuns in New York City doubled in the decade after 1875, reaching 2,000 in 1885. By that time, nuns directly controlled the city's public child-care system, raising over 80 per cent of the dependent children, with Jews and Protestants raising 10 per cent each.[34]

As well as suffering from high rates of poverty, the American Irish in the late nineteenth century retained their reputation as a violent and turbulent people. The Irish were more likely to be arrested for drunk and disorderly behaviour than any other ethnic group. They preserved much of the rich gang life that had arisen earlier in the century, though one that led more directly to politics (as, for example, in the Fourth Avenue Tunnel Gang led by the future boss of Tammany Hall, Richard Croker) than to the type of 'organized crime' associated with Italian and Jewish immigrants from the 1890s onward. The Irish dominated American prize fighting, beginning with John Morrisey (1831–78), a native of Tipperary who became heavyweight champion of the United States in 1853 and was one of several Irish pugilists to commence his career as a street-fighter for the political machine, Tammany Hall. John L. Sullivan (1858–1918), a second-generation Irish-American, won the world heavyweight title in 1882, relinquishing it ten years later to James J. Corbett (1866–1933), born in San Francisco of Irish parents. Americans may have found this expression of Irish violence entertaining, but they reacted differently to Irish involvement in such ominous incidents as the Draft Riots of 1863, the Orange and Green Riots of 1870 and 1871, the notorious Molly Maguire assassinations and executions of the 1870s, and the various acts of violence engaged in by Irish nationalist organizations in both Ireland and the United States from the 1860s onward. On the basis of these events, the much-lampooned comic Irishman of the late nineteenth century was widely believed to have a thinly concealed savage side as well.[35]

The late nineteenth century was also the period when Irish-American ethnic societies came into their own. Among the most prominent national

Irish-American organizations were the Irish Catholic Benevolent Union (1859), the Ancient Order of Hibernians (reorganized on a national basis in 1871), the Catholic Total Abstinence Union (1872), and the Knights of Columbus (1881). Most of these ethnic organizations provided insurance benefits as well as an opportunity for friendship and ethnic self-assertion. Irish-American newspapers like the *Boston Pilot* set up exchange agencies to help immigrants send money back to Ireland, a function fulfilled even more effectively by the Irish Emigrant Savings Bank in New York City in the half-century after its formation in 1851. Organizations with a nominally charitable but primarily social bent included the Friendly Sons of St Patrick, established in the eighteenth century, while those dedicated to cultural and literary pursuits included the Philo-Celtic societies (started in 1873), the American Irish Historical Society (1897) and the Gaelic League (1898). The Irish Protestant equivalent of the American Irish Historical Society was the Scotch-Irish Society of America (1889); the two organizations competed with each other in chronicling the glorious contribution of 'the Irish' (a term whose meaning they hotly contested) to the unfolding of American history. Most of the Catholic organizations were led by the Irish urban middle class, and many replicated their Protestant counterparts by emphasizing hard work, self-discipline, thrift and sobriety. They therefore acted as a vehicle for Irish-American assimilation, defined in a specific, middle-class, respectable manner.[36]

At first sight, this idea of achieving assimilation through ethnic assertiveness and separate, Catholic Irish institutions may appear paradoxical. After all, the primary nativist objection to 'hyphenated' Americans was that their allegiance was divided between the United States and their homelands or, worse yet, the Pope. Nonetheless, a strong argument can be made that most immigrant groups have not only discovered their 'ethnicity' in America, but that the development of some form of ethnic identity has been an integral part of the process through which immigrants have normally become American. The majority of Catholic immigrants from nineteenth-century Ireland appear to have lacked any well-defined sense of national, as distinct from regional or local, identity. Measured in terms of geographical origin or census designation they were certainly Irish; but their own sense of Irishness was invariably rooted in local experience. Most immigrants from Ireland to the United States only gradually arrived at a coherent sense of national and ethnic identity, and they did so in America not Ireland. Their formation of this new sense of ethnic identity was captured in the hybrid term 'Irish-American'. Far from hindering assimilation, the development of an ethnic identity expressed through a rich institutional and associational life was the primary means through which the American Irish assimilated. Acquiring an ethnic identity, in other words, was the first prerequisite for Irish assimilation.[37]

LABOUR AND GENDER

Irish America in the last three decades of the nineteenth century was a place of considerable social diversity. Impoverished immigrants from the West of Ireland lived in the same cities as well-established middle-class Irish Americans of the second and third generations. Some Irish Americans did very well in this period, even as most new arrivals continued to occupy the lower rungs of the social ladder. By the 1870s there was already a small but significant upper and upper-middle class of Irish Americans, among them millionaires like William Grace, who was elected Mayor of New York City in 1880 and 1884, the first Catholic to hold that office. Immigrants from Ulster continued to prosper in the United States in the late nineteenth century, none more so than Alexander T. Stewart (1803–76) of New York City, who ran the world's largest retail store; John T. Pirie (1871–1940) of Chicago, who helped found the department store of Carson, Pirie, Scott; and Thomas W. Mellon (1813–1908) of Pittsburgh, who established a famous banking house and whose son Andrew (1855–1937) went on to acquire one of the world's great art collections, which he eventually donated to the nation to found the National Gallery of Art. Below the upper echelons, there was also a growing class of so-called 'lace curtain' Catholic Irish, who struggled for acceptance in middle-class America and did everything they could to distance themselves from the still-numerous 'shanty Irish' and the masses of recent immigrants from the West and South of Ireland. Many of these respectable Irish worked as clerks, teachers and sales personnel, enjoying higher social status but earning lower wages than the skilled and unionized workers of the first and second generations who increasingly dominated the Irish-American working class.[38]

Unskilled labour, nonetheless, remained the predominant source of employment for Irish *immigrants* to the United States in the late nineteenth century, with domestic service as its female form. Study after study by historians of the American Irish in the Northeast and Midwest has shown that the Irish-born were disproportionately concentrated in menial labour until at least 1890. From Boston and Newburyport, Massachusetts to Poughkeepsie, New York, to Philadelphia and Detroit, Irish immigrants worked much more often in unskilled jobs and much less often in skilled and professional positions than both native-born Americans and Germans, the other principal immigrant group in the United States before the 1880s. Those Irish who did advance socially did not rise suddenly from rags to riches; they did not move from unskilled labour to the ranks of the professionals and independent entrepreneurs, even though by the century's end at least some of their children could hope to do so. Instead, Irish social mobility typically occurred within the working class, from unskilled to semi-skilled or skilled labour. At the same time, local census records show surprisingly high rates of property ownership among Irish immigrants. As they moved from menial to more skilled forms of labour, they often managed to purchase a home. But this outward sign of material prosperity had its costs; every member of the family had to work hard to pay off the mortgage, so that children after the age of twelve, if not sooner, were set to work and deprived of further education. These limited and ambiguous successes are the type historians look for in the history of the nineteenth-century American Irish, rather than spectacular stories of 'rags-to-riches'. The children of Irish immigrants were typically more successful than their parents, though once again this was often a matter of getting a better position within the working class rather than progressing to the upper echelons.[39]

The further west they went, the better the Irish did. Thus, both the first and second generations did better in Philadelphia than in Boston or New York, better in Detroit than in Philadelphia, better in Denver than in Detroit, and best of all in San Francisco. Similarly, while German immigrants did better than the Irish in every city, the gap between them narrowed the further west one went. In Denver, as early as 1890, 30 per cent of Irish-born males were working in skilled trades and 15 per cent in business, the professions and white-collar jobs, figures that were comparable to those of the native-born. In San Francisco the percentage of Irish-born males working in white-collar jobs rose from 15 per cent in 1852 to 20 per cent in 1880, the number in skilled blue-collar jobs remained more or less constant (dropping from 20 to 19 per cent), the number in semi-skilled blue-collar jobs rose from 17 per cent to 30 per cent and the number in unskilled manual labour dropped sharply from 48 per cent to 32 per cent. The second generation did even better, so that by 1880 their social position was slightly higher than the average for the community as a whole. Women did not share in this social advancement, however. The number of Irish-born females employed as domestic servants in San Francisco stayed constant at about 60 per cent between 1852 and 1880.[40]

Women accounted for half of all Irish immigrants to the United States in the second half of the nineteenth century. Most of them were young and single. Only 16 per cent of all Irish immigrants from Ireland between 1887 and 1900 were married. Marriage rates among Irish emigrants to Britain were considerably higher, suggesting that family groups could not afford to travel as far as the United States, whereas unattached individuals could. As the median age of female emigrants from Ireland between 1852 and 1921 was only twenty-one, most Irish women who emigrated were well below the prevailing age for marriage. The American Irish retained much of the economic emphasis that had come to characterize marriages in post-famine Ireland. They married at a higher rate than in Ireland, but at a lower rate than any other American immigrant group. At the same time, rates of widowhood and male absence or desertion were notably higher among the Irish in America than in Ireland, so that a disproportionately high number of Irish women found themselves single and economically self-sufficient in America.[41]

The interpretation of Irish-American women's history in the late nineteenth century turns on how one chooses to explain this distinctive quality. Did their status as unsupported, self-sufficient workers make them more or less independent? Most historians of the subject incline to the former, more optimistic interpretation, seeing Irish women in America as strong, assertive, seekers of economic opportunity, fending for themselves with considerable success. As domestic servants they could observe at first hand the morals and manners of the middle class, passing on what they had learned to their daughters, who tended to avoid service whenever possible. As single women, the servants revelled in their independence; and, if they married, they tended to dominate their husbands, who had little success in elevating themselves from unskilled to skilled labour or the professions. Irishmen consequently had greater difficulty than Irish women adjusting to life in their new country, devoting much of their energy instead to ethnic or nationalist politics and to lamentations, invariably fuelled by too much bad whiskey, on their banishment and exile.[42]

This interpretation has much to offer. But was the economic necessity in which Irish immigrant women were enmeshed really a source of independence? Or was it just another form of dependence, one that differed from the stifling and oppressive conditions in late nineteenth-century Ireland but only by replacing one form of social control with another? Irish women in America did gain certain new freedoms, of course, chief among them freedom from the control of parents, brothers and mothers-in-law. But they were also restricted in new ways by the types of work they did. The critical question is how these women made a living. As early as 1870, 20 per cent of all schoolteachers in New York City were Irish women; other professional careers included nursing and the religious orders. By 1900, daughters of Irish-American parents accounted for 10 per cent of all female teachers of foreign parentage in the United States, exceeding the combined total of those with English and German parents. Second-generation Irish-American women took domestic service jobs much less frequently than the first generation, moving instead into positions in trade, manufacturing and the professions. But most Irish women *immigrants*, like their male counterparts, were unskilled and worked either as domestic servants or in factories or sweatshops.[43]

Domestic service, throughout the second half of the nineteenth century, was the defining activity of Irish women in America, generating the pervasive stereotype of 'Bridget'. As early as the 1850s, 80 per cent of all women who worked in paid household labour in New York City were from Ireland; as late as 1900, fully 61 per cent of all Irish-born women working in the United States did so in domestic capacities. In sharp contrast, most native-born females and immigrants (with the significant exception of Swedes, who entered service jobs at about the same high rate as the Irish) avoided service jobs assiduously. Jewish women, for example, preferred the garment factory and sweatshop to domestic service, no matter how bad wages and conditions might be. Italian women were even more resistant to domestic service. For an Italian girl to have gone to live alone in a stranger's house and work as his servant would have violated a series of taboos and threatened the traditional structure of family life. At the same time, of course, most Jewish and Italian women married young, so that there were fewer single females available to become servants even had their culture condoned that decision. But very few single women, other than the Irish and the Swedes, opted for domestic service. Only 22 per cent of English and Welsh-born women in the United States in 1900, 28 per cent of Scottish and 9 per cent of Italians worked in service.[44]

Why were Irish women so heavily concentrated in domestic service? Wages and conditions were considerably better in service than in factory or sweatshop labour. Servants had no expenses for food and transportation. Their diet was generally much better than that of factory workers, even if it took the form of leftovers. Service was the preferred option for most female Irish immigrants. Unlike other immigrants, single Irish women faced few obstacles – protective fathers and brothers, family taboos – to doing live-in work in other people's homes. And unlike other single immigrant women they apparently saw no stigma in domestic service. Historians have yet to explain adequately why this was so. Indeed, absence of evidence on this matter is usually taken as the starting point for an argument that domestic service was considerably more liberating than oppressive. Domestic service thereby becomes the vehicle for women's self-assertion and liberation.[45]

In the prevailing interpretation, Irish female servants in the United States are seen as anything but servile. Servants, or so the argument goes, worked for good wages in decent conditions, saved plenty of money, delayed marriage or refused it altogether in order to preserve their independence, went shopping on weekends and generally had a good time on their days off, in the process liberating themselves from the stultifying constraints of Irish culture and assimilating fairly easily into American life. They learned the mores and manners of the middle class and passed them on to their own children when they got married. Though they achieved little in the public realm of politics, nationalism and trade unionism, Irish women in America dominated the more important private realm, as self-sufficient individuals or as wives and mothers.[46]

This is certainly an inspiring tale, but how convincing is the portrait of servitude as non-servile? What was it really like to be a servant, to live as a 'Bridget' in the house of the wealthy, as a figure of fun if also of affection? That such a job, at its best, was better than anything available in Ireland does not necessarily entail women's liberation. How did the women themselves regard their servitude? With a fair amount of pride in some cases, the few available sources suggest. But the contrast with most other American women, immigrant and native-born alike, cries out for explanation. Perhaps the Irish differed so much precisely because of the degree of gender and economic oppression they had faced in Ireland, because they started at the bottom in America and because the alternatives to domestic service available to them (including industrial work) were so much worse.

If the degree of social oppression inherent in the servant relationship has been underestimated by historians, the same is likely to be true of the degree of sexual exploitation endured by Irish women in their adopted households. Servants had to fend off the unwanted sexual attentions of their masters and their master's sons, and were frequently subjected to sexual harassment, assault and even rape in the households where they lived. While the exchange of sexual favours could in some cases be liberating, both personally and economically, the distinctive character of domestic service doubtless ensured that coercion too often prevailed over consent. Recent studies have suggested that most Irish prostitutes were ex-servants whose introduction to sex (or at least certain unwanted or bartered forms of it) had come within the households where they worked. The optimistic portrait of domestic service as a safe haven constituting the polar opposite of prostitution is therefore in need of serious revision. Young female immigrants clearly had very good reasons for avoiding service in favour of factory labour, despite the material disadvantages of the latter. Service was surely not the liberating safe haven it has been portrayed to be.[47]

In the last resort the matter comes down to the choices available to immigrant women. It must be remembered that, in Ireland as well as in America, the primary form of employment for young Irish women outside their own homes was domestic service. And conditions for servants were generally better in the United States than in Irish homes or farms. Domestic service in New York or Boston could therefore represent a distinct improvement, opening new forms of opportunity to young Irish women. In this respect, it is striking how favourably the experience of service was described by most Irish immigrant women in their letters home. Service, moreover, was more often a temporary than a permanent condition, a way station on the road to marriage or other forms of employment. Even when its effects were deleterious, then, they might be short-lived. That said, it is surely important not to romanticize domestic service, and to remember that it was based ultimately on domination and subordination.

Looking at service in this way helps explain why roughly the same proportion of Irish immigrant women worked in industry (mainly the so-called 'needle trades') as in domestic positions. Especially in Massachusetts (Lowell, Lawrence, Holyoke, Fall River), Rhode Island, Connecticut and New York (Troy, Cohoes) young Irish women entered the cotton mills and worked there alongside their brothers and fathers until marriage, often returning to the mills when widowed or abandoned. Fires and industrial accidents were very frequent, but employment was more regular than in the 'needle trades' in bigger cities. These trades included a variety of occupations, including sewing, stitching and garment making, much of which could be done at home on a contract or piecework basis and was therefore suitable for women with small children. By the late nineteenth century, however, this work was increasingly done in sweatshops and factories, under very arduous conditions. An abundance of available women workers drove wages ever downward. While work in the 'needle trades' was always more of a necessity than a choice for Irish immigrant women, they accounted for 33.8 per cent of all seamstresses in the United States in 1900 compared to 41.2 per cent of all white domestic servants.[48]

Failure of the Potato Crop, 1846
The feelings of despair and desolation resulting from a spoiled potato crop are vividly portrayed in this image. The potato blight first struck in 1845; here a family inspects the harvest a year later, only to find that it too has been ruined. (*Pictorial Times*, 22 August 1846.)

Bridget O'Donnell and her children, 1849
This is perhaps the archetypal image of suffering in famine-stricken Ireland, the enormity of the tragedy shown by the mother's haggard desperation and the helplessness of her emaciated children. (Engraving. *The Illustrated London News*, 22 December 1849.)

A funeral at Skibbereen, 1847
Many reports of suffering during the Great Famine came from Skibbereen, in west Cork, where mortalities were among the highest. In a scene calculated to shock British opinion, a young famine victim is hauled away to his grave. The 'funeral' lacks dignity and ritual – there is not even a coffin. (Engraving. *The Illustrated London News*, 30 January 1847.)

Eviction scene, 1848
Some half a million Irish were evicted during the Great Famine, especially following the Poor Law Extension Act of 1847 which shifted the burden of famine relief to the landlords. Rather than support poor tenants on their estates, many landlords evicted them. The 'Gregory clause' of the 1847 Act forced tenants with more than a quarter of an acre to give up their land if they wished to receive relief. (Engraving. *The Illustrated London News*, 16 December 1848.)

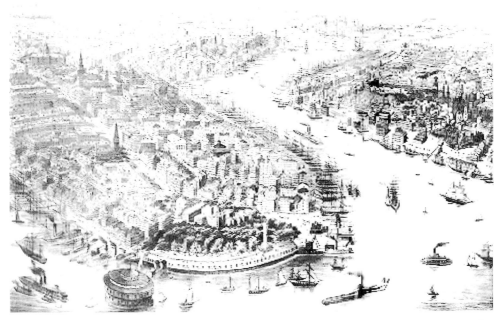

Aerial view of the South Street Seaport, New York, 1856
On arrival in New York, immigrant ships docked at the South Street piers on the East River. After
1855 the immigrants were transported to a clearing center, Castle Garden (in the left foreground).
Run by the city, Castle Garden curbed the worst abuses endured by the immigrants and gave advice
on housing, work and transportation. (*Harper's Weekly*, 26 June 1858.)

Immigrants disembarking at the Battery, Castle Garden, New York, 1847
This famous painting depicts the arrival of an immigrant ship in New York harbor. The scene is set
in 1847, the worst year of the famine, but the passengers appear smart and prosperous. Only the
words 'Pat Murfy, for Ameriky' on the trunk on the right suggest an Irish dimension; but there is no
hint of 'Black '47', the year of the 'coffin ships'. (Painting by Samuel Waugh, ca. 1855. Museum of
the City of New York.)

St. Patrick's Day parade in New York City, ca. 1870
Although the grandeur and pomposity of the parade are surely exaggerated, this lithograph
captures the growing cultural power and self-confidence of the American Irish. St. Patrick's Day
had been celebrated by Protestant Irish immigrants in 18th-century America but became
emblematic of Catholic Irish-American identity thereafter. (Lithograph, ca. 1870. The J. Clarence
Davis Collection, Museum of the City of New York.)

Workers laying tracks at Broadway and 14th Street, New York City, ca. 1880
The Irish experience in 19th-century America could be summed up by one word – 'labour'.
Throughout the US, Irishmen built roads, canals and railroads, mined coal and manned the
factories. Irish women worked in sweatshops and were the chief source of domestic labour.
Here the workers retain their dignity and respectability through back-braking labour regardless
of the admonishments of the finger-pointing gentleman on the left. (Painting by Hughson
Hawley. Museum of the City of New York.)

The 'Molly Maguires'

Twenty young Irish-American men were hanged in Pennsylvania in the late 1870s, convicted of a series of 16 assassinations allegedly committed by a secret society called the 'Molly Maguires'. Demonized by contemporary observers as the embodiment of Irish savagery, here they are uncharacteristically respectable. (Engraving by Paul Frenzeny and Jules Tavernier, *Harper's Weekly*, 31 January 1874. Courtesy of the Perry-Casteñeda Library, The University of Texas, Austin.)

The Orange and Green Riots, New York City, 1871

With the arrival of many Catholic immigrants from Ireland from the 1820s onward, Irish Americans of Ulster Protestant origin formed a separate 'Scotch-Irish' ethnic identity, celebrating 12 July (the anniversary of the Battle of the Boyne) instead of St. Patrick's Day. As in Ireland, 12 July spawned ethnic and sectarian conflict, culminating in 1871 in the deaths of over 60 rioters in New York City. (Engraving. *Frank Leslie's Illustrated Newspaper*, 29 July 1871. State Historical Society of Wisconsin.)

Irish squatters in New York's Central Park, 1880s
Before the park was built in the 1850s the area of Manhattan which is now Central Park was where many Irish lived in tents, shacks, and shanties. The poorest of the Irish continued to be squatters into the 1880s. The figures here are mostly women or children, though it is unclear what this means. Are the men away at work, or have they departed permanently through death or desertion? (The J. Clarence Davis Collection, Museum of the City of New York.)

Domestic servants
Domestic service was the largest category of employment for Irish immigrant women in the 19th and early 20th centuries. Known as 'Bridgets', these Irish servants often stayed in service until they got married or found other work. Many, however, remained servants permanently, sometimes working for the same family over several decades. (Photograph by Charles Van Schaick ca. 1890. State Historical Society of Wisconsin.)

Daniel O'Connell (1775-1847)
The towering figure of Irish nationalism in the first half of the 19th century, he attracted mass support among Irish Americans for his campaign to repeal the Act of Union. (Watercolor by Thomas Heathfield Carrick, 1844. National Gallery of Ireland.)

Charles Stewart Parnell (1846-91)
Leader of the Home Rule movement of the 1880s, he visited the US in 1879-1880, and helped raise money for Irish nationalism, land reform, and famine relief. A master politician known for his austere, aristocratic bearing, Parnell was the 'uncrowned king of Ireland'. (*The Dictionary of National Biography*, Vol. XV.)

Al Smith (1873-1944)
Born in New York City, he served four
terms as   governor of New York and was
the first Catholic to run for president.
(Painting by Alton Tobey. Museum of the
City of New York.)

John F. Kennedy (1917-63)
The great-grandson of an Irish famine
refugee, he was the first Catholic elected
to the US presidency. Kennedy is shown
here receiving his patent of arms during his
visit to Ireland, where he received a raptur-
ous welcome. (*Treasures from the National
Library of Ireland*, The Boyne Valley Honey
Company, Dublin 1994, R26709)

Given the large number of Irish-American women who worked in industry for low wages in dangerous and unsanitary conditions, it is scarcely surprising that they quickly established themselves in the American labour movement. Kate Mullaney successfully organized the Irish collar laundresses in Troy, New York in 1868. Winifred O'Reilly (née Rooney), who came to the United States with her parents as a child in the 1840s, worked as a nursemaid, errand girl and factory collar maker as a child. Widowed young with an infant, she made a living through factory needle work and went on to become an active member of the Knights of Labor. She introduced her daughter, Leonora O'Reilly, to the world of trade unionism as a teenager, and Leonora became an organizer for the United Garment Workers of America and helped found the Women's Trade Union League. Another Irish-born organizer for the Knights was Leonora Barry, an immigrant from County Cork, whose introduction to industrial labour came when she took a job in a New York hosiery mill after being widowed with two small children at the age of thirty-two. Barry was elected to the Knights' committee on Women's Work in 1885. Kate Kennedy, who came to the United States with her brother during the famine, worked as an embroiderer of cloaks and vests to raise the money to bring over her mother and four sisters from Ireland. During this time she also went to school to prepare herself for a career as a schoolteacher. By 1857 the family was reunited in San Francisco, where Kennedy became a school principal and went on to lead one of the first trade unions of public schoolteachers, demanding equal pay for equal work. Other Irish leaders of the movement to unionize schoolteachers included Margaret Healy and Catherine Goggins in Chicago. American-born Mary Kenny O'Sullivan, the daughter of Irish immigrants, began her career in the bookbinding industry, became the first female organizer for the American Federation of Labor in 1892 and established the New York chapter of the Women's Trade Union League in 1904. Also active in radical circles was the Irish-born Populist leader Mary Ellen Lease, famous for her advice to America's farmers, 'Raise less corn and more hell.'[49]

Irish men were even more prominent in the late nineteenth-century American labour movement. John Siney and John Welsh, both Irish-born, led the Workingmen's Benevolent Association in the Pennsylvania anthracite coal region in the 1870s. An estimated one-third of the employees who went on strike in the great railroad strike of 1877 were Irish. Robert Blissert, who was born in England to Irish parents in 1843 and came to the United States in 1868, was active in the American Section of the First International and New York's Amalgamated Trades and Labor Union, and helped found the city's powerful Central Labor Union in 1882. Terence V. Powderly (1849–1924), born in the anthracite region of Pennsylvania to Irish immigrant parents, was the leader of the Knights of Labor, the largest labour organization in the United States in the late 1870s and 1880s. Denis Kearney and Frank Roney, both immigrants from Ireland, dominated the San Francisco labour scene in the late 1870s and 1880s. Socialist P.J. McGuire, the son of Irish immigrants in New York City, organized the Brotherhood of Carpenters and Joiners, helped form the American Federation of Labor in 1886 and is remembered as the 'Father of Labor Day' (established by Congress in 1894). The Irish also dominated the workforce and trade unions in metal work, longshore work and freight-handling in the 1880s and 1890s. The support of Irish-American shoemakers in Massachusetts was crucial in providing the American socialist movement with some of its first electoral victories.[50]

Yet, just as earlier in the nineteenth century, perhaps the most interesting aspect of Irish involvement in the American labour movement in the post-famine era is not so much formal participation in trade unionism as the interaction between trade unionism and older forms of protest rooted in the Irish countryside. Irish branches of the Knights of Labor in the 1880s, for example, sometimes retained practices of secrecy, oath-taking and ostracism that had originated in rural Ireland. The largely Irish District Assembly 49 of the Knights, organized in New York City in 1882, came into direct conflict with the organization's national leadership which, in an attempt to placate the Catholic Church, ordered an end to secrecy the same year. Another tactic imported from Ireland was the distinctive type of boycotting engaged in by Irish workers in New York City in the 1880s. Drawn from the Land War in contemporary Ireland, boycotting was adapted in the industrial United States for use as an economic weapon against manufacturers, newspapers, shipping companies and Chinese-made goods.[51]

The most famous and tragic example of Irish rural strategies being deployed in American industrial conditions was the case of the Molly Maguires. More than fifty Irishmen, accused of belonging to a secret terrorist society, went on trial in the Pennsylvania anthracite region in the late 1870s. They were charged with a string of assassinations, going back to the Civil War, in which at least sixteen mine owners, superintendents, bosses, miners and public officials had been killed. Twenty of the Molly Maguires were executed for capital murder, and most of the rest were sent to prison. The case was cracked by an Irish-born Pinkerton detective, James McParlan, who had been sent into the anthracite undercover to infiltrate the secret society and collect evidence. The episode remains shrouded in ambiguity, as the Molly Maguires left no evidence of their aims and motivations. What has survived instead is a series of very critical accounts of them compiled by nativists, the enemies of organized labour, the Catholic Church (which denounced the Molly Maguires for their secrecy and violence and lamented their impact on American perceptions of ordinary Irish immigrants), the trade union movement (which denounced them for the same reason) and the Pinkerton Detective Agency. These sources reveal a great deal less about the Molly Maguires than about their author's ideologies. The case of the Molly Maguires does make considerable sense, however, when viewed in terms of an Irish rural tradition of retributive justice and secrecy adapted to industrial America, much like the 'Corkonians', 'Fardowners' and 'Ribbonmen' on the canals and public works during the antebellum era.[52]

Throughout the late nineteenth century, Irish trade unionists and labour activists continued to espouse racial exclusion even as they fought for other forms of social justice. While struggles between Irish and black workers persisted in the post-famine era, the most intense form of Irish racial animosity in this period was directed against the Chinese. Organized labour in general, and indeed American society as a whole in the 1870s, shared in this animosity to a remarkable extent, but the hostility of Irish workers to the Chinese was arguably the most intense of all, especially in California where Irish immigrant workers were at the vanguard of a movement to curtail Chinese immigration. As in the case of Irish sentiment against African Americans during the antebellum period, a primary motivation was fear of Chinese labour competition, especially on railroad construction and in menial city jobs. Once again, the validity of this belief was less important than its pervasive hold in Irish working-class circles. Beyond economic concerns, Irish anti-Chinese sentiment was, once again, intimately tied to questions of assimilation, the presence of a new alien minority affording the Irish yet another opportunity to protest and demonstrate their fitness for inclusion in the racial mainstream. The men behind the anti-Chinese agitation in California were both Irish-born: Denis Kearney, leader of the Workingmen's party, and the socialist and ex-Fenian, Frank Roney. Though these two Irishmen differed strongly on labour politics, they shared with most Irish immigrant workers a detestation of the Chinese as a racially inferior source of cheap labour. This Irish-dominated nativist workingmen's movement pushed through a series of stringent anti-Chinese measures in California and was instrumental in the passage of the federal law of 1882 outlawing the further immigration of Chinese labourers to the United States. The pattern has since become grimly familiar in American history, with immigrant groups that have established one foot on the social ladder using the other to kick down those beneath them.[53]

NATIVISM AND POLITICS

If the Irish were capable of such sentiment against the Chinese, it was in part because they were still the targets of an often virulent racial nativism themselves. Some of this opposition came from organized labour, though less so than in earlier periods, for the Irish were by now major players in the labour movement themselves. But anti-Irish and anti-Catholic sentiment were still pervasive in American culture. The degree of racial nativism directed against the Irish in late nineteenth-century America is perhaps best captured in a notorious quote by the visiting English historian Edward A. Freeman: 'This would be a grand land if only every Irishman would kill a Negro, and be hanged for it. I find the sentiment generally approved – sometimes with the qualification that they want Irish and Negroes for servants, not being able to get any other.'[54]

As in earlier periods of the nineteenth century, the Scotch-Irish were often at the center of American nativism. Anti-Catholicism was clearly a very effective means of assimilation for Protestant Irish immigrants. At the heart of New York City's Orange and Green Riots of 1870 and 1871, which left more than seventy dead, was a nativist Protestant conception of the American republic which regarded impoverished Irish immigrants as unsuitable for citizenship. Scotch-Irish participation in American anti-Catholic movements reached its peak in the generation after the Civil War, with the formal establishment in the United States of the Loyal Orange Institution, the first lodge of which was founded in New York City in 1867, followed quickly by branches in Philadelphia and Pittsburgh. In the United States, as one historian puts it, the Orange Order 'abandoned its monarchism but lost none of its Protestant fervor'.[55]

By 1873, the Order claimed 100 lodges and 10,000 members and, by 1914, 364 lodges and 30,000 members. It was open to all Protestants but, predictably, it was overwhelmingly Scotch-Irish in composition. The names of individual American lodges recalled the key events in Ulster's troubled history since 1688: the Apprentice Boys Lodge, the Walls of Derry Lodge, the Sons of William Lodge and many others. American Orangemen established close links with and helped inspire the leading anti-Catholic movements of the late nineteenth century, especially the most important of these organizations, the American Protective Association (APA). Founded in Clinton, Iowa in 1877, the APA claimed 2,500,000 members at its height in 1894, pledged not to hire Catholics, not to go on strike with them and not to vote for them. While its members included American, Canadian, British and Scandinavian Protestants, among others, the Scotch-Irish provided much of its leadership as well as the nucleus of many of its branches. The president of the APA was Canadian-born William Traynor, who had previously served as Deputy Supreme Grand Master of the Loyal Orange Institution.[56]

The period of Reconstruction (1863–77) was notable mainly for its extension of political and civil rights to African Americans, but hand in hand with this democratic impulse went a concerted campaign to limit the political power of immigrants and their political allies, the Democrats. The Enforcement Act of 1870, designed primarily to protect the constitutional rights of blacks, made false registration and repeated voting an offense in federal elections, while the Naturalization Act of the same year tightened federal controls over the issue of naturalization papers by state courts, extended to six months the period before which newly naturalized citizens could vote, and allowed federal judges to appoint commissioners to oversee voter registration and count ballots. All of these measures were intended to undermine the power of political organizations like Tammany Hall, which depended heavily on Irish immigrant support and had perfected the art of political corruption.[57]

The extent of this nativist and Republican backlash against immigrants and Democrats was starkly visible in Jersey City in the 1870s. The Irish had achieved political dominance of the city's government between 1867 and 1870, due to sheer force of numbers. Half of the city's governing aldermen in 1870 were Irish, most of them Irish-born skilled workers and members of the lower middle class. Local Republicans, with the support of many native-born Democrats, responded to the Irish takeover by pushing through the New Jersey legislature a bill abolishing the current system of government. While the mayor and aldermen retained their offices they lost their power, which was transferred to special commissions appointed by the legislature. City wards were also re-drawn in such a way as to minimize Irish influence. In this way, a legislature dominated by native-born Protestants effectively stripped Irish Catholics of their control of Jersey City. Only in 1877 did the repeal of the commission plan lead to a restoration of Irish power. A similar movement in New York City, involving an effort to restore property qualifications for voting on issues of taxation and expenditure, was unsuccessful.[58]

Despite the force of the nativist backlash in the 1870s, its net effect may have been to strengthen Irish support for Democratic machines. The tide of political power was already turning strongly in favour of the Irish, especially in city governments. 'Honest John' Kelly, who succeeded the disgraced William Tweed in 1871, was the first Irish boss of Tammany Hall. Kelly gave way to Richard Croker in 1886, who in turn was replaced by Charles Francis Murphy in 1902. Kelly, Croker and Murphy were the three great Irish bosses of Tammany Hall; together they ran New York City with only minor interruptions for more than fifty years, from 1871 to 1924. The machine over which they presided was the prototype for a brand of late nineteenth-century Irish municipal politics that arose in several other American cities. Among the Irish bosses of the 1890s beyond Tammany Hall were Hugh McLaughlin of Brooklyn, Mike McDonald of Chicago, Christopher Buckley of San Francisco, William Sheehan of Buffalo and 'Little Bob' Davis of Jersey City. In Boston, which was so factionalized that it never developed an effective machine, Irish leaders like Martin Lomasney, Patrick J. Kennedy (father of Joseph P. Kennedy and grandfather of John F. Kennedy), Mike McDonald and John F. 'Honey Fitz' Fitzgerald (grandfather of John F. Kennedy) vied with one another to inherit the mantle of Pat Maguire (d. 1893), and thereby win control of the local Democratic party and, with it, control of city politics.[59]

The Irish political machine had an elaborate organization, designed to reach every voter. Its representative at the lowest level was the 'block captain' or 'ward heeler', who established a personal relationship with everyone in his neighbourhood. Then came the 'precinct captain', the 'ward boss', and on through the ranks to the 'sachems' and the 'grand sachem' of Tammany Hall. The boss of Tammany and most other machines, it should be emphasized, did not become mayor; he was much more powerful than that. By controlling the party caucuses and nominating process, the boss effectively appointed the mayor. That is, the machine selected the candidate for mayor, the electors voted him in, but the boss retained the power and continued to run the city.

The Irish municipal machines of the late nineteenth century perfected forms of politics that were denounced as immoral by their enemies, the reformers. They built and retained their power by meeting the needs of their constituents in ways their detractors condemned as corrupt, especially through the dispensation of favours (money, jobs, protection) in return for votes. They secured citizenship for immigrants who had not completed their five-year term of naturalization, in return for their vote. Tammany Hall, for example, opened its own naturalization bureau, printed its own naturalization applications and certificates, and consolidated its power by creating citizens according to its own needs. The machines paid people to vote; they registered and voted for all sorts of people who were not qualified, including the dead, the departed and the unborn; and they destroyed the ballots of their opponents uncounted. The defeat of the radical mayoral candidate Henry George (1839–97) in New York City in 1886 was blamed by some on widespread fraud, including the destruction of uncounted ballots cast in his favour. The machines used the Irish-dominated police force to prevent voters from entering the polling booths. They intimidated labour and socialist parties into submission, employing gangs of 'plug uglies' against their parades and pressuring judges to deny them permits for their meetings and demonstrations. Several bosses also took advantage of their power to amass great personal fortunes, having started out penniless. Perhaps the two most colourful in this respect were George Washington Plunkitt and Richard Croker.[60]

George Washington Plunkitt was born in New York City of Irish parents in 1842 and raised in the Seneca Village area of what is now Central Park. Although Seneca Village was excoriated by contemporary nativists as a den of iniquity (much like the Five Points district), recent research suggests that its residents, despite great poverty and adversity, did all they could to make it a decent place in which to live and raise their children. Some of its residents were squatters living in shanties, but most were tenants in more durable structures. Nonetheless, it was a very tough environment in which to grow up and surviving it must have equipped Plunkitt rather well for the rough and tumble world of city politics. He first held office as a city alderman, before rising to become a 'sachem' in Tammany Hall and, eventually, as Father of the Council of Tammany, its elder statesman. Plunkitt delivered many of his most insightful sayings on politics from the bootblack stand in the County Courthouse, the best of which were committed to paper by the journalist William Riordan in his book, *Plunkitt of Tammany Hall* (1905). Plunkitt is perhaps best-known for his views on civil service reform and corruption (or what he called 'graft'). The civil service reformers were the bane of his existence. They wanted a standardized, professional city government whose members had to pass entrance examinations. Plunkitt wanted to hand out jobs in government to those who deserved them, in other words his Irish constituents. Civil service reform was a curse, Plunkitt declared, but he predicted that it would never catch on. As it turned out, it was easy enough for the Tammany men to get around it; once they resumed power after a sporadic burst of reform, they simply abolished objective tests for job candidates in favour of 'essays' which they 'graded' as they saw fit.[61]

As for corruption, Plunkitt's position is best expressed in his most famous saying: 'I seen my opportunities, and I took 'em.' Plunkitt distinguished, infamously, between 'honest' and 'dishonest' graft. The latter included things like blackmailing, embezzlement and gambling; a good example of the former was the use of inside information on a forthcoming construction project to buy the land where it was scheduled to take place, and then selling the land at a big profit to the construction company. One would have to be a fool to pass up opportunities like that, Plunkitt believed, and it was through 'honest' graft of this sort that he made his millions. Known as 'the sage of Tammany Hall', George Washington Plunkitt died in New York City in 1924.[62]

Richard Croker was born in Ireland in 1841 and sailed with his parents to the United States as a young boy in the famine year of 1846. Like Plunkitt's, the family found shelter in Seneca Village. Croker grew up in a tenement on the Lower East Side, where he headed a local gang called the Fourth Avenue Tunnel Gang. Through his gang leadership, Croker drew the attention of Tammany, winning its respect on one occasion by reportedly voting for a single candidate seventeen times in one day. 'Vote early and vote often', as one of the more infamous slogans attributed to the nineteenth-century American Irish put it. Elected to the position of alderman in 1869, Croker was acquitted of murder in the early 1870s. Thereafter he held a series of appointed government offices and made his way through the ranks of 'Honest John' Kelly's machine. Croker succeeded Kelly as leader of Tammany in 1886, consolidating his power that year by successfully thwarting the attempt by an insurgent labour party to mobilize the working-class vote. Defeated by reformers in the election of 1894, he sailed for England for a three-year exile on his stud farm, leaving Tammany in the care of a loyal henchman. Croker also owned extensive properties in New York State, Florida and Ireland, having become very rich in office – no doubt through 'honest' graft. He resumed control of Tammany in 1897, successfully running his candidate for mayor of New York City but, after a second political defeat in 1901, Croker departed for Ireland, where he lived out his days as a country gentleman, breeding horses and dispensing philanthropy until his death in 1922.[63]

How did the Irish come to dominate the politics of so many American cities in the late nineteenth century? They were, firstly, the largest or second largest immigrant group in most eastern and mid-western cities from the mid-nineteenth century to the 1890s, and they gradually translated their numerical strength into the actual wielding of political power. Moreover, they had been tightly affiliated since the 1820s with the Democratic party, through which they built most of their political machines. Less tangibly, it has been argued that the Irish were uniquely well-suited to mass democratic politics because they came to America from a country whose social and political structure had molded them for the part. The Irish certainly differed from other immigrant groups because of their fluency in English, a language in which most of them were literate by the post-famine period. They also came from a country in which Daniel O'Connell, with his movements for Catholic Emancipation and Repeal of the Act of Union, had mobilized hundreds of thousands of Irish people in a form of mass democratic politics unprecedented in European history. This precedent was important, though it is hard to measure its influence on Irish immigrants who came to America. Irish-American political machines probably imitated O'Connell's movement to some extent in using the Catholic parish system as the basis of their organization.[64]

More important than O'Connellism, surely, was the Irish tradition of subterranean politics, combined with a pervasive distrust of the law and conventional politics. Tavern keepers of the type who had dominated secret societies in Ireland emerged as the archetypal 'block captains' and 'ward bosses' in American cities. At the same time, their experience of an arbitrary and highly oppressive judicial system in nineteenth-century Ireland had surely predisposed the immigrants to see judicial institutions and conventional political structures as instruments of fraud and tyranny rather than democracy. They would therefore have had few scruples in using politics in ways that horrified middle-class reformers. Turning adversity to their advantage, the American Irish built an urban power base that would endure until the Second World War and beyond.[65]

RELIGION

If Democratic political machines and the labour movement were two of the three most important institutions in Irish-American life in the late nineteenth century, the third was the Catholic Church. By 1880 there were 6 million Catholics in the United States and, by 1890, 7.3 million. One-sixth of the Catholics in 1890 lived in the three heavily Irish cities of New York-Brooklyn, Chicago and Philadelphia. While the leaders of the American Church in the late nineteenth century came from many different ethnic backgrounds, the Irish dominated the hierarchy. They had been elevated to positions of leadership early in the nineteenth century, in part because they were the first Catholic immigrant group to come to the United States in large numbers, and in part because their fluency in English fitted them well for the task. By 1900, two-thirds of the American Catholic bishops were of Irish birth or descent, including those of the most important dioceses, New York, Baltimore, Boston, Philadelphia, Detroit, St Paul and San Francisco. Quite fittingly, the first American Cardinal was Brooklyn-born John McCloskey (1810–85) of New York City, who was selected in 1875. The undisputed leader of American Catholicism after McCloskey's death was James Gibbons (1834–1921), who served as Archbishop of Baltimore from 1878 and Cardinal from 1886 until his death. Other influential Irish leaders of the Church included Bishop John Ireland (1838–1918) of St Paul, Minnesota, a native of County Kilkenny who had come to the United States in 1849 and who represented the progressive wing of the Catholic Church on most causes; his fellow-progressive Bishop John Keane of Richmond, Virginia (1839–1918), who came to the United States in 1845 and, under the patronage of Gibbons, became rector of the newly created Catholic University of America in 1887; and their conservative opponent, American-born Michael Corrigan (1839–1902), who replaced McCloskey as Archbishop of New York City in 1885.[66]

During the second half of the nineteenth century, in both the United States and Ireland, the 'devotional revolution' that had begun at mid-century continued. In the United States its effects were noticeable in a more expressive style of Catholic devotion than the 'plain style' that had prevailed in the early republican period. The most popular devotions included those to the Sacred Heart of Jesus, to Jesus in the eucharist, to the passion of Jesus and to the Immaculate Conception of the Virgin Mary. Other practices included recitation of the rosary, repetition of the Hail Mary, meditation on the life of Jesus and devotion to particular saints (as well as 'novenas', or nine days of prayer, to mark their feast days). Irish Catholic homes in the second half of the nineteenth century typically had a family shrine, a font of holy water, a bible, a crucifix and various images of Jesus, Mary, the saints, the Pope or the American cardinals. Most of these devotional forms were not new, but they were emphasized with renewed vigour under the papacy of Pius IX. The new piety and devotionalism noticeable in late nineteenth-century America and Ireland is best understood as a specific form of a global reformation of Catholicism orchestrated from Rome and propagated by the hierarchy in metropolitan centers on both sides of the Atlantic.[67]

Hand-in-hand with the new devotional style came an increasing emphasis on the hierarchical authority of the Church. Regular attendance by the laity at mass and the sacraments, of course, served to accentuate the authority of the clergy, especially compared to the lax standards of the early nineteenth century. At the same time, the new devotionalism emphasized sin, guilt, confession and reparation, with frequent sermons on hell and purgatory, all of which augmented clerical authority while at the same time devaluing the secular world in favour of the spiritual. The rituals and air of mystery surrounding devotional practices, from candles and incense to bells and liturgical theater, served a similar purpose. This emphasis on clerical authority reached its apogee with the declaration in 1870 of papal infallibility.[68]

The Catholic hierarchy and clergy in the late nineteenth-century United States fell into three broad camps, liberal, conservative and radical. The liberals, led by Cardinal James Gibbons of Baltimore and Archbishop John Ireland of St Paul, were the most powerful. The conservatives came a close second, with the radicals a distant third. The liberals tended to favour the cause of organized labour, if only because opposing it would alienate a large Irish working-class constituency; but they were determined to channel working-class discontent into more moderate movements. They condemned economic privilege and political corruption, but defended capitalism, progress and American-style democracy. They emphasized industry, self-reliance, thrift, temperance and respectability over more traditional values of humility, obedience and fatalism. They favoured dialogue with non-Catholics. Above all, they were 'Americanizers', convinced that the American republic was a friendly rather than a hostile environment for Catholicism, and that the Church itself was fundamentally compatible with the American way of life. Liberal Catholicism of this sort received most of its support from middle-and upper-class Irish Americans, from workers who espoused temperance and other forms of 'self-improvement', and from the residents of those cities and towns where the Irish were most closely integrated into native society. The liberals were therefore rather unlikely leaders for the Irish-speaking peasant immigrants of the 1890s, many of whom gravitated to either the conservative or the radical camp, if they gravitated to the Church at all.[69]

The conservatives were led by Archbishop Michael Corrigan of New York and Bishop Bernard McQuaid (1823–1909) of Rochester. Unlike the liberals, they regarded the American Church as surrounded by hostile forces, adopting a combative and even militant stance in defense of tradition, authority and hierarchy. To this extent, they were the heirs of Archbishop Hughes, just as the liberal 'Americanizers' were part of a tradition established by Bishop Carroll during the revolutionary era. Many of the American conservatives had been trained in Rome, strongly endorsed papal authority and leaned toward ultramontanism (a conservative and authoritarian form of Catholicism).

They condemned ecumenicism (cooperation with other Christian churches, despite doctrinal differences) and opposed lay initiatives in parish government. They preached a gospel of resignation and obedience to authority that was the antithesis of liberal Catholicism. They drew most of their support from big eastern cities with large Irish-born populations, from affluent socially conservative American Catholics, from Irish Americans seeking protection against nativism and from political machines like Tammany Hall.[70]

Radical Catholics, the third major group, were outspokenly critical of the social costs of industrialization and urbanization. Predictably, they had little support in the upper reaches of the hierarchy. The best-known clerical proponent of radicalism in the 1880s was Fr. Edward McGlynn (1837–1900), an Irish-born supporter of social reform on both sides of the Atlantic. McGlynn denounced plutocracy (government based solely on wealth) and machine politics, championed the cause of organized labour, and offered a sustained critique of the workings of Gilded Age capitalism based on anti-monopolist and egalitarian traditions rooted in Irish revolutionary nationalism, the New Testament and the ideas of Henry George and other contemporary labour reformers. McGlynn's involvement in the New York City mayoral election of 1886 got him in trouble with his superior, Archbishop Corrigan, and his refusal to explain himself to Rome led to a sentence of excommunication that lasted until 1892. Many working-class Irish families, including that of the future labour radical Elizabeth Gurley Flynn, left the Church in protest at McGlynn's treatment. The radicals were committed to social reform in part because they feared widespread apostasy among the working class; but they differed from the liberals in arguing that the Church should place itself in the forefront of the movement to reform society. They called for cooperation with Protestants on social and political matters. Despite McGlynn's personal popularity, however, the radicals' strategy of appealing to their working-class Irish adherents as exploited workers first, and persecuted Irishmen second, had limited appeal to a constituency that was courted as well by liberal and conservative Catholic clergymen, by machine politicians and by a vibrant Irish-American nationalist movement.[71]

The differences between Catholic conservatives, liberals and radicals are perhaps most evident in issues concerning education and labour. Conservatives strongly favoured parochial education as a means of isolating Catholic children from Protestantism. They condemned the public schools either as godless institutions that gave no effective religious training or, even worse, as bastions of Protestantism (which they often were). Some conservative clergy denied the sacraments to parents who sent their children to public instead of parochial schools. Moreover, conservatives mistrusted, and sometimes detested, the democratic goal of individual transformation through education, embodied in the idea of a public school system, fearing that it would render children unfit for the station of life into which they had been born. Liberal Catholics, on the other hand, with their general optimism about human nature, believed strongly in the eradication of ignorance and poverty and the uplift and assimilation of Irish Catholic immigrants through education. Sensing the democratic promise of the public school system, they outraged the conservatives by experimenting in ecumenical cooperation with Protestant educators. In Poughkeepsie, New York, for example, the local board of education rented the Catholic school for use during regular hours, while in Minnesota, Bishop Ireland cooperated with the public schools in similar fashion. The radical minority within the clergy took the liberal position to its extreme, rejecting parochial schools altogether as divisive of the working class. Fr. McGlynn, for example, rejected all suggestions that he build a school in his parish.[72]

Led by Bishop Ireland, the liberals emerged triumphant in the debate over education. The Third Plenary Council of the American Catholic Church, meeting at Baltimore in 1884 (known as Baltimore III), struck a compromise by encouraging the establishment of more parochial schools and calling for the removal of priests who failed to establish schools, but refusing to sanction the hard-line position of denying the sacraments to parents who did not comply. Then in 1892 the liberals won a major victory when the papal delegate, Francesco Satolli, visiting from Rome, approved the experiments in cooperation with the public schools pioneered by Bishop Ireland and forbade priests to deny the sacraments to parents whose children attended these schools when no adequate parochial school was available. Satolli's verdict was later upheld in a letter by Pope Leo XIII to Cardinal Gibbons. The liberals had successfully fended off the attacks both of the radicals, who opposed parochial schools altogether and the conservatives, who upheld them to the exclusion of cooperation with Protestants and the public educational system. Joint ventures of the type favoured by Bishop Ireland were few and far between, however, and even his own experiments in educational ecumenicism had failed by the early 1890s. Despite the rhetoric of Baltimore III, only 37 per cent of the nation's Catholic communities in 1900 were supporting their own schools, with parochial schools noticeably more common in the West than the East. Lacking the incentive of language preservation, the Irish had considerably fewer parochial schools than the Germans. The majority of Irish Catholic children in late nineteenth-century America, in short, attended what conservatives continued to denounce as 'godless' (or Protestant) public schools. By the end of the century, however, large numbers of their teachers were second-generation Irish Catholic women).[73]

On questions of labour, the liberals also emerged victorious over both the radicals and the conservatives. While liberal optimists like Cardinal Gibbons could see no major flaws in American society, radicals like Fr. Edward McGlynn vied with conservatives like Archbishop Michael Corrigan in condemning American industrial capitalism as heartless, godless and crassly materialistic. For conservatives, this criticism seemed to be an end in itself, confirmation of the besieged state of the Church in the modern world, whereas for radicals it was the starting point for progressive reform. Liberals, in contrast to those to their left and right, found little to complain of in the social status quo and were more likely to endorse temperance and other means of individual self-improvement as the best means of reform. When it came to labour unions, conservatives were predictably opposed to Catholic membership in such organizations, radicals enthusiastically supported them and liberals trod a prudent middle course.[74]

Matters came to a head in the mid-1880s when Archbishop Corrigan and his fellow conservatives attempted to extend to the United States a Vatican ruling against Canadian Catholics joining the Knights of Labor, the largest labour organization in American history up to that point. They also tried to persuade Rome that Henry George's *Progress and Poverty* (1879), a radical manifesto calling for a tax on landed property that was popular among urban workers in the United States, ought to be placed on the Vatican's Index of forbidden books. When Archbishop Gibbons went to Rome in 1887 to accept the 'red hat' (i.e. become a cardinal), he reiterated his opinion, forwarded by letter some years previously, that the action proposed against labour would be imprudent and would be sure to alienate the Catholic working class. The Vatican responded in 1889 by approving the Knights of Labor and refusing to put George's book on the Index, though at the same time sending a supposedly secret letter to the American hierarchy reaffirming the principle of private property and warning Catholics to 'beware the false theories of Henry George'. Rome also agreed to reopen the case of the excommunicated radical priest Edward McGlynn in 1892, with Bishop Ireland appointed as the man to interview him. Sensing an opportunity to embarrass Corrigan, Ireland persuaded McGlynn to disavow socialism (though the radical priest clung to his belief that the state should tax land to meet its social obligations) and Leo XIII lifted the excommunication. The previous year

(1891), Leo had issued his famous encyclical *Rerum Novarum* ('of new things', i.e. the new social conditions caused by the industrial revolution) outlining a program for social justice in the modern world. While he defended private property in no uncertain terms, the Pope also defended the rights of workers to organize and the obligation of the state to intervene in society to further social justice. This document was enthusiastically received by the American liberals, even if little was done to put its principles into practice in the United States until the twentieth century.[75]

While men like Bishop Ireland were liberal on questions of education and labour, they were noticeably less so when it came to ethnic and national assertiveness within the American Catholic Church. The Church in late nineteenth-century America, as has often been remarked, was 'One, Holy, Apostolic and Irish'. The Irish, of course, claimed to run the Church not for themselves but as a national institution that was in turn part of a world-wide religion based in Rome. There could be little room in the Irish-dominated American Church, however, for the types of ethnic assertiveness that began to surface in the late nineteenth century. Protests against Irish control of the American Church came especially from Germans, who had always insisted on retaining their own language and style of devotion, and Poles, who began arriving in the United States in large numbers in the 1870s and 1880s. Some degree of diversity, including German and Polish parishes, was generally tolerated by both liberals and conservatives, so long as these parishes remained answerable to the Irish-dominated hierarchy. But the idea of formally establishing separate parishes for each linguistic or national group, with their own clergy and equal representation in the hierarchy, was firmly rejected.[76]

German priests stepped up their objections to forced 'Americanization' by the Irish in the 1880s, petitioning Rome for their own parishes and pastors, with the same rights as English-speaking ones. Bishops John Ireland and John J. Keane launched a counterattack against this campaign, arguing that concessions to one national group would lead to concessions to all and to the consequent fragmentation of the American Church. The Vatican eventually responded by recognizing the legitimacy of separate parishes for different language groups (a practice that was already widespread in the United States), but refused to grant further privileges, such as the appointment of German clergy and hierarchy on a proportional basis or the foundation of separate parochial schools. The resolution of further disputes was left to the local bishops.[77]

The question of national rights within the American Church reemerged with renewed intensity in 1891 in a controversy that came to be known as

'Cahenslyism'. Peter Paul Cahensly was a German Catholic layman and member of the Reichstag (Germany's parliament) who devoted most of his time to bettering the conditions of German emigrants abroad. Cahensly and his followers drafted a document called the Lucerne Memorial in 1891 and sent it to the Pope, arguing that each nationality in the America Church should have its own parishes, its own priests, catechetical instruction in the mother tongue, separate parochial schools and equal rights and representation for its clergy within the Church. Bishop Ireland and Cardinal Gibbons condemned this movement forthrightly, and it made little progress in the United States. Predictably, neither Cahensly nor the German Americans succeeded in persuading Rome to change its 'national' policy in the United States. Irish-American liberals had won another victory, but this time through a distinctly illiberal and authoritarian policy which further alienated German Catholics as well as newly arriving immigrants from Poland and Italy.[78]

One final important struggle within the American Catholic Church in the late nineteenth century requires clarification. This was the 'Americanist' controversy of the 1890s, which had implications well into the twentieth century and in some respects foreshadowed the reforms enacted by the second Vatican Council (Vatican II) in the 1960s. 'Americanism', to the extent that it ever existed as a coherent position within the Catholic Church in the United States, was a progressive, liberal philosophy which sought to adapt Catholicism to modern, or 'American', social and cultural conditions. Americanism can be equated, up to a point, with the dominant liberal faction within the American Church, who believed that American democracy was the best form of government the world had yet seen; that the Church should adopt a progressive stance on social questions and establish a dialogue on this and other matters with Protestants; that American Catholics should assimilate into the United States; that the United States should have its own Catholic University (duly founded with papal approval in Washington, DC, in 1887, over the objections of Michael Corrigan, who wanted it to be in New York); and that the American Church could thereby become a model for the rest of the world to follow. Traditionalists in both the United States and Europe bitterly opposed these views, leading to the eventual condemnation of Americanism as a form of heresy.[79]

The controversy began almost by chance when a translation of the life of Isaac Hecker was published in France in 1897. Hecker, a prominent American Catholic convert who had died nine years earlier, had espoused a brand of liberal Catholicism that to some extent presaged the Americanist position. The French translation of his biography came with a preface by Abbé Félix Klein stating a version of Americanism far more extreme than anything espoused by Hecker or subsequent Catholic liberals in the United States. The entire Church, Klein argued, must look to American leadership if it was to survive in the modern world. Monarchists and conservative Catholics throughout France responded with an onslaught against Klein, Hecker and Americanism. While in some ways the conflict reveals more about France than the United States, it resulted in the formation of a special investigative commission in Rome and the issue of a papal encyclical, *Testem Benevolentiae* (1899), condemning the 'Americanist heresy'. The Pope condemned the beliefs that Christian doctrine required modification to bring it into line with the modern world; that the 'natural and active virtues' of the modern world were superior to traditional 'supernatural' and 'passive' virtues; and that the Church's authority and discipline ought to be reduced in any way. At the same time, he took pains to distinguish between three forms of Americanism – the characteristic qualities of the American people, the laws and customs of the United States, and the specific doctrines he had mentioned – insisting that only the third of these was being condemned. And he did not claim that these doctrines were actually contained in either the writings of Isaac Hecker or the views of the current American hierarchy. Thus, while conservatives like Corrigan exulted in this papal verdict, liberals like Ireland and Gibbons could justly deny that they had ever held the views condemned by the Pope. Both sides could claim a victory. The papal ruling did, however, serve as a warning to liberals not to push their philosophy too far, marking the growing power of conservatism within the Catholic Church both globally and in the United States.[80]

NATIONALISM

The final important institution in late nineteenth-century Irish-American life was a flourishing nationalist movement. The origins and nature of this movement have been hotly debated by historians. According to the most influential interpretation, the origins of Irish-American nationalism lay in the loneliness, alienation and poverty of the immigrant experience, which bred 'a pervasive sense of inferiority, intense longing for acceptance and respectability, and an acute sensitivity to criticism'. In their public rhetoric, the nationalists claimed to be fighting for an independent Ireland; but Irish independence was an abstract, distant goal compared to the pressing reality of how to win acceptance and success in America. Irish-American nationalism, in this reading, was 'directed chiefly toward American, not Irish ends'. This was true in two senses: first, a free Ireland would inevitably raise the ethnic status of Irish people in America; second, and much more pragmatically, institutions ostensibly organized to further purely nationalist goals were used as pressure groups for all sorts of other ethnic and political issues, and their mere existence could be cited as evidence of Irish-American acumen for respectable middle-class political pursuits and hence their fitness for inclusion as full, respectable members of the national community.[81]

The model of assimilation here is a plausible one, but only if it is extended to cover the working-class majority of Irish immigrants as well as the small but powerful middle class. The flaw in the model as it stands is that it deals almost exclusively with middle-class Irish-American culture. The Irish-American middle class may well have been (to quote the principal proponent of this view) 'fundamentally conservative', aspiring to little more than respectability within middle-class America. But does this mean that all Irish-American nationalists shared these limited goals? In other words, were there other sources than the emerging middle class for Irish-American nationalism? The prevailing model is one-dimensional: it either ignores the importance of working-class contributions to the nationalist movement, or it implies that working-class nationalists merely wanted to be like their middle-class counterparts. As one historian has pointed out, it 'views working-class life simply as a transitional stage on the road to bourgeois respectability and defines assimilation solely as acquisition of middle-class values that enabled the Irish immigrant to "accommodate . . . to an often hostile environment"'. Working-class Irish-American nationalists were not simply middle-class Irish Americans in the making. Nor was middle-class conservatism the only, or necessarily the dominant, political stance of the nationalist movement. Instead, there was a strong strand of working-class radicalism at the heart of the movement.[82]

The history of Irish-American nationalism in the 1880s is a classic example of one of the principal themes of this book, the manner in which the history of the American Irish was intertwined with developments in Ireland as well as the United States. To understand what happened in the 1880s, it is necessary to think of the American Irish in a trans-national setting, a single, complex and diverse Irish culture that existed simultaneously on both sides of the Atlantic Ocean. In terms of nationalism especially, strikingly similar developments took place in late nineteenth-century Ireland and the United States, featuring many of the same individuals. Nationalists and reformers like Charles Stewart Parnell, Michael Davitt, Patrick Ford and John Devoy, for example, were deeply involved in the political affairs of the Irish in both Ireland and America.

The Fenian Brotherhood, the chief expression of nationalism during the famine era, had barely survived the debacle of the 1860s. Jeremiah O'Donovan Rossa (1831–1915) became Head Center of the organization in New York in 1877. Born in Rosscarbery, Ireland in 1831, O'Donovan Rossa had been imprisoned by the British for his political activities in 1859 and again in 1865. He was released in 1870 on condition that he go into political exile, and spent the rest of his life in New York City, where he led the Fenian movement, edited the *United Irishman* (founded in 1881), fathered fifteen children, launched a disastrous dynamite campaign against British cities and survived an assassination attempt by an Englishwoman on Broadway in 1885. By the late 1870s, the Fenians were overshadowed by a new body, Clan na Gael, founded in New York City by Jerome C. Collins. Under the leadership of John Devoy it soon became the most powerful Irish republican organization on either side of the Atlantic. By the late 1870s it had some 10,000 members, bound to strict secrecy. In 1877 a seven-member Joint Revolutionary Directory was created to bind the Clan to the Irish Republican Brotherhood in Dublin.[83]

The dominant figure among American hard-line republican nationalists was John Devoy (1842–1928). Born in the town of Kill, Co. Kildare, Devoy had spent some time in the French Foreign Legion before accepting an assignment from the Irish Republican Brotherhood to enlist Irish soldiers serving in the British Army. Imprisoned for his political activities in 1866, he was released in 1871 and came to New York City on the same ship as O'Donovan Rossa. But Devoy was of an altogether sterner mettle than the volatile Fenian leader. Settling in New York, he served for a while as foreign editor of the New York *Herald*, and then published two newspapers, the *Irish Nation* (1881–5) and the influential *Gaelic-American* (1903–28), until his death in New York City in 1928. He also turned Clan na Gael into the most formidable exponent of Irish physical-force nationalism to be found anywhere in the world. It was largely through Devoy's fund-raising and organizational efforts in the United States that the Easter rebellion of 1916 became possible. An uncompromising proponent of hard-line republicanism, he has aptly been described by one historian as 'the Lenin of Irish-American nationalism'.[84]

Throughout the late nineteenth century, however, constitutional nationalism remained much more popular than hard-line republicanism on both sides of the Atlantic. Its leader, incongruously enough, was Charles Stewart

Parnell (1846–91), a Protestant landlord with an American mother, who led a mass Catholic movement for Home Rule in the 1880s. Parnell's primary goal was constitutional autonomy for Ireland, rather than republican independence or reform of social conditions. He wanted a restoration of the Irish Parliament that had been abolished in 1801, but within the framework of the British monarchical constitution. Although Parnell was prepared to enter into temporary alliances with the Fenians and Clan na Gael, he was never a man of violence, believing instead in peaceful change through parliamentary democracy. By the same token, he entered into strategic alliances with land reformers as well, but social reforms were always secondary to nationalist ones in his thinking. If he could win constitutional autonomy for Ireland by linking his cause with republicanism or land reform, then so much the better; if not, then neither cause was ultimately of much use to him.

The great land reformer in this period was Michael Davitt (1846–1906). Born into a peasant family in County Mayo during the Great Famine and raised in a factory town near Manchester, England, Davitt was sent to work as a child and lost his right arm in an industrial accident at age eleven. He joined the Fenians in 1865 and became Organizing Secretary of the Irish Republican Brotherhood in 1868. In 1870 he was arrested on arms charges and sentenced to fifteen years' penal servitude. Released in 1877, he travelled to the United States, where he met the radical reformer Henry George in 1880 and was impressed by his ideas on land reform. With the Irish-American nationalist ideologue John Devoy he discussed ways of combining nationalist agitation with the land question, laying the groundwork for what would soon come to be called the New Departure.[85]

Davitt's chief ally in the United States was Patrick Ford (1837–1913), a native of Galway who had moved with his parents to America in 1846. After working in the printing office of William Garrison's abolitionist newspaper, *The Liberator*, he enlisted in the Union Army during the Civil War and lived for a few years thereafter in Charleston, South Carolina before returning to New York City in 1870 to found what quickly became the leading Irish-American newspaper, the *Irish World* (the words *and American Industrial Liberator* were added to the title in 1879). Ford supported the right of labour to organize unions and go on strike, insisted that there had been a grave miscarriage of justice in the case of the Molly Maguires, campaigned against monopoly control of business and endorsed a wide range of radical causes from women's rights to income tax and an eight-hour workday. He argued that labour was the producer of value and ought to be rewarded accordingly, and that non-producers were using their power to appropriate what labour produced. Ford believed that the plight of the rural poor in Ireland and the industrial poor in America were part of the same story. 'The cause of the poor in Donegal is the cause of the factory slave in Fall River', as he put it. The solution in both places, he believed, was the nationalization of landed property, which would link nationalism with radicalism in a potentially powerful ideological combination. His ideas placed him in the mainstream of an American radical tradition stretching from the abolitionists and early feminism through the trade union movement and Radical Reconstruction, belying the characterization of Irish-American culture as inherently conservative and necessarily opposed to reform movements. Patrick Ford, as one historian puts it, spoke 'the traditional language of American radicalism'.[86]

Irish-American support for the different types of nationalism varied widely according to social position and recency of arrival in the United States. It is fair to say that, in general, the 'lace curtain' or middle-class Irish, many of them second-generation, were the least likely to support radicalism or extremism. They had little to gain, and often much to lose, by social reform in either Ireland or the United States; and they denounced the use of violence as providing grist to the nativist mill. Clinging to their hard-earned respectability, they favoured Home Rule and moderate and gradual land reform in place of any form of revolution. They were Parnell's chief supporters in the 1880s. The case of recent immigrants is less clear-cut; one historian has found that those who came from Munster arrived with a well-developed sense of nationalism and were the most likely of all Irish Americans to support hard-line republicanism, whereas Irish-speakers from Connacht evinced little interest in nationalism of any kind, their allegiances still being primarily local. Finally, there was substantial support among the urban working class for tying the cause of nationalism to radical social reform in both Ireland and America. Few Irish-American women appear to have participated in the Irish-American nationalist movement, however, with the exception of the short-lived Ladies' Land League established in 1881. Although Patrick Ford included women's rights on his list of radical causes, feminism was never an important ingredient of Irish-American nationalism.[87]

The various strands in Irish and Irish-American nationalism came together in the so-called New Departure, a brief-lived but potentially very powerful political alliance formed in 1879. An alliance between land reformers, hard-line republicans and constitutional nationalists in Ireland and Irish America would be formidable indeed, but it was no easy task to bring it about. The Irish Republican Brotherhood and Clan na Gael regarded

Home Rule as at best a halfway-house on the road to their goal of national independence, and were interested in land reform only to the extent that it might mobilize the peasantry in behalf of the greater goal of independence. Parnell and the Home Rulers, for their part, found the physical-force republicans too extreme and the reformers too radical. Radicals on both sides of the Atlantic, meanwhile, wanted an overhaul of the Irish tenant system and perhaps even outright ownership of the land by an independent Irish state, with social and labour reform as a concomitant in the United States. Middle-class Irish nationalists on both sides of the Atlantic were determined to resist them.[88]

In its origins, the New Departure appears to have been primarily political rather than social in orientation. That is, its principal goal was Irish national independence rather than a social revolution. The three main parties to the agreement were Devoy, Parnell and Davitt. Devoy evidently believed, or allowed himself to believe, that Parnell's ultimate goal was an independent Ireland. Parnell certainly allowed Devoy and Davitt to believe that he was seeking both independence and land reform, not just constitutional change. In reality, however, he was probably using these causes to exert sufficient pressure on the British government that it would have to concede Home Rule. Davitt, as an ex-Fenian, hoped the New Departure might secure some form of Irish independence, though from 1880 onward he devoted most of his attention to improving the lot of Irish tenants. In New York City, Ford supported Davitt in the hope of reforming Irish America as well, while Devoy was interested in Home Rule and land reform only to the extent that they might be mobilized in support of his uncompromising goal of full republican independence. It is scarcely surprising that so volatile an alliance could not last for long; but during the period of agitation which followed its formation, the alliance represented a very powerful new political force in Irish history.[89]

The period of political and social agitation in Ireland that lasted from 1879 to 1882 is known as the Land War. The principal political organization involved was the Land League, which had branches in both Ireland and the United States. Parnell visited America to raise funds and win support for the Land League late in 1879. He left in March 1880, having covered 16,000 miles, spoken in sixty-two cities, addressed a joint session of Congress and helped raise $300,000 for famine relief in Ireland and for the Land League. Parnell was also instrumental in founding the American Land League in New York City in March 1880 to provide money and moral support for the Irish parent organization. His sister, Fanny, who had emigrated to America in

1874, founded the Ladies' Land League in New York in October 1880. For the radical nationalist, Patrick Ford, these new institutions were the ideal means of publicizing his belief that the cause of the rural poor in Ireland was the same as that of the industrial poor in America, that the Irish poor had a right to own their land and that the American working class had the same right to control the fruits of its own labour. Ford found himself at the vanguard of a radical movement headed by Michael Davitt on one side of the ocean and the trade union movement of New York City on the other. Thus, when Davitt toured the United States from May to December 1880, he sided naturally with Patrick Ford in calling for social as well as nationalist revolution.[90]

Patrick Ford developed his ideas on Irish land and labour in close association with Henry George, the American-born reformer and economist who published the hotly-debated *Progress and Poverty* in 1879. Seeking to understand why poverty intensified along with economic progress, George found the answer in the existence of unproductive landed wealth, and called for a single tax on land as a solution. In 1880, George was introduced to Michael Davitt in Staten Island. The following year, George published a book, *The Irish Land Question* (which had been serialized by the *Irish World* in 1880), claiming that private property in land, rather than the British presence *per se*, was the root of Ireland's problems, and hence that the solution lay in a social rather than an exclusively nationalist revolution. Moreover, since, according to George's theory all of a country's land belongs naturally to its people, tenant reform was merely a smokescreen hiding the necessity of outright ownership of the land by the peasantry or the state. In October 1881, George sailed for Ireland, where he spent a year as the correspondent of Ford's *Irish World*. Among his most fervent supporters in the Irish-American community was Fr. Edward McGlynn.[91]

Matters reached a crisis on both sides of the Atlantic in mid-1882. In May and June, Davitt came out openly in favour of the abolition of private property and the nationalization of land, whereby the state would take control of all land and rent it out on equitable terms to tenant farmers (including the hitherto landless). Parnell condemned this scheme, as did the moderates and conservatives who controlled the Land League in America. The most vehement criticism came from Devoy, who condemned what he saw as the influence of Ford and George, neither of whom he considered genuinely committed to the cause of Irish freedom. He had never been interested in the Land War or the New Departure except to the extent that it might prove useful in achieving his single goal of national independence. Davitt came to

America in June 1882, where his scheme for land nationalization was enthusiastically supported by Patrick Ford and Fr. McGlynn. But under fierce attack by the mainstream Irish-American nationalist movement and increasingly isolated in Ireland, Davitt soon backed down and publicly pledged his support to Parnell.[92]

In both Ireland and the United States the New Departure ended in a showdown between three different conceptions of nationalism – constitutional, physical force and social reform – with socially and politically conservative constitutionalists emerging victorious in both countries. When, in January 1881, the American conservatives successfully insisted that each branch of the American Land League should send its own funds directly to Ireland, rather than through any central organization, Patrick Ford established his own separate Land League, with funds to be transferred to Ireland via the *Irish World*. Ford's newspaper quickly became by far the most important American source of funds to Ireland, dispatching more than $343,000 to the Irish Land League by the autumn of 1882. But, as the New Departure split asunder, conservatives regained control of the nationalist movement on both sides of the Atlantic. Devoy broke with Ford and Davitt in April 1881, while continuing to denounce Home Rule as inadequate. At the same time, as it became clear that the New Departure was no longer politically useful or necessary, Parnell and his supporters in both Ireland and the United States began to distance themselves from both radical reform and republican nationalism, concentrating instead on the single goal of Home Rule. When Parnell was arrested in October 1881 he responded by issuing his famous 'No Rent Manifesto', urging the Irish tenantry to withhold all rent from their landlords. The British government responded by suppressing the Land League (which was then replaced by the Ladies' Land League, recently created with this eventuality in mind). But, after his release from prison, Parnell had decided to call off the agrarian agitation, in return for political concessions from the Liberal government in England. Parnell's withdrawal effectively brought the Land War to an end so that radicals like Michael Davitt in Ireland and Patrick Ford and Henry George in America found themselves confined to the margins of the nationalist movement from 1882 onward.[93]

Yet Ford and George had always been interested in questions of social reform generally, not just in national liberation for Ireland. For Ford, the oppression of the Irish in Ireland was but one instance of a larger form of social oppression, centered on issues concerning land, labour and wealth. He and George stayed active in politics even after conservatives had won control of the Irish-American nationalist movement. In 1886 they had a second showdown with conservatism, this time when Henry George ran for mayor of New York City.[94]

Reaching out to the labour movement of New York City, Ford had already found considerable support for the cause of Ireland among the city's trade unions. Local branches of his Land League had maintained very close links with local union branches, and in January 1882 more than 12,000 representatives of the city's unions had met at Cooper Union to endorse Parnell's 'No-Rent Manifesto'. Out of this meeting emerged a new organization, the Central Labor Union (CLU), led by Robert Blissert, an English immigrant born of Irish parents. The CLU provided much of Henry George's support in 1886, along with Patrick Ford, Fr. McGlynn and the Knights of Labor (whose leader, Terence V. Powderly, was born in Pennsylvania to Irish-born parents). Ranged against the forces of Irish-American radicalism were the conservatives of Tammany Hall and Archbishop Corrigan's Catholic hierarchy. Running on the ticket of the United Labor party, George came second in the race, relegating the Republican candidate, Theodore Roosevelt, to third place; but, despite the makings of an Irish working-class revolt, Tammany held firm and the Democratic candidate, Abram S. Hewitt, won the election.[95]

Thus ended a highly revealing episode in Irish transatlantic history. By the 1890s, with the tragic death of Charles Stewart Parnell in Ireland, the nationalist fervour subsided. As it did so, the 'new immigrants' coming to America in vast numbers from southern and eastern Europe began to outstrip the old immigrants from north-west Europe. In this emerging multi-ethnic environment the Irish would soon find themselves accepted as full Americans, if only by default.

Chapter 5

◆

IRISH AMERICA, 1900–1940

In the first half of the twentieth century, the American Irish left behind them much of the discrimination and impoverishment that had characterized the nineteenth century. The arrival in the United States from the 1880s onward of the 'new immigrants' from southern and eastern Europe was greeted by an upsurge of racial nativism. To many Americans, the cultures, religions and lifestyles of these 'new immigrants' seemed so strange that the Irish must have appeared quite normal by comparison. In racial terms, the Irish were soon begrudgingly included in the superior 'Nordic' or 'Teutonic' category, while southern and eastern Europeans were classified as inferior. The Catholicism of Irish Americans excluded them from full respectability in the United States for decades to come, until the election of John F. Kennedy as president in 1960 finally settled that question. But already, by the early twentieth century, the American Irish had achieved rough occupational and educational equality with the American population as a whole, and they considerably exceeded the 'new immigrants' in social mobility and success.[1] At the same time, they began to make their mark on American literature, played a disproportionately powerful role in the American labour movement, made a greater contribution than ever to Irish nationalism and continued to dominate both the Catholic Church and the politics of American cities. The American Irish, despite the forces of nativism and condescension that still surrounded them, began to come into their own in the first half of the twentieth century.

THE IRISH IN IRELAND AND THE UNITED STATES

The number of Irish emigrants to the United States fell steadily between 1901 and 1950. Between 1901 and 1910 339,065 Irish people arrived, but only 146,181 in the decade 1911–20, when transatlantic emigration was interrupted by the First World War. Ulster emigrants accounted for fully 19 per cent (55,385) of all Irish emigrants to the United States in the period 1900–9, and 25 per cent (26,294) in the five-year period up to the First World War (1910–14). It is safe to assume that at least half of these emigrants, and perhaps many more, were Catholics. An even greater number of Ulster emigrants, most of them Protestants, went to Canada in this period. This preference for Canada was consolidated in the 1920s, when new legislation restricted immigration to the United States and the British government offered inducements to emigrants settling within the Empire. As a result, Ulster Protestant migration to the United States was cut to a trickle. Regionally, the pattern of Irish emigration in the first half of the twentieth century displayed a striking similarity to the dominant pattern throughout the nineteenth century, with the north-central counties of Leitrim, Cavan, Monaghan and Roscommon, along with County Mayo, having the heaviest departure rates.[2]

The destinations of Ireland's emigrants changed markedly during the first half of the twentieth century. In the period 1876 to 1921, 84 per cent went to the United States and only 8 per cent to Britain, 4 per cent to Australia, 3 per cent to Canada and 1 per cent to all other countries. In the period 1926–36, the United States still accounted for 54 per cent of the total net emigration, but that proportion declined thereafter for a number of reasons. The US Immigration Acts of 1921 and 1924 greatly restricted immigration from all countries (and excluded most Asian immigrants altogether). The 1924 Act set an annual quota of 28,567 for the Irish Free State, which was reduced to 17,853 in 1929. All immigrants were now required to obtain a visa from the American Consulate in their country. Then came the Great Depression and the Second World War, which further discouraged immigrants from coming to the United States. Immigration from Ireland to the United States, which had totalled 220,591 in the 1920s, was cut drastically; only 13,167 Irish immigrants arrived in the 1930s and 26,967 in the 1940s. Already by 1930 about three Irish immigrants were going to Great Britain for every one that went to America. With the Atlantic crossing rendered very dangerous by the Second World War, the Irish settled in Britain in record numbers, filling an acute labour shortage there. When overseas migration from Ireland resumed in the late 1940s and 1950s, the numbers of Irish emigrants going to the United States represented only about 10 per cent of the total emigration from Ireland.[3]

The primary cause of Irish emigration in the first half of the twentieth century was much the same as in the late nineteenth century, ongoing problems in agriculture and the landholding system combined with retarded urbanization and industrialization. The long-sought goal of owner-occupancy, whereby tenants were allowed to buy their own farms with loans subsidized by the government, merely consolidated the pattern of late inheritances laid down in the late nineteenth century, discouraging agricultural improvement and encouraging emigration by non-inheriting siblings. Because of late inheritance, many of the inheritors remained permanently single. By 1946, one-third of all Irish farmers were over sixty-five years old. Women accounted for one-sixth of all farmers; nearly half of these were over sixty-five and three-quarters were widows. None of this was conducive to innovation or the creation of a dynamic rural economy. At the same time, when new agricultural techniques were introduced, they tended to be labour-saving devices (tractors, milking machines, etc.) which reduced the demand for labour and thereby encouraged emigration. The number of jobs in Irish agriculture declined by 272,303 between 1926 and 1961, yet only 101,828 non-agricultural jobs were created in this period, for a net loss of 170,475. The worst losses were in the West and Northwest: Galway, Sligo, Leitrim and Donegal lost a combined total of 96,704 agricultural jobs but gained only 4,861 jobs in other sectors. These four counties alone accounted for half the national contraction in employment in the period 1926–61. Nor did Ireland have prosperous, expanding cities to absorb people displaced from the countryside. The urban population increased by only 5 per cent (a mere 46,000 people) from 1881 to 1926; in the same period, by contrast, the urban population of the United States increased 282 per cent, from 14 to 54 million people. While rural dwellers with some education might find opportunity in Dublin, the best option among the young was often to emigrate.[4]

Throughout the first half of the twentieth century, Ireland still had the highest rates of delayed marriage in Europe. Europeans were generally late-marrying (over 30 years old for men, over 26 for women), but Irish grooms (aged 33 on average) and brides (aged 28) were the oldest of all. The percentage of Irish people aged 25 to 34 who were single was by far the highest in Europe, and permanent celibacy was higher among Irish men than women, reversing the dominant trend in Northwest Europe. There appears to have been an inverse relation between rates of postponed marriage and rates of emigration in the first half of the twentieth century, with the proportion of the population that was single increasing as emigration fell.[5]

As the bulk of Irish emigration was deflected to Britain, the Irish proportion of total immigration to the United States fell accordingly, as did the numbers of first and second-generation Irish in the United States. The Irish accounted for just under 5 per cent of America's immigrants in the opening decades of the twentieth century, but for only 2.5 per cent in the 1920s, 1930s and 1940s. Thus, while one in two newcomers to America in the 1840s had been Irish-born, that figure had dropped to one in forty by 1920. There were 1,615,459 Irish-born people in the United States in 1900, down from the historical peak of 1,871,509 in 1890; by 1940 this figure had fallen to 572,031. The number of second-generation Irish Americans (native-born of Irish or mixed parentage) reached its peak at 3,375,546 in 1900 but had fallen to 1,838,920 by 1940. At the same time, of course, the ethnic group had expanded into the third and fourth generations and beyond, though in a way that usually defies standardized measurement.[6]

The American Irish in the first half of the twentieth century remained an overwhelmingly urban people. They also retained their preference for living in the Northeast and the Midwest. This preference was strongest among the Irish-born, an average of 69 per cent of whom lived in the Northeast and 19 per cent in the Central Region between 1900 and 1920, compared to only 8 per cent in the West and 4 per cent in the South.[7] Among Irish Americans born in the United States (the second generation and beyond) there was greater regional diversity, but an estimated two-thirds of them still lived in the Northeast and Midwest. Moreover, fully 80 per cent of all Irish Americans lived in urban areas in 1910, and 90 per cent by 1920, about twice the percentage for the American population as a whole. As the population of American cities rapidly expanded in the early twentieth century, however, the Irish-born share of the urban population decreased considerably. The 203,450 Irish-born residents of New York City in 1920, for example, accounted for only 4 per cent of the city's population, compared to 24 per cent in 1860 and 12 per cent in 1890. The 64,590 Irish-born residents of Philadelphia also accounted for 4 per cent of the city's population, down from 16 per cent in 1860 and 11 per cent in 1890. Boston's 57,011 Irish-born in 1920 made up 8 per cent of the city's population, compared to 26 per cent in 1860 and 16 per cent in 1890. In Chicago, the Irish share of the population (56,786) in 1920 had fallen to only 2 per cent, compared to 18 per cent in 1860 and 6 per cent in 1890. San Francisco's 18,257 Irish-born in 1920 accounted for 4 per cent of the city's population, compared to 16 per cent in 1860 and 10 per cent in 1890. The Irish-born proportion of cities like Pittsburgh, St Louis, Jersey City and Providence declined to a similar proportion. If the second and third generations are taken into account, of course, the Irish-American share of urban populations increases significantly, but by 1920 the Irish *immigrant* presence had clearly declined considerably.[8]

LABOUR

To understand the social position of the American Irish in the early twentieth century, it will be helpful to take a brief retrospective look at the late nineteenth century. In the 1880s and 1890s the number of American Irish confined to manual, unskilled jobs had begun to decline significantly. While the Irish-American occupational structure as late as 1880 had closely resembled that of the 1850s and 1860s, significant progress was made in the last two decades of the century. However, the period 1850–80 is the one that has been most intensively studied by historians, while the period 1880–1900 has yet to get the attention it deserves. This is unfortunate, as the earlier period was dominated by impoverished famine immigrants and culminated in a severe economic depression.[9]

During the last two decades of the nineteenth century, by contrast, both the first and the second generation of American Irish (the immigrants and their offspring) made significant social progress. By 1900, indeed, the Irish (both generations combined) had achieved rough occupational parity with the native-born, and greatly surpassed the 'new immigrants' from southern and eastern Europe. As a predominantly urban people, the American Irish were concentrated much more heavily than the national average in skilled and unskilled labour rather than in agriculture. But, allowing for this urban-rural divide, their occupational structure closely resembled the national average: while 65 per cent of American-Irish males worked in industry and transportation, only 15 per cent were unskilled manual labourers, most of them recent immigrants. About 6 per cent belonged to the middle class and 14 per cent to the lower middle class, while 15 per cent worked in agriculture. Only in New England, with its more rigidly stratified social structure and its long history of nativism, did the American Irish remain heavily concentrated in menial labour. But New England was home to fewer than one-fifth of all Irish Americans in 1900.[10]

Instead of being concentrated in menial labour, as they had been for much of the nineteenth century, the American Irish now worked disproportionately in the skilled trades. Most Irish-American workers were skilled rather than unskilled, and they were disproportionately concentrated in the best-paid and most highly unionized trades. While Irish Americans in 1900 accounted for only 7.5 per cent (one-thirteenth) of the total male workforce in the United States, they provided one-sixth of all teamsters, metal workers and masons; one-fifth of stone cutters, leather tanners, wire-workers, brass-workers, skilled textile workers, paper mill workers, roofers and street rail workers; and almost one-third of all plumbers, steam fitters and boiler-makers. In addition, they exceeded their proportion in almost every other form of skilled and semi-skilled urban employment, providing about 10 per cent of all electricians, miners, glass-blowers and blacksmiths, and one-eighth of machinists, railroad-men, and printers.[11]

Largely because of the arrival of the 'new' immigrants, the Irish were now less concentrated in manual labour than they had been; but many Irish-Americans, especially recent immigrants, continued to work in unskilled labour and rates of social mobility varied widely from region to region. In heavy industries like iron, steel and mining, Irish Americans now dominated blue-collar managerial posts, while the heaviest, lowest-paid labour was done by newly arrived Slavs, Hungarians and Italians. Even as late as 1900, how-ever, 25 per cent of Irish-born males and 17 per cent of American-born Irish males still worked in unskilled, poorly paid and usually non-unionized jobs, and Irish Americans accounted for a disproportionately high percentage (11 per cent) of the nation's casual labourers. Irish economic progress was greatest in the Midwest and Far West, considerable in the dynamic economies of Pennsylvania and New York, and least in the relatively static and socially stratified states of New England.[12]

As for Irish-American women, those who were native-born tended to avoid domestic service for work as secretaries, stenographers, nurses or schoolteachers. In the first decade of the twentieth century, daughters of Irish-born parents made up the largest group of schoolteachers in New York City, over 2,000 out of a total female teaching population of 7,000. Similar patterns were evident in cities throughout the Northeast, and in Chicago and San Francisco. In 1908, to take one example, American-born daughters of Irish parents made up 26.2 per cent of all teachers in Buffalo, 26.4 per cent in Fall River, 49.6 per cent in Worcester, 29.9 per cent in Lowell, 24 per cent in Providence, 38 per cent in Scranton and 15.5 per cent in New Orleans. Immigrant women, however, did less well than the native-born, with a sub-stantial majority of Irish-born females still working either as servants or in textile factories and sweatshops in the early twentieth century. In 1900, 54 per cent of Irish-born women in the American labour force were house ser-vants (compared to only 19 per cent of the second generation Irish), 6.5 per cent were laundresses and most of the remainder worked in industry.[13]

The case of Mary Mallon, the notorious 'Typhoid Mary' of New York City, offers some insights into the position of working-class Irish immigrant women in the United States at the turn of the century. Born in County Tyrone in 1869, Mallon came to the United States at the age of fifteen and, after living briefly with an aunt and uncle, made her own way as a cook in a series of well-to-do households. In 1906 she was working for a rich banker, Charles Henry Warren, at his summer house on Long Island when typhoid fever struck six of the eleven people in the household. Investigators hired by Warren determined that Mary Mallon was the source, but she had already left Warren's employment by this time. She was traced in March 1907 to the home of Walter Bowen in Park Avenue, where she was the cook. After samples of her urine, feces and blood were taken, she was forcibly removed to a hospital, where tests revealed her to be a carrier of high concentrations of typhoid bacilli. Mary Mallon was perfectly healthy herself, but she was capable of spreading the disease to others. While she was only one of probably hundreds of carriers of the disease in New York City at this time, she had the misfortune to be the first healthy carrier tracked down by officials. Mallon was removed to a hospital in Manhattan's East River and, although health officials had no clear legal right to detain her, she was kept there for the next three years. Not all healthy carriers of typhoid were treated in this way; but Mary Mallon was an Irish immigrant, a servant and a single woman, and hence more vulnerable than most.[14]

Mallon was set free in 1910, on condition that she avoided preparing or cooking of food for others. After labouring in a laundry for some time, she disappeared from view, only to resurface in 1915 when typhoid struck at Sloane Maternity Hospital in New York City, affecting twenty-five doctors, nurses and other staff. After two of the afflicted died, the outbreak was traced to a human carrier, a cook named Mrs Brown, who had been working there for three months. Mrs Brown, it emerged, was none other than Mary Mallon who, once the fraud had been exposed, was demonized in the popular imagination as 'Typhoid Mary', a metaphor for contagion and the deliberate spreading of disease, by immigrants generally and the Irish in particular. She was sent back to the hospital on the East River, where she lived alone in a one-room cottage until her death in 1938, insisting to the last that she was a healthy woman who had never transmitted typhoid fever to anybody. On this point she was clearly wrong, just as she was culpable in returning to food preparation after the first outbreak. But the power and resonance of the image of 'Typhoid Mary' in popular culture in the early twentieth century makes sense only if it is remembered that she was a single, working-class, female immigrant as well as a carrier of infectious disease.[15]

Mary Mallon was but one among hundreds of thousands of Irish immigrants trying to make a living in the United States in the early twentieth century. The American Irish by this time had come to dominate the trade union movement of the United States, shaking off most of their nineteenth-century reputation for violence and replacing it with an image of moderation and respectability. The American Irish played a disproportionately large role in the American labour movement at this time, providing more than eighty long-term labour leaders in over fifty prominent unions between 1890 and 1914. Even in trades where they accounted for only a small minority of the workforce, Irish Americans often dominated the union leadership, for example in the Carpenters and Joiners, Brewery Workers and Meat Cutters. 'Numerically,' as one historian puts it, 'the Irish dominated few trades, but politically they dominated a majority.'[16]

While these unions were mainly concerned with 'bread and butter' issues of better wages and conditions, some Irish-American activists continued the tradition of radicalism pioneered by Patrick Ford in the 1880s. That tradition had been carried on in the following decade by men like Hugh O'Donnell, who led the striking steel workers of Homestead, Pennsylvania against the Pinkertons in 1892, and by Sylvester Kelleher, who worked with the socialist leader Eugene V. Debs on the American Railroad Union. The old association of Irish-American workers with violence did re-emerge in the early twentieth century when the MacNamara brothers of the Union of Bridge and Structural Iron Workers allegedly blew up eighty-seven buildings between 1905 and 1911, culminating in the notorious destruction of the offices of the *Los Angeles Times*, with twenty-one fatalities. Many Irish Americans were also involved in the radical anarcho-syndicalist organization, Industrial Workers of the World (IWW), which was founded in 1905 and was widely, if rather hysterically, accused of sustained violence and industrial sabotage throughout the following decade.[17]

Perhaps the best-known Irish radicals involved in American labour circles in the early twentieth century were James Connolly and James Larkin. Born in Edinburgh, Scotland of Irish parents in 1868, Connolly moved to Dublin in 1896, where he founded the Irish Socialist Republican Party. He came to New York in 1902 where he published the *Harp*, established the Irish Socialist Federation and co-founded the Industrial Workers of the World (IWW), before returning to Ireland in 1910. The author of the classic *Labour in Irish History* (1910) and several other works, Connolly formulated a unique synthesis of socialism, republican nationalism and Catholicism, bringing his own Citizen Army to fight in the Dublin insurrection of 1916 in hopes of turning it into a social revolution as well as a nationalist one. A signatory of the Irish Declaration of Independence and a commander of the republican forces in the insurrection, he was executed by the British in the aftermath of the uprising. James 'Big Jim' Larkin (1876–1947) was even more prominent in American labour circles. Born in Liverpool of Irish parents, he organized a series of famous strikes in Belfast and Dublin between 1907 and 1913, before moving to the United States, where he was active in radical causes until his return to Ireland in 1923, devoting much of his energies to the IWW and to the American Communist party, which he helped found in the wake of the Bolshevik revolution of 1917.[18]

While some Irish-American trade unionists, such as John J. Murphy of Central Labor Union in Philadelphia, also pursued a radical course, most Irish labour leaders in the early twentieth century were known for their conservatism. By 1900 Irish immigrants or their descendants held the presidencies of over 50 of the 110 unions in the American Federation of Labor (AFL), the most powerful but also one of the most conservative labour organizations in the country. The typical Irish-American labour activist was not an immigrant from the Irish countryside but a second or third-generation American who had been raised in an industrial town or city. The AFL concentrated on winning better wages and conditions for its members, most of them highly skilled workers. These workers were mainly white, male and of northwest European descent; blacks, women and the 'new immigrants' from southern and eastern Europe were largely excluded from this narrow and restrictive labour movement. Concerned with 'bread and butter' issues, and confined to a skilled elite, the AFL deliberately avoided programs for systematic social reform, let alone revolutionary change.[19]

Irish Americans headed some of the most influential unions within the AFL. Among the most prominent were James O'Connell of the Machinists; Timothy Healy, leader of the International Brotherhood of Stationary Firemen; Frank Duffy and P.J. McGuire of the Carpenters; and James Lynch of the Typographers. McGuire, an erstwhile socialist who had been instrumental in the creation of America's Labor Day, abandoned his earlier radicalism and cooperated with the leader of the AFL, Samuel Gompers, in creating a socially conservative, job-conscious union. Irish-American labour leaders also played an active role in assisting Gompers in his campaign against socialism within the AFL. John Mitchell, the leader of the powerful United Mine Workers of America, formed a special group, the Militia of Christ for Social

Service, to coordinate anti-socialist policies in the labour movement and to gain the support of the Catholic Church. Irish-American unionists like John Hynes of the Sheet Metal Workers and Dan Tobin of the Teamsters also joined Gompers in withdrawing the AFL from the new International Federation of Trade Unions in 1919, on the grounds that involvement in international solidarity could only distract the AFL from its purpose of safeguarding its members' material interests.[20]

By the early twentieth century, Irish-American women as well as men were playing a prominent role in the American labour movement. Leonora O'Reilly (1870–1926), the daughter of the Irish-born labour activist Winifred O'Reilly, was appointed to the board of the National Women's Trade Union League (WTUL) when it was founded in 1903. Mary Kenny O'Sullivan, who had been the first female organizer of the Knights of Labor in the 1880s, established the New York chapter of the WTUL. Agnes Nestor was elected president of the International Glove Workers Union, while Julia O'Connor was chosen to head the telephone operators' department of the International Brotherhood of Electrical Workers in 1912. Cork-born Mary Harris Jones (c.1830–1930), known as 'Mother Jones', was one of the foremost labour activists in the United States. Jailed frequently, she devoted most of her life to helping impoverished and exploited workers, and was particularly active among coal miners. In 1905 she helped found the IWW, where she was joined by Irish-American activist Elizabeth Gurley Flynn (1890–1964). The organization was headed by William 'Big Bill' Haywood (1869–1928), who was also of Irish descent.[21]

The labour struggles of the early twentieth century sometimes involved a generational conflict between established Irish immigrants and the newest arrivals. This was certainly the case in Butte, Montana, the rather unlikely venue for 'the most Irish town in the United States' at this time. In 1900, the first and second generation Irish numbered over 8,000 in a total population of just over 30,000. Thus, in this city fully 2,500 miles away from the nearest eastern seaport, 26 per cent of the residents were either Irish-born or the children of Irish-born. Butte was the largest and most productive copper-mining town in the world. It was settled from the beginning by Irish immigrants, a clear majority of whom came from the western portion of County Cork, where copper was also mined. Working in close cooperation with the legendary Irish-born 'copper king', Marcus Daly, the first generation of immigrants organized themselves in the socially conservative Butte Miners' Union, which emphasized job security, company stock options, the prerogatives of skilled mine workers over the unskilled and the exclusion of 'new immigrants'. The BMU never once launched a strike or work stoppage in its thirty-six-year history.[22]

From the turn of the century onward, however, the BMU faced a mounting challenge from radicals in the IWW and the Western Federation of Miners (WFM). The WFM was led by Donegal-born Ed Boyce, who moved its headquarters from Butte to Denver to escape the BMU. There followed a wave of strikes and labour violence in Butte, in which recent Irish immigrants played a prominent part. The immigrants now came from all over Ireland, supplanting the dominance of the Corkmen who had long constituted a powerful regional enclave within the Irish-American community in Butte. Whereas the older immigrants had been concentrated in mining, the newer ones favoured heavy industry. Differences in cultural background and work experience translated into radically different understandings of labour and social justice. In the words of one historian, 'By 1910 some Irish immigrant workers had been in Butte for thirty years; others for thirty days. To assume that they shared either ethnic or class interests is folly. They arose from and occupied different and mutually hostile worlds.' Shunning existing ethnic institutions like the Ancient Order of Hibernians and the Robert Emmet Literary Association, these 'new' Irish founded their own Pearse-Connolly Independence Club (named after the two most influential leaders of the 1916 rebellion in Ireland), sharing meeting space with the IWW and other radical groups. They were supported in their efforts by Irish socialist Con Lehane, who visited Butte in 1916, and by Jim Larkin, who visited three times between 1915 and 1917. The causes of Irish liberation and social justice in America were inextricably linked, Larkin insisted, echoing James Connolly and Patrick Ford.[23]

After the turbulent opening decades of the twentieth century, when radical movements attained an influence rarely seen before or since in American history, the American Irish continued to play a prominent role in the labour movement. William Z. Foster, the son of immigrants from County Carlow, launched his career in 1919 when he and fellow Irish-American John Fitzpatrick helped organize a great national steel strike. He later became involved in the recently formed Communist Party of America. Mike Quill (1905–66), a former member of the IRA in Ireland, helped establish the powerful Transport Workers Union of America in 1934 and became its first president. Joe Curran, born in 1906 to an impoverished Irish family on New York's East Side, organized the sailors of the East Coast in the 1930s and became the first president of the National Maritime Union in 1937. When the Congress of Industrial Workers (CIO) broke away from the conservative

American Federation of Labor (AFL) in 1936 to organize all workers, not just the skilled elite, its leaders included Irish Americans John Brophy, James B. Carey and Mike Quill. The two most powerful Irish-American labour organizers thereafter were Philip Murray (1886–1952), son of an Irish-born labourer, and William George Meany (1894–1979), the grandson of a famine refugee. As president of the CIO, Murray helped pave the way for its merger with the AFL in 1955. Meany was appointed president of the combined AFL-CIO, and exercised an important influence on American politics. Irish-American influence in the U.S. labour movement was reaching its peak.[24]

NATIONALISM

In the opening two decades of the twentieth century Irish-American nationalism assumed a more powerful and influential form than ever before or since. Americans of Irish descent played an unprecedented role in the affairs of Ireland, making a significant contribution to Ireland's achievement of *de facto* independence by the 1920s. During this decisive period in Irish-American nationalism, the traditional tension between hard-line, physical-force republicanism and gradual, constitutional reform (Home Rule) was a central theme, though the third component of the nationalist struggle, social justice, never regained the prominence it had attained in the 1880s.

Radical nationalists in the 1880s had lamented the existence of class inequality and monopoly, had clashed frequently with conservatives in the Roman Catholic hierarchy and had adopted an egalitarian attitude toward women's rights and women's participation in the nationalist movement. Their ideology had accorded well with the wider American radical tradition emanating from abolitionism, feminism and the labour movement. Conservatives in the 1880s, by contrast, had tended to favour the status quo on questions of class, gender and religion. On these matters, at least, moderate constitutional nationalists of the Parnellite persuasion found common ground with the hard-line republican extremists ranged behind John Devoy. The goals and strategies of these two rival groups — constitutional autonomy through peaceful, legal change versus outright independence by whatever means necessary — could scarcely have been more different. But they had shared a strong antipathy toward social radicalism, in the first case because it threatened the middle-class security of the constitutionalist leaders, and in the second because it was seen as a mere diversion from the single important goal of national independence.[25]

By the mid-1880s, the conservative constitutionalists had fended off the challenge of social reformers and hard-line republicans alike. Yet constitutional nationalism, on both sides of the Atlantic, had gone into serious decline since the rejection of Home Rule by the British parliament and the death in 1891 of Charles Stewart Parnell. With the constitutionalists in disarray, the nationalist movement had been kept alive in America by a small cadre of militant activists led by John Devoy, waiting patiently to test the validity of their belief that 'England's difficulty is Ireland's opportunity'. In other words, should England become involved in war, that would be the best time for Ireland to launch an insurrection. The long-awaited opportunity finally came in 1916.[26]

In the meantime, however, constitutional nationalists on both sides of the Atlantic reorganized themselves, under the leadership of John Redmond (1856–1918), who reunited the various factions within the Irish Parliamentary Party (IPP) at the turn of the century. Redmond visited the United States in 1901, where he helped found the United Irish League of America (UILA), which claimed some 200 branches within a year of its foundation, dedicated to raising funds and generating public support for the cause of Home Rule in Ireland. Like his predecessor Parnell, Redmond deliberately blurred the distinction between his own moderate constitutionalist position and full-fledged republicanism, thereby generating further support in America. The UILA was supported by the *Irish World* and its editor Patrick Ford, who had abandoned his earlier radicalism and now lined up consistently behind the Catholic Church he had once criticized, as well as endorsing a variety of anti-Semitic conspiracy theories (a distorted version of his old attacks on monopoly and international capital). The UILA, composed mostly of Irish Americans of high social standing and often considerable wealth, outspokenly opposed socialism and other radical movements. And, while women did play an active role in the UILA from the beginning, the IPP in Dublin was strongly critical of women's suffrage. In short, the exclusive goal of constitutionalists on both sides of the Atlantic was the restoration of an autonomous Irish parliament, and they rejected both the call for social revolution inherent in the radical position of the 1880s and the demands for full independence issued by physical-force republicans.[27]

Like the constitutionalists, the physical-force republicans were reunited at the turn of the century. One important center of Irish-American republicanism in the early twentieth century was the American Order of Hibernians (AOH), but the most influential was a rejuvenated Clan na Gael. The Clan had split into factions in the 1880s and been discredited with large sectors of the American public by the dynamite campaigns launched in England in the 1880s. In 1900 its factions were brought together again under the leadership of John Devoy and Daniel Cohalan of New York City, and Joseph McGarrity of Philadelphia. Using Devoy's newspaper, *Gaelic American*, the Clan attacked the IPP and UILA and their objective of Home Rule, calling instead for a fully independent republic in Ireland, to be achieved through physical force if necessary. The Clan retained the largely working-class support that had been its basis in the late nineteenth century, yet it was no more interested in advancing the cause of social reform than the UILA was. For John Devoy, social reform could only represent a dilution of the cause to which he dedic-ated his long political life, an independent Irish republic. Moreover, in sharp contrast to the often militantly secular Young Irelanders and Fenians of the mid-nineteenth century and the radicals of the 1880s, the republicans of the early twentieth century were anything but anti-clerical. And on questions of gender, they were typically even more conservative than their constitutional-ist counterparts. The old radical traditions of Irish nationalism in the nine-teenth century, in short, played only a peripheral part in the nationalist movements of the early twentieth century.[28]

The great turning point in the nationalist history of the Irish on both sides of the Atlantic came in 1916. Taking advantage of England's involvement in the First World War, a small but highly determined group of hard-line Irish republicans decided to launch a rebellion, knowing that they would almost certainly sacrifice their own lives but hoping that in so doing they might galvanize the Irish people in support of the republican cause. It was to be a revolution of poets and mystics, shot through with ideas of blood sacrifice and redemption, and timed accordingly for Easter weekend. It was a desperate gamble; and, remarkably, it paid off, largely because the British execution of the rebels outraged a previously indifferent population. Before 1916, the majority of the Irish population in both Ireland and America had supported John Redmond and his crusade for Home Rule rather than the more militant demands of the hard-line republicans. Home Rule even went on the statute books in 1914, only to be postponed for the duration of the First World War. Redmond's moment of greatest triumph was swallowed up in the bloody trenches of Europe, and by the time he died in 1918 his political party was in a shambles. The cause of constitutional nationalism was reduced to the margins of Irish political life, replaced by a vibrant republican tradition which now had the support of the majority of the Irish people on both sides of the Atlantic.[29]

Much of the impetus for the 1916 rebellion had originated in the United States. Some of the leading proponents of Irish physical-force nationalism anywhere in the world were to be found in New York City in the late nine-teenth and early twentieth centuries. The most important organization in this respect was Clan na Gael, which maintained close links with the Irish Republican Brotherhood (IRB) in Dublin. Based in New York City, the Clan was involved in the planning of the insurrection of 1916, and acted as the main link between the rebels and the German government, whom it suc-cessfully asked for arms and ammunition in 1916. Leaders of the Clan and the AOH had fostered close relations with German Americans over the pre-vious decade in anticipation of conflict with Great Britain, and during the war Devoy published pro-German material in his newspaper, *Gaelic American*. The Clan also funded the visit by the Irish nationalist Sir Roger Casement to Germany in order to liaise with the German leadership and to try to raise an Irish brigade from prisoners of war (there being some 154,000 Irishmen serving in the British Army during the war). 'Clearly', as one historian con-cludes, 'the Clan played an important role in providing money, support and, if not leadership, then at least inspiration to the IRB to go ahead with the insurrection'.[30]

Irish-American involvement in the events of 1916 was therefore quite considerable. A remarkable number of the leaders and key participants in the insurrection had lived or travelled in the United States. Thomas J. Clarke and James Connolly had both lived and worked there, while John MacBride and his wife Maud Gonne MacBride, Francis Sheehy-Skeffington, Joseph Plunkett and Sir Roger Casement, had all made tours of one kind or another in the United States. Eamon de Valera, who went on to become the dominant figure in Irish politics for half a century until his death in 1975, escaped execution after the insurrection on the grounds of his dual British-American citizen-ship, having been born to an Irish mother and a Spanish father in New York City in 1882. Another participant, Diarmuid Lynch, also laid claim to Amer-ican citizenship. The experience of these individuals in the United States, combined with the material and political support of Irish Americans, account for the significant phrase in the proclamation issued by the new provisional government of Ireland on Easter Monday 1916, which declared that Ireland had risen up in rebellion 'supported by her exiled children in America'.[31]

In the wake of the insurrection and executions, Irish-American national-ism became a mass movement for the first time since the 1880s. News of the Easter Rebellion all but destroyed what remained of the UILA, as Irish Americans united almost unanimously behind the physical-force tradition. Clan na Gael sponsored an Irish Race Convention, which met in New York City in 1916 and out of it emerged the Friends of Irish Freedom (FOIF), which claimed more than 275,000 members at its peak in 1919. Between 1916 and 1921 Irish Americans raised an estimated $10 million in support of Irish independence. Also active in Irish-American nationalist circles at this time was the left-leaning Irish Progressive League which, much like James Connolly in Ireland, sought to inject a social-revolutionary content into the struggle for Irish freedom, though to no avail. If social radicalism was largely in abeyance, however, republican extremism was resurgent, so much so that the more outspoken Irish-American republicans became targets of government suspicion after the United States entered the First World War as an ally of Great Britain. Both John Devoy's *Gaelic American* and Jeremiah O'Leary's *Bull* were banned from the mails under the Espionage, Sabotage and Sedition Acts of 1917–18 for their militant denunciations of Britain. But, although the American Irish were only in the process of emerging into full respectability at this time, they never faced the types of popular persecution endured by German Americans during the war. With the massive victory of the republican political party, Sinn Féin, in the Irish general election of 1918, accompanied by the triumph of the hard-line position of Clan na Gael and FOIF in the United States, physical-force republicanism assumed the dimensions of a mass, popular movement on both sides of the Atlantic.[32]

When the war in Europe ended late in 1918, FOIF pressed the case for Irish independence as part of the postwar settlement. No sooner had the armistice been declared in November than FOIF proclaimed the second week in December 'Irish Self-Determination Week'. Mass meetings and demonstrations were held throughout the United States in support of Irish freedom. Another Irish Race Convention met in Philadelphia on 22 and 23 February 1919, demanding recognition of the right of Ireland to form a government of its own. Eighty-five-year-old Cardinal Gibbons of Baltimore, the revered Irish leader of the American Catholic Church, addressed the convention, calling for national self-determination for Ireland, and a delegation was appointed to meet with President Wilson in New York in March to press him to intervene on Ireland's behalf at the Peace Conference. The meeting drew little response from Wilson, and the delegation then chose three of its number to go to the Peace Conference in Paris under the title of the American Commission on Irish Independence to apply direct pressure. Petitions arrived at the White House from Irish groups all over the United States and from as far away as Australia and Argentina. In June 1919 the Senate passed a resolution requesting the American diplomats to secure a hearing for the Irish delegation before the Peace Conference. Wilson, however, simply forwarded the resolution without comment to the conference chairman,

Georges Clemenceau, and nothing more was heard of it. When the treaty that eventually emerged from the negotiations in Versailles made no mention of Ireland, Irish Americans lobbied actively against it in Senate hearings and in meetings and demonstrations nationwide. That Woodrow Wilson was proudly conscious of his own Ulster Presbyterian background and held a correspondingly low opinion of Irish Catholics served to heighten still further the existing tension between him and the nationalists. The FOIF distributed 1,300,000 pamphlets, took out numerous newspaper advertisements, and issued full-page rebuttals of the President's speeches in favour of the League of Nations as he toured the country. Their well-publicized hostility to the treaty contributed to the rising tide of disillusionment with the treaty and its eventual defeat in November 1919.[33]

Among the most outspoken opponents of Irish-American nationalism at this time were the Scotch-Irish. Though immigration from Ulster declined rapidly after 1900, Scotch-Irish identity survived through a variety of cultural institutions, especially in New York and Pennsylvania. The Orange Order continued to flourish, and many Scotch-Irish Americans expressed their solidarity with the Protestants of Ulster in their opposition to Home Rule. When the Home Rule Act finally passed in 1914, the Scotch-Irish in the United States actively sympathized with Ulster's fierce opposition to the measure. Irish-American demands for an independent and united Ireland after 1916, similarly, provoked a vigorous Scotch-Irish reaction, as organizations like the Loyal Orange Order exerted themselves to refute the arguments of Daniel F. Cohalan's Friends of Irish Freedom. After the Order's Twelfth of July parade in New York City in 1919, a meeting was held to draw up resolutions for transmission to Senator Henry Cabot Lodge, chairman of the Senate Foreign Relations Committee, which was then conducting hearings on the Treaty of Versailles. The resolutions protested the committee's granting of a hearing to representatives from the self-styled Irish Republic, accused Irish republicans of conspiring with Germany during the First World War, and denied that Ireland had any cause for independence. Scotch-Irish agitation against Irish independence tapered off quickly after the creation of a self-governing state of Northern Ireland within the Union.[34]

Within the nationalist ranks, serious differences soon emerged between republicans based in Ireland and their Irish-American counterparts. The preeminent Irish republican leader, Eamon de Valera, escaped from a British prison in February 1919, made his way to Ireland where he was elected president of Dáil Eireann (the parliament of the *de facto* Irish republic), and then left for the United States, where he would spend the next eighteen months and raise over $5 million in bond certificates to fund the new Irish republic (though only about half that figure ever reached Ireland). After meeting with Devoy, Cohalan and other hard-liners, de Valera issued a press statement declaring the Irish republican government to be the only lawful government of Ireland. Ireland, he declared, did not need to be granted the right of self-determination by any council of international powers; it already possessed that right and had exercised it in the insurrection of 1916 and again in the election of 1918. Devoy and especially Cohalan, on the other hand, insisted that Ireland's right to self-determination needed formal international recognition to be meaningful, and were very angry at Woodrow Wilson for ignoring this demand.

De Valera increasingly came to regard Cohalan's obsession with American and international politics as a digression from the path necessary for the attainment of Irish independence. Irish Americans, he believed, should stop devoting their time and money to opposing the Versailles treaty, and should concentrate instead on directly helping Ireland in its war of independence against the British. To secure control over American funds, and to redirect the impetus of Irish-American nationalism, de Valera decided in the summer of 1920 to bypass the FOIF and, with the help of dissident Irish-American republican Joseph McGarrity, set up his own organization, the American Association for the Recognition of the Irish Republic (AARIR). This organization rapidly eclipsed the FOIF, claiming some 800,000 members at its height in 1921. The bitter dispute between de Valera and Cohalan culminated in the summer of 1920, when each side sent a rival delegation to the Republican convention in Chicago. The convention took advantage of these divisions by deciding to ignore Ireland altogether in its platform. Later that year, the Democrats did the same. Only against this background of conflict between de Valera and Irish-American republicans is it possible to understand why Cohalan and Devoy, ostensibly arch-republicans, threw their support behind Michael Collins (1890–1922) and the pro-treaty forces, and against de Valera and his hard-line republican allies, when civil war broke out in the newly created Irish Free State in 1922.[35]

The Irish Civil War was fought over the question of sovereignty and not, as is sometimes assumed, over Ulster. In 1920, Ireland had been partitioned into two unequal parts: the twenty-six counties of the Republic and the six northeastern counties of Armagh, Down, Antrim, Derry, Tyrone and Fermanagh. That these six counties of Northern Ireland would remain part of the United Kingdom was never a contested issue in the negotiations in 1921 for a treaty to end the Anglo-Irish war. By that time, the creation of a separate Northern Ireland was a foregone conclusion. Instead, the sticking point was the sovereignty of the remaining twenty-six counties. Would this part of Ireland constitute a republic, as the men of 1916 had declared? Or would it retain some loose allegiance to the British Empire, such that its government members would be required to swear a formal oath of allegiance to the British crown? When Michael Collins, the architect of the Irish Republican Army (IRA) and the chief negotiator on the Irish side, returned to Dublin with a treaty providing for the latter rather than the former, he announced pragmatically that it had given Ireland the 'freedom to achieve freedom'. Rejecting the treaty, he warned, might lead to a British invasion. But de Valera and his republican followers rejected the treaty on principle and a brief but nasty civil war ensued (April 1922 to April 1923), resulting in victory for the pro-treaty forces.

Only a small minority of diehard Irish Americans opposed the treaty. But many embittered republican exiles made their way from Ireland to America, where they tried to keep their militant tradition alive in exile. Joseph McGarrity, who had sided with de Valera in the internecine quarrels with John Devoy and Daniel Cohalan, continued to support the hard-line republican side in the 1920s and 1930s, even as de Valera reentered the mainstream of Irish constitutional politics and assumed control of the Irish government. McGarrity was born in County Tyrone, in the heart of Ulster, in 1874 and had emigrated to the United States at the turn of the century. He settled in Philadelphia, where he made a fortune in business. During the Anglo-Irish War and the Irish Civil War, he supplied money and munitions to the IRA, and in the 1930s he joined Irish militants in supporting a bombing campaign in English cities to demand a united, thirty-two county Irish republic. In response to this campaign, de Valera outlawed the IRA and imprisoned many of its leaders, reneging on the last of his hard-line republican principles and abandoning his erstwhile ally Joseph McGarrity. But if McGarrity expected popular support among the majority of Irish Americans he was to be disappointed. The bombing campaign proved very unpopular with the American Irish and had very few supporters outside McGarrity's circle. Not until the 1960s would the physical-force tradition re-surface as a major force in Irish and Irish-American nationalism.[36]

ALCOHOL AND CULTURE

The general profile of the Irish-American community in the early twentieth century is somewhat contradictory. On the one hand, the American Irish had achieved occupational and educational parity with the population as a whole. In the decade 1910–20, according to one historian, Catholic Irish Americans for the first time exceeded the national average in college attendance and graduation, and in professional and white-collar careers. Americans of Irish Protestant descent, it should be noted, were at this time close to the national average on these measures, and above average in white-collar careers, though they would decline in both categories thereafter, even as Irish-American Catholics continued to prosper. On the other hand, Irish immigrants were still reported to have very high rates of pauperism in the early twentieth century. According to one US government report in 1901 the Irish had more inmates in all penal and charitable institutions than any other immigrant group in the country. And in 1910 a sociological study found that the Irish-born accounted for by far the largest number of paupers in the country (1,048.5 per 100,000), more than twice the rate for the next immigrant group, the Swiss.[37]

Rates of alcoholism among the American Irish, both first and second-generation, were also demonstrably higher than for all other Americans in the early twentieth century. One study of admissions to the Worcester, Massachusetts State Hospital in 1900 discovered the following percentages of alcoholic cases among the total male admissions for each ethnic group: Irish, 37; German, English and Scottish, 20–25; Massachusetts-born, 14; and Jewish, 5. A study by the same author of admissions to Manhattan State Hospital, New York in 1908 showed Americans of Irish descent again well to the front for alcoholism with 27.7 per cent, whereas those of German, native-born and English descent had rates of only 11.4 to 11.9 per cent, Italians 7.7 per cent and Jews 3 per cent. For the entire United States (except Montana) in 1920, the rate of alcoholism (measured by 'alcoholic first admissions' to state hospitals, i.e. alcoholic psychoses, paranoid states, hallucinosis) was computed as follows: Irish 17.1 per cent, Austrian 14.0, Canadian 7.6, Polish 6.3, Scotch 6.0, all other foreign-born 5.8. Standardized tests for alcoholic psychosis per 100,000 population in New York state mental hospitals in the period 1929–31 revealed a figure as high as 30.5 per cent (males 50.1, females 11.0) for the Irish, with only 7.9 for Scandinavians, 4.8 for English, 4.6 for native-born whites of white parentage, 4.3 for Italians and 3.8 for Germans.[38]

The susceptibility of the Irish on both sides of the Atlantic to alcohol abuse and alcoholism is well known, but scholars have yet to offer an adequate explanation. Historians and others who have researched the subject agree that the American Irish did not, and do not, drink significantly more than other Americans. Why, then, have the Irish suffered higher rates of alcohol addiction and alcohol-related illnesses? Some historians have argued that the negative stereotype of the violent Irish drunk – and its positive counterpart, the happy-go-lucky Irish drunk – have been imposed by the dominant Anglo culture on either side of the Atlantic. This thesis is certainly valid up to a point, but it cannot really be proved or disproved, and it ultimately fails to confront the brute fact that the American Irish did suffer from remarkably high levels alcoholism.

It is very difficult to explain why this was so, but the one historian who has tackled the question at length has placed Irish-American drinking squarely in the context of the formation of a new ethnic identity in the United States. Heavy drinking outside the home, he finds, was already common in Ireland and became more so in the United States. Public drinking, especially among males, was central to becoming Irish-American; the more one drank, and was seen to drink, the more Irish one became. Irish-American manhood, in particular, came to be associated with heavy drinking, as distinct from drunkenness; a man who could hold his liquor was truly a man, and truly Irish. All-male drinking was the norm, an expression of pride in ethnicity. But, even though rates of alcoholism were much higher for males than for females, Irish women also appear to have drunk more in America than in Ireland. Drinking was ultimately a component of Irish, not just masculine, identity. From the fact of Irish drinking emerged the stereotype of the Irish drunk, violent or comic, epitomized by the 'stage Irishman' of popular theater. In a process as circular as it was culturally effective, this argument concludes, Irish immigrants assimilated as Americans by conforming to that stereotype and adopting the ethnic identity of Irish drinker. There may well be something to this line of inquiry, though as it stands it seems rather stilted and artificial as an explanation of any social activity, let alone one so convivial as drinking. The historical experience of colonization and displacement might yield a more plausible explanation but is notoriously difficult to document in its particulars.[39]

One profitable line of inquiry would be to examine the distinctive Irish style of drinking, and the central role of alcohol in the definition of Irish-American ethnic identity, in comparative perspective with other ethnic groups. Italian Americans, for example, apparently consumed about as much alcohol as the Irish, but without succumbing to illness. The difference between the Irish and the Italians lay, as it continues to lie, in the style and purpose of their drinking. The Italians drank wine with their food, and indeed treated the wine as a food, rarely if ever consuming alcohol away from the dinner table. The Irish drank beer and whiskey, usually on its own rather than with food; and Irish men liked to drink in public places, preferably in all-male groups. Irish-American women drank too, but less publicly. The most salient attribute of the Irish, it appears, is not that they drink more than others but that they drink differently. But even this approach, it should be noted, can offer at best only a partial answer to why roughly the same alcohol intake led to illness in some ethnic groups but not in others. This question demands, but perhaps ultimately defies, thorough historical investigation.[40]

The character of the hard-drinking, if harmless, comic Irishman was one of the most pervasive in American popular culture from the mid-nineteenth century onwards. As early as the 1850s, Irish farces had become a staple of the American theater, generating the pervasive character of the 'stage Irishman', slow-witted but endearing, blundering his way through an impossibly convoluted plot. The most popular Irish-American playwrights of the late nineteenth century had been Dion Boucicault (1820–1920) and the team of Edward Harrigan (1844–1911) and Anthony Hart (1855–1891), whose popular and humorous 'Mulligan Series' contributed to the development of the American musical. The dim-witted comic Irishman gradually faded from the American stage in the early twentieth century, but continued to flourish in the movies for a generation thereafter, with actors like Barry Fitzgerald specializing in the comic role of the hard-drinking 'Mick' or 'Paddy'.

A whiskey bottle, it has been observed, is the most important object in the room for the entire family throughout Eugene O'Neill's masterpiece, *Long Day's Journey into Night*. The dominant figure in twentieth-century American theater, O'Neill (1888–1953) was the son of an Irish immigrant who had fled the famine in 1846 and prospered as an actor in the United States. In 1936, he became the first and only American dramatist to win the Nobel Prize. Surveying the state of American theater in the second decade of the twentieth century, O'Neill was appalled by the comic tradition of 'stage' Irishmen and Irish 'bulls' (logical blunders) that had been in place since the late nineteenth century. Equally opposed to the prevailing 'Pat 'n' Mike' stereotype was the Ancient Order of Hibernians (AOH). But O'Neill's stern realism entailed a harsh portrait of the American Irish which could find few supporters in the nationalist AOH, whose cultural moralism and ethnic chauvinism he found repugnant. This chauvinism was manifested most unpleasantly in 1911 when members and supporters of the AOH, accompanied by Irish nationalists led by John Devoy, rioted against John Millington Synge's drama, *The Playboy of the Western World*, when it was brought to America by W.B. Yeats's Abbey Theatre players.

(The play had also faced riots and demonstrations when it was staged in Dublin in 1907.) Devoy condemned the play as a 'vile libel on Irish womanhood and a gross misrepresentation of their religious feelings'. O'Neill, repulsed equally by the stereotypical 'stage' Irishman and the puritanism of Irish-American cultural nationalists, set out to re-invent Irish-American theater.[41]

O'Neill drew most of his themes from his own life: his childhood, his alcoholism, his tortured relationship with his father, the nature of families and marriage, and his sentiments as an Irish American toward Protestant Yankees. Focusing on what he saw as quintessentially Irish-American themes of sexual repression, shame, romantic pride, patriarchy and alcoholism, he produced a series of plays with universal resonance and appeal. Stricken by Parkinson's disease in 1939, O'Neill wrote three major plays in a sustained burst of creativity over the next two years, *The Iceman Cometh*, *Long Day's Journey into Night*, and *A Moon for the Misbegotten*, the first two of which are usually regarded as his finest works.[42]

The dominant Irish-American novelists in the first half of the twentieth century were F. Scott Fitzgerald (1896–1940), John O'Hara (1905–70), and James T. Farrell (1904–79). Fitzgerald, a third-generation Irish American, came from a well-established family in St Paul, Minnesota. Educated at Princeton and readily accepted into the Protestant social elite, he drew on his experiences of this world in writing his masterpiece *The Great Gatsby* (1925), along with *Tender is the Night* (1934) and several others works, before succumbing to alcoholism. O'Hara came from a very different background. Born in Pottsville, in the heart of the Pennsylvania anthracite country, he missed out on the prep-school and Ivy League education he cherished, and never fulfilled his goal of acceptance in the upper levels of society where Fitzgerald moved so easily. The inarticulate rage of the Irishman excluded from the world of the Protestant elite can be heard in much of his work. As one of the characters in his novel *BUtterfield 8* (1935) explains to his WASP girlfriend: 'I wear Brooks clothes and I don't eat salad with a spoon and I probably could play five-goal polo in two years, but I am a Mick. Still a Mick ... there are not two kinds of Irishmen. There's only one kind ... We're Micks, we're non-assimilable, we Micks'. This blend of 'pride and grievance that the lubricants of alcohol and ambition have failed to smooth away', as one recent historian puts it, lay at the heart of O'Hara's social predicament. Despite this predicament, *BUtterfield 8* was a big popular success, while a second novel, *Ten North Frederick*, won the National Book Award in 1955.[43]

James T. Farrell, the son of an Irish-born teamster, had few of O'Hara's social pretensions and none of Fitzgerald's social standing. He grew up in a tough Irish neighbourhood on the South Side of Chicago and drew on his upbringing to write of a world that neither Fitzgerald nor O'Hara had ever known, in the trilogy *Studs Lonigan* (1932–35) and his subsequent pentalogy on the character Danny O'Neill (1936–43). Farrell's chief concern was what he saw as the cultural and spiritual bankruptcy of lower-class Irish-American life, which he blamed in large measure on the Catholic Church. In their very different ways, the careers of these three novelists, along with Eugene O'Neill (and the immensely popular playwright, Philip Barry) indicated the extent to which Irish Americans had moved from the margins to the mainstream of the American literary world.[44]

RELIGION

Throughout the first half of the twentieth century, the Irish continued to dominate the American Catholic Church, just as Catholicism remained central to Irish-American culture. In 1908, Pope Pius X removed the Church in the United States from the jurisdiction of the *Congregatio de Propaganda Fide*; in other words, America was no longer to be regarded by Rome as missionary territory and was to be placed instead on a basis of equality with such ancient national churches as those of Italy, France and Germany. Built largely by Irish immigrants over the previous century, the American Church was prospering as never before. By 1900, there were an estimated 12 million Catholics in the United States, by 1915 there were 15 million and by the 1950s the number would rise to somewhere between 33 and 40 million members.[45]

A small minority of clergymen in the early twentieth century carried on the radical tradition within American Catholicism that had been pioneered by men like Fr. Edward McGlynn in New York City in the 1880s. Chief among these radicals at the turn of the century was Fr. Peter Yorke, an Irish-born graduate of the Maynooth seminary (Ireland), who applied for a position in the American mission and was posted to San Francisco in 1888. Appointed editor of the local Catholic newspaper, he forcefully defended his countrymen and co-religionists against the attacks of the nativist American Protective Association in the 1890s. In 1901, when the major employers in San Francisco banded together in a lockout designed to break union labour, Yorke sided with the workers and became one of their leaders in the bitter struggle that followed. Yorke helped plan strategy, gave public speeches, printed pamphlets and news reports, and eventually assisted in settling the strike. Throughout the dispute, he faced the concerted opposition of the Irish-American upper-middle class as well as the Irish-American political establishment and Catholic hierarchy, led by the mayor, James D. Phelan and the Archbishop, Patrick Riordan. Citing the papal encyclical *Rerum Novarum* (1891), Yorke insisted that the power to form unions was a natural right that workers should not have to extract as a concession from employers. After the lockout of 1901, Yorke stayed active in radical circles, editing a pro-labour newspaper, the *Leader*, and following in the footsteps of Edward McGlynn and Patrick Ford by explicitly linking the cause of social reform with that of national liberation in Ireland. Another radical Catholic priest active in the West was Fr. Thomas J. Hagerty, who helped found the radical labour organization, the Industrial Workers of the World in 1905.[46]

Also inspired by the papal encyclical *Rerum Novarum* was Monsignor John Ryan (1869–1945), the most influential Catholic social theorist in the first half of the twentieth century. Ryan was the oldest of eleven children born to Irish immigrant parents in Vermillion, Minnesota. He was influenced in his early years by the writings of the reformer, Henry George, the Irish-American radical journalist, Patrick Ford and the Irish-American Populist leader, Ignatius Donnelly, who was elected to the House of Representatives from the district where Ryan lived. *Rerum Novarum* was the decisive moment in his intellectual and spiritual development, merging Catholicism and Populism as he understood them. After ordination at St Paul Seminary, Minnesota, Ryan obtained a doctorate in moral theology at the Catholic University of America. His dissertation, 'A Living Wage' (published in 1906), invoked *Rerum Novarum* to defend the notion of decent wages as a basic human right. On the strength of this dissertation, Ryan joined the faculty of St Paul seminary, teaching social ethics through a sophisticated mixture of economics, sociology and theology.[47]

During the Progressive Era (1900–17), Ryan's views were at the vanguard of social reform. He favoured a minimum wage, an eight-hour workday, laws to protect peaceful picketing, municipal housing, and the rights of women and children, along with insurance against unemployment, accidents, illness and old age. He also supported public ownership of utility companies, mines and forests, the regulation or dismantling of monopolies and the prohibition of speculation on the stock and commodity exchanges. In 1916 Ryan published his major synthesis of ethics and economics, *Distributive Justice: The Right and Wrong of our Present Distribution of Wealth*, and three years later he was appointed to the faculty of the Catholic University of America, where he taught for the rest of his life.[48]

In the aftermath of the First World War, Ryan was chosen by the Catholic hierarchy to draw up a report outlining Catholic social policy for the postwar era. The result was 'The Bishops' Program of Social Reconstruction', issued under the auspices of the National Catholic War Council (NCWC), which had been founded in 1917 to coordinate the Catholic response to American entry into the First World War. The 'Bishops' Program' was a radical blueprint for a future America, the most progressive document compiled by any religious group, not just the Catholic Church, during the Progressive Era. It urged the government to maintain the employment and labour arbitration boards set up during the war; to promote the principles of the family living wage, and the right of labour to organize and bargain collectively; to regulate monopolies; to give women equal pay for equal work; to raise wages so that individuals could protect their families against sickness, accidents, invalidism and old age; to build public housing; and to provide insurance schemes for the citizenry. Ryan's document, however, came at an inopportune moment, for the Progressive Era had spent most of its energy by 1917 and the following decade would be marked by political conservatism rather than continued reform. Ryan's report, moreover, attracted the opposition of big business and of powerful conservative elements within the Church for its alleged 'socialist' tendencies. It would not be until the New Deal of the 1930s that something like Ryan's vision of social justice began to go into effect.[49]

Ryan was an enthusiastic supporter of President Franklin Delano Roosevelt's New Deal, even if he did not exert the influence that some of his more zealous champions have sometimes claimed. After initial hesitation, Ryan supported Roosevelt in 1932 and quickly emerged as the foremost Catholic apologist for the New Deal, which eventually enacted the core of Ryan's own programs: the Wagner Act, granting federal recognition to trade unions; the Social Security Act, setting up old-age and unemployment insurance; and the Fair Labor Standards Act, providing for minimum wages and hours. But these laws were more of a beginning than an end for Ryan. In the late 1930s, he and his colleagues at the NCWC prepared another and even more advanced (and more coherent and articulate) statement, *The Church and the Social Order*, updating the 1918–19 effort. This document endorsed all the major reforms Ryan had been promoting for the past two decades, warning about industry's abuse of power, reaffirming the legitimacy of unions and the right to strike, and calling not just for a 'living wage' but also for a 'saving wage' as protection against sickness, death and unemployment. The document was presented as a 'middle way' between socialism and individualism, partly to counter accusations from certain employers and conservatives that Ryan's ideas were mere left-wing propaganda.[50]

John Ryan's philosophy was an effective blend of liberal Catholicism with elements of a wider American reform tradition running from Populism through Progressivism to the New Deal. In the latter tradition he found an emphasis on social and economic intervention by the government in the name of greater social justice and efficiency; in the former he found, in particular, the teachings of Thomas Aquinas on social responsibility and social cohesion. The result was a formidable intellectual synthesis. But, precisely because it was so intellectually formidable, Ryan's program of 'Catholic Social Action' had very little impact on the great majority of the American Catholic laity. And, despite the precedent of *Rerum Novarum*, it encountered stiff opposition from conservative clergyman. One such clergyman in particular proved much more popular with the public throughout most of the 1930s. Ryan attacked this clergyman's economic theories as quackery in 1936, and condemned him for anti-Semitism two years later, warning Catholics that the same tactics might be used against them as were being employed against the Jews. But even attacks of this gravity had little short-term impact, for Ryan's antagonist was formidable indeed: Fr. Charles Coughlin, the 'radio priest' of Royal Oak, Michigan, one of the great populist demagogues of American history.[51]

A native of Canada, Charles Coughlin (1891–1979) had taught as a professor in a theological college in Windsor, Ontario before being appointed to the diocese of Detroit in 1920. He began broadcasting over the radio in support of his new parish, Royal Oak, in 1926 and it was through radio that he would rise to national prominence. Like Ryan, Coughlin began as a social radical, inspired by the Populist heritage. From that heritage, however, he ultimately extracted not a progressive emphasis on social justice through big government, but an undercurrent of nativism, anti-Semitism and conspiratorial thinking that historians have often pointed to as one side of the American populist tradition. It has been but a short step, in this tradition, from theories of an international banking conspiracy to outright anti-Semitism. Once the connection between banking and Jewishness is made, a small but persistent strain of American populism has always tended to drift into conspiracy theory. The old Irish radical of the 1880s, Patrick Ford, had fallen into this trap late in his career, and so too did Charles Coughlin, whose early social radicalism had congealed by the mid-1930s into an ugly blend of anti-Semitism and proto-fascism.

Fr. Coughlin nonetheless retained considerable appeal throughout the 1930s, not only to Irish Americans but to Catholic Americans generally, reaching millions in his weekly radio broadcasts. He initially supported Roosevelt and the New Deal, but broke away to found the National Union for Social Justice, which ran its own candidate for president in 1936. Listening to the radio, however, should not be equated with political preference, let alone behaviour; Coughlin may have attracted an audience of some 5 million to his weekly radio broadcasts, but fewer than 1 million voted for his favoured candidate, William Lemke, in 1936, compared to just under 23 million for the victor, Franklin Delano Roosevelt and almost 17 million for the runner-up, Alfred M. Landon. After the debacle of 1936, Coughlin combined attacks on the 'Communism' of the New Deal with attacks on Jews, resurrecting the fraudulent 'Protocols of the Elders of Zion', founding a new anti-Semitic Christian Front and condemning the war against Germany as a conspiracy by Jews and Communists. His superior in the 1930s, Bishop Michael Gallagher of Detroit, had tolerated Coughlin's behavior, but the populist priest was eventually silenced during the Second World War by Gallagher's successor, Archbishop Edward Mooney.[52]

Coughlin's support was apparently strongest among middle-class and 'respectable' working-class Irish Americans and German Americans, hard hit by the depression and not fully assimilated into the American mainstream despite several generations in the country. Tensions between Irish Catholics and Jews were common in the early and mid-twentieth century, with many cases of property damage, insults, beatings and desecration of Jewish burial grounds. Neighbourhood Irish gangs, especially in the Bronx, Brooklyn, Boston and Dorchester, Massachusetts, fought street battles with Jews and invaded Jewish neighbourhoods in the 1930s and 1940s. Fr. Coughlin's minor counterpart on the East Coast was a Fr. Edward Lodge Curran, who organized and encouraged anti-Semitic demonstrations. Many of them were held under the auspices of the Christian Front, which met in Hibernian Hall in Roxbury, Boston. Nazi sympathizer Joseph E. McWilliams propagated similar ideas through his American Destiny party in New York.[53]

While some Irish Catholics were undoubtedly at the forefront of American anti-Semitism in the 1930s, it must be emphasized that American Catholics continued to endure a remarkable degree of discrimination themselves during this period, at both the popular and the intellectual level. Anti-Catholicism had been a major component of the successful drive for immigration restriction in the early 1920s, and the virulently anti-Catholic Ku Klux Klan claimed anywhere between three and five million members in the 1920s. Anti-Catholicism, in short, was an integral element of American politics and culture in the 1920s and beyond. As for elite culture, it has been remarked justly that anti-Catholicism was the one intellectually respectable form of bigotry in the United States in the first half of the twentieth century. The equation of Catholicism with anti-democracy and anti-republicanism has long roots in American history, stretching back to the Revolution and beyond. But what is surprising is the extent to which this form of anti-Catholicism survived into the twentieth century, especially among intellectuals. Indeed, Catholic 'authoritarianism' was generally construed as so clearly the opposite of the democratic ideal that anti-Catholicism became a central component of the liberal creed. In the 1930s, liberal intellectuals pointed repeatedly to the apparent links between fascism and Catholicism in Europe, allegations that were only strengthened by the outpourings of Fr. Charles Coughlin. Anglo-Saxon Protestantism, with its emphasis on civil liberties, individualism and experimental science, was held to be the perfect barrier against fascism, whereas the hierarchical (some said 'authoritarian') element in Catholicism weakened individualism and freedom, clearing the way to totalitarian government. As the Catholic Church exerted its influence over Hollywood producers through censorship, resisted the sale of birth-control devices and engineered the firing of the British philosopher Bertrand Russell from his post at City College, New York in 1940, leading members of the liberal intelligentsia charged that Catholicism was antithetical with American democracy. Against the prevailing philosophy of pragmatism, which held truth to be partial, tentative and verifiable only in practice, the Church was criticized as absolutist, dogmatic and all-encompassing in its philosophical claims, embodying the intellectual equivalent of totalitarianism. Given that pragmatism was widely seen as the one quintessentially American philosophy, the Catholic Church could therefore be characterized as both anti-democratic and un-American.[54] Until at least the 1950s, Catholicism remained anathema to large sectors of the American intelligentsia.

POLITICS

The final great theme in the history of the American Irish in the first half of the twentieth century is their continuing domination of urban politics. In the late nineteenth century, Irish-American political bosses had built a first generation of Democratic machines in cities like New York, Brooklyn, San Francisco, Albany and Jersey City. While some of these machines had been weakened by political reforms and realignments in the 1890s, the Irish constructed a second generation of 'reformed' machines in New York, Albany, Jersey City and elsewhere during the Progressive Era. These cities had large

Irish voting populations and were located in states with friendly Democratic governors. They never had sufficient resources and patronage positions to satisfy their constituents, however, and lived with the constant fear of working-class revolts, as for example in New York City in 1886.[55]

By 1890 Irish bosses ran most of the big-city machines constructed in the 1870s and 1880s. These bosses included Tammany Hall's Kelly and Croker, Brooklyn's McLaughlin, the Bay Area's Buckley, Buffalo's Sheehan, Jersey City's Davis and Albany's Patrick McCabe. The Irish also dominated the Democratic party in cities where effective centralized machines had not been built, including Chicago where the Democrats were led by Mike McDonald, and Boston where Pat Maguire temporarily emerged to the forefront among several quarrelling factions. Boston never developed a centralized machine on the Tammany model, but the Irish still managed to control the city from the turn of the century onward. The mayors of Boston from 1903 to 1945 were Patrick Collins (1903–5), John 'Honey Fitz' Fitzgerald (1906–8, 1910–14), James M. Curley (1915–19, 1922–6, 1930–4), Frederick W. Mansfield (1934–8), Maurice J. Tobin (1938–42, 1944), and John E. Kerrigan (1945). All but Collins, who was born in Ireland, were American-born. From New York to Chicago and San Francisco, the Irish also dominated the lower echelons of the urban Democratic party. This conquest of power rested on the mobilization of ethnic voting, which the Irish achieved more quickly and successfully than any other group in the late nineteenth and early twentieth centuries.[56]

A second generation of longer-lived Irish machines emerged during the Progressive Era. This second generation of machines replaced the old nineteenth-century hostility to reform with a much more pragmatic approach, favouring Progressive labour and social welfare legislation as a way of con-solidating power among its increasingly diverse working-class constituents. Tammany Hall once again led the way in this respect, led by its latest Irish-American boss, Charles F. Murphy (1858–1924), who succeeded Richard Croker in 1902. By incorporating social reforms into their own program, rather than seeing them as a threat to their power, the machines strengthened their position. At the same time, they enthusiastically supported such reforms as municipal control over utility companies, aware that strengthen-ing their control over big business would create a bigger pool of patronage jobs, not to mention donations, 'insider' information and 'kickbacks'. With a wider patronage pool, the machines drew Irish voters ever closer into their fold. They also began to mobilize the so-called 'new immigrants' – Jews, Italians and Slavs – whom the older machines had simply ignored. By and large, however, the best jobs and most resources went to the Irish. The 'new ethnics' tended to get poorer jobs and fewer resources; most often, indeed, they were accorded symbolic rather than material recognition, a practice perhaps best captured by the image of the Irish boss attending a Jewish funeral in the morning, complete with yarmulke, before moving on to an Italian wedding and sundry other duties that afternoon and evening. Eventually the 'new ethnics' would demand more power, with critical consequences for the Irish machines in the 1930s.[57]

Before the revolt of the 'new ethnics', however, the American Irish built a generation of political machines that were even more powerful than those of the late nineteenth century. Among the great Irish bosses of the first half of the twentieth century were Charlie Murphy of New York City, Frank Hague (1876–1956) of Jersey City, Thomas Pendergast (1872–1945) of Kansas City, Edward J. Kelly (1876–1950) of Chicago and David L. Lawrence (1889–1966) of Pittsburgh. Murphy consolidated Tammany's control over New York City, reversing the defeats suffered by Boss Croker towards the end of his reign, so that the Irish machine continued to run the city until 1933. The Tammany system reached a peak of both power and style when the flamboyant Jimmy Walker was elected mayor of New York in 1925 and 1929. In Jersey City, Frank Hague built one of the most powerful and repressive machines in the United States, running his city and dominating the politics of his state until 1949. Pendergast built an equally powerful machine in Kansas City, forming a powerful alliance with President Franklin Delano Roosevelt in 1932. Pendergast helped launch the political career of Harry Truman, who also received valuable support from the Bronx Democratic leader, Ed Flynn. As a graduate of Fordham University, Flynn represented a powerful new mixture of college education and political clout. He dominated the Bronx, and exerted considerable influence over city and national Democratic politics from the early 1920s until his death in 1953. Pendergast, meanwhile, got into trouble for engaging in what George Washington Plunkitt used to call 'honest graft'. His Ready-Mixed Concrete Company received an endless supply of contracts for city and state construction companies. There were also widespread allegations of electoral fraud. As the corruption scandals deepened, Roosevelt abandoned Pendergast and in 1939 he was indicted for income tax invasion and sent to prison for fifteen months. Finally, the most durable of all the machines founded in the early twentieth century was that of Dan O'Connell in Albany, which survived into the 1990s. Compared to the nineteenth-century machines, these new organizations borrowed and spent much more money, and controlled substantially more patronage jobs, thereby consolidating their control over the electorate and especially over the Irish. To give one example: local government employment in the three machine cities of New York, Jersey City and Albany rose from 59,202 in 1900 to 158,453 in 1930, with the number of Irish on the payroll climbing from 21,749 to 82,116.[58]

How exactly did the Irish machines build and retain their power? Their success rested in large measure on their ability to perform functions and meet needs that were inadequately addressed by the existing social and political structure. By fulfilling these functions, the machines posed a major dilemma for all reform movements that tried to clean up city politics by driving machines out of existence. To some extent, the machines can be seen as creations of the people as well as for the people; they were extremely responsive to what their constituents wanted and, despite the complaints of reformers, often served their constituents well. Abolishing the machines could never, in itself, be an effective policy, unless some new system were devised to replace them. Only by meeting the social needs the machines addressed could the reformers hope to bring about genuine and long-lasting reform. Three areas of particular importance in this respect were welfare, business and social mobility.[59]

Throughout the nineteenth century there was practically no welfare system available to help the neediest Americans. Federal welfare was non-existent until the New Deal. The modern system of old-age pensions, federal unemployment assistance and direct aid to the indigent elderly and to mothers with dependent children, was introduced only in 1935. Until the first decade of the twentieth century, the great bulk of assistance was provided by private charities, with limited assistance from individual states and cities. The machine therefore filled an important vacuum, dispensing material assistance to the needy in the form of cash and jobs, and collecting their votes in return.[60]

The machines also fulfilled an important function in relation to big business. They awarded contracts to public utility companies, railroads, local transportation companies, electric light companies and communications corporations, and protected these businesses from competition. In return, businesses allocated jobs to be filled by the machine as patronage positions, made large financial contributions to election campaigns, and submitted bids for city work that greatly exceeded the cost of the work to be done, so that the bosses could skim off the excess funds. The irony here is that anti-machine reformers actually strengthened the position of the bosses by placing utility companies and other corporations under tightened municipal control.

Once the reformers left office and the bosses came back in, the machines were able to exploit the tighter relationship with the corporations to their mutual benefit.[61]

The third area in which historians have identified a critical function fulfilled by the machine was the provision of some degree of social mobility to its supporters, mainly in the form of jobs. At the heart of machine politics lay a highly developed form of patronage. In the language of political science, this entailed distributing 'separable goods' or 'divisible benefits', rather than delivering 'inseparable' or 'public goods' (also referred to as 'indivisible benefits'). In other words, Irish leaders distributed their rewards to individuals rather than to the community as a whole. They delivered jobs, cash, contracts and other benefits, rather than general services like pollution control. They did, of course, build roads, transit systems, schools and hospitals, which benefited everybody in the community, but in such a way as to reward individual contractors in the process. The bulk of the patronage went to the Irish, who typically got most of the best jobs. This policy was highly effective as long as the Irish controlled the cities, but would prove fatal to the machines in the 1930s when the 'new immigrants' from southern and eastern Europe began to demand and gain the type of power once monopolized by the Irish.[62]

There were two types of patronage: direct (provision of government jobs) and indirect (provision of jobs in private sector companies doing work for the government). But were these jobs really a source of social mobility? Direct patronage jobs were typically working-class or lower middle-class, e.g. firemen, policemen and clerks. Likewise, jobs provided through indirect patronage (e.g. in construction, utility companies and municipal transportation companies with government contracts) were almost always working-class. Even if the machines provided plenty of employment for the Irish, it cannot convincingly be said that they provided a means of upward mobility. Indeed, it might even be argued that the machines perpetuated existing patterns of employment, holding the Irish back more than helping to advance them. Irish political success, in other words, may have hindered rather than assisted Irish economic advancement – except, of course, for bosses like Plunkitt and Croker, who became very rich in office.[63]

While the power of the machines was based in large measure on the needs they fulfilled, their continued operation also depended on a distinctive political style. The key to this style was an emphasis on personal, reciprocal relationships between the machines and their constituents. The Irish political machines treated people above all as individuals, not as clients, or bureaucratic cases or members of social classes. They paid attention to their personal needs and wants, rather than applying abstract, universal rules of the type a judge, a social worker or a bureaucrat might use. Working-class families received jobs, money, food, coal and help with the law or government. Because the individuals in question received personal attention rather than the cold, clinical processing dispensed by bureaucracies, they could be relied upon to deliver their votes.[64]

Irish machine politics has often been characterized as non-ideological, in the sense that it was highly pragmatic, concerned with getting the job done by whatever means necessary. Viewed from this perspective, municipal politics was something of a game, an end in itself, its sole object being to get and then to keep power. Irish machine bosses generally opposed social reform movements, unless enacting such reforms became unavoidable, as for instance during the Progressive Era and the New Deal. But opposition to social engineering, of course, does not necessarily equate with non-ideological politics. To oppose social reform in a society like the United States in the early twentieth century was an ideological position in itself. It is no coincidence that the machines opposed not only progressive reformers, on the one hand, but radical working-class movements, on the other. Irish machine politicians were usually very conservative on social matters, embracing reform only when they thought it could consolidate their hold on power.[65]

Perhaps the most colourful figure in Irish-American politics in this period was James Michael Curley, who dominated the politics of Boston for most of his political career. Unlike other American cities, Boston never transcended political factionalism to produce a single, dominant, machine. In the late nineteenth and early twentieth centuries, four political chieftains, John F. 'Honey Fitz' Fitzgerald, Patrick Kennedy, Martin Lomasney and James Michael Curley, battled for control of the city. It was Curley who emerged victorious in the long run, going on to dominate Boston politics for almost half a century. Curley was first elected to office in 1899, a seat on the Boston City Council. Over the next fifty years, he was elected four times to Congress, served four terms as mayor of Boston, held several other offices from alderman to governor, and was defeated once for the House of Representatives, once for the Senate, twice for the governorship, and six times for mayor. Lacking the city-wide system of ward leaders and precinct captains of a centralized machine, Curley never became a 'boss' in the sense pioneered by Tammany Hall and epitomized by his contemporaries, Frank Hague of Jersey City, Tom Pendergast of Kansas City and Dan O'Connell of Albany. This explains why he actually held elected office, rather than controlling things from behind the scenes. As an elected politician, he was enormously popular with the people of Boston, and was immortalized in literature in Edwin O'Connor's novel, *The Last Hurrah* (1956).[66]

James Michael Curley was born in a Boston slum to parents who had come to the United States from Galway. After his father died when he was ten years old, his mother worked as a scrubwoman to support him and his ten-year old brother. Curley received no formal education beyond grade school. He sold newspapers as a schoolboy, worked long hours as a delivery boy in a neighbourhood drugstore and was later employed in a piano factory and by a tinsmith. At the age of seventeen, he took a job with a grocer, and worked for the next eight years preparing orders and delivering them in a horse-drawn wagon, getting to know the city of Boston inside out. Curley worked his way through the rough and tumble world of Boston's political clubs, suf-fering an early reverse that might have disillusioned many others. With a characteristically Irish disdain for civil service reform, he had agreed to take a civil service examination for the position of letter carrier in place of a con-stituent, having first consulted the law books to determine that the only penalty if he were caught would be prevention from taking any civil service exams in the future. But Curley had misinterpreted the law, and instead found himself in jail for sixty days. During his time in jail he was elected to Boston's Board of Aldermen, setting the tone for a long political career to come.[67]

After being elected to Congress in 1910 and 1912, Curley turned his atten-tion back to Boston, announcing that he would run for mayor in 1913 against the incumbent John 'Honey Fitz' Fitzgerald (grandfather of the future presid-ent, John Fitzgerald Kennedy). 'Honey Fitz' had been mayor for six of the previous eight years, after succeeding Patrick Collins, the first American-born son of Irish parents to hold the office. Fitzgerald, however, decided to withdraw from the race in 1913, and did not hold political office again. Endorsed by the powerful Irish-American boss of the West End, Martin Lomasney, Curley defeated his fellow-Irishman Thomas J. Kenny, by 43,000 votes to 37,000, carrying 16 of Boston's 26 wards and winning in all the lower-income sections of the city. He was defeated for reelection in 1917 by a coalition of Irish factions, but served as mayor again in 1921–5 and 1929–33, and Governor of Massachusetts from 1934 to 1936. He would have been reelected easily as mayor in 1925 and 1933, but the state legislature had changed the law to forbid successive terms by the same man. These years from 1920 to 1936 were the period of Curley's greatest power. As mayor and governor, he spent substantial sums on hospitals, beaches, playgrounds, stadiums, recreational facilities, subways and street repairs, thereby providing tangible benefits to the electorate while at the same time creating thousands of patronage jobs.[68]

While James Michael Curley was in many ways the most powerful man in Boston for most of his political career, he had an uncomfortable and ambivalent relationship with the 'other' Boston, the Boston of Yankee privilege and culture. He boasted that when one of his sons was admitted to Harvard, he destroyed the letter of acceptance and sent him instead to Holy Cross, the Jesuit school in nearby Worcester. Holy Cross and Boston College, rather than Harvard, held the loyalties of most Boston Irish, their alumni competing with Harvard graduates in city business, the professions, insurance, real estate and stock brokerage, while holding a clear advantage in municipal politics. At the same time, however, Curley wanted the support of Harvard and its alumni in his campaigns, actively sought the respectability that their approbation could bring and spoke frequently on the Harvard campus.[69]

After supporting FDR in 1932, Curley eventually broke with him in 1936, serving in the meantime as governor of Massachusetts and supporting a wide range of social legislation. His break with the New Deal administration was followed, in rapid succession, by defeat in his campaigns for the US Senate in 1936, for mayor of Boston in 1937 and for governor of Massachusetts in 1938. The usual explanation for these sudden political reverses is that the New Deal welfare state – social security, unemployment compensation, minimum wages, trade union recognition – had eroded Curley's position. Combined with insurgent movements by 'new ethnics', these developments had gravely undermined the position of Tammany Hall in New York in the 1930s. But, just as new political machines arose in Pittsburgh and Chicago during and after the New Deal, Curley rebounded from the defeats of 1937 and 1938, being elected congressman in 1942 and mayor of Boston, one last time, in 1945 at the age of seventy. Defeated in a hard-fought battle for reelection in 1949, he ran token campaigns for mayor (his ninth and tenth) in 1951 and 1955, designed primarily for purposes of fund-raising and publicity rather than to seek office. When Curley died in 1958, his net estate was only $3,768, insufficient to cover the bequests he had made. 'He was in the game,' as one historian puts it, 'not for money, but for power and the thrill of its exercise'.[70]

If James Michael Curley weathered the storm of the 1930s, Tammany Hall faced a more sustained and serious challenge. There were two principal aspects to this challenge: the political mobilization of the 'new ethnics', and the passage of federal welfare legislation that threatened to undercut the function of the machines. With the arrival of the 'new immigrants' from about

1890 onward, the machines had been forced to adapt to new circumstances. They succeeded in doing so to some extent, but never sufficiently, doling out certain benefits to the 'new immigrants' but reserving most of their resources and nearly all the best jobs for their loyal Irish followers. While the Irish received tangible benefits (jobs and money), Jews and Italians got more minimal rewards (money for food, coal or rent, business licenses, minor party posts). They were also rewarded with symbolic gestures, such as speeches against literacy tests and immigration restriction, or visits by the bosses to weddings and funerals. This policy of exclusion proved disastrous with the onset of the Great Depression in 1929, however, when the machines had to fire thousands of employees, with Jews and Italians the first to go. At the same time, the drying up of the patronage pool alienated many of the Irish. The 'new immigrant' supporters of Anton Cermak defeated Chicago's Irish machine in 1931, while a 'new ethnic' coalition led by the Italian American, Fiorello La Guardia, dealt a crushing defeat to Tammany Hall in 1933, removing it from power for the next twelve years.[71]

The primary causes of the decline of the Irish political machines during the New Deal of the 1930s, according to most historians, were the radical new provisions for job creation, unemployment benefits and social security enacted by the federal government, together with the demands of the 'new immigrants' for greater power and representation. The troubles of Tammany Hall in the 1930s certainly had a lot to do with the historic increase in government social intervention, and the consequent reduction in the patronage power of the machine, combined with a well-timed revolt by the 'new ethnics'. What is less well understood is the extent to which some of the machines survived the crisis of the New Deal, turning the new government measures to their advantage. To the extent that they could take charge of dispensing the new federal funds sent to individual cities and states, the machines could win control over an unprecedented source of patronage.[72]

This transformation was especially noticeable in cities like Jersey City, Albany, Pittsburgh and Chicago, where powerful and durable new machines emerged in the 1930s. In Jersey City, Boss Hague kept the new immigrants at bay until 1949. In Albany, Dan O'Connell's machine survived unscathed in part because there were fewer new immigrants, and in part because so many of the city's employees worked directly for the state government, and hence unemployment and welfare needs were lower. In Pittsburgh, David Lawrence built a new machine in the 1930s, combining Irish and 'new ethnic' support, which ran the city until 1969. And in Chicago the Irish forged a similar alliance to regain control of the city in 1933, paving the way for the last of the great Irish bosses, Richard Daley, who ruled the city as mayor uninterruptedly from 1955 to 1976. The key to the success of these machines was control over the new welfare and job-creation funds provided by the federal government.[73]

In the 1920s and 1930s, the Irish began to make their mark on national as well as urban politics for the first time. Already by 1920, Irish-born members of Congress outnumbered by more than two to one all other foreign-born representatives, but very few Irish Catholics were appointed to important executive or judicial posts in the federal government prior to the New Deal of the 1930s. Compared to their domination of urban politics by the early twentieth century, it took the Irish considerably longer to have an impact on national affairs. It is fitting, however, that it was a product of Tammany Hall who blazed the trail towards national politics. His name was Alfred Emmanuel Smith and, when asked about his credentials, he liked to answer that he was a graduate of the Fulton Street Fish Market in lower Manhattan.

Born in New York City in 1873 of Irish, German and Italian stock, Al Smith worked first at a variety of odd jobs as a teenager, before securing employment as a clerk at the Fulton Fish Market in 1892, for $12 a week and all the fish he could eat. Although he worked on Fulton Street for only a year, his name would always be associated with it. Like many young Irishmen in New York City, Smith became involved in his local Democratic club, canvassing before elections and running errands for ward leaders. He soon became a favourite of the Tammany boss, Charlie Murphy, and from 1904 to 1915 he served as one of Tammany's men in the state assembly, where he formed an alliance with an up-and-coming young lawyer-politician, Robert F. Wagner. In 1911, when the Democrats captured the governorship and both houses of the legislature, Smith was elected majority leader and became chairman of the Ways and Means Committee. Wagner, by then a senator, was elected leader in the upper house. The same year, 146 women lost their lives in the Triangle Shirt Waist factory fire in New York City, and the legislature created a Factory Commission with Wagner as chairman and Smith as vice-chairman to investigate the tragedy and the variety of problems and abuses lying behind it. As a result, the state's labour code was revised to improve the condition of New York City's workers generally. Building on his popularity among the people of the city, Smith was elected governor of New York in 1918, with the active support of Tammany. After a narrow defeat in 1920, he was re-elected governor in 1922, 1924 and 1926.[74]

The culmination of Al Smith's career was his involvement in presidential politics. He made his first bid for the Democratic nomination in 1924, only to fall prey to an ugly resurgence of anti-Irish and anti-Catholic nativism. He secured the Democratic nomination four years later but, in a campaign marked by frequent outbursts of anti-Catholic bigotry, he was defeated by the Republican candidate, Herbert Hoover. Smith won in only eight states and failed to carry even his home state, New York. The campaign of 1928, nonetheless, marked an important turning point in American political history, as Smith was the first Catholic ever to be nominated as a presidential candidate. And, while his Catholicism was certainly unattractive to large numbers of voters, most historians and political scientists would agree that the Democrats stood little chance of winning the presidency in 1928, regardless of the candidate and his religion. Smith's unsuccessful candidacy, however, may have paved the way for the victory of Franklin Delano Roosevelt in 1932 by solidifying the support of the Democratic party among urban voters and immigrants. After the election of 1928, Smith returned to New York City, where he died in 1944, though not before leaving the Democratic party in 1940 in protest at the policies of the New Deal. He retained his enormous popularity among the people of the city, who gave him the unofficial title of 'First Citizen'.[75]

Thus, while the American Irish had suffered some major political defeats in the 1930s – chief among them the demise of Tammany Hall – they had also scored some major victories. Not only did they lay the basis for a third generation of municipal machines, they had also begun to make their mark on national politics for the first time. During the New Deal, the American Irish started to be appointed and elected to important offices in the federal government. President Roosevelt included Irish Americans like Thomas G. Corcoran (1900–77), James A. Farley (1888–1976), Frank Murphy (1890–1949), and Joseph P. Kennedy (1888–1969) among his close advisors. As his Attorney General, he chose Senator Thomas Walsh of Montana, while James A. Farrell became Paymaster-General and chairman of the Democratic National Committee. Irish-American senators elected in 1932 included Augustine Lonergan from Connecticut, Ryan Duffy from Wisconsin and Pat McCarran from Nevada. Politics at the national level, rather than simply in the cities, would be a major theme in the history of the American Irish for the remainder of the century, culminating in the historic election of an Irish-American Catholic, John F. Kennedy, to the presidency in 1960.[76]

Chapter 6

◆

IRISH AMERICA SINCE THE SECOND WORLD WAR

By the 1940s, Britain had replaced the United States as the major destination for Irish emigration. Although substantial numbers of Irish people came to the United States in the 1950s and again in the 1980s, they made up only a small percentage of total Irish emigration and a tiny percentage of American immigration in the second half of the twentieth century. In the 1970s and 1990s, moreover, emigration dwindled in the face of unprecedented economic prosperity in Ireland. In the postwar era, therefore, the history of the American Irish was a history concerned not with immigrants so much as with established members of the ethnic group, from the second generation and beyond. It was these well-established, American-born Irish who set the tone for the history of the American Irish as a whole in this period, continuing to dominate the American Catholic Church, playing a prominent role in local and federal politics, and once again making a substantial contribution to the nationalist struggle in Ireland.

PROSPERITY

Rates of emigration from Ireland to the United States between 1945 and 1980 varied widely, as the Irish economy alternated between cycles of stagnation and prosperity, and as American immigration laws were reformed in ways that both benefited and hurt the Irish. In the 1940s, 26,967 Irish immigrants arrived in the United States, followed by 57,332 in the 1950s; 37,461 came in the 1960s, but only 6,559 in the 1970s. In 1965 Congress passed a new immigration law, overturning the old national origins quota system in place since the 1920s. Under the new system, Ireland's quota increased slightly, from 17,000 to a maximum allowable figure of 20,000 (the figure now assigned to every nation). But the rules for admission changed, with preference given to potential immigrants who either had close family ties to US citizens or possessed skills needed in the United States. Most Irish people in the 1960s and 1970s could meet neither of these qualifications. At the same time, the Irish economy was exceptionally strong in these two decades, due in part to intelligent government planning, with a heavy emphasis on exports and the attraction of foreign investment through various incentives (including loans, grants and exemption from taxation on profits for firms that exported their products). In 1961–71, for the first time since the foundation of the Irish state, the number of jobs created outside the agricultural sector exceeded the number lost within it. At the same time, Ireland's entry into the European Common Market (today's European Union) in 1973 made it a more attractive base for foreign firms wishing to export to European markets, and Ireland soon became a major recipient of EU development funds. As a result, emigration in the 1960s and 1970s was very low.[1]

Mainly because of this unprecedented economic prosperity, Ireland's long-standing pattern of population loss was reversed. For the first time since the Great Famine, the natural increase in population exceeded the figure for emigration. There was a net inflow of people into Ireland in the 1970s of 104,000, including 63,000 married persons returning with children, most of whom had apparently emigrated to Britain as single people in the 1950s. As a result, the country's population rose rather than fell. Counties like Cavan, Donegal, Mayo, Roscommon and Sligo recorded population increases for the first time since the 1840s. As the population expanded, however, job creation could not keep pace (even with 97,000 new jobs created between 1971 and 1979). As a result, unemployment increased sharply to 7.6 per cent in 1975 and 15.6 per cent in 1983. Predictably, the cycle of emigration resumed from the late 1970s onward, reaching significant proportions again in the following decade.[2]

As the relative prosperity of the Irish economy in the 1960s and 1970s gave way to economic stagnation and high unemployment in the 1980s, emigration to the United States picked up once again. Between 1980 and 1990, net outward migration from Ireland totalled 216,000, with the bulk of the emigrants leaving after 1985. Between 1986 and 1990, the average outflow was 34,000. Special immigration laws passed in the United States in 1986 and 1990 enabled Ireland to send more immigrants to America. The Immigration Reform and Control Act of 1986 provided 40,000 special visas to countries that had been the traditional sources of emigration to the United States and had been adversely affected by the 1965 act. Known as Donnelly visas after the Irish-American Congressman who sponsored the scheme, they were offered to applicants randomly selected from a mailing list and did not require skills, jobs offers or family connections. Of the 40,000 green cards issued under this scheme, 16,329 went to Irish applicants. The Immigration Act of 1990 established a new lottery system (the 'Morrison' visas) that guaranteed Ireland 48,000 'Morrison' green cards over three years.[3]

Official figures greatly underestimate the number of Irish immigrants to the United States in the 1980s, counting only those who came to the country legally. From 1980 to 1985, those figures varied between only 900 and 1,400 immigrants a year. Thereafter, the numbers rose to roughly 1,900 in 1986, 3,000 in 1987, 3,500 in 1988, 9,900 in 1989 and 4,500 in 1990. The great majority of these legal immigrants in the late 1980s were admitted under Donnelly and Morrison visas. But tens of thousands of Irish who entered the United States in the 1980s on temporary tourist visas failed to return home once their visas had expired, staying indefinitely and working without proper documentation. They settled especially in New York, Boston, Chicago and San Francisco, where vibrant underground communities of 'new Irish' emerged, often in rundown inner cities areas like the South Bronx.[4]

Within the two population flows from Ireland in the 1980s, one legal and the other illegal, four types of emigrant have been identified. The first were self-consciously economic refugees, citing lack of work and opportunity as the main reason for their departure from Ireland. Most of this first group were working-class or lower-middle-class, and they included many illegal as well as documented immigrants. The second group, by contrast, was composed mainly of young middle-class Irish who went to the United States on tourist visas and then took an extended, illegal working holiday. Most did not see any particular risk in this, as they did not intend to stay in the country permanently; many, however, doubtless ended up staying as they put down roots. The third group was also middle-class or upper-middle-class but, unlike the previous two, was almost always legal; it consisted primarily of university graduates and professionals, and constituted a substantial 'brain drain' from Ireland. A remarkable 36 per cent of those who earned primary university degrees in Ireland in 1988, for example, went on to emigrate, including 48 per cent of engineering graduates, 43 per cent of arts and social science graduates and 42 per cent of architecture graduates. Most of these highly trained young emigrants, dubbed *Eirepreneurs* by one historian, went to Britain, the United States and the European Union (in that order), settling in the major cities of the western economy, where opportunity was readily available to them. The members of the fourth and final category of Irish emigrants in the 1980s were all documented, as they were the winners of Donnelly and Morrison visas. Most of these visas went to Irish residents rather than the illegal Irish already in America, and many chose not to exercise the option of going to the United States; many of those who did cross the Atlantic did so only temporarily each year for a specified period, until such time as the visa became permanent, without ever giving up their residence in Ireland.[5]

In the 1990s Ireland entered a period of unprecedented economic prosperity, reversing the demographic trends of the previous decade. With a highly educated young population, booming consumer spending and annual growth rates as high as 7 per cent, the new economy was dubbed the 'Celtic Tiger'. Lacking an industrial past, Ireland did not have to deal with post-industrial devastation of cities and the environment, nor the problems of economic adjustment faced by many other countries. As one popular saying put it: 'The Industrial Revolution is the best thing that never happened to Ireland.' At the same time, Ireland received billions of dollars in subsidies and aid from the European Union (EU) in the 1980s and 1990s, using the funds to build highways and a new infrastructure. One Irish motorist quoted in a newspaper recalled his reaction to the new highways, with their EU logos: 'God bless the German taxpayer'. Ireland's small-farm-based agriculture was very well suited to benefit from the EU Common Agricultural Policy, while EU funds were also used very effectively to attract multinational companies in information technology and pharmaceuticals with generous development deals and low tax rates. Thus, while Ireland's recent prosperity threatened to bring to an end its status as a major recipient of EU funds, those funds were being used to build the basis of a potentially durable economic prosperity.[6]

At the heart of this prosperity was the emergence of a high-tech economy that probably benefited the majority of Ireland's population, but left behind a core of impoverished, poorly educated urban dwellers. In the course of the 1990s, Ireland became one of the major computer-servicing, hardware assembling and software-producing centers in Europe. Sixty per cent of all business-application software and 40 per cent of all personal-computer packaged software sold in Europe in the late 1990s was made in Ireland. Dublin became the European center for tele-servicing computer problems, with calls from all over Europe routed to international operators located there. Ireland also became the leading European manufacturer of 'anti-virus' and 'anti-crash' devices. Major American manufacturers of personal computers, like Gateway and Dell, established their European manufacturing, distribution and service centers in Ireland. Even with as many as 45,000 new jobs a year being created, however, unemployment remained in the region of 10 to 12 per cent, the hardest hit being unskilled, poorly educated inner-city slum dwellers and residents of working-class, tower-block suburbs. In parts of inner-city Dublin in the late 1990s, unemployment was as high as 70 per cent, and violent crime and drug addiction were endemic, even as most middle- and upper-middle-class Irish people prospered as never before.[7]

Not surprisingly, the net result of this overall prosperity was a reversal in Ireland's historical pattern of emigration and population loss, to an even greater extent than in the 1970s. Well aware of how many skilled workers had been lost to Ireland through emigration in the 1980s, the government launched a campaign to get them back. Eighteen of the twenty members of the School of Architecture graduating class at University College, Dublin (UCD) in 1984 had emigrated, for example, as had fourteen of the sixteen members of the engineering class at Trinity College, Dublin (TCD) in 1986. Now a series of government-sponsored posters in airports and other loca-tions announced 'We Need You Back in Ireland'. In the 1990s, for only the second time since the Famine, more people entered Ireland than left it, and the overall population grew rather than declined. Whereas almost 71,000 people had emigrated from Ireland (for all destinations) in 1989, only 21,200 emigrated in 1998 and 44,000 people migrated into the country. Among them were not only Irish people returning from Britain or America, but also a substantial proportion of immigrants from eastern Europe and Africa. Ireland, for the very first time in its history, was becoming a nation of immig-rants rather than emigrants, with the attendant problems of racism and intol-erance that have classically accompanied the process of immigration in other countries. The irony was perhaps best captured in a cartoon in *The Irish Times* in August 1998 depicting a group of Romanian gypsies who had recently been smuggled into the country and bearing the caption 'No Romanians Need Apply'.[8]

THE IRISH-AMERICAN COMMUNITY

With the decline in Irish immigration, the number of first and second-generation Irish Americans fell rapidly in the second half of the twentieth century. There were 572,031 Irish-born Americans in 1940, compared to only 251,375 in 1970 and 197,817 in 1980. The number of second-generation American Irish (American-born of Irish or mixed parentage) also dropped, from 1,838,920 in 1940 to 1,198,845 in 1970. The extent and nature of this demographic change can be illustrated by considering the case of New York

City, where the first and second-generation Irish population dropped substantially after the Second World War. As late as 1940, they had together accounted for half a million people, but by 1960 that number had dropped to 312,000 and by 1970 to 220,000. In 1980 (before the sizeable influx of the following decade), only 42,000 New Yorkers were Irish-born, with another 600,000 identifying themselves as being of primary or partial Irish origin (second-generation and beyond), out of a total population of 7 million. Most of the metropolitan area's Irish-American population now lived outside the city proper, which went from being 90 per cent white in 1940 to less than half white in the 1990s. The suburbs of Long Island, Westchester and New Jersey held the heaviest concentrations of Irish-Americans by the 1990s, most of them financially well-off members of the third generation and beyond. Of the city boroughs, Queens had the largest concentration of Irish Americans (about one-third of the city's total in 1980 and 1990), with Brooklyn second.[9]

The share of the Irish-American population living in the sunbelt states, especially Florida, Arizona and California rose rapidly after 1950, even more quickly than the share of the American population as a whole. Between 1960 and 1980, the number of Americans living in the sunbelt states rose from 23 to 27 per cent, while the number of Irish Americans living there almost doubled, rising from 9 to 16 per cent. Thus, after almost a century in which the Irish-American population had been virtually stationary, with about 60 per cent living in the states of Massachusetts, New York, Pennsylvania and Illinois, that population by the 1990s was moving with the general population flow of the United States. This fragmentation of the old geographical concentration was contributing to a significant erosion of ethnic identity among Irish Americans.[10]

Like other urban 'ethnics', the American Irish took full advantage of postwar federal legislation on highway construction, home ownership and mortgage financing, each of which made significant contributions to the rapid growth of suburbanization in the United States. The combined metropolitan areas of Boston, Chicago and New York were home to between 54 and 58 per cent of all Irish immigrants to the United States in the twentieth century, and as recently as 1980 they contained 17 per cent of those native-born Americans who identified themselves as being of Irish ancestry. But large numbers of the American Irish had moved out from the inner areas of these cities by that time, settling in their metropolitan suburbs and beyond. The only significant inner-city Irish neighbourhoods in Chicago by 1980, for example, were Beverly and Morgan Park on the far Southwest Side, along with remnants of the famous 'Back of the Yards' community in Bridgeport. Most other Irish inner-city communities in Chicago had been settled by African Americans and Latinos from the 1960s onward, as had much of the Bronx, Prospect Park and other Irish areas in New York City. Attracted by the relative prosperity and racial segregation of the suburbs, Irish families moved in their thousands out of the inner cities. This Irish flight to the suburbs was facilitated, as in the case of other white Americans who moved out of cities, by affluence; the income of Irish immigrant families in New York City and Chicago was only 6 to 7 per cent less than that of native-born families of native parentage, while the income of second-generation Irish families was 6 to 14 per cent higher than the native-born average. In Boston suburbanization was slower, partly because of lower rates of black and Hispanic migration and partly because the Irish had a lower economic status, with Irish immigrants earning 20 per cent less than the native-born average and second-generation families earning only 2 per cent more. Overall, despite heavy suburbanization – especially by members of the second generation and beyond – the American Irish moved to the suburbs more slowly than the American population as a whole. They thereby retained some of their historical preference for city life, even as the substantial drift to the suburbs tended to fragment their sense of a cohesive ethnic identity.[11]

Irish-American suburbanization coincided with a steady climb up the occupational ladder in the second half of the twentieth century. Much of this upward social mobility can be attributed to Catholic colleges like Fordham, Boston College and Georgetown, founded by the Church in the wake of the famine immigration of the mid-nineteenth century with the express intention of expanding opportunity for Irish Americans through higher education. Although they remained lower on the occupational ladder than any of the older (pre-1890) immigrant groups in 1950, the American Irish were distributed more evenly in the occupational structure than ever before. Seventy-three per cent of first-generation Irish-American men worked in blue-collar jobs in that year, including 20 per cent who were employed as craftsmen. Just under 14 per cent worked as unskilled labourers. In semi-skilled and service positions, the Irish-born were most heavily represented as porters or cleaners, followed by firemen and policemen. Among those who held professional jobs (4.2 per cent of the first generation and 9.5 per cent of the second) the most important position was clergyman, while those who worked as managers (7.6 per cent and 11.6 per cent) tended to be superintendents of buildings. Irish-born women continued to work disproportionately in service, predominantly in private households.[12]

Compared to the Irish-born, second-generation Irish Americans in 1950 displayed considerable upward mobility, though still at a slower rate than most other immigrant groups. Men with one or more Irish-born parents moved into the professional ranks, generally as accountants, clergymen or lawyers, at an impressive rate. But relative to other blue-collar workers of foreign parentage, Irish Americans were over-represented in the protective services (policemen and firemen). Second-generation women were dispersed widely throughout the occupational structure, with a concentration in the protective services. In white-collar fields Irish Americans were over-represented in law, engineering, teaching and clerical work. In Boston, admittedly, the Irish (along with the Italians) continued to lag behind all other white groups in the 1950s and 1960s, holding three times their share of unskilled labouring jobs, and disproportionately fewer professional, managerial and proprietorship positions. If one thing is certain about twentieth-century Irish-American social history, however, it is that the Boston Irish cannot be held to typify the American Irish; on the contrary, they were exceptionally disadvantaged. Moving beyond Boston to the United States as a whole, Americans of Irish descent in 1970 were over-represented, compared with the general population, in law, medicine and the sciences and had clearly left behind most of the disadvantages associated with the earlier immigrant generations.[13]

The Irish share of total immigration to the United States fell drastically in the twentieth century, so that those who arrived in the 1940s accounted for 2.6 per cent of all immigrants, those of the 1950s accounted for 2.3 per cent and those of the 1960s for only 1.1 per cent. As the immigrant flow was cut off, the demographic profile of the Irish-American ethnic group was transformed. The 1950s were a turning point in this respect. One-third of the Irish-born in the United States in 1950, and one-quarter of the offspring of Irish immigrants, had died by 1960. The ratio of second- to first-generation grew to over four to one in the same decade, and the median age of Irish-born Americans reached almost sixty years. The 'typical' Irish American by 1960 belonged to the third and later generations, not to the immigrant group and its children. With the decline in Irish immigration in the 1960s, the number of first-generation immigrants continued to fall, and by 1970 almost one in three Irish-born Americans was over seventy years old. This 'graying' of Irish America, along with the rapid reduction of immigration from Ireland and the exodus to the suburbs, was in large part responsible for the significant diffusion and erosion of Irish-American ethnicity in the second half of the twentieth century.[14]

Several aspects of the late nineteenth-century Irish-American family structure had survived well into the 1950s, but began to disintegrate thereafter. Up to the 1950s, the median age at first marriage for Irish immigrants or their children was still higher than for any other major immigrant group in the United States. Rates of permanent celibacy also remained unusually high, and the American Irish typically had larger families and fewer divorces than any other foreign-born group in the United States. The high rates of marital fertility of the late nineteenth century survived, so that as late as 1960 Irish-born mothers were second only to women born in Mexico in the number of children they bore. But already by 1960 Irish Americans of the first and second generation were more likely to marry outside their ethnic group than within it, whereas three-quarters of all Irish immigrants in the United States in 1920 had married other Irish people (of either Irish or American birth). The patterns of matrimony (late marriage and in-group marriage), high fertility and permanent celibacy that had characterized the Irish in America since the post-famine era had all but disappeared by 1970, replaced by distinctively American patterns of social and geographical mobility, education and marriage. The implications for the cohesion of the ethnic group and the maintenance of ethnic identity are obvious.[15]

While most Irish-Americans by this time were American-born, there was still a substantial immigrant presence, especially in the 1950s and again in the 1980s. Among those Irish visitors to the United States in the 1980s who ended up staying permanently, there were two distinct groups. Alongside the legally documented immigrants, who included a well-educated elite of so-called *Eirepreneurs*, was an illegal community whose size in the 1980s has been estimated at between 40,000 and 200,000. The latter figure, cited by activists for immigration law reform, is a clear exaggeration but the former is an underestimate; a figure of between 40,000 and 100,000 is most likely. Paradoxically, each of these two groups, legal and illegal, was 'invisible' in its own way. The professional elite were comfortably ensconced in the upper echelons of the American business world, and often had few if any links with other Irish immigrants or Irish Americans. The illegals, on the other hand, were compelled by their status to work in an 'informal', undocumented economy, even as they revitalized the blighted urban areas in which they settled. Putative bonds of ethnicity among the better-off legal immigrants were easily severed by their integration into native-born professional and business elites, and by the facility and frequency with which they could fly home to Ireland, temporarily or permanently. Those who stayed in America assimilated quickly and did not coalesce into a separate ethnic community. Illegals, on the other hand, who clustered together in the same neighbourhoods, could not leave the country and relied on existing ethnic networks, did quickly form a vibrant new Irish-American community, but one that was necessarily concealed from the authorities and the outside world.[16]

The illegals found work primarily in the construction industry, restaurants and bars, typically working for Irish Americans who had immigrated in the 1950s or who belonged to second and third-generation families. Construction work, in particular, had traditionally been heavily Irish in its workforce and management, and had long operated on the basis of parallel 'formal' and 'informal' economies. Independent contractors, working without licenses and depending on non-union labour, were especially likely to hire undocumented immigrants, thereby saving on tax and social security obligations. Irish dominance of construction unions also meant that unionized construction sites often turned a blind eye to illegal immigrant labourers, so long as they came from Ireland. Irish-born illegals were paid less than other construction workers, both unionized and non-unionized, but generally fared much better than illegals from other countries. Similarly, young Irish men and women living illegally in the United States turned to Irish-owned bars and restaurants as a primary source of employment, in an under-the-counter arrangement that was of benefit, in the short-term at least, to employer and employee alike.[17]

Female Irish immigrants, both legal and illegal, were excluded from most construction jobs, but joined males in bar and restaurant work and found jobs as nannies and nurses in private homes. Demand for Irish nannies was considerable among two-career families in the urban centers of the Northeast where most illegals worked. A majority of all Irish women who came to New York City in the 1980s worked in private homes looking after children and the elderly. Live-in nannies and nurses had free meals and lodging, but they earned only half what construction workers did, while working much longer hours. Though work of this kind was often the only option for many illegal female immigrants, it was clearly not a source of long-term opportunity.[18]

While there was often a symbiotic relationship in the 1980s and 1990s between the new immigrants and the established Irish-American community, with the latter providing jobs and the former providing labour as well as revitalizing old inner-city neighbourhoods, there was also considerable tension. Much of this tension was generational, with the old Irish regarding the new as rude, lazy and ungrateful. But there was also considerable cultural conflict, as neither side conformed to the other's definition of Irishness. Many of the

young new Irish found native-born Irish Americans to be reactionary, puritanical and romantic in their conception of Ireland, while established Irish
Americans found the newcomers to be disrespectful, irreligious and lacking
in patriotism to both Ireland and the United States. On questions of gay
rights in particular, the two generations disagreed bitterly.[19]

Despite their political differences, the newcomers and the established
community came together to form a united front on the issue of illegal immigration. The Irish Immigration Reform Movement (IIRM), founded in 1987
to lobby on behalf of illegal Irish immigrants, depended heavily on the financial resources, facilities and lobbying power of established Irish Americans,
including the United Irish Counties Association, the AOH, the Irish-
American Labor Coalition (IALC), the Brehon Law Society and prominent
clergymen and businessmen. The Irish Immigration Working Committee
(IIWC), founded under the auspices of the Irish Consulate in New York City,
coordinated lobbying efforts for a series of immigration reform bills introduced into the House and Senate between 1987 and 1990. After 1990 the
issue diminished in importance, as illegals in the United States got visas and
the economy in Ireland began to expand dramatically.[20]

One other, more ambivalent bond between the established community
and the newcomers throughout the second half of the twentieth century was
alcohol. Spending much of their spare time in bars in an effort to duplicate
the social camaraderie they had enjoyed in Ireland, the immigrants drank
every bit as much as members of the established community. The image of
the hard-drinking Irish American, however, continued to be in part a cultural
stereotype as well as a social fact. According to researchers who have examined the topic, the American Irish drank no more than Americans of British
descent, only slightly more than Italian Americans and less than people in
France. Yet they had much higher rates of alcoholism and alcohol-related
psychoses than any of these groups. Unless there is some valid genetic explanation for this (a possibility that has not been considered in the historical
literature), then the best line of inquiry remains cultural, focusing on the
centrality of hard drinking to Irish-American masculinity and ethnic identity.
At the same time, alcohol abuse has been linked to a variety of emotional disorders. As late as 1950, newcomers from Ireland retained the highest rates of
mental illness (usually alcoholic psychoses) among all foreign- and native-
born whites. The children of Irish immigrants had significantly fewer
psychological problems than their parents, but still exceeded all second-
generation Americans in rates of mental disorders at this time. As in previous
years, rates of mental illness among the Irish in America also seem to have

been higher than in Ireland. Again, the explanations for this are far from clear, though some social psychiatrists have pointed to a greater degree of emotional and sexual repression as well as alcoholism among the American Irish compared to other ethnic groups in the United States.[21]

Questions of emotion, sexuality, family and alcoholism were, predictably, among the prominent themes in the vast body of Irish-American literature produced since the Second World War. This literature has generally been even more distinctively ethnic than that of Irish-American authors earlier in the twentieth century, more concerned with specifically Irish-American issues. Among its highlights are Edwin O'Connor's classic political novel, *The Last Hurrah* (1956); William Gibson's vivid rendition of growing up Irish in America in the 1920s, *A Mass for the Dead* (1968); Elizabeth Cullinan's memorable portrait of a dominant Irish matriarch in *A House of Gold* (1970); Tom McHale's account of affluent Irish Americans in Philadelphia, *Farragan's Retreat* (1971); Wilfrid Sheed's political novel, *People Will Always Be Kind* (1973); Maureen Howard's ambivalent memoir of her childhood and parents, *Facts of Life* (1978); and the various works of Mary Gordon, Pete Hamill, Jimmy Breslin and William Kennedy. Recent novels by younger authors include Alice McDermott's *That Night* (1987), set in lower-middle-class suburban Long Island in the 1960s, and *Charming Billy* (1998), which dealt with the familiar themes of alcoholism, family and memory and won a National Book Award; Tom Grimes's *A Stone of Heart* (1990), which dealt with a disintegrating Irish-Italian family in Queens, New York; and Thomas E. Kennedy's *Crossing Border* (1990), which raised themes of home, family and the difficulty of communicating emotion that had long been central to Irish-American literature.[22]

Irish-American literature in the 1990s also displayed a renewed sense of history, both personal and general. One of the best-selling books of the late 1990s was Frank McCourt's poignant, harrowing, yet ultimately optimistic memoir, *Angela's Ashes* (1996), in which he related the story of his childhood in Brooklyn and then Limerick in the 1930s. Thomas Cahill's best-selling *How the Irish Saved Civilization* (1995), an account of Irish monastic scholarship in the 'Dark Ages', also became a major best-seller. Peter Quinn's panoramic and dramatic novel of the Irish in Civil War New York, *Banished Children of Eve* (1994), memorably brought to life the central themes in Irish transatlantic history in the mid-nineteenth century. New cultural institutions, like the New York Irish History Roundtable and the Ireland House at New York University were founded to promote awareness of Irish and Irish-American history and culture. And from March through October 1996, the

Museum of the City of New York ran a major exhibit called 'Gaelic Gotham', giving a detailed and sophisticated portrayal of the history of Irish New York. Irish Studies programs at American universities prospered as never before. Together, these and many similar developments constituted a renaissance in Irish–American culture comparable in many ways to the remarkable Irish artistic flowering taking place in both Ireland and England in the same period.

RELIGION

According to polls conducted in the 1970s and 1980s, just over half of Americans whose primary ethnic allegiance was Irish were Protestant. This finding is at first sight quite surprising to most people. But it must be borne in mind that the Protestant Irish arrived in America earlier than the Catholics, while many of the latter who came before 1800 appear to have converted to Protestantism. While Protestant individuals accounted for considerably less than a quarter of all Irish immigrants to the present-day United States, their high share of the Irish-American population as a whole seems to be due mainly to their earlier arrival in America and a consequent multiplier effect. Significant numbers of Protestants also continued to arrive in the United States from Ireland in the nineteenth century. Irish-American Protestants in the late twentieth century were more likely than Catholics to belong to families with deep American roots, third or fourth-generation or beyond. In a poll conducted by the National Opinion Research Center in the 1970s, only 41 per cent of Irish-American Catholics interviewed were fourth-generation or beyond, compared to 83 per cent of American-Irish Protestants.[23]

Even more surprising than the slight majority of Protestants is the finding that Irish-American Catholics as a group tended by the late twentieth century to be better educated and wealthier than their Protestant counterparts. This is certainly unusual in the context of Irish history or American history before 1900. By the turn of the twentieth century, however, Irish Catholics had caught up with the population as a whole in terms of work and education, and they soon surpassed Irish Protestants and most immigrant groups in both respects. Within the context of American regional history, on the other hand, the current Irish Catholic advantage over Irish Protestants makes considerable sense. Irish-American Catholics, although dispersed throughout the country by the late twentieth century, remained heavily concentrated in the Northeast and Midwest, whereas more than half of Irish-American

Protestants lived in the South, where so many of their forebears had settled. Until at least the 1960s, the South was the most impoverished region in the United States; only thereafter did its relative disadvantage to the rest of the country begin to decline. Partly as a result, Irish-American Catholics in the 1970s were twice as likely as Irish-American Protestants to be university graduates, had significantly higher family incomes and were almost three times as likely to live in cities. The income and educational levels of Catholic Irish Americans exceeded not only those of the Protestant Irish but also of the American population generally, leading one sociologist to the perhaps overstated conclusion that the Catholic Irish are 'the most affluent gentile group in America'.[24]

The Catholic Church retained its powerful position at the heart of Irish-American history in the decades after the Second World War, though not quite to the extent that it had over the previous century. Irish Americans continued to dominate the upper echelons of the American Catholic Church in the postwar era, the principal figure during the Cold War being Cardinal Francis J. Spellman (1889–1967). The son of a small-town, Irish-American grocer, he graduated from Fordham College in 1911, was ordained a priest in 1919 and dominated the hierarchy from his appointment as Archbishop of New York in 1939 and Cardinal in 1946 until his death in 1967. Deeply conservative, he carved out an effective synthesis of Catholic orthodoxy and American patriotism, supporting McCarthyism, the Vietnam war and anti-communism generally, while also crusading for censorship in popular culture. Spellman's successors in New York City were two more Irish-American conservatives, Terence Cooke (1921–83), who became Cardinal in 1969, and John O'Connor (b.1920), who became Cardinal in 1985. At the other end of the political spectrum from the New York conservatives was Cardinal Richard J. Cushing (1895–1970) of Boston, a conventional liberal who maintained close ties to the Kennedy family. Born into a working-class, Irish-American family in Boston, he succeeded Irish-American William O'Connell as Archbishop and became Cardinal in 1958. Cardinal Timothy Manning of Los Angeles, born in County Cork in 1909, also aligned himself with the liberal tradition in Irish-American Catholicism, supporting the efforts of César Chavez to unionize Mexican-American agricultural workers in California in the late 1960s.[25]

Not every member of the American Catholic hierarchy in the late twentieth century was Irish-American, of course. Dennis Dougherty, a staunch Irish-American conservative who forbade his parishioners from watching Hollywood movies, was succeeded as Archbishop of Philadelphia in 1960 by the Polish American, John Krol. Similarly, the Portuguese American, Humberto Medeiros, succeeded Cardinal Cushing in Boston in 1970. As the twentieth century drew to a close, and new immigrant groups (especially Latinos) began to demand and gain more power within the Church, the Irish retained their prominence in the American hierarchy and clergy but not the dominance they once regarded as their birthright. Still, as late as 1970, over 50 per cent of the American bishops and 34 per cent of the priests had an Irish background, at a time when Americans of Irish descent made up less than 20 per cent of all American Catholics.[26]

The traditional American liberal antipathy toward Catholicism reached a peak in the 1940s, but faded in the 1950s. In the 1940s, many American intellectuals still tended to believe that Catholicism was fundamentally antithetical to democracy, because its alleged authoritarianism and absolutism could not be reconciled with American political practice and philosophical thought. One of the best-selling books of the late 1940s, for example, was Paul Blanshard's *American Freedom and Catholic Power*, which charged Catholicism with anti-democratic social policies, intolerance, and 'separatist or un-American' features, drawing praise from prominent liberal intellectuals. In *The Authoritarian Personality* (1950), the transplanted German intellectual Theodore Adorno included Catholics in his general category of restrictive, religious families whose children might channel their frustration into fascist politics. Adorno also reiterated the alleged connection between Catholicism and support for Nazism, while Seymour Martin Lipset cited Catholics' support for McCarthyism in the 1950s as proof of their susceptibility to authoritarianism (ignoring the fact that most Catholics remained Democratic in this period). The Harvard social psychologist, David C. McClelland, argued that the lack of economic success in Catholic countries could be explained by their religion's stifling of children's initiative and autonomy. And a study funded by the Social Science Research Council frankly compared Catholicism to Communism, claiming that the adherents of both were dogmatic, intolerant and anti-democratic.[27]

It was precisely the looming threat of communism, however, that rescued American Catholics from their status as suspect citizens. The philosopher Sidney Hook, who as recently as 1940 had described Catholicism as 'the oldest and greatest totalitarian movement in history', pointed out in the early 1950s that the most urgent threat to American freedom now came from the Kremlin, not the Vatican. Leaving aside the issue of whether Americans in the 1950s exaggerated the Soviet threat, it remained true that the Pope had no atomic bombs. From about 1950 onward American liberals moved toward a cautious acceptance of Catholicism combined with forthright denunciations of communism and calls for national unity in the face of communist expansionism. Thus, when Will Herberg published his influential study *Protestant-Catholic-Jew: An Essay in American Religious Sociology* (1955), he included Catholics as an integral element of an 'American religion' constituted by three complementary faiths. Certain issues continued to rankle among American liberals, of course, chief among them Catholic demands for government assistance for educational projects. Separate schools were particularly unpopular among liberals in the 1950s, partly because they were believed to fracture the national cultural unity so earnestly demanded during the early Cold War, and partly because the idea of religiously segregated schools sat poorly with the mounting drive for racially integrated education from the middle of the decade onward. Nonetheless, John F. Kennedy was able to overcome anti-Catholicism in 1960 to very narrowly win the presidency of the United States. The Church won greater acceptance in the United States in the wake of the second Vatican Council (Vatican II, 1962–5), an international convention that resulted in a wide variety of reforms in Catholic doctrine and practice. But, while it pleased many American Catholics, Vatican II alienated many others, especially those to the left and right of its liberal agenda. Radical Catholics protested that the reforms had not yet gone far enough; conservatives, by contrast, were alarmed that the reforms had already conceded too much.[28]

As Irish-American Catholics became ever more American than Irish, they inevitably began to rethink the meaning of Catholicism in the United States, a process that could only be intensified by Vatican II. For many American Catholics in the 1960s the result was a crisis of identity, with some responding to the new liberalism by dropping their faith altogether, and others taking the opportunity to renew their commitment to Catholicism (whether in opposition to, or in agreement with, the reforms). Complicating the American response to Vatican II was the ongoing process of suburbanization, which was undermining the inner-city parish base and its system of parochial education. As the American Irish moved in large numbers to the suburbs in the 1950s and 1960s, many of the older urban parish schools were forced to close. While the new suburban parishes tried to imitate the urban model by placing a church and school at the center of parish life, the bonds of ethnic community were inevitably sundered by suburbanization. The new model of a single family home with one or more automobiles stood in sharp contrast to the traditional insular, ethnic enclaves of the cities. To the extent that suburban life eroded the differences between various (white) ethnic groups, it simultaneously eroded the social base of the Catholic school system. Many Irish suburban parents turned away from the parochial school system altogether, seeking commonality for their children in the public schools. One result was a stark decline by the 1970s in the numbers of young men and women enrolling in seminaries and convents. Bishop John Hughes, the great champion of Catholic schools in the mid-nineteenth century, would have been outraged by all of these developments. But his age was long gone, for by now the accent in the term 'Irish-American' was decidedly on the American.[29]

In the 1980s and 1990s the preeminent position of the Catholic Church in the Irish-American community came under bitter attack in certain quarters. The teachings of the Church on matters of sexuality and abortion alienated many young Irish Americans, especially recent arrivals from Ireland. One of the chief flashpoints was the question of gay rights, which ranged older Irish Americans and Irish immigrants of previous generations against younger Irish Americans from both the United States and Ireland, but primarily the latter. The question came into sharp focus in 1991 when the committee in charge of organizing New York City's St Patrick's Day parade, dominated by the Ancient Order of Hibernians, refused to let the Irish Lesbian and Gay Organization (ILGO) take part. In an effort to reach a compromise, Division 7 of the Manhattan AOH invited ILGO to march with them, but under Division 7's banner rather than its own. Mayor David Dinkins then decided to march with Division 7 and ILGO rather than in the mayor's customary place at the head of the parade, and during the parade he was booed and pelted with beer cans. Cardinal O'Connor did not take a public stance, though he clearly disapproved of homosexuality and of Dinkins's decision. Many who opposed ILGO regarded the parade as a celebration not just of Irishness but of Catholicism. Many members of ILGO were themselves Catholic, of course, but their opponents wanted them excluded for their violation of the official teachings of the Church.[30]

Matters came to a head when the AOH once again banned ILGO in 1992 and ILGO demanded the right not only to march but to do so under its own banner. The city's Human Rights Commission protested the AOH's decision, and the city eventually removed the right to organize the parade from the AOH division that had been running it for a century, giving it instead to the state division. But the state body then also insisted on banning ILGO and, when ILGO and the Dinkins administration took the case to court, a federal judge upheld the denial of ILGO's right to march. Dinkins and others refused to march that year and ILGO staged a protest march instead, with numerous arrests. In 1994, with ILGO still banned, the new mayor, Rudolph Giuliani, registered his disagreement with his predecessor's position by marching with the AOH parade. The dispute between ILGO and the AOH remained unresolved in the late 1990s, as did similar battles in Boston and other cities. And in an irony that did not escape the agitators, the eroding power of the Catholic Church in Ireland had by that time made Ireland far more conducive a place for homosexual culture than Irish America.[31]

MUNICIPAL POLITICS

In the three decades after the Second World War, the Irish continued to dominate politics in cities like Chicago, Pittsburgh and Albany. The age of Irish machine politics had not simply come to an abrupt end during the New Deal, even if Tammany Hall had suffered a debilitating reverse. On the contrary, several machines had strengthened their position in the 1930s, and after the war they oversaw massive urban renewal and development projects, often financed by federal funds, thereby creating new supplies of municipal jobs and revenue. In many ways, these machines seemed as powerful as ever. Ultimately, however, they succumbed to demographic and political forces that were strikingly similar to those which had undermined Tammany Hall and other machines in the 1930s. From the 1960s onwards, black and Hispanic residents demanded a greater share of political power, just as the 'new immigrants' had done a generation or two before. With white Americans, including the Irish, moving in huge numbers to the suburbs, blacks and Hispanics soon found themselves with the demographic potential to wield considerable political power. When the old machines proved unwilling or unable to meet their demands, black and Hispanic urban dwellers challenged them directly. By the 1980s, African-American voters had helped elect black mayors in Chicago, Philadelphia and New York, and were posing a serious threat to Irish power in Boston. But not before the Irish machines of the postwar era had produced some of their more memorable displays of power.[32]

The Irish retained a strong grip on American city politics in the decades following the Second World War. New York City, like Boston and Chicago, was still a very Irish city. Its mayor from 1946 to 1950 was Irish-born William O'Dwyer. Significantly, he had risen to power through the police department rather than Tammany Hall. The police and fire departments of New York City, Boston, Chicago and many other cities were still predominantly Irish at this time. Although Tammany went down to defeat at the hands of Italian-American boss Carmine de Sapio in 1949, William O'Dwyer was re-elected mayor that year (only to resign in 1950 over allegations linking him to organized crime). Robert Wagner, Jr., whose mother was Irish, became the last Irish mayor of New York City when he was elected in 1953 with the help of Tammany, but turned against the organization during his bid for a third term in 1961. Thus ended the almost century-long domination of Manhattan politics by the Irish. In the Bronx, the Irish retained control of Democratic politics until 1963, led by the bosses Edward Flynn (1891–1953) and Charles Buckley (1890–1967). The Irish also controlled the Democratic party in Staten Island, and in the heavily Irish suburban Long Island counties of Nassau and Suffolk. Similarly in Boston, which never developed a political machine on the New York model, the mayors between 1945 and 1993 were all Irish-Americans (with one brief exception): James M. Curley (1946–50), John B. Hynes (1950–2, 1952–60), John F. Collins (1960–8), Kevin H. White (1968–84) and Raymond L. Flynn (1984–93). Flynn's Italian-American successor, Thomas M. Menino depended heavily for his election on Irish support within the local Democratic party.[33]

Irish urban political power reached its twentieth-century acme in Chicago. The Chicago Irish had begun to take control of Democratic politics in the early 1880s, built a machine in the early twentieth century, fought off an ethnic revolt in the early 1930s, and then built an even more powerful machine during the New Deal, paving the way for three successive Irish-American mayors, Martin Kennelly, Edward Kelly and Richard Daley (who ruled uninterruptedly from 1955 until his death in 1976). The degree of Irish political mobilization and organization in Chicago was such that they continued to exert an influence on politics quite disproportionate to their share of the city's population. In the early 1960s, for example, Irish Americans accounted for only about 10 per cent of Chicago's population, but 12 of the city's 50 aldermen were Irish-American, along with 21 of its 50 ward commissioners and almost half of its state attorneys. In 1964, 41 of the 72 highest administrative positions in the Chicago Police Department were held by Irishmen, and of the 35 police commissioners in Chicago in the century up to that point at least 21 were of Irish origin. The man presiding over this remarkable display of Irish political domination was Richard Daley (1902–76), the last of the great Irish-American machine politicians.[34]

Richard Daley was one of the most formidable figures in twentieth-century American politics. His personality, as one of his biographers noted, was based in equal measure on his family, his faith, his neighbourhood, his ethnicity, his party and his city. A devout Roman Catholic, he was the only child of working-class Irish Catholic parents, and raised his own family in the same traditions. In his biographer's words, 'He is Irish to the core. He was born, grew up, and has lived all his life in Bridgeport, one of Chicago's authentic Back-of-the-Yards neighborhoods. He has always been a Democrat. And he is a life-long resident of Chicago, a city he has always believed to be the greatest metropolis in the world.' A committed family man, he married a neighbourhood girl named Eleanor Guilfoyle, and together they raised seven children, educating them in parochial schools and Catholic 'subway' universities like Loyola and St Paul. He was a moderate drinker who disliked drunks, off-colour stories and swearing. Unlike many previous Irish bosses he was scrupulously honest and never enriched himself personally in politics; he did, however, regard nepotism as one of his political duties and took good care of his relatives. According to one source, over a hundred of them held government jobs. He loved the neighbourhood of Bridgeport, where he was born and baptized, attended school and served as an altar boy, got married and raised his family. The neighbourhood was working-class and heavily Irish; no black families lived there. Daley was very proud of being Irish. All his close friends and most of his political advisors were Irish. St Patrick's Day, when the river was dyed green and he led the city's great parade, was always his finest day.[35]

How did this distinctive personal style translate into politics? Daley was a master at the personal touch, the key to machine politics. He was an expert in the mechanics of politics, organization and campaigning. He was cautious and conservative, dismissive of reform and social engineering. Daley was a Democrat, but of the old, pre-New Deal kind. Although he was a very powerful figure in the national Democratic party in the 1960s, he had no time for its association with the welfare state, with civil rights and with an interventionist foreign policy. Daley may have ruled one of the world's greatest cities, but his style was parochial. In his heart, he never left Bridgeport. As his leading biographer puts it: 'He conceives his city and world as a series of Bridgeports – communities in which God-fearing, decent, hard-working people strive to keep the community stable, hold onto the values of their fathers, and fulfill their obligations as citizens to the neighborhood, the *polis*, and the nation.' This was a worldview that inevitably brought Daley into opposition with the anti-war and counter-cultural movements of the late 1960s. Entirely unable to understand them, he took at face value the threats of youthful protestors at the Democratic convention of 1968 that they would turn the city he had built into a circus. He treated them as though they were a genuinely revolutionary force and unleashed the full and awesome power of the Chicago police and the National Guard against them. At the same time, he tried to silence the anti-war Democratic delegates inside the convention hall, using heavy-handed tactics. The nation watched it all on television. As the Democrats went down to defeat by Richard Nixon in the presidential election later that year, Daley lost much prestige within the national party and faced an emerging challenge to the power of his machine in Chicago.[36]

Daley's machine reached its peak in the early 1960s, but began to decline thereafter in the face of attack by its erstwhile allies, the labour movement and racial and ethnic 'minorities'. He opposed public employee unionization and collective bargaining for obvious reasons; they could only weaken the patronage system on which his power depended. He did support organized labour (and secured its vote) in other ways, providing massive downtown public works projects, guaranteeing the prevailing wage for craft union members on the city payroll and appointing labour representatives to most of the city's boards and commissions. But he bitterly opposed public-sector unions. Chicago's teachers, who had long been excluded from machine patronage, were the first to organize, forcing Daley to agree eventually to collective bargaining. Fire fighters and transit workers followed suit in the 1970s, against bitter opposition from Daley. In much the same way, police officers, fire fighters and other municipal workers in Albany threatened the power of Dan O'Connell's long-lived political machine in the 1970s.[37]

If public-sector unions posed one threat to Daley's machine, an even more powerful challenge was posed by Chicago's black and Latino voters. Black voters had provided Daley's margin of victory in 1955 and 1963, but got little in return. Then in 1964 the Civil Rights Act prohibited job discrimination on the basis of race, a measure that was extended in 1972 to cover state and local government employment. Blacks in Chicago brought suit in federal court to end the discriminatory hiring and promotion practices of Daley's police and fire departments. After a bitter court fight and lengthy negotiations, the machine was forced to back down. Reformers also took a successful class action suit, filed by independent candidates, taxpayers and voters, objecting to the fact that half the 40,000 jobs in the city and county were given to party stalwarts. The Chicago machine was enjoined from using partisan criteria in government hiring and firing. At the same time, the local revenue base was eroding by the 1970s, due to the flight of population and capital. As white people moved to the suburbs, so did business and industry. Foreign competition was also contributing during this period to the de-industrialization of the frost-belt cities of the Midwest.[38]

In both Chicago and Albany the city payroll fell in the 1970s, with fewer jobs meaning fewer votes controlled. The surviving machines had also lost their hold over federal welfare funds by this time. Without controlling the distribution of social services to poor families, most of whom were now black and Hispanic, the machine politicians could not count on 'minority' support. On the contrary, Daley's patronage practices and his racist public housing policies, which denied racial 'minorities' the best public jobs and consigned them to segregated tower-block housing, eventually led to a successful revolt against his machine. Daley died in 1976 with his machine intact, but African-American Harold Washington built a 'rainbow coalition' of blacks, Hispanics and white liberals in 1983 to defeat Daley's Irish-American successor, Mayor Jane Byrne, and his son, Richard M. Daley, in the Democratic primary and went on to be elected mayor. Daley's son did become mayor in the 1990s, continuing the tradition of Irish domination of the city's politics. But the heyday of machine politics in Chicago, over which his father had presided, was at an end.[39]

NATIONAL POLITICS

As the last of the Irish political machines started to decline in the 1960s, the American Irish were making a significant impact on national politics, especially in the legislative and executive branches of government. Thus, while Tammany Hall suffered its final defeat in New York City in 1961, nine of the nineteen Congressmen elected from the city the following year were Irish-American, as were one-third of the delegates sent by New York state to the Democratic convention in 1960. The two most powerful Irish-American politicians in the 1950s were the anti-communist crusader, Senator Joseph McCarthy, and Senator John F. Kennedy, who in 1960 became the first Catholic elected president of the United States.[40]

Unlike most Irish Americans at the time, Joseph McCarthy was a Republican, not a Democrat. A graduate of Marquette University, he represented the state of Wisconsin in the US Senate. As an anti-communist crusader, he lent his name to the crusade against internal subversion that swept across the United States in the late 1940s and early 1950s. McCarthy drew much of his support from the same places where support for Fr. Charles Coughlin had been strongest in the 1930s. He and Coughlin shared a following among Irish Americans, many of them Irish-born and most of them middle-aged or older, in the poorer districts of Boston, New York, Philadelphia and Chicago. Irish Americans supported McCarthy in part because of their concerns for Catholics in communist eastern Europe, and in part because of their suspicions about the patriotism of liberals and intellectuals. McCarthy, however, was a Republican, and most Irish Americans retained their allegiance to the Democrats. Irish-American machine politicians typically avoided the question of McCarthyism altogether. Very few Irish defected permanently to the Republican party during the McCarthyite era, though many voted for Eisenhower. The mass defection of the Irish came only from the mid-to-late-1960s onward, as part of the nationwide political realignment following the passage of the Civil Rights Act in 1964. McCarthyism transcended party political lines; it was as much an anti-elitist and anti-intellectual movement as an anti-communist one. McCarthy's Irish-American supporters typically found themselves ranged against a political and social establishment they regarded with resentment and suspicion. In an ironic twist that was noted at the time, the sons of the Protestant elite, educated in the Ivy League, were being interrogated for their 'un-American' activities by Irish Catholic graduates of universities like Marquette, Fordham and Notre Dame.[41]

One Irish-American politician for whom McCarthyism posed an acute dilemma was Senator John F. Kennedy (1917–63), a Democrat who represented the state of Massachusetts in the US Senate in the 1950s. Most of Kennedy's Irish Catholic constituents supported McCarthy, as did several members of his family. His younger brother, Robert, was actively engaged in the investigations into communism and worked for a time on the staff of McCarthy's investigative committee. His father invited McCarthy to the family retreat at Hyannisport on a number of occasions. The young Kennedy had to balance local and ethnic concerns against national political ambitions, and never supported Joseph McCarthy in public. On the other hand, for Kennedy to have criticized him openly would have been to alienate his constituents and members of his family. Kennedy faced a dilemma in 1954 when McCarthy, whose star was now rapidly falling, faced a censure vote in the Senate. As it turned out, Kennedy was in hospital awaiting a back operation, when the vote was taken. He later revealed that he would have voted against McCarthy, but on narrow and technical grounds, and that he feared that his vote would have a large negative impact on his support among the American Irish.[42]

The great-grandson of a famine refugee who had died fourteen years after landing in Boston, John Fitzgerald Kennedy embodied the dream of Irish success in the United States. He did so, moreover, in Boston, the city where the Irish had always experienced the most bigotry and had made the least social progress. But Kennedy was anything but typical of the American Irish.

Raised in privilege and educated at Harvard, he had lived as a student in London, where his father Joseph P. Kennedy was American ambassador. As the grandson of two of Boston's most storied turn-of-the-century political chieftains, Patrick J. Kennedy and John 'Honey Fitz' Fitzgerald, and the son of an intensely ambitious and immensely wealthy father, Kennedy grew up steeped in politics. Joseph P. Kennedy had seen his own political fortunes dwindle in the late 1930s after he miscalculated the state of world politics by supporting Germany in the encroaching European conflict. He was eventually removed from office by President Roosevelt and never entered politics again, but he had extremely high ambitions for his sons. After his eldest son, Joseph, died in action in the Second World War, Joseph P. Kennedy focused his ambitions on his next son, John, known affectionately as Jack.

These ambitions came to be realized from the 1950s onward, though the prospect of Jack Kennedy running for president raised the major dilemma of how voters would react to his religion. No Catholic had ever been elected President of the United States, and the obstacles to be faced by an Irish Catholic candidate had been clearly revealed in the bigotry directed against Al Smith in the 1920s. To become president, Kennedy would have to overcome more than a century of discrimination against Irish Catholics and persuade the American public that somebody of his religious background was fit to hold the highest political office. Kennedy made his first bid for power at the Democratic convention of 1956, when he sought the nomination for vice-president and was narrowly defeated. His father astutely regarded this defeat as a good thing, realizing that a Democratic defeat (which looked likely because the popular Dwight D. Eisenhower was running for a second term) might well be blamed on the religion of his son. Had Kennedy won the nomination for Vice-President in 1956 he might never have won the presidential nomination four years later.[43]

Kennedy's Catholicism was one of the central issues in the campaign of 1960. With considerable political skill, he decided to address the issue head-on during the primaries, beginning in May 1960 at the West Virginia primary. Aware that voters there were deeply suspicious of Catholicism, he reassured them in a live telecast debate with Franklin Delano Roosevelt, Jr. that the oath of office of the President of the United States is, among other things, an oath to support the separation of church and state, and that to break this oath would be a crime against the Constitution and against God. The telecast was immensely successful, persuading many Protestants that their fears were groundless. At the same time, Kennedy could count on the support of most of America's Catholics (estimated at between 35 and 43 million out of a total population of 171 million), though many clergymen and conservative laity are thought to have supported Kennedy's Republican opponent, Vice President Richard Nixon, in 1960.[44]

After winning the Democratic nomination and proceeding to the campaign against Nixon in the summer of 1960, Kennedy had to deal more than ever with the question of religion. If there was a single location where he finally laid this question to rest, it was Houston, Texas, on 12 September 1960. Anxious to address the issue, Kennedy had accepted an invitation from the Greater Houston Ministerial Association to discuss his religion. He was to make an opening statement and then submit himself to questioning by the 300 assembled ministers along with an audience of 300 more. In his opening statement, Kennedy briefly pointed to what he regarded as the central issues of the election – communism, poverty, education and the space program, in that order – before turning to the question of religion.

The real issues in the campaign, Kennedy began, had once again been obscured by his Catholicism, so the time had come for Americans to listen as he stated unequivocally 'not what kind of church I believe in, for that should be important only to me, but what kind of America I believe in'. Kennedy professed his belief in an America where the separation of church and state was absolute, where clergy could not tell politicians or voters how to act, where churches or religious schools were not granted any public funds and where nobody was denied office because of his or her religion. 'I believe,' he continued, 'in a President whose views on religion are his own private affair, neither imposed upon him by the nation or imposed by the nation upon him as a condition to holding that office'. He would resign from office, he told his listeners, if his religion ever interfered with his stewardship of the national interest. But it would not and could not interfere, Kennedy assured his listeners for, 'contrary to common newspaper usage, I am not the Catholic candidate for President. I am the Democratic Party's candidate for President, who happens also to be a Catholic. I do not speak for my church on public matters – and the church does not speak for me'. Kennedy's performance not only won the sympathy and applause of a hostile audience that evening in Houston; it was shown on television around the nation the following day and by Kennedy's staff and volunteers throughout the remainder of the campaign.[45]

Since Kennedy's election, the American Irish have continued to operate on the national political stage, while losing power in the local arena. Eugene J. McCarthy (b.1916) and Robert F. Kennedy (1925–68), for example, both ran for the presidential nomination of the Democratic party in 1968. In the period from the late 1960s to the late 1990s, Irish-Americans like Daniel P. Moynihan (b.1927) and Edward Kennedy (b.1932) served with distinction in the US Senate, as did Thomas 'Tip' O'Neill (1912–94) in the House. In America's cities, however, the Irish lost influence, for example in San Francisco, New York City and post-Daley Chicago. There was also a substantial drift away from the Democratic party, beginning with Roosevelt's pro-British policies in the early 1940s, and proceeding from there through Irish support for McCarthyism and Eisenhower to the major political realignment following the signing of the Civil Rights Act of 1964 by Democratic President, Lyndon B. Johnson. In 1980, a majority of American Catholics voted Republican for the first time, helping to elect Ronald Reagan to the presidency; and, in the elections of 1994, Irish Americans cast a majority of their congressional ballots for Republicans for the first time since the 1920s, helping that party win majorities in both houses of Congress.[46]

The importance of John F. Kennedy's election to the presidency in 1960, however, lies as much in the broader realm of identity and culture as in the field of electoral politics. Narrow though his margin of victory was, it was a historic turning point in the history of the American Irish, marking their final acceptance as full Americans. Given the degree of anti-Irish and anti-Catholic bigotry that had survived through the twentieth century, one might also argue that it was in 1960 rather than 1860 that the American Irish finally became 'white', if by that term one means full racial and cultural respectability, a final acceptance by white American Protestants of Irish-American Catholics as their equals in all things important. This process of acceptance and integration is always a mixed blessing, however, for it tends inevitably to be accompanied by an erosion and fragmentation of racial or ethnic identity. The price of full assimilation for American immigrant groups has often been the sundering of ties between their ethnic identity and their past. For the Irish, 'becoming American' was in this sense a matter of being cut adrift; Ireland became a distant, soft, romantic place, while the often grim realities of the Irish-American past receded gently into the mist.

NATIONALISM, I

One area of Irish-American history where there was substantial continuity from the 1790s to the 1990s, however, was the participation by the American Irish in struggles for the national liberation and reunification of Ireland. Irish-American nationalism reached its historical low point in the 1930s and 1940s, before reviving in the period since 1968. When Eamon de Valera refused to open Ireland's ports to the British Navy during the Second World War in return for a dubious promise by Winston Churchill to end partition, he looked to the Irish in the United States for support, encouraging the formation of the American Friends of Irish Neutrality in 1940 to lobby against a possible British invasion of Ireland. Ireland's neutrality in the Second World War, however, caused serious problems for Americans of Irish descent. While American troops were dying by the tens of thousands fighting the Nazis, de Valera made formal complaints about the presence of GIs in Northern Ireland, gaining little support among Irish-American Catholics and irritating Americans of Ulster Protestant descent who interpreted the stationing of troops as tantamount to American recognition of the partition of Ireland. The image of the Irish government in American public opinion reached its nadir in 1945, when de Valera drove home his insistence on Irish neutrality by formally visiting the German embassy in Dublin to pay his condolences on the occasion of Hitler's death.[47]

It was not until the 1960s that the American Irish once again began to play an active role in the affairs of Ireland. Since the partition of the country in 1920, Northern Ireland had survived (with heavy British subsidies) as essentially a fiefdom of the Orange Order, with Unionist Protestants exerting a stranglehold on political and socio-economic power and the sizeable Catholic minority confined to a subordinate position. Toward the end of the 1960s, Catholic student activists launched a civil rights movement, modelled to some extent on the civil rights movement in the American South. The students demanded an end to discrimination in employment and housing, along with recognition of full civil and political rights for Ulster's Catholic minority. The main organizations involved in this phase of the conflict were the Northern Ireland Civil Rights Association (NICRA, founded 1967); the Social Democratic Labour Party (SDLP, founded 1970), with John Hume as one of its principal leaders; and People's Democracy (PD), a revolutionary organization dedicated to the formation of an Irish socialist republic, founded by Bernadette Devlin. Singing American protest songs like 'We Shall Overcome', and marching from Belfast to Derry in the manner pioneered by Dr Martin Luther King, the protestors were met with baton-charges and high-powered water-cannon. Whereas the civil rights movement in the United States had used its tactic of non-violent response to police brutality to capture the moral high ground and topple the old Jim Crow system of segregation and disenfranchisement, in Ireland the result was a long-term intensification of violence rather than a peaceful resolution. With the British Army called in to impose order, what began as a civil rights movement gave way to an armed struggle for a thirty-two county republic. Single-minded physical-force nationalism, in other words, had re-emerged as a major political force. Unionist extremists also formed their own paramilitary groups, and over the next thirty years, a period known as 'The Troubles', more than 3,000 people would be killed.[48]

How were these developments greeted by the Irish in the United States? Descendants of the Scotch-Irish had faded from public view since the Second World War, so that the staunch Unionist sentiment so evident among many Ulster Protestants in the late 1960s had little by way of a counterpart among Protestant Irish Americans. Thus, when the Reverend Ian Paisley, a hard-line Ulster Unionist, visited the United States in 1969 to publicize his cause, he aroused much less enthusiasm among Protestant Irish Americans committed to the Union than among southern fundamentalist Christians of various ethnic backgrounds who hailed him as an anti-communist crusader. Nevertheless, when a subcommittee of the House of Representatives Committee on Foreign Relations held hearings on Northern Ireland in 1972, a variety of Scotch-Irish organizations appeared before it or submitted statements, including the Scotch-Irish Foundation, the Loyal Orange Order of the United States, Ulster American Loyalists and the Northern Ireland Service Council. Although the impact of the Scotch-Irish on the politics of Northern Ireland since the 1960s has been minimal compared to that of Catholic Irish Americans, the existence of groups like these suggested the survival of at least some coherent sense of Scotch-Irish identity. Indeed, at the level of the individual rather than the collective, that identity was probably much stronger than is commonly supposed, especially in the South.[49]

The reaction among Catholic Irish Americans to the events in Northern Ireland was to rebuild both of the primary nationalist traditions, constitutionalist and republican. Already by 1967, a lawyer from Buffalo named James Heaney had founded the American Congress for Irish Freedom (ACIF), which had twenty-five chapters and 3,000 members nationwide by 1969. The ACIF sponsored speaking tours by civil rights activists from the SDLP, but was generally conservative on American political matters, its members often supporting the war in Vietnam and opposing civil rights for African Americans even as they endorsed the cause of civil rights for Ulster Catholics. Nationalism, once again, had triumphed over social radicalism. The phrase 'Brits out of Belfast, Niggers out of Boston' was reportedly chanted by Irish Americans in Massachusetts in the late 1960s and early 1970s. Much more progressive in its politics was a second Irish-American nationalist organization, the National Association for Irish Justice (NAIJ), founded in 1969 by Brian Heron, a grandson of the revolutionary socialist of 1916, James Connolly. The NAIJ had thirty-one affiliates by 1969, and had established student groups at universities like Columbia and Fordham. But it was never as powerful as the ACIF, representing a distinctly minority radical view. The dominant position became starkly evident in August 1969 in the furor surrounding the visit of Ulster republican activist Bernadette Devlin to the United States.[50]

Bernadette Devlin had been elected to the British Parliament amid considerable fanfare in 1969 at the age of only twenty-two. She arrived in New York City on 21 August 1969, to the adulation of the American press. Mayor John Lindsay presented her with a golden key to the city, and she arranged an impromptu meeting with UN Secretary-General, U Thant. But she quickly outlived her welcome in the United States, deliberately stirring up conflicts and divisions among the American Irish. Socially conservative organizations like the ACIF, the AOH and the Irish Counties Association wanted Devlin to concentrate on purely Irish and purely nationalist issues. Encouraged by the radical members of the NAIJ, Devlin chose instead to condemn the lack of support by Irish-American nationalists for African Americans, to emphasize her own socialist ideals and to criticize the Catholic Church. In Los Angeles, she was heckled by an Irish-American audience when she spoke in favour of black civil rights, and in Detroit, where leaders of the Irish Association tried to exclude African Americans from a rally, she refused to speak until they were admitted. The local AOH, which had presented her with a large sum of money, waited until after press photographers had captured the event, then took back the money and sent it to the Catholic Church in Ireland instead. Having already nicknamed the police chief in her native Derry 'Mayor Daley', she reserved her harshest attacks for her visit to Daley's Chicago, comparing Irish-American racists there to the Orangemen in Ulster. Repeating her message on subsequent visits to the United States, Devlin alienated the majority of Irish-Americans and the mainstream press with her socialism and her radicalism on the question of American civil rights.[51]

Developments in Irish-American nationalism over the subsequent violent quarter-century closely paralleled developments in Ireland. In 1969, the IRA and its political wing, Sinn Féin, split into 'Official' and 'Provisional' camps, the former dedicated to the pursuit of a socialist Irish republic through mainly political means, and the latter sanctioning the use of armed struggle. Devlin and the more militant NICRA activists supported the new 'Provos', while the more moderate constitutionalist nationalists organized a new political party, the Social Democratic Labour Party (SDLP) in 1970 to pursue the cause of civil rights for Catholics through peaceful means. In the United States, an Official IRA network, composed mainly of old, left-leaning IRA veterans and the remnants of the radical NAIJ (which collapsed in 1970) coalesced in the James Connolly Clubs of New York and Massachusetts, which reorganized under Official Sinn Féin supervision into the Irish Republican Clubs (IRC) of the United States in 1971. The IRC endorsed the foundation of a socialist republic in Ireland, strongly supported the cause of civil rights in America, condemned the Vietnam War, and expressed its solidarity with the liberation movements of the Third World. Once again, however, this leftist orientation repelled all but a minority of Irish Americans, who were much more likely to support the moderate SDLP or, increasingly, the hard-line physical-force tradition based on the exclusive aim of Irish unification by whatever means necessary. The massacre of thirteen innocent protestors by British paratroopers at a civil rights demonstration in Derry on 'Bloody Sunday' (30 January 1972), combined with the abandonment under Unionist pressure of the brief-lived Sunningdale peace agreement in 1974, served to galvanize the cause of physical-force republicanism on both sides of the Atlantic.[52]

The dominant figure in the physical-force tradition in the United States was an Irish immigrant and veteran of the Irish Civil War, Michael Flannery. At the age of fourteen, Flannery had joined the Irish Volunteers in his native County Tipperary. During the War of Independence he fought the Black and Tans, and during the Civil War he was on the side of the anti-treaty men. Captured and imprisoned by the Free State forces, he left for New York City on his release in 1927, and within two years he had become a leading figure in what remained of Clan na Gael. For the next forty years, Flannery pursued a relatively peaceful career with the Metropolitan Life Insurance Company. When the Troubles erupted in Ulster, he joined ACIF but, frustrated by its moderate approach, he soon left to form the Irish Action Committee, composed of militant nationalists. In 1969, Flannery travelled to Belfast to meet leaders of the newly emerging Provisional IRA and was asked to lead a fundraising organization to support a renewed military campaign aimed at uniting Ireland. In April 1970, at a press conference in New York, Flannery announced the formation of the Northern Ireland Aid Committee, better-known by its acronym NORAID.[53]

NORAID proved very successful in raising funds. Although the organization always insisted that the funds were used for 'humanitarian relief', it is generally believed that they were employed mainly for the purchase of arms and ammunition, or at least that they freed other IRA funds to be spent in this manner. Irish bars in cities throughout the US served as the principal bases of NORAID fund-raising. At least one tavern, in New Jersey, was opened with the primary purpose of sending whatever profits it made and funds it collected back to Ireland. Money was also raised through dinner dances and direct-mail solicitations. Irish-dominated locals of the Teamsters', Carpenters' and Longshoremen's unions were among the major contributors to NORAID. Virtually every penny that NORAID raised, aside from what was needed to cover expenses in America, was sent to Ireland in the form of money orders, bank drafts or direct deposits. NORAID publicized its activities and fund-raising events in a newspaper, the *Irish People*, based in the Bronx. With the collapse of the moderate constitutionalist group, the ACIF, in 1970, NORAID and its hard-line position had emerged by the early 1970s as the dominant and most popular form of Irish-American nationalism. By 1972 it claimed 100 chapters and 80,000 members. A second very influential Irish-American nationalist group from this period was the Irish National Caucus (INC), founded as an umbrella organization for various nationalist and republican groups in the United States in 1974.[54]

During the 1970s, Irish Americans furthered the physical-force tradition by sending guns as well as money to Ulster. Armed with an obsolete arsenal of Second World War rifles, Thompson submachine guns and even shotguns, the provisional IRA (the 'Provos') turned to America for help. One of the principal suppliers of arms to the IRA in the early 1970s was George Harrison, a veteran of the anti-treaty forces in the Irish Civil War. According to one government report, over 6,900 weapons and 1.2 million rounds of ammunition were stolen between 1971 and 1974 from the Marine Corps base at Camp Lejeune and from Fort Bragg, North Carolina, most of which ended up in the hands of the IRA. Of course, in addition to masterminding direct thefts of weaponry from the US military, agents of the IRA in the United States could simply visit one of the more than 160,000 gun shops in the country in 1972 to buy a variety of arms and supplies and then smuggle them into Ireland. Harrison and other gun runners sent their merchandise by cargo ships, concealed in household and office furniture, or 'machine parts'. Longshoremen in ports where the American Irish still dominated the labour force often turned a blind eye to these shipments. According to British Army and Ulster police sources, about 90 per cent of the IRA's new arms supplies between 1970 and 1980 came from the United States, and 75 per cent of all killings by the IRA had been carried out with American weapons.[55]

Concerned by the growing appeal of physical-force nationalism in the 1970s, some of the most prominent and powerful Irish Americans responded by reviving the peaceful, constitutionalist tradition. Irish diplomats in the United States joined with Irish-American business and civic leaders to create the Ireland Fund in 1976. Designed to undercut the appeal of NORAID, the Ireland Fund was founded to raise money for use in peaceful projects in Northern Ireland. The driving force behind this scheme was the former international rugby star, Tony O'Reilly, a national hero in Ireland and president of the H.J. Heinz Company. Through direct mail solicitations and expensive dinners attended by business leaders, politicians and other prominent Irish Americans, the Ireland Fund had raised $50 million by 1992, supporting hundreds of development initiatives, cultural projects and charities in Northern Ireland. At the same time, Ulster's preeminent constitutional nationalist, John Hume of the SDLP, used his friendship with Senator Edward Kennedy to make contact with other influential Irish-American politicians, including Representative 'Tip' O'Neill, Senator Daniel Patrick Moynihan and Governor Hugh Carey of New York. Kennedy, O'Neill, Moynihan and Carey came to be known as the 'Four Horsemen' of Irish-American politics, working closely with John Hume to formulate a coherent position on Ulster and to issue a joint condemnation of the IRA in 1977. With the influence of NORAID beginning to decline by the late 1970s, the more moderate position of the 'Four Horsemen' looked as though it was about to provide a palatable alternative to violence. [56]

Everything changed, however, with the hunger strikes launched by IRA prisoners in Northern Ireland in 1981, in which ten men eventually starved to death in protest at being denied the status of political prisoners. As the hunger strikes progressed throughout the first half of the year, Irish Americans united as rarely before in defense of Irish republicanism. In New York City, a flotilla of anti-British protestors followed the yacht of the visiting Prince Charles through the city's harbour and crowds of demonstrators disrupted his visit to the ballet at Lincoln Center. Throughout May 1981, following the death of the first hunger striker, Bobby Sands, there were daily demonstrations on the streets of New York City. The International Longshoremen's Union, led by Irish American Teddy Gleason, imposed a 24-hour boycott on British ships to protest Sands's death, affecting vessels from Maine to Texas. An Irish-American Labor Coalition was formed to coordinate trade union activities in support of the hunger strikers, organizing boycotts against British goods and a mass demonstration to greet the ocean liner *Queen Elizabeth II* when it sailed into New York in May 1981. On 27 April 1981 Cardinal Terence Cooke of New York sent a message to British Prime Minister Margaret Thatcher, urging her to concede the demands

of the hunger strikers. As each of the ten hunger strikers died, commem-
oration services were held in St Patrick's Cathedral, New York City. In
Massachusetts, the state legislature passed a resolution condemning the
government of Mrs Thatcher for its insensitivity to the value of human
life and the real issues of Ireland's divisive struggle. On 6 May 1981, the
'Four Horsemen' sent a telegram to Thatcher, which was made public in the
American and British press, strongly condemning her 'intransigence' and
urging her to end the 'posture of inflexibility that must lead inevitably to
more senseless violence and more needless deaths'. Predictably, the net result
of the hunger strikes was a resurgence in support for NORAID and the
hard-line position.[57]

In the early 1980s, physical-force nationalism flourished in the United
States as never before or since the era of 1916. The major organizations were
NORAID, a newly-militant AOH and long-dormant chapters of Clan na
Gael which reemerged to raise money and conduct enthusiastic publicity
campaigns. The republican movement also won significant victories between
1979 and 1982 when American courts acquitted George Harrison, the leading suspected supplier of arms to the IRA, on charges of gun-running and
agreed that fugitive IRA men such as Peter Gabriel McMullan and Dessie
Macken were political refugees entitled to asylum. The high point of the
physical-force tradition came, perhaps, when the martyred hunger striker
Bobby Sands was elected grand marshal of the New York City St Patrick's
Day parade in 1982, followed by Michael Flannery of NORAID the following year. The 1983 parade attracted a record attendance and Flannery was
cheered all along Fifth Avenue by groups waving pro-IRA placards and flags.
Cardinal Terence Cooke refused to give his traditional blessing, appearing on
the steps of St Patrick's Cathedral twenty minutes after Flannery had passed,
to be greeted by a hostile crowd who booed and hissed him and chanted 'Up
the Provos'.[58]

This upsurge in physical-force nationalism, needless to say, was not without its critics in the American government. The 'Four Horsemen' drew considerable attention for their rejection of violence in favour of a moderate,
constitutional approach. Less visible but perhaps more intriguing were those
members of the Reagan administration, starting with the president himself,
who were willing to play the Irish card whenever it seemed expedient, yet
presided over arguably the most anti-Irish administration since the presidency of Woodrow Wilson. Ronald Reagan, his Secretary of State, Al Haig,
and the head of the CIA, William Casey, all identified themselves as thoroughly Irish-American. The presidential election of 1981 was a major turning

point in US electoral politics, as a majority of American Catholics voted Republican for the first time. Anxious to consolidate this new support, Ronald Reagan made a famous tour of Ireland in 1984, where he unearthed an unlikely ancestor or two, much to the skepticism of most Irish onlookers. Unlike President Kennedy, who had been greeted in Ireland with genuine and enormous enthusiasm, President Reagan faced protests at US foreign policy, along with a boycott by some faculty and students when he was awarded an honorary degree at University College, Galway. Moreover, despite his bow toward 'Irishry' in an electoral year, Reagan followed a consistently pro-British policy throughout his two terms in office, maintaining an exceptionally close relationship with Margaret Thatcher. He supported Thatcher against the hunger strikers early in his first term, for example, and during his second term he pressed for the deportation of IRA men and signed a stringent new extradition treaty with Britain. Only in an age of confused and diluted Irish-American ethnicity, perhaps, could so pro-British and anti-Irish a president have masqueraded as an Irishman.[59]

The contrast with President Clinton could not be starker. A southern Protestant with some Irish roots, Clinton made no pretense to be a Catholic Irishman. But the end of the Cold War in the early 1990s exposed as never before the fictions of the alleged 'special relationship' between the United States and Britain, allowing Clinton to ignore British interests whenever necessary. He visited both the Republic of Ireland and Northern Ireland late in 1995, receiving a tumultuous welcome in Dublin that reminded many of the Kennedy visit. And, although Unionist politicians had called for a boycott of Clinton's activities in the North, he was received very warmly by Protestants and Catholics alike in Belfast, Derry and other parts of the province. Greeted as a symbol of peace and reconciliation, Clinton went on to become a principal architect of the decisive changes that would finally occur in Northern Ireland in the late 1990s.

NATIONALISM, II

Even as support for physical-force nationalism reached one of its historical peaks among the American Irish in the early 1980s, major changes were already underway within the republican movement in Ireland that would help transform the political structure of Northern Ireland in the following decade. Gerry Adams, the leader of Provisional Sinn Féin (the political wing of the Provisional IRA) had become convinced by the early 1980s that a military campaign by the IRA would never on its own be sufficient to bring about the withdrawal of the British from Northern Ireland. He embarked on a campaign to add a dynamic political component to the republican agenda, hoping thereby to displace the moderate Social Democratic Labour Party (SDLP) as the main representative of northern nationalists and to attract wider support in the Irish Republic. Sinn Féin therefore endorsed a new policy of achieving republican independence with 'a ballot box in one hand and an armalite [rifle] in the other'. Sinn Féin politicians, including Adams, were elected to seats in the British Parliament (which, as republican Irishmen, they declined to occupy) and in the general election of 1983, Sinn Féin won 43 per cent of the Catholic vote in Northern Ireland. While these electoral victories greatly encouraged Irish-American republicans, they also heralded a move away from pure violence toward mainstream politics, which would result in the declaration of cease-fires by the IRA in the 1990s and the eventual arrival at a peace settlement in 1998.[60]

The tide began to turn against the hard-liners from the mid-1980s onward. While Flannery's appointment as grand marshal in 1983 had been popular with many, it had also been very unpopular in certain quarters. Mayor Ed Koch, Governor Mario Cuomo, Senator Alphonse D'Amato and Representative Geraldine Ferraro had all marched in the parade, despite pressure from the Irish government not to do so. But the Friends of Ireland, a moderate nationalist group formed in 1981 by prominent Irish-American politicians, had urged a boycott of the parade. The Irish Taoiseach (Prime Minister), Garret Fitzgerald, and his Ambassador to the United States, Tadhg O'Sullivan, had condemned the republican exploitation of St Patrick's Day. The Irish national airline, Aer Lingus, had withdrawn its financial sponsorship. Cardinal Cooke had snubbed Flannery by refusing to greet him on the steps of St Patrick's. And Senator Daniel Patrick Moynihan and ex-Governor Hugh Carey, two very prominent Irish Americans who had always been honoured guests at the parade, refused to attend that year.[61]

Irish-American physical-force republicanism suffered a series of reverses after the high point of Flannery's grand marshalship. In 1986, a second-generation Irish American, William Quinn, who had joined the IRA after a spell in NORAID and conducted bombing campaigns in Britain, was denied the political asylum he had expected, because Britain and the United States had recently agreed on a more restrictive extradition treaty. Quinn was duly handed over by the American authorities to the British on charges of murdering a policeman. Escaped IRA man Joseph Patrick Doherty was sent back to a British prison in Ulster in 1993, after a protracted, eleven-year legal struggle involving the Immigration and Naturalization Service as well as the

Attorney General's office. Moreover, a variety of IRA gunrunners were convicted and sentenced to long terms in prison in Massachusetts and Florida between 1986 and 1991.[62]

More important than these individual reverses to the republican cause were the shifting permutations of politics in Ireland and Great Britain. The Anglo-Irish Agreement of 1985 for the first time recognized some role for the government of the Irish republic in the affairs of Northern Ireland. Its central provision was the creation of an Intergovernmental Conference at which officials of the Irish and British governments would periodically discuss the affairs of Northern Ireland. This agreement gave new life to the embattled cause of constitutional nationalism, led by John Hume of the SDLP, who continued to reach out to European and American politicians with his message of peaceful, gradual change. At the same time, Gerry Adams led a faction within the republican movement that was increasingly interested in restoring questions of civil rights and social justice to the agenda, without reneging on the ultimate goal of a thirty-two county republic. This was no easy strategy to pursue. It led to splits within Sinn Féin, with some republicans (especially the breakaway body, Republican Sinn Féin) refusing to compromise on their single goal of a united Ireland. These divisions were mirrored in the United States, where hard-liner Michael Flannery withdrew from NORAID to protest its endorsement of Adams's position. Flannery formed a new organization, Cumann na Saoirse ('Society of Freedom'), to support Republican Sinn Féin, while Martin Galvin retained the leadership of NORAID. The process set in motion by Adams culminated in the declaration of a cease-fire by the IRA in August 1994, which was approved by NORAID, though not without additional divisions and defections.[63]

If a single Ulster politician deserved most credit for the cessation of violence in the 1990s it was John Hume. He stuck fast to his principles of civil rights, social justice and constitutional reform from his emergence on the political scene in the 1960s to the transformation of the 1990s, even as the violence of the intervening period made his position look untenable to many. In talks with Gerry Adams in the early 1990s, he urged the republican leader to consider a negotiated settlement, at the same time persuading the British and Irish governments in 1993 to declare formally that Sinn Féin would be guaranteed a seat at future discussions on the fate of Northern Ireland if the IRA renounced its campaign of violence. Once the cease-fire had taken effect, Adams was granted a visa to enter the United States (having been excluded as a terrorist up to that point); following in the footsteps of Parnell,

Davitt, Redmond and de Valera, he embarked on a triumphal tour of the country. The American government, especially President Clinton and his unofficial emissary, ex-Senator George Mitchell, played a critical role in bringing about the peace agreement that was finally signed in 1998.[64]

The Belfast (or 'Good Friday') Agreement of May 1998 enshrined the idea of 'consent' as the central principle of politics in Northern Ireland. In other words, it guaranteed that the province would not change its current status unless a majority of its population voted to do so, while at the same time holding out the possibility of that eventually happening. The agreement also created a series of new constitutional and political bodies, including a Northern Ireland assembly and executive elected on the basis of proportional representation, a Ministerial Council composed of government members from northern and southern Ireland to discuss matters of mutual interest, a Council composed of representatives of the various legislative assemblies in the British Isles, and regular high-level conference meetings between the heads of the British and Irish governments. Finally, the agreement included important new provisions on human rights, along with recommendations for reforming the police and judicial systems.

The agreement might best be described as a major triumph for constitutional nationalism, with a strong republican inflection. This would explain why most of the opposition to it came from extreme Protestant Unionists rather than the Catholic side. Apart from some ominous splinter groups from IRA, support for the agreement among Catholics in both the North and the Republic was overwhelming. Its main effect was to restore questions of social justice, civil rights and political equality to the agenda, while at the same time allowing the Irish government an unprecedented degree of involvement in the affairs of Northern Ireland. While hard-line republican critics argued that the agreement reneged on the goal of a united Ireland, from the point of view of Gerry Adams and his followers it merely postponed the achievement of that goal rather than abandoning it. Combining the best of the two nationalist traditions, constitutional and republican, the agreement won the overwhelming support of the Catholic Irish on both sides of the Atlantic. As the twentieth century drew to a close, the implementation of the agreement was by no means certain. But two hundred years after Ireland's great insurrection of 1798, the dominant tone among Irish nationalists from New York and Boston to Dublin and Belfast was one of cautious optimism. As the long history of the Troubles had demonstrated over the previous thirty years, the histories of Ireland, Irish America and the United States were still bound very closely together.

CONCLUSION

◆

The chronological arrangement of this book has hopefully rendered the course of Irish-American history clearer than a strictly thematic analysis could have done. Nonetheless, the chronological approach has its pitfalls, not least of which is the tendency to impose on the past a greater narrative coherence than it could possibly have had, along with the related problem of teleology in which history is plotted as heading toward a pre-determined end. In the latter regard, the specter haunting the story told in these pages is that of social mobility and, through it, assimilation. Nineteenth-century Irish Americans were by and large poor, alienated and often despised; late twentieth-century Irish Americans are about as well-off, educated and Americanized as anybody else. Is the narrative of Irish-American history therefore one of uncomplicated progress, a tale of inevitable assimilation through social mobility? And, to the extent that the case of the Irish is exemplary of broader patterns in American historical development, what does the answer to this question imply about the history of other immigrant groups, past, present and future?

Although the American Irish undoubtedly advanced in socio-economic terms and 'became American' in the process, the story that has been told here is not necessarily a 'Whiggish' one. According to the much-maligned 'Whig' interpretation of history, the past is simply the unfolding of a better future; it is an as-yet unrealized and incomplete version of the better present in which we live today. The history of how one American ethnic group moved from poverty to middle-class prosperity, and from racial inferiority to solid respectability, might clearly be made to fit this 'Whig' mold. But America is a multi-racial, multi-ethnic society; the history of no single ethnic group occurs in a vacuum. American history as a whole, and with it Irish-American history, has been first and foremost a history of contestation and struggle over power, rather than neutral progress from bad to good to even better.

Irish-American identity emerged from a crucible of social, political and cultural conflict both within the ethnic community and between it and other elements of the host society. The formation of a dominant ethnic identity was possible only through the suppression of less palatable alternative forms of Irishness, among them those of the Molly Maguires, of Fr. Edward

McGlynn and Mother Jones, of James Connolly and William Z. Foster, and of civil rights workers, gays and lesbians in the late twentieth century. The struggle to define Irish-American ethnicity was a twofold process. Irish people generally were seeking acceptance in a wider American society that had initially shunned them socially even as it depended on them economically. But the terms of acceptance were largely dictated by the dominant society, which demanded and tolerated only certain forms of identity and behaviour on the part of the immigrant minority.

The result was a power struggle within the immigrant community to define an ethnic identity on the basis of which some form of incorporation into the dominant society would be accepted. Providing the link between the two arenas, ethnic and national, was a process of middle-class formation which provided the route to wealth, power and respectability in both the immigrant community and the society at large. Ranged against this dominant trajectory of assimilation were a minority of dissenting voices – labour activists, political radicals, agnostics and, in recent years, gays and lesbians – who embodied different meanings of ethnicity and, by implication, a different sense of what Irish America was or could become.

At the same time, the Catholic Irish faced a variety of opponents in the wider American society that played host to them, especially in the nineteenth century. Their religion was deeply suspect to most Americans when they began to arrive in large numbers in the 1830s and it remained so until at least 1960, serving as the principal *raison d'être* for a variety of nativist movements, many of them manned and led by Scotch-Irishmen. As labour radicals and rioters, and as street politicians, the Catholic Irish were both feared and despised during most of the nineteenth century. And, from the moment they arrived in the United States as immigrants, they were classified as racially inferior, consigned to a social category that could not be considered fully human. It took them until at least 1900 to shake off this mantle (or, as recent historians have put it, not only to 'embrace whiteness' but to be recognized as fully white by the dominant society). Yet it is worth recalling that a principal cause of Irish entry into the ranks of full racial respectability was the massive influx from the 1880s onward of 'new immigrants' from southern and eastern Europe who were regarded by most native-born Americans as much stranger and much more threatening than the Irish had ever been. Far from being a 'Whiggish' tale of seamless, inevitable progress, the incorporation of the Irish as full-fledged Americans can be explained only in terms of a new phase in the wider history of racial and cultural subordination in the United States.

Yet there is also a more positive and optimistic side to this story. Although the incorporation of the Irish into the ranks of full racial respectability became possible only because of the racialization of the 'new immigrants', the Irish presence in the United States had decisively altered the terms of the racial and cultural debate over the meaning of America. Despite (or perhaps because of) the vehemence of nativist attacks, the Irish had 'become American' without, for the most part, sacrificing their religion, their culture, their heritage. They thereby helped establish the primacy of cultural pluralism over more repressive models of assimilation such as 'Anglo-conformity' (enforced entry into the American 'melting-pot'). The Irish assimilated into American life, but they did so either through the medium of their own ethnic institutions, most notably the Church and the various nationalist movements, or by joining organizations that served as bridges between their community and the mainstream, especially the labour movement and the Democratic party and its urban machines (thereby transforming these organizations in the process). In creating a new ethnic identity that was simultaneously Irish and American, the immigrants expanded the meaning and limits of American culture as a whole. Although the 'new immigrants' faced intensified forms of racial discrimination and prejudice that had originated in the anti-Irish nativism of the early nineteenth century, they also benefited in some ways from precedents set by the Irish on questions of race, ethnicity and assimilation. Their chances of 'becoming American', as they gradually did in the twentieth century, had been greatly increased by the earlier struggles of the Irish.

In this respect, the history of the American Irish has a particular relevance for the present. Since 1965, the United States has entered another period of mass immigration. Seven million immigrants entered the United States legally in the 1980s alone, more than for any decade in American history except 1901–10, when 8.8 million arrived. If an estimated average of 300,000 to 500,000 undocumented aliens a year is added to the figures, the total for the 1980s exceeds that for 1901–10 and becomes the highest ever in American history, in absolute numbers if not proportion. It is estimated that about 10 million more legal immigrants came to the United States in the 1990s. The Latino population of the United States has almost tripled since 1960, reaching 20 million in 1990, while the Asian population reached 7.3 million in the same year, the majority of them immigrants from Korea, China and India. With the return of mass migration has come a national debate over culture, history, language and immigration restriction. It might be argued that history holds no lessons for the present, or at least none that will be listened to. But in the name of toleration and open-mindedness about the meaning of being American, some familiarity with the Irish-American experience would surely be indispensable in grappling with current dilemmas. Every aspect of that experience, from chain migration to urban settlement, from nativist attack to ethnic response, from nationalism to religious pluralism, and from political involvement to social mobility and labour activism, bears an instructive parallel for the present.

As Mexican Americans and other Latinos begin to assimilate in the late twentieth century, the question arises of where the lines of racial exclusion have thus far been drawn in American history. First the Irish, then the 'Orientals,' then the 'new immigrants' of the period 1880–1920, and then, in the late-twentieth century, the massive wave of immigrants from Latin America, Asia and Africa, have all been subject to considerable racial discrimination in the United States. Yet, with the partial exception of Asians, no immigrant group has been treated in a manner approaching that inflicted on African Americans. Not only were black Americans in the antebellum North (leaving aside slavery altogether for a moment) considerably more disadvantaged than the Irish, they remained the most oppressed and disadvantaged group in American society as a whole as the twentieth century drew to a close.

The historically radical forms of freedom that have been so central to the history of the United States since its foundation have always depended on equally radical forms of un-freedom. In terms of both social practice and the ideological explanation of that practice, the freedom of some Americans has been predicated on the racial oppression of others. Both the Irish in the nineteenth century, and Latinos and Asians in the late twentieth century, 'became white' in large part by measuring their position in American society against that of African Americans. Thus, while the move toward cultural pluralism inaugurated by the arrival of the Catholic Irish in the United States in the early nineteenth century had important and liberating consequences for the history of American immigration, ethnicity and even race, there is a point beyond which the ideological fortress of race has remained impregnable. It is at precisely this point that one leaves behind the particular history of immigration for the general history of the United States. America is indeed a land of immigrants, but only in part.

Finally, a word on Ireland. The theme of emigration is central to any understanding of modern Ireland and its history. No other country contributed a higher percentage of its population to the United States. Significantly more Irish people migrated to North America than live in Ireland today. In some ways, emigration is the dominant theme of modern Irish history. The structure of landholding, the nature of religion and the patterns of politics and nationalism would all have been fundamentally different in the absence of mass emigration, especially in the second half of the nineteenth century. Without emigration, modern Ireland would not be as it is. For every Irish generation since the famine, emigration has been a rite of passage, an anticipated if not always inevitable stage in the life cycle. Countless thousands drifted into emigration without any clear sense of intention, moving inexorably from villages to towns, towns to cities (often London or Liverpool rather than Dublin or Cork), and then on to America or Australia. Others went with a plan, joining friends or relatives. For both, it was the natural thing to do. This sustained outflow of emigrants, so many of them young and single, imparts to Irish history over the last century-and-a-half a peculiar poignancy, a sense of departure, exile and longing most clearly evoked, perhaps, by the sight throughout rural Ireland today of extensive pasture land populated by sheep and cattle grazing among the ruins of abandoned cottages. It is a reminder that the population of the country was once almost twice as large, a reminder of the millions who joined the Irish exodus to America. The story of these nameless millions conjures up feelings of sadness and indignation, mingled with pride and wonder and occasional bewilderment, at what they became once they settled in America.

BIBLIOGRAPHY

———— ◆ ————

An exhaustive bibliography of Irish-American history would fill an entire volume. Listed below are the books and articles that were consulted in the writing of this book. This list includes most of the best works published in the field over the last forty years, as well as several older ones. Doctoral dissertations, master's theses and many journal articles have been omitted for reasons of space, but the list that follows is nonetheless a comprehensive and representative guide to the historiography.

Adams, William F. *Ireland and the Irish Emigration to the New World from 1815 to the Famine.* 1932. New York: Russell & Russell, 1967.

Akenson, D.H. 'Ontario: Whatever Happened to the Irish?' *Canadian Papers in Rural History*, 2 (1982), 204–56.

———. 'An Agnostic View of the Historiography of the Irish Americans.' *Labour/Le Travail*, 14 (Fall 1984), 123–59.

———. *The Irish in Ontario: A Study in Rural History.* Montreal: McGill-Queen's University Press, 1984.

———. *Being Had: Historians, Evidence and the Irish Exodus to North America.* Port Credit, Ontario: P.D. Meany, 1985.

———. 'Data: What is Known About the Irish in North America.' In Oliver MacDonagh and William F. Mandle, eds. *Ireland and Irish-Australia: Studies in Cultural and Political History.* London: Croom Helm, 1986.

———. 'The Historiography of the Irish in the United States of America.' In Patrick O'Sullivan, ed. *The Irish World Wide. History, Heritage, Identity.* Vol. II. *The Irish in the New Communities.* Leicester, England: Leicester University Press, 1992.

———. *The Irish Diaspora: A Primer.* Belfast: The Institute of Irish Studies, Queens University, Belfast; and Toronto: P.D. Meany, 1996.

Allen, Theodore W. *The Invention of the White Race.* Vol. 1. *Racial Oppression and Social Control.* New York: Verso, 1994.

Anbinder, Tyler. *Nativism and Slavery: The Northern Know Nothings and the Politics of the 1850s.* New York: Oxford University Press, 1992.

Arnesen, Eric. 'Up from Exclusion; Black and White Workers, Race, and the State of Labor History.' *Reviews in American History*, 26 (March 1998), 146–67.

Athearn, Robert G. *Thomas Francis Meagher: An Irish Revolutionary in America.* New York: Arno Press, 1976.

Bailyn, Bernard. *The Peopling of British North America: An Introduction.* New York: Vintage Books, 1988.

———. *Voyagers to the West: A Passage in the Peopling of America on the Eve of the Revolution.* New York. Vintage Books, 1988.

Baird, W. David. 'Violence Along the Chesapeake Canal: 1839.' *Maryland Historical Magazine*, 66 (Summer 1971), 121–34.

Baker, Jean. *Affairs of Party: The Political Culture of Northern Democrats in the Mid-Nineteenth Century*. Ithaca, NY: Cornell University Press, 1983.

Bardon, Jonathan. *A History of Ulster*. Belfast: The Blackstaff Press, 1992.

Bayor, Ronald H. and Timothy J. Meagher, eds. *The New York Irish*. Baltimore, MD: Johns Hopkins University Press, 1996.

Beatty, Jack. *The Rascal King: The Life and Times of James Michael Curley*. Reading, MA: Addison-Wesley, 1992.

Belchem, John. 'Nationalism, Republicanism and Exile: Irish Emigrants and the Revolutions of 1848.' *Past and Present*, 146 (February 1995), 103–35.

Bellows, Barbara L. *Benevolence Among Slaveholders: Assisting the Poor in Charleston, 1670–1860*. Baton Rouge, LA: Louisiana State University Press, 1993.

Bennett, David H. *The Party of Fear: From Nativist Movements to the New Right in American History*. Chapel Hill, NC: University of North Carolina Press, 1988.

Benson, Lee. *The Concept of Jacksonian Democracy: New York as a Test Case*. Princeton, NJ: Princeton University Press, 1961.

Bernstein, Iver. *The New York City Draft Riots: Their Significance for American Society and Politics in the Age of the Civil War*. New York: Oxford University Press, 1990.

Berthoff, Rowland W. *British Immigrants in Industrial America*. Cambridge, MA: Harvard University Press, 1953.

——. 'Celtic Mist Over the South.' *Journal of Southern History*, 52 (November 1986), 523–46.

Billington, Ray Allen. *The Protestant Crusade, 1800–1860*. Chicago: Quadrangle Books, 1964.

Bimba, Anthony. *The Molly Maguires*. New York: International Publishers, 1932.

Birdwell-Pheasant, Donna. 'The Early Twentieth-Century Stem Family: A Case Study from County Kerry.' In Marilyn Silverman and P.H. Gulliver, eds. *Approaching the Past: Historical Anthropology through Irish Case Studies*. New York: Columbia University Press, 1992.

——. 'Irish Households in the Early Twentieth Century: Culture, Class, and Historical Contingency.' *Journal of Family History*, 18 (1993), 19–38.

Blessing, Patrick J. 'Irish.' In Stephan Thernstrom, ed. *The Harvard Encyclopedia of American Ethnic Groups*. Cambridge, MA: Belknap Press of Harvard University Press, 1980.

——. 'Culture, Religion and the Activities of the Committee of Vigilance, San Francisco 1858.' Working paper, series 8, no. 3, Charles and Margaret Hall Cushwa Center for the Study of American Catholicism, University of Notre Dame, 1980.

——. 'Irish Emigration to the United States, 1800–1920: An Overview.' In P.J. Drudy, ed. *The Irish in America: Emigration, Assimilation, Impact*. (Irish Studies, 4). Cambridge, England: Cambridge University Press, 1985.

——. *The Irish in America: A Guide to the Literature and the Manuscript Collections*. Washington, DC: Catholic University of America Press, 1992.

Blethen, H. Tyler and Curtis W. Wood, Jr., eds. *From Ulster to Carolina: The Migration of the Scotch-Irish to Southwestern North Carolina*. Cullowhee, NC: Western Carolina University Press, 1986.

——. *Ulster and North America: Transatlantic Perspectives on the Scotch-Irish.* Tuscaloosa, Alabama: University of Alabama Press, 1997.

Bodnar, John E., ed. *The Ethnic Experience in Pennsylvania.* Lewisburg, PA: Bucknell University Press, 1973.

Bolger, Stephen G. *The Irish Character in American Fiction, 1830–1860.* New York: Arno Press, 1976.

Boyce, D. George. *Nineteenth-Century Ireland: The Search for Stability.* Dublin: Gill and Macmillan, 1990.

Boyce, D. George and Alan O'Day, eds. *The Making of Modern Irish History: Revisionism and the Revisionist Controversy.* London: Routledge, 1996.

Bradshaw, Brendan. 'Nationalism and Historical Scholarship in Modern Ireland.' *Irish Historical Studies*, 26 (November 1989), 329–51.

Brady, Ciaran, ed. *Interpreting Irish History: The Debate on Historical Revisionism.* Dublin: Irish Academic Press, 1994.

Bric, Maurice J. 'The Irish and the Evolution of the "New Politics"'. In P.J. Drudy, ed. *The Irish in America: Emigration, Assimilation, Impact.* (Irish Studies, 4). Cambridge, England: Cambridge University Press, 1985.

Brinkley, Alan. *Voices of Protest: Huey Long, Father Coughlin, and the Great Depression.* New York: Knopf, 1982.

Broehl, Wayne G., Jr. *The Molly Maguires.* Cambridge, MA: Harvard University Press, 1964.

Brooke, Peter. *Ulster Presbyterianism: The Historical Perspective, 1610–1970.* Dublin: Gill and Macmillan, 1987.

Brown, Thomas N. *Irish-American Nationalism, 1870–1890.* Philadelphia: Lippincott, 1966.

Browne, Henry J. *The Catholic Church and the Knights of Labor.* New York: Arno Press, 1976.

Browne, Joseph. 'The Greening of America: Irish-American Writers.' *Journal of Ethnic Studies*, 2 (Winter 1975), 71–6.

Brundage, David. 'Denver's New Departure: Irish Nationalism and the Labor Movement in the Gilded Age.' *Southwest Economy and Society*, 5 (Winter 1981), 10–23.

——. 'Irish Land and American Workers: Class and Ethnicity in Denver, Colorado.' In Dirk Hoerder, ed. *Struggle a Hard Battle: Essays on Working Class Immigrants.* DeKalb, IL: Northern Illinois University Press, 1986.

——. *The Making of Western Radicalism: Denver's Organized Workers, 1878–1905.* Urbana, IL: University of Illinois Press, 1994.

——. '"In Time of Peace Prepare for War": Key Themes in the Social Thought of New York's Irish Nationalists, 1890–1916.' In Ronald H. Bayor and Timothy J. Meagher, eds. *The New York Irish.* Baltimore, MD: Johns Hopkins University Press, 1996.

Buckley, John Patrick. *The New York Irish: Their View of American Foreign Policy, 1914–1921.* New York: Arno Press, 1976.

Burchell, Robert A. *The San Francisco Irish, 1848–1880.* Manchester, England: Manchester University Press, 1979.

——. 'The Historiography of the American Irish.' *Immigrants and Minorities*, 1 (November 1982), 281–305.

Campbell, Malcolm. 'The Other Immigrants: Comparing the Irish in Australia and the United States.' *Journal of American Ethnic History*, 14 (Spring 1995), 3–22.

Canny, Nicholas. *The Elizabethan Conquest of Ireland: A Pattern Established, 1565–76*. New York: Barnes & Noble, 1976.

——. *Kingdom and Colony: Ireland in the Atlantic World, 1569–1800*. Baltimore, MD: Johns Hopkins University Press, 1988.

——, ed. *The Oxford History of the British Empire*. Vol. 1. Oxford: Oxford University Press, 1998.

Carroll, Francis M. 'America and Irish Political Independence.' In P.J. Drudy, ed. *The Irish in America: Emigration, Assimilation, Impact*. (Irish Studies, 4). Cambridge, England: Cambridge University Press, 1985.

Casey, Daniel J. and Robert E. Rhodes. *Modern Irish-American Fiction. A Reader*. Syracuse, NY: Syracuse University Press, 1989.

Casey, Marion. 'The Irish.' In Kenneth Jackson, ed. *The Encyclopedia of New York City*. New Haven, CT: Yale University Press, 1995.

Clark, Dennis. *The Irish in Philadelphia: Ten Generations of Urban Experience*. Philadelphia: Temple University Press, 1973.

——. 'Urban Blacks and Irishmen: Brothers in Prejudice.' In Miriam Ershkowitz and Joseph Zikmund, II, eds. *Black Politics in Philadelphia*. New York: Basic Books, 1973.

——. 'Babes in Bondage: Indentured Irish Children in Philadelphia in the Nineteenth Century.' *Pennsylvania Magazine of History and Biography*, 101 (October 1977), 475–86.

——. 'Ethnic Enterprise and Urban Development.' *Ethnicity*, 5 (June 1978), 108–18.

——. *The Irish Relations: Trials of an Immigrant Tradition*. London and Toronto: Associated University Presses, 1982.

——. *Hibernia America: The Irish and Regional Cultures*. Westport, CT: Greenwood Press, 1986.

——. *Erin's Heirs: Irish Bonds of Community*. Lexington, KY: University Press of Kentucky, 1991.

Clark, Terry N. 'The Irish Ethnic Identity and the Spirit of Patronage.' *Ethnicity*, 2 (December 1975), 305–59.

Cogley, John. *Catholic America*. New York: The Dial Press, 1973.

Coleman, James Walter. *The Molly Maguire Riots: Industrial Conflict in the Pennsylvania Coal Region*. Richmond, VA: Garrett & Massie, 1936.

Coleman, Terry. *Going to America*. New York: Doubleday, 1973.

Collins, Brenda. 'Proto-industrialization and Pre-famine Emigration.' *Social History*, VII (1982), 127–46.

Connable, Alfred and Edward Silbefard. *Tigers of Tammany*. New York: Holt, Rinehart & Winston, 1967.

Connell, K.H. *The Population of Ireland, 1750–1845*. Oxford: Oxford University Press, 1950.

——. 'Peasant Marriage in Ireland After the Great Famine.' *Past and Present*, 12 (1957), 76–91.

——. 'Peasant Marriage in Ireland: Its Structure and Development Since the Famine.' *Economic History Review*, 2nd Ser., 14 (1962), 502–23.

——. *Irish Peasant Society: Four Historical Essays*. Oxford: Clarendon Press, 1968.

Connolly, James J. *The Triumph of Ethnic Progressivism: Urban Political Culture in Boston, 1900–1925*. Cambridge, MA: Harvard University Press, 1998.

Connolly, S.J. *Priests and People in Pre-Famine Ireland, 1780–1845*. New York: St Martin's Press, 1982.

——. 'Ulster Presbyterians: Religion, Culture, and Politics, 1660–1850.' In H. Tyler Blethen and Curtis W. Wood, Jr., eds. *Ulster and North America: Transatlantic Perspectives on the Scotch-Irish*. Tuscaloosa, Alabama: University of Alabama Press, 1997.

Corcoran, Mary. 'Emigrants, *Eirepreneurs*, and Opportunists: A Social Profile of Recent Irish Immigration in New York City.' In Ronald H. Bayor and Timothy J. Meagher, eds. *The New York Irish*. Baltimore, MD: Johns Hopkins University Press, 1996.

Cousens, S.H. 'The Regional Pattern of Emigration during the Great Irish Famine.' *Transactions of the Institute of British Geographers*, 28 (1960), 25.

——. 'Emigration and Demographic Change in Ireland, 1851–1861.' *The Economic History Review*, XIV (December 1961), 275–88.

——. 'The Regional Variations in Population Changes in Ireland, 1861–1881.' *The Economic History Review*, XVII (December 1964), 301–21.

——. 'The Regional Variations in Emigration from Ireland between 1821 and 1841.' *Transactions of the Institute of British Geographers*, 37 (1965), 15–30.

Crawford, E. Margaret, ed. *Famine: The Irish Experience, 900–1900*. Edinburgh: John Donald, 1989.

Crawford, E. Margaret, ed. *The Hungry Stream: Essays on Emigration and Famine*. Belfast: The Institute for Irish Studies, Queens University, Belfast; and the Centre for Emigration Studies, Ulster-American Folk Park, 1997.

Crawford, W.H. 'Landlord-Tenant Relations in Ulster, 1609–1920.' *Irish Economic and Social History*, 2 (1975), 5–21.

Cronin, Harry C. *Eugene O'Neill: Irish and American: A Study in Cultural Context*. New York: Arno Press, 1976.

Cross, Ira B., ed. *Frank Roney: An Autobiography*. 1931. New York: Arno Press, 1976.

Cross, Robert D. *The Emergence of Liberal Catholicism in America*. 1958. Chicago: Quadrangle Books, 1968.

Crozier, Alan. 'The Scotch-Irish Influence on American English.' *American Speech*, 59 (1984), 310–31.

Cullen, L.M. *An Economic History of Ireland Since 1660*. London: Batsford, 1972.

——. *The Emergence of Modern Ireland, 1600–1900*. London: Batsford Academic Press, 1981.

Curley, James Michael. *I'd Do It Again: A Record of All My Uproarious Years*. New York: Arno Press, 1976.

Curtis, Lewis Perry. *Apes and Angels: The Irishman in Victorian Caricature*. 1971; Washington, DC: Smithsonian Institution Press, 1997 (revised edition).

Daly, Mary. *The Famine in Ireland*. Dundalk, Ireland: Dundalgan Press, 1986.

——. 'Revisionism and Irish History: The Great Famine.' In D. George Boyce and Alan O'Day, eds. *The Making of Modern Irish History*. London: Routledge, 1996.

Darroch, A. Gordon and Michael D. Ornstein. 'Ethnicity and Occupational Structure in Canada in 1871: The Vertical Mosaic in Historical Perspective.' *Canadian Historical Review*, 61 (September 1980), 305–33.

D'Arcy, Frank. *The Story of Irish Emigration*. Cork: Mercier Press, 1999.

D'Arcy, William. *The Fenian Movement in the United States, 1858–1866*. New York: Russell & Russell, 1971.

Davis, Graham. 'Models of Migration: The Historiography of the Irish Pioneers in South Texas.' *Southwestern Historical Quarterly*, 99 (January 1996), 326–48.

Day, Mark R. 'The Passion of the San Patricios.' *Irish America Magazine* (May/June 1993), 44–8.

Dayton, Cornelia H. *Women Before the Bar: Gender, Law, and Society in Connecticut, 1639–1789*. Chapel Hill, NC: University of North Carolina Press, 1995.

de Crèvecouer, J. Hector St John. *Letters from an American Farmer and Sketches of Eighteenth-Century America*. 1782. New York: Penguin Books, 1981.

de Nie, Michael. 'Curing "The Irish Moral Plague".' *Éire-Ireland*, 32 (Spring 1997), 63–85.

Deutsch, Sarah. *Women and the City: Gender, Space, and Power in Boston, 1870–1940*. Forthcoming. New York: Oxford University Press, 2000.

Dickson, David. *Arctic Ireland: The Extraordinary Story of the Great Frost and Forgotten Famine of 1740–41*. Belfast: The White Row Press, 1997.

Dickson, R.J. *Ulster Emigration to Colonial America, 1718–1775*. London: Routledge and Kegan Paul, 1966.

Diner, Hasia. *Erin's Daughters in America: Irish Immigrant Women in the Nineteenth Century*. Baltimore, MD: Johns Hopkins University Press, 1983.

Dinneen, Joseph F. *The Purple Shamrock: The Hon. James Michael Curley of Boston*. New York: Norton, 1949.

Dolan, Jay P. *The Immigrant Church: New York's German and Irish Catholics, 1815 to 1865*. Baltimore, MD: Johns Hopkins University Press, 1975.

——. *The American Catholic Experience: A History From Colonial Times to the Present*. Garden City, NY: Doubleday, 1985.

Doan, Robert. 'Green Gold to the Emerald Shores: Irish Immigration to the United States and Transatlantic Monetary Aid.' Unpublished Ph.D. dissertation, Temple University, 1998.

Donnelly, James S., Jr. 'Hearts of Oak, Hearts of Steel.' *Studia Hibernica*, 21 (1981), 7–73.

——. 'The Administration of Relief, 1846–7.' In W.E. Vaughan, ed. *A New History of Ireland*. Vol. V. *Ireland Under the Union, I, 1801–70*. Oxford: Clarendon Press, 1989.

——. 'The Great Famine and its Interpreters, Old and New.' *History Ireland*, 1 (Autumn 1993), 27–33.

——. 'Mass Eviction and the Great Famine.' In Cathal Póirtéir, ed. *The Great Irish Famine*. Cork: Mercier Press, 1995.

——. '"Irish Property Must Pay for Irish Poverty": British Public Opinion and the Great Irish Famine.' In Chris Morash and Richard Hayes, eds. *Fearful Realities: New Perspectives on the Famine*. Dublin: Irish Academic Press, 1996.

Dowling, Linda Almeida. '"And They Still Haven't Found What They're Looking For": A Survey of the New Irish in New York City.' In Patrick O'Sullivan, ed. *The Irish World Wide. History, Heritage, Identity*. Vol. I. *Patterns of Migration*. Leicester, England: Leicester University Press, 1992.

Doyle, David Noel. 'The Irish and American Labour, 1880–1920.' *Saothar: Journal of the Irish Labour History Society*, 1 (1975), 42–53.

——. *Irish-Americans, Native Rights, and National Empires: The Structure, Divisions, and Attitudes of the Catholic Minority in the Decade of Expansion.* New York: Arno Press, 1976.

——. *Ireland, Irishmen, and Revolutionary America, 1760–1820.* Cork: The Mercier Press, 1981.

——. 'The Regional Bibliography of Irish America, 1800–1930: A Review and Addendum.' *Irish Historical Studies,* 23 (May 1983), 254–83.

——. 'Catholicism, Politics and Irish America Since 1890: Some Critical Considerations.' In P.J. Drudy, ed. *The Irish in America: Emigration, Assimilation, Impact.* (Irish Studies, 4). Cambridge, England: Cambridge University Press, 1985.

——. 'The Irish in Australia and the United States: 1800–1939: Some Comparisons.' *Irish Economic and Social History,* 16 (1989), 73–94.

——. 'The Irish in North America, 1776–1845.' In W.E. Vaughan, ed. *A New History of Ireland.* Vol. V. *Ireland Under the Union, I, 1801–70.* Oxford: Clarendon Press, 1989.

——. 'The Irish as Urban Pioneers in the United States, 1850–1870.' *Journal of American Ethnic History,* 10 (Fall 1990–Winter 1991), 36–59.

—— and Owen Dudley Edwards, eds. *America and Ireland, 1776–1976: The American Identity and the Irish Connection, 1776–1976.* Westport, CT: Greenwood Press, 1980.

Drudy, P.J., ed. *The Irish in America: Emigration, Assimilation, Impact.* (Irish Studies, 4). Cambridge, England: Cambridge University Press, 1985.

Drudy, P.J. 'Irish Population Change and Emigration Since Independence.' In P.J. Drudy, ed. *The Irish in America: Emigration, Assimilation, Impact.* (Irish Studies, 4). Cambridge, England: Cambridge University Press, 1985.

Dublin, Thomas. *Women at Work: The Transformation of Work and Community in Lowell, Massachusetts, 1826–1860.* New York: Columbia University Press, 1979.

Dudley Edwards, Owen. 'The American Image of Ireland: A Study of its Early Phases.' *Perspectives in American History,* IV (1970), 199–282.

Dudley Edwards, R. and T. Desmond Williams. *The Great Famine: Studies in Irish History, 1845–52.* Dublin: Browne and Nolan, 1956.

Dudden, Faye. *Serving Women: Household Service in Nineteenth Century America.* Middletown, CT: Wesleyan University Press, 1983.

Duff, John B. *The Irish in America.* Belmont, CA: Wadsworth, 1971.

Dumenil, Lynn. '"The Tribal Twenties": "Assimilated" Catholics' Response to Anti-Catholicism in the 1920s.' *Journal of American Ethnic History,* 11 (Fall 1991), 21–49.

Dunaway, Wayland F. *The Scotch-Irish of Colonial Pennsylvania.* Chapel Hill, NC: University of North Carolina Press, 1944.

Ehrlich, Richard, ed. *Immigrants in Industrial America, 1850–1920.* Charlottesville, VA: University of Virginia Press, 1977.

Eid, Leroy V. 'The Colonial Scotch-Irish: A View Accepted Too Readily.' *Éire-Ireland,* XXI (Winter 1986), 81–105.

——. 'Irish, Scotch, and Scotch-Irish: A Reconsideration.' *American Presbyterian,* LXIV (Winter 1986), 211–25.

——. '"No Freight Paid So Well": Irish Emigration to Pennsylvania on the Eve of the American Revolution.' *Éire-Ireland,* XXVII (Summer 1992), 35–59.

Ellis, John Tracy. *American Catholics and Intellectual Life.* 1956. Chicago: University of Chicago Press, 1969.

Emmer, P.C. and M. Mörner, eds. *European Expansion and Migration: Essays on the Intercontinental Migration from Africa, Asia, and Europe*. New York: Berg, 1992.

Emmons, David M. *The Butte Irish: Class and Ethnicity in an American Mining Town, 1875–1925*. Urbana, IL: University of Illinois Press, 1989.

——. 'Faction Fights: The Irish Worlds of Butte, Montana, 1875–1917.' In Patrick O'Sullivan, ed. *The Irish World Wide. History, Heritage, Identity*. Vol. II. *The Irish in the New Communities*. Leicester, England: Leicester University Press, 1992.

Erie, Steven P. *Rainbow's End: Irish Americans and the Dilemmas of Urban Machine Politics, 1840–1985*. Berkeley, CA: University of California Press, 1988.

Ernst, Robert. *Immigrant Life in New York City, 1825–1863*. 1949. Syracuse, NY: Syracuse University Press, 1994.

Evans, E. Estyn. 'Cultural Relics of the Ulster Scots in the Old West of the United States.' *Ulster Folklife*, XI (1965), 33–8.

——. 'The Scotch-Irish: Their Cultural Adaptation and Heritage in the Old American West.' In E.R.R. Green, ed. *Essays in Scotch-Irish History*. London: Routledge & Kegan Paul, 1969.

——. *Ireland and the Atlantic Heritage: Selected Writings*. Dublin: The Lilliput Press, MLMXCVI.

Fallows, Marjorie R. *Irish-American Identity and Assimilation*. Englewood Cliffs, NJ: Prentice-Hall, 1979.

Fanning, Charles, ed. *The Exiles of Erin: Nineteenth-Century Irish-American Fiction*. South Bend, Indiana: University of Notre Dame Press, 1987.

——. *The Irish Voice in America: Irish-American Fiction from the 1760s to the 1980s*. Lexington, KY: University of Kentucky, 1990.

——. 'The Heart's Speech No Longer Stifled: New York Irish Writing Since the 1960s'. In Ronald H. Bayor and Timothy J. Meagher, eds. *The New York Irish*. Baltimore, MD: Johns Hopkins University Press, 1996.

Fischer, David H. *Albion's Seed: Four British Folkways in America*. New York: Oxford University Press, 1989.

Fitzgerald, Maureen. 'Charity, Poverty, and Child Welfare.' *Harvard Divinity Bulletin*, 25 (1996), 12–17.

Fitzgerald, Patrick. 'The Scotch-Irish and the Eighteenth-Century Irish Diaspora.' *History Ireland*, 7 (Autumn 1999): 37–41.

Fitzpatrick, David. 'Irish Emigration in the Later Nineteenth Century.' *Irish Historical Studies*, XXII, 86 (1980), 126–43.

——. *Irish Emigration, 1801–1921. Studies in Irish Economic and Social History*, No.1. Dundalk, Ireland: The Economic and Social History Society of Ireland, 1984.

——. 'Emigration, 1801–70.' In W.E. Vaughan, ed. *A New History of Ireland*. Vol. V. *Ireland Under the Union, I, 1801–70*. Oxford: Clarendon Press, 1989.

Foner, Eric. *Free Soil, Free Labor, Free Men: The Ideology of the Republican Party Before the Civil War*. New York: Oxford University Press, 1970.

——. 'Class, Ethnicity, and Radicalism in the Gilded Age: The Land League and Irish-America.' In Eric Foner, *Politics and Ideology in the Age of the Civil War*. New York: Oxford University Press, 1980.

Foster, R.F. 'History and the Irish Question.' *Royal Historical Society Transactions*, 5th Ser., 32 (1983), 169–92.

——. *Modern Ireland, 1600–1972*. London: Allen Lane Penguin, 1988.

Franchot, Jenny. *Roads to Rome: The Antebellum Protestant Encounter with Catholicism.* Berkeley, CA: University of California Press, 1994.

Freedman, Samuel G. *The Inheritance: How Three Families and America Moved from Roosevelt to Reagan and Beyond.* New York: Simon and Schuster, 1996.

Funchion, Michael J. *Chicago's Irish Nationalists, 1881–1890.* New York: Arno Press, 1976.

Garrett, Stephen. *The Irish Character in American Fiction, 1830–1860.* New York: Arno Press, 1976.

Gerber, David A. *The Making of an American Pluralism: Buffalo, New York, 1825–1860.* Urbana, IL: University of Illinois Press, 1989.

Gerstle, Gary. 'Liberty, Coercion, and the Making of Americans.' *The Journal of American History*, 84 (September 1997), 524–58.

Gibson, Florence E. *The Attitudes of the New York Irish Toward State and National Affairs.* New York: Columbia University Press, 1951.

Gilje, Paul A. *The Road to Mobocracy: Popular Disorder in New York City, 1763–1834.* Chapel Hill, NC: University of North Carolina Press, 1987.

Gitelman, Howard M. 'No Irish Need Apply: Patterns of and Responses to Ethnic Discrimination in the Labor Market.' *Labor History*, 14 (Winter 1973), 56–68.

Gleason, Philip. *Catholicism in America*. New York: Harper & Row, 1967.

Golway, Terry. *Irish Rebel: John Devoy and America's Fight for Ireland's Freedom.* New York: St Martin's Press, 1998.

Gordon, Michael. 'The Labor Boycott in New York City, 1880–1886.' *Labor History*, 16 (1975), 184–229.

——. 'Irish Immigrant Culture and the Labor Boycott in New York City, 1880–86.' In Richard Ehrlich, ed. *Immigrants in Industrial America, 1850–1920.* Charlottesville, VA: University of Virginia Press, 1977.

——. *The Orange Riots: Irish Political Violence in New York City in 1870–1871.* Ithaca, NY: Cornell University Press, 1993.

Gray, Peter. '*Punch* and the Great Famine.' *History Ireland*, 1 (Summer 1993), 26–33.

——. 'Potatoes and Providence: British Government Responses to the Great Famine.' *Bullán: An Irish Studies Journal*, 1 (Spring 1994), 75–90.

——. *The Irish Famine*. New York: Abrams, 1995.

——. 'Ideology and the Famine.' In Cathal Póirtéir, ed. *The Great Irish Famine.* Cork: Mercier Press, 1995.

——. 'Famine Relief Policy in Comparative Perspective: Ireland, Scotland, and Northwestern Europe, 1845–1849.' *Éire-Ireland*, 32 (Spring 1997), 86–108.

Greeley, Andrew M. *The Catholic Experience.* New York: Doubleday, 1967.

——. *That Most Distressful Nation.* Chicago: Quadrangle Books, 1972.

——. 'The American Irish: A Report from Great Ireland.' *International Journal of Comparative Sociology*, XX (March–June 1979), 67–81.

——. *The Irish-Americans: The Rise to Money and Power.* New York: Harper & Row, 1981.

——. 'The Success and Assimilation of Irish Protestants and Irish Catholics in the United States.' *Sociology and Social Research*, 72 (July 1988), 229–36.

Green, E.R.R. 'The Scotch-Irish and the Coming of the Revolution in North Carolina.' *Irish Historical Studies*, VII (September 1950), 77–86.

———. 'The "Strange Humours" That Drove The Scotch-Irish to America, 1729.' *William and Mary Quarterly*, 3rd Ser., 12 (January 1955), 113–23.

———. 'The Irish American Business and Professions.' In David N. Doyle and Owen Dudley Edwards, eds. *America and Ireland, 1776–1976: The American Identity and the Irish Connection*. Westport, CT: Greenwood Press, 1980.

———, ed. *Essays in Scotch-Irish History*. London: Routledge & Kegan Paul, 1969.

Greene, Jack P. 'Independence, Improvement, and Authority: Toward a Framework for Understanding the Histories of the Southern Backcountry during the Era of the American Revolution.' In Ronald Hoffman, Thad W. Tate, and Peter J. Albert, eds. *An Uncivil War: The Southern Backcountry during the American Revolution*. Charlottesville, VA: The University Press of Virginia, 1985.

———. *Imperatives, Behaviors, and Identities: Essays in Early American Cultural History*. Charlottesville, VA: The University Press of Virginia, 1992.

Gribben, Arthur, ed. *The Great Famine and the Irish Diaspora in America*. Amherst, MA: University of Massachusetts Press, 1999.

Griffen, Clyde. 'Making it in America: Social Mobility in Mid-Nineteenth Century Poughkeepsie.' *New York History*, LI (October 1970), 479–99.

—— and Sally Griffen. *Natives and Newcomers: The Ordering of Opportunity in Mid-Nineteenth Century Poughkeepsie*. Cambridge, MA: Harvard University Press, 1978.

Griffin, William D. *A Portrait of the Irish in America*. New York: Scribner's, 1981.

Groneman Pernicone, Carol. 'Working-Class Immigrant Women in Mid-Nineteenth-Century New York: The Irish Woman's Experience.' *Journal of Urban History*, 4 (1978), 255–73.

Gudelunas, William A., Jr. and William G. Shade. *Before the Molly Maguires: The Emergence of the Ethno-Religious Factor in the Politics of the Lower Anthracite Region, 1844–1872*. New York: Arno Press, 1976.

Guinnane, Timothy. *The Vanishing Irish: Households, Migration, and the Rural Economy in Ireland, 1850–1914*. Princeton, NJ: Princeton University Press, 1997.

Handlin, Oscar. *Boston's Immigrants*. 1941. New York: Atheneum, 1976.

Haney Lopez, Ian. *White by Law: The Legal Construction of Race*. New York: New York University Press, 1996.

Hanlon, Gerard. 'Graduate Emigration: A Continuation or a Break With the Past?' In Patrick O'Sullivan, ed. *The Irish World Wide. History, Heritage, Identity*. Vol. I. *Patterns of Migration*. Leicester, England: Leicester University Press, 1992.

Hansen, Marcus Lee. *The Atlantic Migration, 1607–1860*. Cambridge, MA: Harvard University Press, 1940.

Harmon, Morris, ed. *Fenians and Fenianism*. Seattle, WA: University of Washington Press, 1970.

Harris, Ruth-Ann M. *The Nearest Place That Wasn't Ireland: Early Nineteenth-Century Irish Labor Migration*. Ames, Iowa: Iowa State University Press, 1994.

Hernon, Joseph M., Jr. *Celts, Catholics and Copperheads: Ireland Views the American Civil War*. Columbus, OH: Ohio State University Press, 1968.

Higham, John. *Strangers in the Land: Patterns of American Nativism, 1860–1925*. New York: Atheneum, 1965.

Hill, J. Michael. 'The Origin of the Scottish Plantation of Ulster to 1625.' *Journal of British Studies*, 32 (January 1993), 24–43.

Hoffman, Ronald, Thad W. Tate, and Peter J. Albert, eds. *An Uncivil War: The Southern Backcountry during the American Revolution*. Charlottesville, VA: The University Press of Virginia, 1985.

Hogan, Michael F.X. *The Irish Soldiers of Mexico*. Guadalajara, Mexico: Fondo Editorial Universitario, 1997.

Hooker, Richard J., ed. *The Carolina Backcountry on the Eve of the Revolution. The Journal and Other Writings of Charles Woodmason, Anglican Itinerant*. Chapel Hill, NC: University of North Carolina Press, 1953.

Horn, James. 'British Diaspora: Emigration from Britain, 1680–1815.' In P.J. Marshall, ed. *The Oxford History of the British Empire*. Volume II. *The Eighteenth Century*. Oxford: Oxford University Press, 1998.

Hoppen, K. Theodore. *Ireland Since 1800: Conflict and Conformity*. New York: Longman, 1989.

Horsman, Reginald. *Race and Manifest Destiny: The Origins of American Racial Anglo-Saxonism*. Cambridge, MA: Harvard University Press, 1981.

Hoy, Suellen. 'The Journey Out: The Recruitment and Emigration of Irish Religious Women to the United States, 1812–1914.' *Journal of Women's History*, 6 and 7 (Winter/Spring 1995), 64–98.

Hueston, Robert F. *The Catholic Press and Nativism, 1840–1860*. New York: Arno Press, 1976.

Ibson, John Duffy. *Will the World Break Your Heart? Dimensions and Consequences of Irish-American Assimilation*. New York: Garland Publishing, 1990.

Ignatiev, Noel. *How the Irish Became White*. New York: Routledge, 1995.

Jackson, Carlton. *A Social History of the Scotch-Irish*. Lanham, KY: Madison Books, 1993.

Jackson, Kenneth T. *Crabgrass Frontier: The Suburbanization of the United States*. New York: Oxford University Press, 1985.

——, ed. *The Encyclopedia of New York City*. New Haven, CT: Yale University Press, 1995.

Jackson, Pauline. 'Women in Nineteenth-Century Irish Emigration.' *International Migration Review*, 18 (Winter 1984), 1004–20.

Jacobson, Matthew F. *Special Sorrows: The Diasporic Imagination of Irish, Polish, and Jewish Immigrants in the United States*. Cambridge, MA: Harvard University Press, 1995.

——. *Whiteness of a Different Color: European Immigrants and the Alchemy of Race*. Cambridge, MA: Harvard University Press, 1998.

Jenkins, Brian. *Fenians and Anglo-American Relations During Reconstruction*. Ithaca, NY: Cornell University Press, 1969.

Johnson, J.H. 'Harvest Migration from Nineteenth-Century Ireland.' *Transactions and Proceedings of the Institute of British Geographers*, 20 (1965), 97–112.

Jones, Maldwyn A. 'Ulster Emigration, 1783–1815.' In E.R.R. Green, ed. *Essays in Scotch-Irish History*. London: Routledge & Kegan Paul, 1969.

——. 'Scotch-Irish.' In Stephan Thernstrom, ed. *The Harvard Encyclopedia of American Ethnic Groups*. Cambridge, MA: Belknap Press of Harvard University Press, 1980.

——. 'The Scotch-Irish in British America.' In Bernard Bailyn and Philip D. Morgan, eds. *Strangers Within the Realm: Cultural Margins of the First British Empire*. Chapel Hill, NC: University of North Carolina Press, 1991.

Joyce, William L. *Editors and Ethnicity: a History of the Irish-American Press*. New York: Arno Press, 1976.

Kane, Paula M. *Separatism and Subculture: Boston Catholicism, 1900–1920*. Chapel Hill, NC: University of North Carolina Press, 1994.

Kennedy, Robert E. *The Irish: Emigration, Marriage, and Fertility*. Berkeley, CA: University of California Press, 1973.

Kenny, Kevin. 'Religion and Immigration: The Irish Community in New York City, 1815–40.' *The Recorder: A Journal of the American-Irish Historical Society*, 3 (Winter 1989), 4–49.

——. 'Nativism, Labor and Slavery: The Political Odyssey of Benjamin Bannan.' *The Pennsylvania Magazine of History and Biography*, CXVIII (October 1994), 326–61.

——. 'The Molly Maguires and the Catholic Church.' *Labor History*, 37 (Summer 1995), 345–76.

——. 'The Molly Maguires in Popular Culture.' *The Journal of American Ethnic History*, 14 (Summer 1995), 27–46.

——. *Making Sense of the Molly Maguires*. New York: Oxford University Press, 1998.

Kinealy, Christine. *This Great Calamity: The Irish Famine, 1845–1852*. Dublin: Gill and Macmillan, 1994.

——. *A Death-Dealing Famine: The Great Hunger in Ireland*. London and Chicago: Pluto, 1997.

Klein, Rachel N. 'Frontier Planters and the American Revolution: The South Carolina Backcountry, 1775–1782.' In Ronald Hoffman, Thad W. Tate, and Peter J. Albert, eds. *An Uncivil War: The Southern Backcountry during the American Revolution*. Charlottesville, VA: The University Press of Virginia, 1985.

——. *Unification of a Slave State: The Rise of the Planter Class in the South Carolina Backcountry, 1760–1808*. Chapel Hill, NC: University of North Carolina Press, 1990.

Knobel, Dale T. *Paddy and the Republic: Ethnicity and Nationality in Antebellum America*. Middletown, CT: Wesleyan University Press, 1986.

Larkin, Emmet. 'The Devotional Revolution in Ireland.' *American Historical Review*, 77 (June 1972), 625–52.

——, trans. and ed. *Alexis de Tocqueville's Journey in Ireland, July–August, 1835*. Washington, DC: The Catholic University of America Press, 1990.

Larkin, James. *Ireland and the Irish in the U.S.A.* New York: Transport Workers of America, CIO, 1947.

Laurie, Bruce, Theodore Hershberg and George Alter. 'Immigrants and Industry: The Philadelphia Experience.' In Richard Ehrlich, ed. *Immigrants in Industrial America, 1850–1920*. Charlottesville, VA: University of Virginia Press, 1977.

Laurie, Bruce. *Workingmen of Philadelphia, 1800–1850*. Philadelphia: Temple University Press, 1980.

Leavitt, Judith Walzer. *Typhoid Mary: Captive to the Public's Health*. Boston: Beacon Press, 1996.

Lebsock, Suzanne. *The Free Women of Petersburg: Status and Culture in a Southern Town, 1784–1860*. New York: Norton, 1984.

Lees, Lynn and John Modell. 'The Irish Countryman Urbanized: A Comparative Perspective on Famine Migration.' *Journal of Urban History*, 3 (August 1977), 391–408.

Levine, Edward M. *The Irish and Irish Politicians: A Study in Social and Cultural Alienation.* South Bend, Indiana: University of Notre Dame Press, 1966.

Leyburn, James G. *The Scotch-Irish: A Social History.* Chapel Hill, NC: University of North Carolina Press, 1962.

Light, Dale B. 'The Role of Irish-American Organisations in Assimilation and Community Formation.' In P.J. Drudy, ed. *The Irish in America: Emigration, Assimilation, Impact.* (Irish Studies, 4). Cambridge, England: Cambridge University Press, 1985.

Lockhart, Audrey. *Some Aspects of Emigration from Ireland to the North American Colonies between 1660 and 1775.* New York: Arno Press, 1976.

Lott, Eric. *Love and Theft: Blackface Minstrelsy and the American Working Class.* New York: Oxford University Press, 1995.

McAvoy, Thomas T. *The Americanist Heresy in Roman Catholicism, 1895–1900.* South Bend, Indiana: University of Notre Dame Press, 1963.

——. *History of the Catholic Church in the United States.* South Bend, Indiana: University of Notre Dame Press, 1969.

McCaffrey, Lawrence. *The Irish Diaspora in America.* Bloomington, Indiana: Indiana University Press, 1976.

——. *Irish Nationalism and the American Contribution.* New York: Arno Press, 1976.

——. *Textures of Irish America.* Syracuse, NY: Syracuse University Press, 1992.

McCurry, Stephanie. *Masters of Small Worlds: Yeoman Households, Gender Relations, and the Political Culture of the Antebellum South Carolina Low Country.* New York: Oxford University Press, 1995.

MacDonagh, Oliver. 'The Irish Catholic Clergy and Emigration During the Great Famine.' *Irish Historical Studies*, V (September 1947), 287–302.

——. 'Irish Emigration to the United States and the British Colonies during the Famine.' In R. Dudley Edwards and T. Desmond Williams, eds. *The Great Famine: Studies in Irish History, 1845–52.* Dublin: Browne and Nolan, 1956.

——. *A Pattern of Government Growth, 1800–60: The Passenger Acts and their Enforcement.* London: MacGibbon & Kee, 1961.

——, ed. *Emigration in the Victorian Age: Debates on the Issues from 19th-Century Critical Journals.* Farnborough, Hants., England: Gregg International Publishers, 1973.

——. 'The Irish Famine Emigration to the United States.' *Perspectives in American History*, X (1976), 357–446.

—— and William F. Mandle, eds. *Ireland and Irish-Australia: Studies in Cultural and Political History.* London: Croom Helm, 1986.

McDonald, Ellen Shapiro and Forrest McDonald. 'The Ethnic Origins of the American People, 1790.' *William and Mary Quarterly*, 3rd Ser., XXXVII (January 1980), 179–99. With communications by Francis Jennings and Rowland Berthoff and a reply by the McDonalds, 700–3.

McDonald, Forrest and Grady McWhiney. 'The Antebellum Southern Herdsman: A Reinterpretation.' *The Journal of Southern History*, 41 (May 1975), 147–66.

——. 'Celtic Origins of Southern Herding Practices.' *The Journal of Southern History*, 51 (1985), 165–82.

McDonald, Sister Justille. *History of the Irish in Wisconsin in the Nineteenth Century.* Washington, DC: Catholic University Press, 1954.

McGimpsey, Christopher. 'Internal Ethnic Friction: Orange and Green in Nineteenth-Century New York, 1868–1872.' *Immigrants and Minorities*, 1 (March 1982), 39–59.

McGreevy, John T. 'Thinking on One's Own: Catholicism in the American Intellectual Imagination, 1928–1960.' *The Journal of American History*, 84 (June 1997), 97–131.

MacKay, Donald. *Flight from Famine: The Coming of the Irish to Canada.* Toronto: McClelland & Stewart, 1990.

McPherson, James M. *The Battle Cry of Freedom: The Civil War Era.* New York: Oxford University Press, 1988.

McWhiney, Grady. *Cracker Culture: Celtic Ways in the Old South.* Alabama: University of Alabama Press, 1988.

—— and Perry Jamieson. *Attack and Die: Civil War Military Tactics and the Southern Heritage.* University, Alabama: University of Alabama Press, 1982.

Mageean, Deirdre M. 'Emigration from Irish Ports.' *Journal of American Ethnic History*, 13 (Fall 1993), 6–30.

Man, Albon P., Jr. 'The Irish in New York in the Early Eighteen-Sixties.' *Irish Historical Studies*, 7 (September 1950), 87–108.

——. 'Labor Competition and the New York City Draft Riots of 1863.' *Journal of Negro History*, 36 (October 1951), 376–405.

Mason, Matthew E. '"The Hands Here are Disposed to be Turbulent": Unrest Among the Irish Trackmen of the Baltimore and Ohio Railroad, 1829–1851.' *Labor History*, 39 (August 1998), 253–72.

Melville, Herman. *Redburn: His First Voyage.* 1849. London: Jonathan Cape, 1937.

Merton, Robert K. 'Latent Functions of the Machine.' In Alexander Callow, comp., *American Urban History.* New York: Oxford University Press, 1969.

Miles, Robert. 'Labour Migration and Racism: The Case of the Irish.' In Robert Miles, *Racism and Migrant Labour.* London: Routledge & Kegan Paul, 1982.

Miller, David W. 'Irish Catholicism and the Great Famine.' *Journal of Social History*, 9 (1975), 81–98.

Miller, Kerby A. *Emigrants and Exiles: Ireland and the Irish Exodus to North America.* New York: Oxford University Press, 1985.

——. 'Assimilation and Alienation: Irish Emigrants' Responses to Industrial America, 1871–1921.' In P.J. Drudy, ed. *The Irish in America: Emigration, Assimilation, Impact.* (Irish Studies, 4). Cambridge, England: Cambridge University Press, 1985.

——. 'Class, Culture, and Immigrant Group Identity in the United States: The Case of Irish-American Ethnicity.' In Virginia Yans-McLaughlin, ed. *Immigration Reconsidered: History, Sociology, and Politics.* New York: Oxford University Press, 1990.

—— and Bruce D. Boling. 'Golden Streets, Bitter Tears: The Irish Image of America During the Era of Mass Migration.' *Journal of American Ethnic History*, 10 (Fall 1990–Winter 1991), 16–35.

—— with Bruce Boling and David N. Doyle. 'Emigrants and Exiles: Irish Cultures and Irish Emigration to North America, 1790–1922.' *Irish Historical Studies*, XXII (1980), 97–125.

——., with David N. Doyle and Patricia Kelleher. '"For Love and Liberty": Irish Women, Migration and Domesticity in Ireland and America, 1815–1920.' In Patrick

O'Sullivan, ed. *The Irish Worldwide: History, Heritage, Identity.* Volume 4. *Irish Women and Irish Migration.* Leicester: Leicester University Press, 1995.

Miller, Robert Ryal. *Shamrock and Sword: The Saint Patrick's Battalion in the U.S.-Mexican War.* Norman, Oklahoma: University of Oklahoma Press, 1997.

Mitchell, Brian C. *The Paddy Camps: The Irish of Lowell, 1821–61.* Urbana, IL: University of Illinois Press, 1988.

Mokyr, Joel. 'Industrialization and Poverty in the Netherlands.' *Journal of Interdisciplinary History,* 10 (Winter 1980), 429–58.

——. *Why Ireland Starved: A Quantitative and Analytical History of the Irish Economy, 1800–1850.* London: Allen and Unwin, 1985.

Montgomery, David. 'The Shuttle and the Cross: Weavers and Artisans in the Kensington Riots of 1844.' *Journal of Social History,* 5 (1972), 411–46.

——. 'The Irish and the American Labor Movement.' In David Noel Doyle and Owen Dudley Edwards, eds. *America and Ireland, 1776–1976: The American Identity and the Irish Connection.* Westport, CT: Greenwood Press, 1980.

Montgomery, Michael. 'The Roots of Appalachian English: Scotch-Irish or British Southern?' *Journal of the Appalachian Studies Association,* 3 (1991), 177–91.

——. 'The Scotch-Irish Element in Appalachian English: How Broad? How Deep?' In H. Tyler Blethen and Curtis W. Wood, Jr., eds. *Ulster and North America: Transatlantic Perspectives on the Scotch-Irish.* Tuscaloosa, Alabama: University of Alabama Press, 1997.

Morash, Chris and Richard Hayes, eds. *Fearful Realities: New Perspectives on the Famine.* Dublin: Irish Academic Press, 1996.

Morris, Charles R. *American Catholic: The Saints and Sinners Who Built America's Most Powerful Church.* New York: Times Books/Random House, 1997.

Moynihan, Daniel Patrick. 'The Irish.' In Nathan Glazer and Daniel Patrick Moynihan, eds. *Beyond the Melting Pot.* Cambridge, MA: MIT Press, 1963.

Murray, Frank. 'The Irish and Afro-Americans in US History.' *Freedomways,* 22 (First Quarter, 1982), 21–30.

Niehaus, Earl F. *The Irish in New Orleans, 1800–1860.* Baton Rouge, LA: Louisiana State University Press, 1965.

Nolan, Janet. *Ourselves Alone: Women's Emigration from Ireland, 1885–1920.* Lexington, KY: The University Press of Kentucky, 1989.

O'Broin, Leon. *Fenian Fever.* New York: New York University Press, 1971.

O'Casey, Daniel J. and Robert E. Rhodes, eds. *Modern Irish-American Fiction: A Reader.* Syracuse, NY: Syracuse University Press, 1989.

O'Connell, Maurice. 'O'Connell, Irish Americans and Negro Slavery.' *The Recorder. A Journal of the American Irish Historical Society,* 3 (Winter 1988), 61–8.

O'Connor, Edwin. *The Last Hurrah.* Boston: Little, Brown, 1956.

O'Connor, Len. *Clout: Mayor Daley and His City.* Chicago: H. Regnery Co., 1975.

——. *Requiem: The Decline and Demise of Mayor Daley and his Era.* Chicago: Contemporary Books, 1977.

O'Connor, Thomas H. *The Boston Irish: A Political History.* Boston: Northeastern Press, 1995.

O'Day, Alan. 'Revising the Diaspora.' In D. George Boyce and Alan O'Day, eds. *The Making of Modern Irish History: Revisionism and the Revisionist Controversy.* London: Routledge, 1996.

O'Dea, Thomas. *American Catholic Dilemma.* New York: The New American Library, 1962.

O'Donnell, Edward T. *Henry George for Mayor! Irish Nationalists, Labor Radicalism, and Independent Politics in Gilded Age New York City.* Forthcoming. Columbia University Press, *c.* 2000.

O'Gallagher, Marianna. *Grosse Île: Gateway to Canada, 1832–1937.* Québec City: Carraig Books, 1984.

O'Gráda, Cormac. 'Seasonal Migration and post-Famine Adjustment in the West of Ireland.' *Studia Hibernica,* 13 (1973), 48–76.

——. 'A Note on Nineteenth-century Emigration Statistics.' *Population Studies,* 29 (1975), 143–9.

——. 'Irish Emigration to the United States in the Nineteenth Century.' In David Noel Doyle and Owen Dudley Edwards, eds. *America and Ireland, 1776–1976: The American Identity and the Irish Connection.* Westport, CT: Greenwood Press, 1980.

——. *Ireland Before and After the Famine: Explorations in Economic History, 1800–1925.* Manchester, England: Manchester University Press, 1988.

——. *Ireland: A New Economic History, 1780–1939.* Oxford: Clarendon Press, 1994.

——. *Black '47 and Beyond.* Princeton, NJ: Princeton University Press, 1999.

O'Grady, Joseph P. *How the Irish Became American.* New York: Twayne, 1973.

——. *Irish-Americans and Anglo-American Relations, 1880–1888.* New York: Arno Press, 1976.

O'Hanlon, Ray. *The New Irish Americans.* Niwot, Colorado: Roberts Rinehart, 1998.

O'Neill, Kevin. *Family and Farm in Pre-Famine Ireland: The Parish of Killashandra.* Madison, WI: The University of Wisconsin Press, 1984.

Opler, Marvin K. 'The Influence of Ethnic and Class Subcultures on Child Care.' *Social Problems,* 3 (July 1955), 12–21.

——. 'Cultural Differences in Mental Disorders: An Italian and Irish Contrast in the Schizophrenias.' In Marvin K. Opler, ed. *Culture and Mental Health: Cross-Cultural Studies.* New York: Macmillan, 1959.

—— and Jerome L. Singer. 'Ethnic Differences in Behavior and Psychopathology: Italian and Irish.' *International Journal of Social Psychiatry,* 2 (Summer 1956), 11–23.

Osofsky, Gilbert. 'Abolitionists, Irish Immigrants and the Dilemmas of Romantic Nationalism.' *The American Historical Review,* 80 (October 1975), 889–97.

O'Sullivan, Patrick. *The Irish World Wide. History, Heritage, Identity.* Vol. I. *Patterns of Migration.* Leicester, England: Leicester University Press, 1992.

——. *The Irish World Wide. History, Heritage, Identity.* Vol. II. *The Irish in the New Communities.* Leicester, England: Leicester University Press, 1992.

——. *The Irish World Wide. History, Heritage, Identity.* Vol. III. *The Creative Migrant.* Leicester, England: Leicester University Press, 1993.

——. *The Irish World Wide. History, Heritage, Identity.* Vol. IV. *Irish Women and Irish Migration.* Leicester, England: Leicester University Press, 1995.

Perceval-Maxwell, M. *The Scottish Migration to Ulster in the Reign of James I.* Belfast: Ulster Historical Foundation, 1990.

Póirtéir, Cathal, ed. *The Great Irish Famine.* Cork: Mercier Press, 1995.

Potter, George W. *To the Golden Door: The Story of the Irish in Ireland and America.* Boston: Little, Brown, 1960.

Purvis, Thomas L., Donald H. Akenson and Forrest and Ellen McDonald. 'The Population of the United States, 1790: A Symposium.' *William and Mary Quarterly*, 3rd Ser., 41 (1984), 85–135.

Purvis, Thomas L. 'Patterns of Ethnic Settlement in Late Eighteenth-Century Pennsylvania.' *Western Pennsylvania Historical Magazine*, LXX (1987), 107–22.

Quigley, David. 'Reconstructing Democracy: Politics and Ideas in New York City, 1865–80.' Unpublished Ph.D. dissertation, New York University, 1997.

Quigley, Michael. 'Grosse Île: Canada's Famine Memorial.' *Éire-Ireland*, 32 (Spring 1997), 7–19.

Quinn, Peter. *Banished Children of Eve.* New York: Penguin, 1994.

——. 'Introduction', William L. Riordan, ed. *Plunkitt of Tammany Hall: A Series of Very Plain Talks on Very Practical Politics.* New York: Signet, 1995.

——. 'Introduction: An Interpretation of Silences.' *Éire-Ireland*, 32 (Spring 1997), 7–19.

——. 'The Tragedy of Bridget Such-a-One.' *American Heritage* (December 1997), 36–51.

Rakove, Milton L. *Don't Make No Waves – Don't Back No Losers: An Insider's Analysis of the Daley Machine.* Bloomington, IL: Illinois University Press, 1975.

Reedy, George E. *From the Ward to the White House: The Irish in American Politics.* New York: Scribner's, 1991.

Riach, Douglas. 'Daniel O'Connell and American Anti-Slavery.' *Irish Historical Studies*, XX (March 1976), 3–25.

Rice, Madeleine Hooke. *American Catholic Opinion in the Slavery Controversy.* New York: Columbia University Press, 1944.

Riordan, William L., ed. *Plunkitt of Tammany Hall: A Series of Very Plain Talks on Very Practical Politics.* With an introduction by Peter Quinn. New York: Signet, 1995.

Robinson, Philip. *The Plantation of Ulster: British Settlement in an Irish Landscape, 1600–1670.* New York: St Martin's Press, 1984.

Rodechko, James P. 'Irish-American Society in the Pennsylvania Anthracite Region: 1870–1880.' In John Bodnar, ed. *The Ethnic Experience in Pennsylvania.* Lewisburg: Bucknell University Press, 1973.

——. *Patrick Ford and His Search for America: A Case Study of Irish-American Journalism.* New York: Arno Press, 1976.

Roediger, David. *The Wages of Whiteness: Race and the Making of the American Working Class.* New York: Verso, 1991.

Roohan, James Edmund. *American Catholics and the Social Question, 1865–1900.* New York: Arno Press, 1976.

Rowland, Thomas J. 'Irish-American Catholics and the Quest for Respectability in the Coming of the Great War.' *Journal of American Ethnic History*, 15 (Winter 1996), 3–31.

Salaman, Redcliffe. *The History and Social Influence of the Potato.* 1949. Cambridge, England: Cambridge University Press, 1989.

Saxton, Alexander. *The Indispensable Enemy: Labor and the Anti-Chinese Movement in California.* Berkeley, CA: University of California Press, 1971.

Scally, Robert J. *The End of Hidden Ireland: Rebellion, Famine, and Emigration.* New York: Oxford University Press, 1995.

Schlesinger, Arthur, Jr. *A Thousand Days: John F. Kennedy in the White House*. Boston: Houghton Mifflin, 1965.

Schrier, Arnold. *Ireland and the American Migration, 1850–1900*. Minneapolis: University of Minnesota Press, 1958.

Shannon, James P. *Catholic Colonization on the Western Frontier*. New Haven, CT: Yale University Press, 1957.

Shannon, William V. *The American Irish*. New York: Macmillan, 1963.

Shaw, Douglas V. *The Making of an Immigrant City: Ethnic and Cultural Conflict in Jersey City, New Jersey, 1850–1877*. New York: Arno Press, 1976.

——. 'Political Leadership in the Industrial City: Irish Development and Nativist Response in Jersey City.' In Richard Ehrlich, ed. *Immigrants in Industrial America, 1850–1920*. Charlottesville, VA: University of Virginia Press, 1977.

Silver, Christopher. 'A New Look at Old South Urbanization: The Irish Worker in Charleston, South Carolina, 1840–1860.' In Samuel P. Hines and George W. Hopkins, eds. *South Atlantic Urban Studies*, Vol. 3. Columbia, SC: University of South Carolina Press, 1979.

Smyth, William J. 'Irish Emigration, 1700–1920.' In P.C. Emmer, and M. Mörner, eds. *European Expansion and Migration: Essays on the Intercontinental Migration from Africa, Asia, and Europe*. New York: Berg, 1992.

Stansell, Christine. *City of Women: Sex and Class in New York, 1789–1860*. New York: Knopf, 1986.

Stivers, Richard. *The Hair of the Dog: Irish Drinking and American Stereotype*. University Park, PA: Pennsylvania State University Press, 1976.

Strong, George Templeton. *Diary of George Templeton Strong*. Ed. Allan Nevis and Milton Haley Thomas. Abridged by Thomas J. Pressly. Seattle, WA: University of Washington Press, 1988.

Tansill, Charles C. *America and the Fight for Irish Freedom, 1866–1922*. New York: Devin-Adair, 1957.

Taylor, Philip. *The Distant Magnet*. New York: Harper & Row, 1971.

Thernstrom, Stephan. *Poverty and Progress: Social Mobility in a Nineteenth-Century City*. 1964. New York: Atheneum, 1970.

——. *The Other Bostonians: Poverty and Progress in the American Metropolis, 1860–1970*. Cambridge, MA: Harvard University Press, 1973.

——, ed. *The Harvard Encyclopedia of American Ethnic Groups*. Cambridge, MA: Belknap Press of Harvard University Press, 1980.

Thomas, Brinley. *Migration and Economic Growth*. Rev. edn. Cambridge, England: Cambridge University Press, 1973.

Tucker, Gilbert. 'The Famine Immigration to Canada, 1847.' *The American Historical Review*, XXXVI (1930–1), 533–49.

Turbin, Carole. *Working Women of Collar City: Gender, Class and Community in Troy, 1864–86*. Urbana, IL: University of Illinois Press, 1992.

Vaughan, W. E., ed. *A New History of Ireland*. Vol. V. *Ireland Under the Union, I, 1801–70*. Oxford: Clarendon Press, 1989.

Vinyard, Jo Ellen McNergney. *The Irish on the Urban Frontier: Nineteenth-Century Detroit, 1850–80*. New York: Arno Press, 1976.

Wakin, Edward. *Enter the Irish-American*. New York: Crowell, 1976.

Walkowitz, Daniel J. *Worker City, Company Town: Iron and Cotton-Worker Protest in Troy and Cohoes, New York, 1855–1884*. Urbana, IL: University of Illinois Press, 1972.

Walsh, Brendan M. 'A Perspective on Irish Population Patterns.' *Éire-Ireland*, IV (Autumn 1969), 3–21.

——. 'Marriage Rates and Population Pressure: Ireland, 1871 and 1911.' *The Economic History Review*, XXIII (April 1970), 148–62.

Walsh, Francis R. 'Who Spoke for Boston's Irish? The *Boston Pilot* in the Nineteenth Century.' *Journal of Ethnic Studies*, 10 (Fall 1982), 21–36.

Walsh, James P. 'American Irish: East and West.' *Éire-Ireland*, 6 (Summer 1971), 25–32.

——. *The Irish: America's Political Class*. New York: Arno Press, 1976.

Walsh, Victor A. ' "A Fanatic Heart": The Cause of Irish-American Nationalism in Pittsburgh During the Gilded Age.' *Journal of Social History*, 15 (1981), 187–204.

——. 'Irish Nationalism and Land Reform: The Role of the Irish in America.' In P.J. Drudy, ed. *The Irish in America: Emigration, Assimilation, Impact*. (Irish Studies, 4). Cambridge, England: Cambridge University Press, 1985.

——. ' "Drowning the Shamrock": Drink, Teetotalism, and the Irish Catholics of Gilded-Age Pittsburgh.' *Journal of American Ethnic History*, 10 (Fall 1990–Winter 1991), 60–79.

Ward, Alan J. *Ireland and Anglo-American Relations, 1899–1921*. Toronto: University of Toronto Press, 1969.

Way, Peter. 'Shovel and Shamrock: Irish Workers and Labor Violence in the Digging of the Chesapeake and Ohio Canal.' *Labor History*, 30 (Fall 1989), 489–517.

——. 'Evil Humors and Ardent Spirits: The Rough Culture of Canal Construction Laborers.' *Journal of American History*, 79 (March 1993), 1397–1428.

——. *Common Labour: Workers and the Digging of the North American Canals, 1780–1860*. Cambridge, England: Cambridge University Press, 1993.

Wells, Ronald A. 'Aspects of Northern Irish Migration to America: Definitions and Directions.' *Ethnic Forum*, 4 (1984), 49–63.

White, Theodore. *The Making of the President, 1960*. New York: Atheneum, 1961.

Wilentz, Robert Sean. 'Industrializing America and the Irish: Towards the New Departure.' *Labor History*, 20 (Fall 1979), 579–95.

Wilson, Andrew J. *Irish America and the Ulster Conflict, 1968–1995*. Belfast: The Blackstaff Press, 1995.

Wilson, David A. *United Irishmen, United States: Immigrant Radicals in the Early Republic*. Ithaca, NY: Cornell University Press, 1998.

Winsberg, Morton D. 'Irish Settlement in the United States, 1850–1980.' *Éire-Ireland*, 20 (Spring 1985), 7–14.

——. 'The Suburbanization of the Irish in Boston, Chicago and New York.' *Éire-Ireland*, 21 (Fall 1986), 90–104.

Wittke, Carl. *The Irish in America*. 1956. New York: Russell and Russell, 1970.

Wokeck, Marianne. *Trade in Strangers: The Beginnings of Mass Migration to North America*. University Park, PA: Pennsylvania State University Press, 1999.

NOTES

◆

Chapter 1: The Eighteenth Century

1. These rough estimates are drawn from Kerby A. Miller, *Emigrants and Exiles: Ireland and the Irish Exodus to North America* (New York, 1985), 137.
2. Miller, *Emigrants and Exiles*, 137, 149.
3. David Noel Doyle, *Ireland, Irishmen, and Revolutionary America, 1760–1820* (Cork, 1981), 51–2; David Noel Doyle, 'The Irish in North America, 1776–1845', in W.E. Vaughan, ed. *A New History of Ireland*. Vol. V. *Ireland Under the Union, I, 1801–70* (Oxford, 1989), 692; quote from E.R.R. Green, 'The Scotch-Irish and the Coming of the Revolution in North Carolina', *Irish Historical Studies*, VII (September 1950), 77. Kerby Miller places the eighteenth-century migration in its wider geographical and temporal contexts better than any other historian; but see also Ronald A. Wells, 'Aspects of Northern Irish Migration to America: Definitions and Directions', *Ethnic Forum*, 4 (1984), 49–63.
4. Patrick J. Blessing, 'Irish', in Stephan Thernstrom, ed. *The Harvard Encyclopedia of American Ethnic Groups* (Cambridge, MA, 1980), 525; Miller, *Emigrants and Exiles*, 139, 140, 144. The larger the agricultural enterprise, the more likely it was to employ slaves; smallholders still found it less risky to hire a few servants than to make the more expensive investment of buying a single slave.
5. Blessing, 'Irish', 525, 527; Miller, *Emigrants and Exiles*, 139.
6. Blessing, 'Irish', 525, 527; Miller, *Emigrants and Exiles*, 139.
7. James G. Leyburn, *The Scotch-Irish: A Social History* (Chapel Hill, NC, 1962), 3–46, 99–101; Carlton Jackson, *A Social History of the Scotch-Irish* (Lanham, KY, 1993).
8. Leyburn, *Scotch-Irish*, 47–61, 101–7.
9. R.J. Dickson, *Ulster Emigration to Colonial America, 1718–1775* (London, 1966), 2–3; Leyburn, *Scotch-Irish*, 83–107; Maldwyn A. Jones, 'Scotch-Irish', in Thernstrom, ed. *Harvard Encyclopedia of American Ethnic Groups*, 896; Maldwyn A. Jones, 'The Scotch-Irish in British America', in Bernard Bailyn and Philip D. Morgan, eds. *Strangers Within the Realm: Cultural Margins of the First British Empire* (Chapel Hill, NC, 1991), 288–91; Jackson, *Social History*, 13–24.
10. Jones, 'Scotch-Irish', 896; Jones, 'Scotch-Irish in British America', 288–91; Jackson, *Social History*, 13–24; Leyburn, *Scotch-Irish*, 83–107; Dickson, *Ulster Emigration*, 2–3; S.J. Connolly, 'Ulster Presbyterians: Religion, Culture, and Politics, 1660–1850', in H. Tyler Blethen and Curtis W. Wood, Jr., eds. *Ulster and North America: Transatlantic Perspectives on the Scotch-Irish* (Tuscaloosa, Ala., 1997), 39–40.
11. Connolly, 'Ulster Presbyterians', 28–9 and *passim*.
12. Miller, *Emigrants and Exiles*, 40.
13. Miller, *Emigrants and Exiles*, 40, 51; Oliver MacDonagh, 'The Irish Famine Emigration to the United States', *Perspectives in American History*, X (1976), 357–446.

14. Miller, *Emigrants and Exiles*, 27–8, 54.

15. For what little has been written on Scotch-Irish women, see Leyburn, *Scotch-Irish*, 32, 148–9, 263.

16. Cf. Leyburn, *Scotch-Irish*, 142–3.

17. Figures from Dickson, *Ulster Emigration*; Jones, 'The Scotch-Irish', 896; Miller, *Emigrants and Exiles*, 149–60. The standard sources on the migration from Ulster in the colonial period are Dickson, *Ulster Emigration*; Leyburn, *Scotch-Irish*, 157–83; Miller, *Emigrants and Exiles*, 149–60; Jones, 'Scotch-Irish', 895–902; Jones, 'Scotch-Irish in British America', 292–3; and Wayland F. Dunaway, *The Scotch-Irish of Colonial Pennsylvania* (Chapel Hill, NC, 1944), 28–43. Jackson, *Social History*, 35–55, gives a useful summary; Blethen and Wood, eds. *Ulster and North America* (especially the essay by Graeme Kirkham, 76–117) add some useful revisions on the pre-1720 migration.

18. Dickson, *Ulster Emigration*, 15–18, 116–80; E.R.R. Green, 'The Scotch-Irish and the Coming of the Revolution in North Carolina', *Irish Historical Studies*, VII (September 1950), 78–9; Bernard Bailyn, *The Peopling of British North America: An Introduction* (New York, 1988), 72–3; Bernard Bailyn, *Voyagers to the West: A Passage in the Peopling of America on the Eve of the Revolution* (New York, 1988), 55.

19. Jones, 'Scotch-Irish', 897; Jones, 'Scotch-Irish in British America', 291–2; Miller, *Emigrants and Exiles*, 159–60; Connolly, 'Ulster Presbyterians', 25–8; Leyburn, *Scotch-Irish*, 164–8.

20. Connolly, 'Ulster Presbyterians', 27–8.

21. Dickson, *Ulster Emigration*, 6–7, 19–31; Jones, 'Scotch-Irish', 896–7; Jones, 'Scotch-Irish in British America', 291–2; Miller, *Emigrants and Exiles*, 158–9; Connolly, 'Ulster Presbyterians', 25–8; Leyburn, *Scotch-Irish*, 160–4, 168–70; Blethen and Wood, eds. *Ulster and North America*, 77 (essay by Kirkham).

22. David Dickson, *Arctic Ireland: The Extraordinary Story of the Great Frost and Forgotten Famine of 1740–41* (Belfast, 1997); Peter Gray, *The Irish Famine* (New York, 1995), 16.

23. Dickson, *Ulster Emigration*, 10–15, 48–53; Miller, *Emigrants and Exiles*, 142.

24. Leyburn, *Scotch-Irish*, 169–73; Wells, 'Aspects of Northern Irish Migration to America', 53–4; Bailyn, *Voyagers to the West*, 43–4; Miller, *Emigrants and Exiles*, 152–5; Dickson, *Ulster Emigration*, 10–15, 48–59.

25. Jones, 'Scotch-Irish', 897; Jones, 'Scotch-Irish in British America', 292–3; Miller, *Emigrants and Exiles*, 152–5; Dickson, *Ulster Emigration*, 8–10, 60–81.

26. Miller, *Emigrants and Exiles*, 155; Connolly, 'Ulster Presbyterians', 33–4; James S. Donnelly, Jr., 'Hearts of Oak, Hearts of Steel', *Studia Hibernica*, 21 (1981), 7–73.

27. Dickson, *Ulster Emigration*, 181–200; Jones, 'Scotch-Irish', 898; Bailyn, *Peopling of British North America*, 37; Blethen and Wood, eds. *Ulster and North America*, 41. K.H. Connell, *The Population of Ireland, 1750–1845* (Oxford, 1950) attributed Irish population growth to increased marital fertility, with early marriage facilitated by the potato and greater ease of acquiring land holdings; but cf. R.F. Foster, *Modern Ireland, 1600–1972* (London, 1988), 217–19. Timothy Guinnane, *The Vanishing Irish: Households, Migration, and the Rural Economy in Ireland, 1850–1914* (Princeton, NJ, 1997), 81–5 also favours increased marital fertility.

28. Though Ulster grew its own flax, seed had to be imported from America because of the nature of linen production. Potash is an alkaline substance consisting mainly of impure potassium carbonate derived originally from burnt plant material.
29. Dickson, *Ulster Emigration*, 16–17, 98–116, 201–20; Jones, 'Scotch-Irish', 897; Miller, *Emigrants and Exiles*, 153; Dunaway, *Scotch-Irish of Colonial Pennsylvania*, 43–6.
30. Dickson, *Ulster Emigration*, 86–94; Jones, 'Scotch-Irish', 898; Miller, *Emigrants and Exiles*, 155.
31. Jones, 'Scotch-Irish', 898; Bailyn, *Voyagers to the West*, 166–75; Miller, *Emigrants and Exiles*, 144.
32. Jones, 'Scotch-Irish', 898; Miller, *Emigrants and Exiles*, 151, 154, 155; Leyburn, *Scotch-Irish*, 176. 'Redemptioners' paid (or 'Redeemed') their fare on arrival, often with the help of a relative.
33. Miller, *Emigrants and Exiles*, 170–1; Jones, 'Scotch-Irish', 902.
34. Miller, *Emigrants and Exiles*, 142–5, 167–8.
35. For purposes of convenience, the term 'Scotch-Irish' is used in this chapter to describe the Ulster Scots from the moment of their arrival in the American colonies; but see the discussion of the term and its contentious history below, and in the Introduction.
36. E. Estyn Evans, *Ireland and the Atlantic Heritage: Selected Writings* (Dublin, MLMXCVI), 110–17; Jones, 'Scotch-Irish', 899; Jones, 'Scotch-Irish in British America', 293; Jackson, *Social History*, 57–9; Mather quote in Leyburn, *Scotch-Irish*, 328.
37. Jones, 'Scotch-Irish', 899; Jones, 'Scotch-Irish in British America', 294; Leyburn, *Scotch-Irish*, 236–42; Jackson, *Social History*, 59–60.
38. Jones, 'Scotch-Irish', 899; Jones, 'Scotch-Irish in British America'; Leyburn, *Scotch-Irish*, 236–42; Jackson, *Social History*, 59–60.
39. Dunaway, *Scotch-Irish of Colonial Pennsylvania*, 50–6; Jackson, *Social History*, 60–4; Dickson, *Ulster Emigration*, 223–6.
40. Leyburn, *Scotch-Irish*, 186–200; Dunaway, *Scotch-Irish of Colonial Pennsylvania*, 56–64; Jackson, *Social History*, 76–7.
41. Miller, *Emigrants and Exiles*, 161; Jackson, *Social History*, 89–92; Blethen and Wood, eds. *Ulster and North America*, 147 (essay by Russel L. Gerlach).
42. Jones, 'Scotch-Irish', 899; Jones, 'Scotch-Irish in British America', 294; Miller, *Emigrants and Exiles*, 161; Bailyn, *Voyagers to the West*, 27 (quote); Leyburn, *Scotch-Irish*, 200–23, 232–3; Dunaway, *Scotch-Irish of Colonial Pennsylvania*, 72–88, 102–13; Blethen and Woods, *Ulster and North America*, 147 (essay by Gerlach).
43. David H. Fischer, *Albion's Seed: Four British Folkways in America* (New York, 1989), 643–4.
44. Rachel N. Klein, *Unification of a Slave State: The Rise of the Planter Class in the South Carolina Backcountry, 1760–1808* (Chapel Hill, NC, 1990), 14, 15, 38, 47–8; Fischer, *Albion's Seed*, 646–8.
45. For a useful survey of the complexities and ironies of American immigration history, including a discussion of how the invention of ethnic identities becomes a vehicle of Americanization, see Gary Gerstle, 'Liberty, Coercion, and the Making of Americans', *The Journal of American History*, 84 (September 1997), 524–58, especially 539–44.

46. Jones, 'Scotch-Irish', 895–6; Jones, 'Scotch-Irish in British America', 284–7; Carl Wittke, *The Irish in America* (1956; New York, 1970), vi–vii; Jackson, *Social History*, 9–10; Dunaway, *Scotch-Irish of Colonial Pennsylvania*, 4–7; and, especially, Leyburn, *Scotch-Irish*, 327–34.

47. Michael Montgomery, 'The Roots of Appalachian English: Scotch-Irish or British Southern?' *Journal of the Appalachian Studies Association*, 3 (1991), 177–91; Michael Montgomery, 'The Scotch-Irish Element in Appalachian English: How Broad? How Deep?' in Blethen and Wood, eds. *Ulster and North America*; Alan Crozier, 'The Scotch-Irish Influence on American English', *American Speech*, 59 (1984), 310–31. I am grateful to Jim Sidbury and Michael Hall for their comments on this matter.

48. Jones, 'Scotch-Irish', 899.

49. Leyburn, *Scotch-Irish*, 190–1, 205; Jones, 'Scotch-Irish', 297.

50. Jones, 'Scotch-Irish', 296. For the role of the Ulster Scots as a buffer, and the connection of this role to the evolution of transatlantic racial identities, see Theodore W. Allen, *The Invention of the White Race*. Vol. 1. *Racial Oppression and Social Control* (New York, 1994).

51. Leyburn, *Scotch-Irish*, 223–35; Dunaway, *Scotch-Irish of Colonial Pennsylvania*, 119–23.

52. Leyburn, *Scotch-Irish*, 223–35; Jones, 'Scotch-Irish', 296; Dunaway, *Scotch-Irish of Colonial Pennsylvania*, 122–3, 152–5.

53. Dunaway, *Scotch-Irish of Colonial Pennsylvania*, 165–75, 196–8; Leyburn, *Scotch-Irish*, 256–72; Jones, 'Scotch-Irish in British America', 299–301.

54. Jones, 'Scotch-Irish in British America', 301; Evans, *Ireland and the Atlantic Heritage*, 105–7. I am grateful to Michael Hall, Jim Sidbury and Neil Kamil for their comments on this paragraph.

55. Jones, 'Scotch-Irish', 900; Evans, *Ireland and the Atlantic Heritage*, 105–6; J. Hector St John de Crèvecouer, *Letters from an American Farmer and Sketches of Eighteenth-Century America* (1782; New York, 1981), 84, 85.

56. E. Estyn Evans, 'Cultural Relics of the Ulster Scots in the Old West of the United States', *Ulster Folklife*, XI (1965), 34; Evans, *Ireland and the Atlantic Heritage*, 103–4, 106; Jones, 'Scotch-Irish', 900; Dunaway, *Scotch-Irish of Colonial Pennsylvania*, 184–8; Leyburn, *Scotch-Irish*, 258–63.

57. Cf. Evans, 'Cultural Relics', 105–6.

58. Leyburn, *Scotch-Irish*, 263; Dunaway, *Scotch-Irish of Colonial Pennsylvania*, 188–9.

59. See, for example, Suzanne Lebsock, *The Free Women of Petersburg: Status and Culture in a Southern Town, 1784–1860* (New York, 1984); Cornelia H. Dayton, *Women Before the Bar: Gender, Law, and Society in Connecticut, 1639–1789* (Chapel Hill, NC, 1995); Stephanie McCurry, *Masters of Small Worlds: Yeoman Households, Gender Relations, and the Political Culture of the Antebellum South Carolina Low Country* (New York, 1995).

60. On the communal and recreational aspects of backcountry life see, for example, Dunaway, *Scotch-Irish of Colonial Pennsylvania*, 184, 191–200; Leyburn, *Scotch-Irish*, 259, 264.

61. Dunaway, *Scotch-Irish of Colonial Pennsylvania*, 48–9; Thomas L. Purvis, 'Patterns of Ethnic Settlement in Late Eighteenth-Century Pennsylvania', *Western Pennsylvania Historical Magazine*, LXX (1987), 107–22, especially 119–20; E.R.R. Green, 'The Irish American Business and Professions', in David N. Doyle and Owen Dudley

Edwards, eds. *America and Ireland, 1776–1976: The American Identity and the Irish Connection* (Westport, CT, 1980), 195.

62. Jones, 'Scotch-Irish', 896, 901; Jones, 'Scotch-Irish in British America', 302; Leyburn *Scotch-Irish*, 293–4.

63. Jones, 'Scotch-Irish', 901; Jones, 'Scotch-Irish in British America', 302–3; Leyburn, *Scotch-Irish*, 274–7.

64. Leyburn, *Scotch-Irish*, 281–4.

65. Jones, 'Scotch-Irish', 901; Jones, 'Scotch-Irish in British America', 303–4.

66. Jones, 'Scotch-Irish', 901; Jones, 'Scotch-Irish in British America', 303–4; Miller, *Emigrants and Exiles*, 165–6; Connolly, 'Ulster Presbyterians', 40.

67. Evans, *Ireland and the Atlantic Heritage*; Jones, 'Scotch-Irish', 901; Jones, 'Scotch-Irish in British America', 308–9; Dunaway, *Scotch-Irish of Colonial Pennsylvania*, 213, 218–28; Leyburn, *Scotch-Irish*, 277, 319–21.

68. Dunaway, *Scotch-Irish of Colonial Pennsylvania*, 119–29; Leyburn, *Scotch-Irish*, 231; Jackson, *Social History*, 116–17. The Paxton Boys were so-called because they came from Paxton (or Paxtang) Township in Dauphin County, which adjoins Lancaster County (site of the Conestoga Massacre) to the south.

69. Dunaway, *Scotch-Irish of Colonial Pennsylvania*, 119–29; Leyburn, *Scotch-Irish*, 231; Jackson, *Social History*, 116–17.

70. Jones, 'Scotch-Irish in British America', 309; Miller, *Emigrants and Exiles*, 163–4; Leyburn, *Scotch-Irish*, 301–4; Jackson, *Social History*, 137–8.

71. Rachel N. Klein, 'Frontier Planters and the American Revolution: The South Carolina Backcountry, 1775–1782', in Ronald Hoffman, Thad W. Tate and Peter J. Albert, eds. *An Uncivil War: The Southern Backcountry during the American Revolution* (Charlottesville, VA, 1985); Klein, *Unification of a Slave State*; Jack P. Greene, 'Independence, Improvement, and Authority: Toward a Framework for Understanding the Histories of the Southern Backcountry during the Era of the American Revolution', in Hoffman, Tate and Albert, eds. *An Uncivil War*.

72. Klein, 'Frontier Planters'; Klein, *Unification of a Slave State*; Greene, 'Independence, Improvement, and Authority'. On the antebellum Irish and race, see Chapter 2 of the present work.

73. Jones, 'Scotch-Irish', 902; Leyburn, *Scotch-Irish*, 304–12; cf. Dunaway, *Scotch-Irish of Colonial Pennsylvania*, 155.

74. Miller, *Emigrants and Exiles*, 166; Jones, 'Scotch-Irish', 902; Jones, 'Scotch-Irish in British America', 309–10.

75. Jones, 'Scotch-Irish in British America', 310–11; Jones, 'Scotch-Irish', 902.

76. Hooker, ed. *Carolina Backcountry*, 13–14, 30, 34.

77. Maurice J. Bric, 'The Irish and the Evolution of the "New Politics"', in P.J. Drudy, ed. *The Irish in America: Emigration, Assimilation, Impact.* (Irish Studies, 4) (Cambridge, England, 1985), 147 (quote).

78. Bric, 'The Irish and the Evolution of the "New Politics"'; David A. Wilson, *United Irishmen, United States: Immigrant Radicals in the Early Republic* (Ithaca, NY, 1998).

79. David Noel Doyle, *Ireland, Irishmen, and Revolutionary America*, 51–2; Doyle, 'The Irish in North America, 1776–1845', 692; Leyburn, *Scotch-Irish*, 182–3; Jackson, *Social History*, x–xi.

80. See, for example, Ellen Shapiro McDonald and Forrest McDonald, 'The Ethnic Origins of the American People, 1790', *William and Mary Quarterly*, 3rd Ser., XXXVII (January 1980), 179–99, with communications by Francis Jennings and Rowland Berthoff and a reply by the McDonalds, 3rd Ser., XXXVII (October 1980), 700–3; Forrest McDonald and Grady McWhiney, 'The Antebellum Southern Herdsman: A Reinterpretation', *The Journal of Southern History*, 41 (May 1975), 152–3; Forrest McDonald and Grady McWhiney, 'Celtic Origins of Southern Herding Practices', *The Journal of Southern History*, 51 (1985), 165–82; Grady McWhiney, *Cracker Culture: Celtic Ways in the Old South* (Tuscaloosa, Alabama, 1988); Grady McWhiney and Perry Jamieson, *Attack and Die: Civil War Military Tactics and the Southern Heritage* (University, Alabama, 1982); Leroy V. Eid, 'The Colonial Scotch-Irish: A View Accepted Too Readily', *Eire-Ireland*, XXI (Winter 1986), 81–105; Leroy V. Eid, 'Irish, Scotch, and Scotch-Irish: A Reconsideration', *American Presbyterian*, LXIV (Winter 1986), 211–25.

81. Jones, 'Scotch-Irish in British America', 285–7; Thomas L. Purvis, Donald H. Akenson and Forrest and Ellen McDonald, 'The Population of the United States, 1790: A Symposium', *William and Mary Quarterly*, 3rd Ser., 41 (1984), 85–135; and, especially, Rowland Berthoff, 'Celtic Mist Over the South', *Journal of Southern History*, 52 (November 1986), 523–46.

82. Leyburn, *Scotch-Irish*, 327–34; Dunaway, *Scotch-Irish of Colonial Pennsylvania*, 5 (quotes).

83. Leyburn's *Scotch-Irish* (1962) remains the standard work and was re-printed in 1989.

Chapter 2: Before the Famine

1. Kerby A. Miller, *Emigrants and Exiles: Ireland and the Irish Exodus to North America* (New York, 1985), 169, 170, 193, 197; Oliver MacDonagh, 'The Irish Famine Emigration to the United States', *Perspectives in American History*, X (1976), 392, 393; Patrick J. Blessing, 'Irish', in Stephan Thernstrom, ed. *The Harvard Encyclopedia of American Ethnic Groups* (Cambridge, MA, 1980), 529.

2. Miller, *Emigrants and Exiles*, 29, 35, 58, 178, 218; K.H. Connell, *The Population of Ireland, 1750–1845* (Oxford, 1950); cf. R.F. Foster, *Modern Ireland, 1600–1972* (London, 1988), 217–19 and Timothy Guinnane, *The Vanishing Irish: Households, Migration, and the Rural Economy in Ireland, 1850–1914* (Princeton, 1997), 81–5.

3. Kevin Kenny, *Making Sense of the Molly Maguires* (New York, 1998), especially Chapter 1; Miller, *Emigrants and Exiles*, 61–9.

4. Miller, *Emigrants and Exiles*, 37–8 (quote on 'imaginary line', 37) and *passim* for the overarching thesis on the commercialization of nineteenth-century Irish agriculture; S.J. Connolly, *Priests and People in Pre-Famine Ireland, 1780–1845* (New York, 1982), 19, 20 (quote on 'peasant society'); MacDonagh, 'Irish Famine Emigration', 361; L.M. Cullen, *An Economic History of Ireland Since 1660* (London, 1972), 81, 110–12, 117.

5. Miller, *Emigrants and Exiles*, 48–51; Cullen, *Economic History*, 110–11; Connolly, *Priests and People*, 15–20; K. Theodore Hoppen, *Ireland Since 1800: Conflict and Conformity* (New York, 1989), 33.

6. Miller, *Emigrants and Exiles*, 48, 49; Connolly, *Priests and People*, 19–20.

7. Miller, *Emigrants and Exiles*, 49–50.

8. Kenny, *Making Sense of the Molly Maguires*, 32–4; Robert J. Scally, *The End of Hidden Ireland: Rebellion, Famine, and Emigration* (New York, 1995), 13, 29–30, 76; S.H. Cousens, 'The Regional Pattern of Emigration during the Great Irish Famine', *Transactions of the Institute of British Geographers*, 28 (1960), 125.

9. Miller, *Emigrants and Exiles*, 51 and Chapter 2; Connolly, *Priests and People*, 19; MacDonagh, 'Irish Famine Emigration', 361–2.

10. Cousens, 'Regional Pattern of Emigration during the Great Irish Famine', 18; Miller, *Emigrants and Exiles*, 198. See, also, Ruth-Ann M. Harris, *The Nearest Place That Wasn't Ireland: Early Nineteenth-Century Irish Labour Migration* (Ames, Iowa, 1994).

11. Miller, *Emigrants and Exiles*, especially Chapters 1 to 6.

12. Blessing, 'Irish', 529; Connolly, *Priests and People*, 21; Miller, *Emigrants and Exiles*, 207–15; Guinnane, *Vanishing Irish*, 34. For more on the potato, see Chapter 3 of the present work.

13. Miller, *Emigrants and Exiles*, 207–8 (quote, 208); Brenda Collins, 'Proto-industrialization and Pre-famine Emigration', *Social History*, VII (1982), 127–46; Guinnane, *Vanishing Irish*, 35–6.

14. Collins, 'Proto-industrialization'; S.H. Cousens, 'The Regional Variations in Emigration from Ireland between 1821 and 1841', *Transactions of the Institute of British Geographers*, 37 (1965), 15–30.

15. MacDonagh, 'Irish Famine Emigration', 418–27; Collins, 'Proto-industrialization', 142–3; Hasia Diner, *Erin's Daughters in America: Irish Immigrant Women in the Nineteenth Century* (Baltimore, 1983), Chapter 1.

16. Miller, *Emigrants and Exiles*, 54–5, 58, 115; Diner, *Erin's Daughters*, Chapter 1.

17. Emmet Larkin, trans. and ed. *Alexis de Tocqueville's Journey in Ireland, July–August, 1835* (Washington, DC, 1990), 3 (quote), 7 (quote), 25–6, 29–30, 40–2, 49–50, 79–84, 112–27, 129–36; Joel Mokyr, *Why Ireland Starved: A Quantitative and Analytical History of the Irish Economy, 1800–1850* (London, 1985), 11; Guinnane, *Vanishing Irish*, 37.

18. Blessing, 'Irish', 529; Miller, *Emigrants and Exiles*, 205 and Chapters 3 and 6 for the conception of emigration as exile by the Irish-speaking poor in this period.

19. MacDonagh, 'Irish Famine Emigration', 395.

20. MacDonagh, 'Irish Famine Emigration', 394–5; Robert Ernst, *Immigrant Life in New York City, 1825–1863* (1949; Syracuse, NY, 1994), 34–5; George Potter, *To the Golden Door: The Story of the Irish in Ireland and America* (Boston, 1960), 188–90; Miller, *Emigrants and Exiles*, 188. The definitive reading of these emigrant letters, highlighting the tension between exile and opportunity, is Miller, *Emigrants and Exiles*.

21. Potter, *Golden Door*, 125–6; Miller, *Emigrants and Exiles*, 216, 238.

22. Miller, *Emigrants and Exiles*, 193–4; MacDonagh, 'Irish Famine Emigration', 396–8.

23. David N. Doyle, 'The Irish in North America, 1776–1845', in W.E. Vaughan, ed. *A New History of Ireland. Vol. V. Ireland Under the Union, I, 1801–70* (Oxford, 1989), 704–5; E.R.R. Green, 'The Irish American Business and Professions', in David N. Doyle and Owen Dudley Edwards, eds. *America and Ireland, 1776–1976: The American Identity and the Irish Connection* (Westport, CT, 1980), 195–8; Earl F. Niehaus, *The Irish in New Orleans, 1800–1860* (Baton Rouge, LA, 1965), 5–11.

24. Potter, *Golden Door*, 137–8; Carl Wittke, *The Irish in America* (1956; New York, 1970), 14.

25. Potter, *To the Golden Door*, 152; Miller, *Emigrants and Exiles*, 197, 253–5; MacDonagh, 'The Irish Famine Emigration to the United States', 400. Fares rose by about 10 shillings in each category after passage of the Passenger Act of 1842, which required ship-owners to spend more on the passenger holds and furnish some of the provisions.

26. Miller, *Emigrants and Exiles*, 253–4; Scally, *End of Hidden Ireland*, especially Chapter 9.

27. Miller, *Emigrants and Exiles*, 255–6; MacDonagh, 'Irish Famine Emigration', 399; Potter, *Golden Door*, 46.

28. Wittke, *Irish in America*, 14; Barbara L. Bellows, *Benevolence Among Slaveholders: Assisting the Poor in Charleston, 1670–1860* (Baton Rouge, LA, 1993), 105; Christopher Silver, 'A New Look at Old South Urbanization: The Irish Worker in Charleston, South Carolina, 1840–1860', in Samuel P. Hines and George W. Hopkins, eds. *South Atlantic Urban Studies*, Vol. 3 (Columbia, SC, 1979), 141, 144, 149; Niehaus, *Irish in New Orleans*, v, 23–34.

29. Graham Davis, 'Models of Migration: The Historiography of the Irish Pioneers in South Texas', *Southwestern Historical Quarterly*, 99 (January 1996), 326–48; Potter, *Golden Door*, 206. With the Texan bid for independence from Mexico in the mid-1830s, the Irish were forced to choose sides. As Mexican citizens and Catholics, many of them sided with Mexico at first, but most took the Texan side eventually.

30. Blessing, 'Irish', 528. Percentages rounded up to the nearest one.

31. George E. Reedy, *From the Ward to the White House: The Irish in American Politics* (New York, 1991), 63; Wittke, *Irish in America*, 45; Potter, *Golden Door*, 242; Niehaus, *Irish in New Orleans*, 31–3.

32. Ernst, *Immigrant Life in New York City*, 39, 57–9; Paul A. Gilje, *The Road to Mobocracy: Popular Disorder in New York City, 1763–1834* (Chapel Hill, NC, 1987), 127–8, 160–2. I am grateful to Ed O'Donnell for information on the recent excavation of Five Points. Tyler Anbinder's forthcoming book on Five Points is likely to be the definitive study.

33. For comparisons of Irish and German immigrants in the nineteenth century, see, for example, Ernst, *Immigrant Life in New York City*; Jay P. Dolan, *The Immigrant Church: New York's German and Irish Catholics, 1815 to 1865* (Baltimore, 1987); David A. Gerber, *The Making of an American Pluralism: Buffalo, New York, 1825–1860* (Urbana, IL, 1989); Bruce Laurie, Theodore Hershberg and George Alter, 'Immigrants and Industry: The Philadelphia Experience', in Richard Ehrlich, ed. *Immigrants in Industrial America, 1850–1920* (Charlottesville, VA, 1977); Stephan Thernstrom, *The Other Bostonians: Poverty and Progress in the American Metropolis, 1860–1970* (Cambridge, MA, 1973); Jo Ellen McNergney Vinyard, *The Irish on the Urban Frontier: Nineteenth-Century Detroit, 1850–80* (New York, 1976).

34. Peter Way, *Common Labour: Workers and the Digging of the North American Canals, 1780–1860* (Cambridge, England, 1993), 90 (Emerson quote); David Roediger, *The Wages of Whiteness: Race and the Making of the American Working Class* (New York, 1991), 145; Bruce Laurie, *Workingmen of Philadelphia, 1800–1850* (Philadelphia, 1980), 159; Ernst, *Immigrant Life in New York City*, 67, 71–8.

35. Christine Stansell, *City of Women: Sex and Class in New York, 1789–1860* (New York, 1986), 156–61, 178; Ernst, *Immigrant Life in New York City*, 66, 68; Faye Dudden, *Serving Women: Household Service in Nineteenth Century America* (Middletown, CT, 1983), 5–6.

36. Silver, 'A New Look at Old South Urbanization', 150, 156–7; Roediger, *Wages of Whiteness*, 146; Niehaus, *Irish in New Orleans*, 47–56; quotes from Olmsted in Frank Murray, 'The Irish and Afro-Americans in US History', *Freedomways*, 22 (First Quarter, 1982), 26, and Roediger, *Wages of Whiteness*, 146.

37. Way, *Common Labour*, 13–14, 25–6, 86–90 (Dickens quote, 90); Dennis Clark, *Hibernia America: The Irish and Regional Cultures* (Westport, CT, 1986), 15–16; Potter, *Golden Door*, 193; Wittke, *Irish in America*, 27; Niehaus, *Irish in New Orleans*, 46 (song).

38. On Irish canal labourers, see Way, *Common Labour*; Peter Way, 'Shovel and Shamrock: Irish Workers and Labor Violence in the Digging of the Chesapeake and Ohio Canal', *Labor History*, 30 (Fall 1989), 489–517; Peter Way, 'Evil Humors and Ardent Spirits: The Rough Culture of Canal Construction Laborers', *Journal of American History*, 79 (March 1993), 1397–1428.

39. Way, *Common Labour*, especially Chapters 6, 7 and 8; Wittke, *Irish in America*, 33; W. David Baird, 'Violence Along the Chesapeake Canal: 1839', *Maryland Historical Magazine*, 66 (Summer 1971), 121–2; Noel Ignatiev, *How the Irish Became White* (New York, 1995), 93–4; Niehaus, *Irish in New Orleans*, 46; Potter, *Golden Door*, 327–31; Way, *Common Labour*, Chapter 6. On Irish railroad track layers, see Matthew E. Mason, '"The Hands Here are Disposed to be Turbulent": Unrest Among the Irish Trackmen of the Baltimore and Ohio Railroad, 1829–1851', *Labor History*, 39 (August 1998), 253–72.

40. Potter, *Golden Door*, 327, 331; Baird, 'Violence Along the Chesapeake Canal', 122–34; Ignatiev, *How the Irish Became White*, 94; Way, *Common Labour*, Chapter 7.

41. Way, *Common Labour*, Chapters 7, 8; Ignatiev, *How the Irish Became White*, 103–6; Miller, *Emigrants and Exiles*, 275–6; David Montgomery, 'The Shuttle and the Cross: Weavers and Artisans in the Kensington Riots of 1844', *Journal of Social History*, 5 (1972), 411–46.

42. Ernst, *Immigrant Life in New York City*, 104–5; Ignatiev, *How the Irish Became White*, 120; Roediger, *Wages of Whiteness*, 134, 147–8.

43. Theodore W. Allen, *The Invention of the White Race*. Vol. 1. *Racial Oppression and Social Control* (New York, 1994); Roediger, *Wages of Whiteness*; Ignatiev, *How the Irish Became White*; Matthew Frye Jacobson, *Whiteness of a Different Color: European Immigrants and the Alchemy of Race* (Cambridge, MA, 1998). For graphic depictions of the Irish in racial terms, see, for example, the illustrations in Dale T. Knobel, *Paddy and the Republic: Ethnicity and Nationality in Antebellum America* (Middletown, CT, 1986) and Iver Bernstein, *The New York City Draft Riots: Their Significance for American Society and Politics in the Age of the Civil War* (New York, 1990). For some textual equivalents of these images, see (among many other sources) Knobel, *Paddy and the Republic, passim* and Jacobson, *Whiteness of a Different Color*, especially 48–9.

44. Roediger, *Wages of Whiteness*, Chapter 6; Eric Lott, *Love and Theft: Blackface Minstrelsy and the American Working Class* (New York, 1995), *passim*; Ignatiev, *How the Irish*

Became White, 42; Kenny, *Making Sense of the Molly Maguires*, 98. For the idea that 'becoming white' was a matter of 'strategy', see Ignatiev, *How the Irish Became White*, 1–3 and *passim*.

45. To the extent that the eighteenth-century Scotch-Irish can be included in the story of Irish-American racial formation, it will clearly be less useful to place them in the context of a pre-existing racial hierarchy. Much more than the Catholic Irish immigrants of the nineteenth century, they helped create that context. I am grateful to my colleague Prasannan Parthasarathi for pointing this out to me.

46. Eric Foner, *Free Soil, Free Labour, Free Men: The Ideology of the Republican Party Before the Civil War* (New York, 1970), Chapter 7; Tyler Anbinder, *Nativism and Slavery: The Northern Know Nothings and the Politics of the 1850s* (New York, 1992); Ian Haney Lopez, *White by Law: The Legal Construction of Race* (New York, 1996), especially Chapters 1 and 2; Jacobson, *Whiteness of a Different Color*, especially 22, 222–45.

47. Eric Arnesen, 'Up from Exclusion: Black and White Workers, Race, and the State of Labor History', *Reviews in American History*, 26 (March 1998), 162–7.

48. For the racial iconography of the American Irish, see, for example, the illustrations in Knobel, *Paddy and the Republic*; Bernstein, *New York City Draft Riots*; Jacobson, *Whiteness of a Different Color*.

49. See, for example, Allen, *Invention of the White Race*, Vol. 1. For the insights in this paragraph, I am indebted to Kevin O'Neill.

50. Jay P. Dolan, *The American Catholic Experience: A History From Colonial Times to the Present* (Garden City, NY, 1985), 69–97.

51. Miller, *Emigrants and Exiles*, 147; Connolly, *Priests and People*. The figure of 25,000, of course, may reflect the inaccuracy of the estimate as well as a falling-away from religion.

52. Miller, *Emigrants and Exiles*, 147.

53. Dolan, *American Catholic Experience*, 96–111.

54. Dolan, *American Catholic Experience*, 112–23.

55. Dolan, *American Catholic Experience*, 166–7, 170–2, 189–93; Blessing, 'Irish', 535; Andrew M. Greeley, *The Catholic Experience* (New York, 1967), 82–5; Thomas T. McAvoy, *History of the Catholic Church in the United States* (South Bend, Indiana, 1969), 92–122. There would be a return to greater lay involvement in American Catholicism in the twentieth century.

56. Jay P. Dolan, *The Immigrant Church: New York's German and Irish Catholics, 1815 to 1865* (Baltimore, 1975), especially Chapters 1 and 2; Dolan, *American Catholic Experience*, 161–9; Greeley, *Catholic Experience*, 37.

57. Kenneth Jackson, ed. *The Encyclopedia of New York City* (New Haven, CT, 1995), 573; Kevin Kenny, 'Religion and Immigration: The Irish Community in New York City, 1815–40', *The Recorder: A Journal of the American-Irish Historical Society*, 3 (Winter 1989), 16–18.

58. Dolan, *Immigrant Church*, 7–8.

59. Dolan, *Immigrant Church*, 57 (quote); Connolly, *Priests and People*, especially Chapter 3; Kenny, *Making Sense of the Molly Maguires*, Chapter 1; Miller, *Emigrants and Exiles*, 73–4. On the 'Devotional Revolution' see Chapter 3 of the present work.

60. Ernst, *Immigrant Life in New York City*, 35–6; Dolan, *Immigrant Church*, especially Chapter 7.
61. Dolan, *Immigrant Church*, 122–7; Edward M. Levine, *The Irish and Irish Politicians: A Study in Social and Cultural Alienation* (South Bend, Indiana, 1966), 91–3.
62. Blessing, 'Irish'; Dolan, *American Catholic Experience*, 251–2, 263; Ernst, *Immigrant Life in New York City*; McAvoy, *History of the Catholic Church in the United States*, 143–4.
63. Ernst, *Immigrant Life in New York City*, 169; McAvoy, *History of the Catholic Church in the United States*, 143–4; John Tracy Ellis, *American Catholics and Intellectual Life* (1956; Chicago, 1969), 68–9; Greeley, *Catholic Experience*, 113–18 (on Hughes's provocation of the nativists).
64. Ellis, *American Catholics and Intellectual Life*, 89–90; Greeley, *Catholic Experience*, 39–40; Madeleine Hooke Rice, *American Catholic Opinion in the Slavery Controversy* (New York, 1944), especially Chapters 1, 4, 5.
65. Edward Wakin, *Enter the Irish-American* (New York, 1976), 70–81; Dennis Clark, *The Irish in Philadelphia: Ten Generations of Urban Experience* (Philadelphia, 1973), 20–2; William V. Shannon, *The American Irish* (New York, 1963), 41–5; Miller, *Emigrants and Exiles*, 322–3; Potter, *To the Golden Door*, 241–69.
66. Doyle, 'The Irish in North America', 706; Clark, *Irish in Philadelphia*; Gilje, *Road to Mobocracy*, 134–8; Christopher McGimpsey, 'Internal Ethnic Friction: Orange and Green in Nineteenth-Century New York, 1868–1872', *Immigrants and Minorities*, 1 (March 1982), 40–4; Potter, *Golden Door*, 215; Ernst, *Immigrant Life in New York City*, 168; Maldwyn A. Jones, 'Scotch-Irish', in Thernstrom, ed. *Harvard Encyclopedia of American Ethnic Groups*, 906.
67. Clark, *Irish in Philadelphia*, 21–2; Potter, *Golden Door*, 420–9; Montgomery, 'Shuttle and the Cross', *passim*; Ernst, *Immigrant Life in New York City*, 102–4; Roediger, *Wages of Whiteness*, 149. On Hughes, see Greeley, *Catholic Experience*, 121 and Ellis, *American Catholics and Intellectual Life*, 68–9. Hughes was referring to Napoleon's invasion of Russia in 1812 when the residents of Moscow reportedly set fire to the city rather than submit, thereby helping to turn back the invasion.
68. Ernst, *Immigrant Life in New York City*, 294; Peter Quinn, 'Introduction', William L. Riordan, ed. *Plunkitt of Tammany Hall: A Series of Very Plain Talks on Very Practical Politics* (New York, 1995), xiii–xv; Reedy, *From the Ward to the White House*, 87; Shannon, *American Irish*, 49–50. The machines are discussed in detail in Chapter 4 of the present work.
69. Levine, *Irish and Irish Politicians*, Introduction; Roediger, *Wages of Whiteness*, 140–1; Jean Baker, *Affairs of Party: The Political Culture of Northern Democrats in the Mid-Nineteenth Century* (Ithaca, NY, 1983), 180; Shannon, *American Irish*, 50–2.
70. Gilbert Osofsky, 'Abolitionists, Irish Immigrants and the Dilemmas of Romantic Nationalism', *The American Historical Review*, 80 (October 1975), 890–3.
71. Osofksy, 'Dilemmas of Romantic Nationalism', 896–9; Roediger, *Wages of Whiteness*, 135; Potter, *Golden Door*, 395.
72. On Irish-Americans and abolitionism generally, see Potter, *Golden Door*, Chapter 34.
73. Osofsky, 'Dilemmas of Romantic Nationalism', 899–901; Potter, *Golden Door*, 384–5.
74. Osofsky, 'Dilemmas of Romantic Nationalism', 908.
75. Roediger, *Wages of Whiteness*, 138.

76. Douglas Riach, 'Daniel O'Connell and American Anti-Slavery', *Irish Historical Studies*, XX (March 1976), 10, 11, 21; Osofsky, 'Dilemmas of Romantic Nationalism', 901–2.

77. Potter, *Golden Door*, 396–404; Osofksy, 'Dilemmas of Romantic Nationalism', 901, 904–5.

78. Osofksy, 'Dilemmas of Romantic Nationalism', 903, 905 (quote); Riach, 'Daniel O'Connell and American Anti-Slavery', 15–18; Potter, *Golden Door*, 396–404; cf. Roediger, *Wages of Whiteness*, 135–6.

Chapter 3: The Famine Generation

1. Peter Gray, *The Irish Famine* (New York, 1995), 34–5; Oliver MacDonagh, 'The Irish Famine Emigration to the United States', *Perspectives in American History*, X (1976), 405; Kerby A. Miller, *Emigrants and Exiles: Ireland and the Irish Exodus to North America* (New York, 1985), 281–8.

2. Timothy Guinnane, *The Vanishing Irish: Households, Migration, and the Rural Economy in Ireland, 1850–1914* (Princeton, NJ, 1997), 85–8; Patrick J. Blessing, 'Irish', in Stephan Thernstrom, ed. *The Harvard Encyclopedia of American Ethnic Groups* (Cambridge, MA, 1980), 528.

3. On the famine of 1740–1, see Chapter 1.

4. MacDonagh, 'Irish Famine Emigration', 362–5; Gray, *Irish Famine*, 31–2; Guinnane, *Vanishing Irish*, 86.

5. Gray, *Irish Famine*, 32; Miller, *Emigrants and Exiles*, 205; MacDonagh, 'Irish Famine Emigration', 365; Guinnane, *Vanishing Irish*, 36–7.

6. Miller, *Emigrants and Exiles*, 282; MacDonagh, 'Irish Famine Emigration', 405–7.

7. For revisionist accounts of the famine see, for example, Mary Daly, *The Famine in Ireland* (Dundalk, Ireland, 1986); Mary Daly, 'Revisionism and Irish History: The Great Famine', in D. George Boyce and Alan O'Day, eds. *The Making of Modern Irish History* (London, 1996); R. Dudley Edwards and T. Desmond Williams, *The Great Famine: Studies in Irish History, 1845–52* (Dublin, 1956); R.F. Foster, *Modern Ireland, 1600–1972* (London, 1988), 318–44. On Irish revisionism generally, see Boyce and O'Day, eds. *The Making of Modern Irish History*; Brendan Bradshaw, 'Nationalism and Historical Scholarship in Modern Ireland', *Irish Historical Studies*, 26 (November 1989), 329–51; R.F. Foster 'History and the Irish Question', *Royal Historical Society Transactions*, 5th Ser., 32 (1983), 169–92; Ciaran Brady, ed. *Interpreting Irish History: The Debate on Historical Revisionism* (Dublin, 1994).

8. See, for example, E. Margaret Crawford, ed. *Famine: The Irish Experience, 900–1900* (Edinburgh, 1989); Cathal Póirtéir, ed. *The Great Irish Famine* (Cork, 1995); Chris Morash and Richard Hayes, eds. *Fearful Realities: New Perspectives on the Famine* (Dublin, 1996); Gray, *Irish Famine*; Peter Gray, '*Punch* and the Great Famine', *History Ireland*, 1 (Summer 1993), 26–33; Peter Gray, 'Potatoes and Providence: British Government Responses to the Great Famine', *Bullán: An Irish Studies Journal*, 1 (Spring 1994), 75–90; Peter Gray, 'Ideology and the Famine', in Póirtéir, ed. *Great Irish Famine*; Peter Gray, 'Famine Relief Policy in Comparative Perspective: Ireland, Scotland, and Northwestern Europe, 1845–1849', *Éire-Ireland*, 32 (Spring 1997),

86–108; James S. Donnelly, Jr., 'The Administration of Relief, 1846–7', in W.E. Vaughan, ed. *A New History of Ireland,* Vol. V. *Ireland Under the Union, I, 1801–70* (Oxford, 1989); James S. Donnelly, Jr., 'The Great Famine and its Interpreters, Old and New', *History Ireland,* 1 (Autumn 1993), 27–33; James S. Donnelly, Jr., 'Mass Eviction and the Great Famine', in Póirtéir, ed. *Great Irish Famine;* James S. Donnelly, Jr., 'Irish Property Must Pay for Irish Poverty': British Public Opinion and the Great Irish Famine', in Morash and Hayes, eds. *Fearful Realities;* Christine Kinealy, *This Great Calamity: The Irish Famine, 1845–1852* (Dublin, 1994); Christine Kinealy, *A Death-Dealing Famine: The Great Hunger in Ireland* (London, 1997); Joel Mokyr, 'Industrialization and Poverty in the Netherlands', *Journal of Interdisciplinary History,* 10 (Winter 1980), 429–58; Joel Mokyr, *Why Ireland Starved: A Quantitative and Analytical History of the Irish Economy, 1800–1850* (London, 1985); Cormac O'Gráda, *Ireland Before and After the Famine: Explorations in Economic History, 1800–1925* (Manchester, 1988); Cormac O'Gráda, *Ireland: A New Economic History, 1780–1939* (Oxford, 1994); Michael de Nie, 'Curing "The Irish Moral Plague"', *Éire-Ireland,* 32 (Spring 1997), 63–85; Peter Quinn, 'Introduction: An Interpretation of Silences', *Eire-Ireland,* 32 (Spring 1997), 7–19; Peter Quinn, 'The Tragedy of Bridget Such-a-One', *American Heritage* (December 1997), 36–51.

9. See the sources listed in note 7.
10. Gray, 'Famine Relief Policy'.
11. Póirtéir, ed. *Great Irish Famine;* Gray, *Irish Famine,* 65–9; Miller, *Emigrants and Exiles,* 287; S.H. Cousens, 'The Regional Pattern of Emigration during the Great Irish Famine', *Transactions of the Institute of British Geographers,* 28 (1960), especially 127–8, 133.
12. Póirtéir, ed. *Great Irish Famine,* 104–34; Gray, *Irish Famine,* 65–9; Cousens, 'Regional Pattern', especially 127–8, 133; Miller, *Emigrants and Exiles,* 287; Guinnane, *Vanishing Irish,* 61–2.
13. Póirtéir, ed. *Great Irish Famine,* 98, 116, 155–73.
14. Gray, 'Famine Relief Policy', *passim* (both quotes, 105).
15. de Nie, 'Curing "The Irish Moral Plague"', 67 (quote) and *passim.*
16. de Nie, 'Curing "The Irish Moral Plague"', 70–83. While the size of Irish landholdings was drastically changed by the famine and continued to change thereafter, it is important to note that Ireland never followed England in having a majority of landless agricultural labourers; instead, it became a land first of medium-sized tenant farmers and, in the early twentieth century, of small proprietors (in a land purchase scheme engineered by the British government).
17. MacDonagh, 'Irish Famine Emigration', 361.
18. MacDonagh, 'Irish Famine Emigration', 411–17; Gray, *Irish Famine,* 94; Miller, *Emigrants and Exiles,* 284, 291–2.
19. Miller, *Emigrants and Exiles,* 291–2; Gilbert Tucker, 'The Famine Immigration to Canada, 1847', *The American Historical Review,* XXXVI (1930–31), 533–49.
20. MacDonagh, 'Irish Famine Emigration', 421, 423, 427; Miller, *Emigrants and Exiles,* 284–8, 297; Cousens, 'Regional Pattern of Emigration'; S.H. Cousens, 'Emigration and Demographic Change in Ireland, 1851–1861', *The Economic History Review,* XIV (December 1961), 275–88.

21. MacDonagh, 'Irish Famine Emigration', 380, 423; Miller, *Emigrants and Exiles*, 296, 297, 302; Cousens, 'Regional Pattern of Emigration', 126–8. The trans-atlantic fare was roughly equivalent to a farm servant's annual wage, or half the annual conace fee, in the 1840s (Miller, *Emigrants and Exiles*, 220). A conservative estimate of the number of people who could speak Irish in Ireland as a whole at this time is 25 per cent, though perhaps only 5 per cent spoke it monolingually.

22. Miller, *Emigrants and Exiles*, 295.

23. MacDonagh, 'Irish Famine Emigration', 428–30.

24. Cousens, 'Regional Pattern of Emigration', 121–3; Gray, *Irish Famine*, 101; Robert J. Scally, *The End of Hidden Ireland: Rebellion, Famine, and Emigration* (New York, 1995), Chapters 3 and 6; Miller, *Emigrants and Exiles*, 296; George Potter, *To the Golden Door: The Story of the Irish in Ireland and America* (Boston, 1960), 126–8; MacDonagh, 'Irish Famine Emigration', 395. Holdings with a rateable value of less than £5 were eligible for poor law funds to assist emigration.

25. Scally, *End of Hidden Ireland*, 176–88. Although many Irish emigrants crossed the Irish Sea next to cargoes of exported food, it should be noted that imports of food exceeded exports by three-to-one in the period 1846–50: see Daly, 'Revisionism and Irish History', 79–80.

26. Scally, *End of Hidden Ireland*, 181–2, 218–19.

27. Scally, *End of Hidden Ireland*, 200 (quote) and Chapter 9; Herman Melville, *Redburn: His First Voyage* (1849; London, 1937), 162–3 (quote), 214–17.

28. MacDonagh, 'Irish Famine Emigration', 396; Gray, *Irish Famine*, 103, 108; Melville, *Redburn*, 292.

29. Melville, *Redburn*, 317–27 (quote 319).

30. Donald MacKay, *Flight from Famine: The Coming of the Irish to Canada* (Toronto, 1990); Marianna O'Gallagher, *Grosse Île: Gateway to Canada, 1832–1937* (Québec, 1984); Michael Quigley, 'Grosse Île: Canada's Famine Memorial', *Éire-Ireland*, 32 (Spring 1997), 7–19; Tucker, 'Famine Immigration to Canada'; MacDonagh, 'Irish Famine Emigration', 411; Miller, *Emigrants and Exiles*, 316.

31. MacDonagh, 'Irish Famine Emigration', 410–11; Scally, *End of Hidden Ireland*, 39, 219; Miller, *Emigrants and Exiles*, 287, 316.

32. MacKay, *Flight from Famine*; O'Gallagher, *Grosse Île*; Quigley, 'Grosse Île'; Tucker, 'Famine Immigration to Canada'; Miller, *Emigrants and Exiles*, 316; MacDonagh, 'Irish Famine Emigration', 411.

33. On the interpretation of emigration as exile, see Miller, *Emigrants and Exiles*, *passim* and 306 (quote).

34. Blessing, 'Irish', 528; Edward Wakin, *Enter the Irish-American* (New York, 1976), 8, 31; David Fitzpatrick, *Irish Emigration, 1801–1921* (Dundalk, Ireland, 1984), 31.

35. Robert Ernst, *Immigrant Life in New York City, 1825–1863* (1949; Syracuse, NY, 1994), 20–30; Carl Wittke, *The Irish in America* (1956; New York, 1970), 19–20.

36. Wittke, *Irish in America*, 23–4; D.H. Akenson, 'An Agnostic View of the Historiography of the Irish Americans', *Labour/Le Travail*, 14 (Fall 1984), 127–8, 153–5; David Noel Doyle, 'The Irish as Urban Pioneers in the United States, 1850–1870', *Journal of American Ethnic History*, 10 (Fall 1990–Winter 1991), 36–53; A. Gordon Darroch and Michael D. Ornstein, 'Ethnicity and Occupational

Structure in Canada in 1871: The Vertical Mosaic in Historical Perspective', *Canadian Historical Review*, 61 (September 1980), 305–33; Patrick J. Blessing, 'Irish Emigration to the United States, 1800–1920: An Overview', in P.J. Drudy, ed. *The Irish in America: Emigration, Assimilation, Impact* (Cambridge, England, 1985), 23; Lynn Lees and John Modell, 'The Irish Countryman Urbanized: A Comparative Perspective on Famine Migration', *Journal of Urban History*, 3 (August 1977), 391–408. Akenson's challenge to the idea that the American Irish were predominantly urban during the famine era is decisively refuted by Doyle, 'The Irish as Urban Pioneers'.

37. Blessing, 'Irish Emigration to the United States', 23; Blessing, 'Irish', 531; Dennis Clark, *The Irish in Philadelphia: Ten Generations of Urban Experience* (Philadelphia, 1973), 29; Dennis Clark, *Hibernia America: The Irish and Regional Cultures* (Westport, CT, 1986), 119–26, 144–50.

38. Christopher Silver, 'A New Look at Old South Urbanization: The Irish Worker in Charleston, South Carolina, 1840–1860', in Samuel P. Hines and George W. Hopkins, eds. *South Atlantic Urban Studies*, Vol. 3 (Columbia, SC, 1979); Earl F. Niehaus, *The Irish in New Orleans, 1800–1860* (Baton Rouge, LA, 1965), 23–35; Wittke, *Irish in America*, 67–71; Doyle, 'The Irish as Urban Pioneers', 44.

39. Ronald H. Bayor and Timothy J. Meagher, eds. *The New York Irish* (Baltimore, 1996), 91–117; Albon P. Man, Jr., 'The Irish in New York in the Early Eighteen-Sixties', *Irish Historical Studies*, 7 (September 1950), 90–4; Miller, *Emigrants and Exiles*, 319; Morton D. Winsberg, 'Irish Settlement in the United States, 1850–1990', *Éire-Ireland*, 20 (Spring 1985), 7–12; Blessing, 'Irish Emigration to the United States', 23; Jay P. Dolan, *The Immigrant Church: New York's German and Irish Catholics, 1815 to 1865* (Baltimore, 1975), 27, 29; Ernst, *Immigrant Life in New York City*, 184.

40. Bayor and Meagher, *New York Irish*, 114; Man, 'Irish in New York', 92–4; Miller, *Emigrants and Exiles*, 310–20; Dolan, *Immigrant Church*, 33; Ernst, *Immigrant Life in New York City*, 53–6; Hasia Diner, *Erin's Daughters in America: Irish Immigrant Women in the Nineteenth Century* (Baltimore, 1983), 107; Wittke, *Irish in America*, 45–6.

41. David A. Gerber, *The Making of an American Pluralism: Buffalo, New York, 1825–1860* (Urbana, IL, 1989), 130; Niehaus, *Irish in New Orleans*, 26, 144; Blessing, 'Irish Emigration to the United States', 24.

42. Gerber, *Making of an American Pluralism*, 132; Ernst, *Immigrant Life in New York City*, 58; Man, 'Irish in New York', 94; Bayor and Meagher, eds. *New York Irish*, 114–17; Niehaus, *Irish in New Orleans*, 59–65; William V. Shannon, *The American Irish* (New York, 1963), 33; Douglas V. Shaw, 'Political Leadership in the Industrial City: Irish Development and Nativist Response in Jersey City', in Richard Ehrlich, ed. *Immigrants in Industrial America, 1850–1920* (Charlottesville, VA, 1977), 87. The Draft Riots and the Orange and Green Riots are discussed below, the Molly Maguires in Chapter 4.

43. Howard M. Gitelman, 'No Irish Need Apply: Patterns of and Responses to Ethnic Discrimination in the Labor Market', *Labor History*, 14 (Winter 1973), 56–68; Bruce Laurie, Theodore Hershberg and George Alter, 'Immigrants and Industry: The Philadelphia Experience', in Ehrlich, ed. *Immigrants in Industrial America*, 141–2; Douglas V. Shaw, *The Making of an Immigrant City: Ethnic and Cultural Conflict in Jersey*

City, New Jersey, 1850–1877 (New York, 1976), 22; Shaw, 'Political Leadership in the Industrial City', 87; Bayor and Meagher, eds. *New York Irish*, 97, 109; David Montgomery, 'The Irish and the American Labor Movement', in David Noel Doyle and Owen Dudley Edwards, eds. *America and Ireland, 1776–1976* (Westport, CT, 1980), 208; Man, 'Irish in New York', 95; Jo Ellen McNergney Vinyard, *The Irish on the Urban Frontier: Nineteenth-Century Detroit, 1850–80* (New York, 1976); Blessing, 'Irish', 531; Robert A. Burchell, *The San Francisco Irish, 1848–1880* (Manchester, England, 1979); David Brundage, *The Making of Western Radicalism: Denver's Organized Workers, 1878–1905* (Urbana, IL, 1994), 45. The theme of geographical and social mobility is taken up in greater detail in Chapter 4 of the present work.

44. David Noel Doyle, 'The Irish and American Labour, 1880–1920', *Saothar: Journal of the Irish Labour History Society*, 1 (1975), 42; Bayor and Meagher, eds. *New York Irish*, 109; Gerber, *Making of an American Pluralism*, 125–6; Iver Bernstein, *The New York City Draft Riots: Their Significance for American Society and Politics in the Age of the Civil War* (New York, 1990), 114; Wittke, *Irish in America*, 25.

45. Wittke, *Irish in America*, 217; Bayor and Meagher, *New York Irish*, 97; Clark, *Irish in Philadelphia*, 63–87; Laurie, Hershberg and Alter, 'Immigrants and Industry'; Thomas Dublin, *Women at Work: The Transformation of Work and Community in Lowell, Massachusetts, 1826–1860* (New York, 1979), 132–64; Montgomery, 'Irish and the American Labor Movement', 210.

46. Christine Stansell, *City of Women: Sex and Class in New York, 1789–1860* (New York, 1986), 156–67.

47. Carol Groneman Pernicone, 'Working-Class Immigrant Women in Mid-Nineteenth-Century New York: The Irish Woman's Experience', *Journal of Urban History*, 4 (1978), 258–62; Wittke, *Irish in America*, 25–7, 217–18; Bayor and Meagher, eds. *New York Irish*, 109, 121–2; Ernst, *Immigrant Life in New York City*, 65–78; Diner, *Erin's Daughters*, 41, 60–2, 73–5.

48. Gerber, *Making of an American Pluralism*, 135, 254; Way, *Common Labour*, Chapter 8; Kevin Kenny, *Making Sense of the Molly Maguires* (New York, 1998).

49. Wittke, *Irish in America*, 217; Bayor and Meagher, eds. *New York Irish*, 109; Bernstein, *New York City Draft Riots*, 119–20; Man, 'Irish in New York', 87–95; Albon P. Man, Jr., 'Labor Competition and the New York City Draft Riots of 1863', *Journal of Negro History*, 36 (October 1951), 392–5; Montgomery, 'Irish and the American Labor Movement', 210; Dublin, *Women at Work*, 206–7; Kenny, *Making Sense of the Molly Maguires*, Chapter 4; Blessing, 'Irish', 538.

50. James Edmund Roohan, *American Catholics and the Social Question, 1865–1900* (New York, 1976), 5–6; Miller, *Emigrants and Exiles*, 331–2; Blessing, 'Irish', 534.

51. Emmet Larkin, 'The Devotional Revolution in Ireland', *American Historical Review*, 77 (June 1972), 625–52; Dolan, *Immigrant Church*, 56–7; David W. Miller, 'Irish Catholicism and the Great Famine', *Journal of Social History*, 9 (1975), 81–98; S.J. Connolly, *Priests and People in Pre-Famine Ireland, 1780–1845* (New York, 1982), especially Chapters 3 and 4.

52. Miller, *Emigrants and Exiles*, 333.

53. Jay P. Dolan, *The American Catholic Experience: A History From Colonial Times to the Present* (Garden City, NY, 1985), 263–9, 324; Suellen Hoy, 'The Journey Out: The

Recruitment and Emigration of Irish Religious Women to the United States, 1812–1914', *Journal of Women's History*, 6 and 7 (Winter/Spring 1995), 64–70.

54. Madeleine Hooke Rice, *American Catholic Opinion in the Slavery Controversy* (New York, 1944), 92–3; Thomas T. McAvoy, *History of the Catholic Church in the United States* (South Bend, Indiana, 1969), 171–3; MacDonagh, 'Irish Famine Emigration', 434; Christopher McGimpsey, 'Internal Ethnic Friction: Orange and Green in Nineteenth-Century New York, 1868–1872', *Immigrants and Minorities*, 1 (March 1982), 42–3.

55. McGimpsey, 'Internal Ethnic Friction', 43; Edward Wakin, *Enter the Irish-American* (New York, 1976), 53 (quote).

56. Tyler Anbinder, *Nativism and Slavery: The Northern Know Nothings and the Politics of the 1850s* (New York, 1992); Kevin Kenny, 'Nativism, Labor and Slavery: The Political Odyssey of Benjamin Bannan', *The Pennsylvania Magazine of History and Biography*, CXVIII (October 1994), 326–61; Eric Foner, *Free Soil, Free Labor, Free Men: The Ideology of the Republican Party Before the Civil War* (New York, 1970); McAvoy, *History of the Catholic Church*, 169–74; Niehaus, *Irish in New Orleans*, 84–96.

57. Kenny, 'Nativism, Labor and Slavery'; Kenny, *Making Sense of the Molly Maguires*, 73–9.

58. George Templeton Strong, *Diary of George Templeton Strong*, edited by Allan Nevins and Milton Haley Thomas and abridged by Thomas J. Pressly (Seattle, WA, 1988), 244, 245, entry for 19 July 1863; Matthew Frye Jacobson, *Whiteness of a Different Color: European Immigrants and the Alchemy of Race* (Cambridge, MA, 1998), 48–50, 54–5; Dolan, *American Catholic Experience*, 202; Patrick J. Blessing, 'Culture, Religion and the Activities of the Committee of Vigilance, San Francisco 1858', Working paper, series 8, no. 3, Charles and Margaret Hall Cushwa Center for the Study of American Catholicism, University of Notre Dame, 1980; Miller, *Emigrants and Exiles*, 323; Burchell, *San Francisco Irish*, 124–5.

59. William V. Shannon, *The American Irish* (New York, 1963), 50–2; Edward M. Levine, *The Irish and Irish Politicians: A Study in Social and Cultural Alienation* (South Bend, Indiana, 1966), 36–51; Noel Ignatiev, *How the Irish Became White* (New York, 1995), 76–7; Steven P. Erie, *Rainbow's End: Irish Americans and the Dilemmas of Urban Machine Politics, 1840–1985* (Berkeley, CA, 1988), 26–7.

60. Ignatiev, *How the Irish Became White*, 77–9 (quote, 79); Shannon, *American Irish*, 51–5; David Roediger, *The Wages of Whiteness: Race and the Making of the American Working Class* (New York, 1991), Chapter 4, especially 75, 77, 80.

61. Foner, *Free Soil, Free Labor, Free Men*.

62. Rice, *American Catholic Opinion*, 118–21.

63. Erie, *Rainbow's End*, 26–7; Burchell, *San Francisco Irish*, 186.

64. Erie, *Rainbow's End*, 51–6; George E. Reedy, *From the Ward to the White House: The Irish in American Politics* (New York, 1991), 65–7.

65. Michael F.X. Hogan, *The Irish Soldiers of Mexico* (Guadalajara, Mexico, 1997); Robert Ryal Miller, *Shamrock and Sword: The Saint Patrick's Battalion in the U.S.–Mexican War* (Norman, Oklahoma, 1997); Mark R. Day, 'The Passion of the San Patricios', *Irish America Magazine* (May/June 1993): 44–8; George Potter, *To the Golden Door: The Story of the Irish in Ireland and America* (Boston, 1960), 473–98; *Irish Times*, 14 January 1991, p.1.

66. Hogan, *Irish Soldiers*; Day, 'Passion of the San Patricios'; Miller, *Shamrock and Sword*; Potter, *To the Golden Door*, 473–98; *Irish Times*, 14 January 1991, p.1.

67. Day, 'Passion of the San Patricios'.

68. Wittke, *Irish in America*, 147–9; Blessing, 'Irish', 536; Niehaus, *Irish in New Orleans*, 157–62; Joseph P. O'Grady, *How the Irish Became American* (New York, 1973), 46–7.

69. Blessing, 'Irish', 536; O'Grady, *How the Irish Became American*, 46–7; Shannon, *American Irish*, 56–9; Wittke, *Irish in America*, 135–44.

70. For arguments that the Irish embraced 'whiteness' as a means of assimilation, see Ignatiev, *How the Irish Became White*; Roediger, *The Wages of Whiteness*, especially Chapter 7; cf. the discussion in Chapter 2 of the present work. On the racialization of the Irish in the wake of the draft riots of 1863, see the *New York Times*, 15 July 1863, and the *New York Tribune*, 14–17 July 1863, as analyzed (along with other contemporary sources) by Jacobson, *Whiteness of a Different Color* (Cambridge, MA, 1998), 52–6.

71. Rice, *American Catholic Opinion*, 118–21.

72. Man, 'Irish in New York', 87–9; Man, 'Labor Competition', 376–402; Bernstein, *New York City Draft Riots*, 114–20.

73. James M. McPherson, *The Battle Cry of Freedom: The Civil War Era* (New York, 1988), 606–11.

74. Bernstein, *New York City Draft Riots*; Kenny, *Making Sense of the Molly Maguires*, 82–102; Man, 'Labor Competition', 396–402; McPherson, *Battle Cry of Freedom*, 606–11. Police records cite only 119 dead, and this is the figure most commonly cited by recent historians (e.g. Bernstein); but, if the contemporary figure of 1,500 was an exaggeration produced by nativists like George Templeton Strong, it is possible that scores, perhaps even hundreds, of casualties ended up uncounted in the rivers on either side of Manhattan.

75. Foster, *Modern Ireland*, 310–16; Miller, *Emigrants and Exiles*, 310–11, 334–5; Potter, *Golden Door*, 498–508.

76. Foster, *Modern Ireland*, 314; Thomas N. Brown, *Irish-American Nationalism, 1870–1890* (Philadelphia, 1966), 27; Miller, *Emigrants and Exiles*, 311, 338–9, 341, 343; Wittke, *Irish in America*, 83–4.

77. Foster, *Modern Ireland*, 312; Wittke, *Irish in America*, 82–3.

78. Miller, *Emigrants and Exiles*, 335–6.

79. Miller, *Emigrants and Exiles*, 337–8. For more on Clan na Gael, see Chapters 4 and 5.

80. McGimpsey, 'Internal Ethnic Friction'; Michael Gordon, *The Orange Riots: Irish Political Violence in New York City in 1870–1871* (Ithaca, NY, 1993).

81. Gordon, *Orange Riots*.

Chapter 4: After the Famine

1. Patrick J. Blessing, 'Irish', in Stephan Thernstrom, ed. *The Harvard Encyclopedia of American Ethnic Groups* (Cambridge, MA, 1980), 528.

2. Cormac O'Gráda, 'Irish Emigration to the United States in the Nineteenth Century', in David Noel Doyle and Owen Dudley Edwards, eds. *America and Ireland, 1776–1976: The American Identity and the Irish Connection* (Westport, CT, 1980), 93–4; Kerby A. Miller, *Emigrants and Exiles: Ireland and the Irish Exodus to North America*

(New York, 1985), 346–8; Kerby A. Miller, 'Assimilation and Alienation: Irish Emigrants' Responses to Industrial America, 1871–1921', in P.J. Drudy, ed. *The Irish in America: Emigration, Assimilation, Impact* (Cambridge, England, 1985), 87; David Fitzpatrick, *Irish Emigration, 1801–1921* (Dundalk, Ireland, 1984), 11–13; Timothy Guinnane, *The Vanishing Irish: Households, Migration, and the Rural Economy in Ireland, 1850–1914* (Princeton, NJ, 1997), 101. The term 'overseas' emigration excludes the 'internal' migration from Ireland to elsewhere in the United Kingdom.

3. Donald H. Akenson, 'An Agnostic View of the Historiography of the Irish Americans', *Labour/Le Travail*, 14 (Fall 1984), 148–9; Donald H. Akenson, 'The Historiography of the Irish in the United States of America', in Patrick O'Sullivan, ed. *The Irish World Wide. History, Heritage, Identity*. Vol. II. *The Irish in the New Communities* (Leicester, England, 1992), 104–5; Maldwyn A. Jones, 'Scotch-Irish', in Thernstrom, ed. *Harvard Encyclopedia of American Ethnic Groups*, 905; Miller, *Emigrants and Exiles*, 349–50, 370–9; Fitzpatrick, *Irish Emigration*, 9–13; Arnold Schrier, *Ireland and the American Migration, 1850–1900* (Minneapolis, 1958), 4–9; S.H. Cousens, 'Emigration and Demographic Change in Ireland, 1851–1861', *The Economic History Review*, XIV (December 1961), 275–88; S.H. Cousens, 'The Regional Variations in Population Changes in Ireland, 1861–1881', *The Economic History Review*, XVII (December 1964), 301–21; Brendan M. Walsh, 'A Perspective on Irish Population Patterns', *Éire-Ireland*, IV (Autumn 1969), 3–21.

4. Miller, *Emigrants and Exiles*, 349–51, 397–402, 469–81; Miller, 'Assimilation and Alienation', 88; Cousens, 'Emigration and Demographic Change'; Cousens, 'Regional Variations'; Cormac O'Gráda, 'Seasonal Migration and post-Famine Adjustment in the West of Ireland', *Studia Hibernica*, 13 (1973), 48–76; Walsh, 'Perspective'.

5. Guinnane, *Vanishing Irish, passim*.

6. Miller, *Emigrants and Exiles*, 346, 361–70; Robert E. Kennedy, *The Irish: Emigration, Marriage, and Fertility* (Berkeley, CA, 1973), 1; Guinnane, *Vanishing Irish*, 121–4.

7. Miller, *Emigrants and Exiles*, 380–402; Guinnane, *Vanishing Irish*, 38–42.

8. Miller, *Emigrants and Exiles*, 380–402.

9. Oliver MacDonagh, 'The Irish Famine Emigration to the United States', *Perspectives in American History*, X (1976), 358; Miller, *Emigrants and Exiles*, 380–422.

10. K.H. Connell, 'Peasant Marriage in Ireland After the Great Famine', *Past and Present*, 12 (1957), 76–91; K.H. Connell, 'Peasant Marriage in Ireland: Its Structure and Development Since the Famine', *The Economic History Review*, 2nd Ser., 14 (1962), 502–23; K.H. Connell, *Irish Peasant Society: Four Historical Essays* (Oxford, 1968); Kennedy, *Emigration, Marriage, and Fertility*; Hasia Diner, *Erin's Daughters in America: Irish Immigrant Women in the Nineteenth Century* (Baltimore, MD, 1983), 1–29; Janet Nolan, *Ourselves Alone: Women's Emigration from Ireland, 1885–1920* (Lexington, KY, 1989), 9–42; Pauline Jackson, 'Women in Nineteenth-Century Irish Emigration', *International Migration Review*, 18 (Winter 1984), 1010, 1018.

11. Connell, 'Peasant Marriage in Ireland After the Great Famine'; Connell, 'Peasant Marriage in Ireland: Its Structure and Development Since the Famine'; Connell, *Irish Peasant Society*; Kennedy, *Emigration, Marriage, and Fertility*; Diner, *Erin's Daughters*, 1–29; Nolan, *Ourselves Alone*, 9–42; Jackson, 'Women in Nineteenth-Century Irish

Emigration'; cf. Guinnane's critique of the Connell thesis, *Vanishing Irish*, 15, 48–51, 73–4, 82–5, 92–6, 133–65, 195, 225–33 and *passim*. Demographers typically use the technical term 'celibacy' to refer to non-marriage rather than total absence of sexual relations, though the latter was apparently more likely to follow from the former in postfamine Ireland than elsewhere.

12. Guinnane, *The Vanishing Irish*, *passim*. See, also, Donna Birdwell-Pheasant, 'The Early Twentieth-Century Stem Family: A Case Study from County Kerry', in Marilyn Silverman and P.H. Gulliver, eds. *Approaching the Past: Historical Anthropology through Irish Case Studies* (New York, 1992), 205–35; Donna Birdwell-Pheasant, 'Irish Households in the Early Twentieth Century: Culture, Class, and Historical Contingency', *Journal of Family History*, 18 (1), 19–38.

13. Miller, *Emigrants and Exiles*, 417–69, 481–92.

14. Miller, *Emigrants and Exiles*, 350–1; Guinnane, *Vanishing Irish*, 104–7.

15. Miller, *Emigrants and Exiles*, 351–3; O'Gráda, 'Irish Emigration'; Kennedy, *Emigration, Marriage, and Fertility*, 76–85; Nolan, *Ourselves Alone*, 2–6, 26–54; Blessing, 'Irish', 529; Patrick J. Blessing, 'Irish Emigration to the United States, 1800–1920: An Overview', in Drudy, ed. *Irish in America*, 19; Diner, *Erin's Daughters*, 31–3; Jackson, 'Women in Nineteenth-Century Irish Emigration', 1006; Fitzpatrick, *Irish Emigration*, 7–8; Guinnane, *Vanishing Irish*, 105–6, 176–9, 181–6.

16. Diner, *Erin's Daughters*, Chapter 2.

17. Diner, *Erin's Daughters*, Chapter 2; Jackson, 'Women in Nineteenth-Century Irish Emigration'; Kennedy, *Emigration, Marriage, and Fertility*, 76–85; Guinnane, *Vanishing Irish*, 53–5, 94–101, 166–76, 266–7, Chapter 7. On the coercive and patriarchal dimension to emigrant remittances see Robert Doan's recent dissertation, 'Green Gold to the Emerald Shores: Irish Immigration to the United States and Transatlantic Monetary Aid, 1854–1923' (unpublished Ph.D. dissertation, Temple University, 1998).

18. Guinnane, *Vanishing Irish*, 110; Miller, *Emigrants and Exiles*, 356–7, 415; Diner, *Erin's Daughters*, 35; Schrier, *Ireland and the American Migration*, 15; Fitzpatrick, *Irish Emigration*, 18–20, 29.

19. Miller, *Emigrants and Exiles*, 354–5; Guinnane, *Vanishing Irish*, 110.

20. Schrier, *Ireland and the American Migration*, 66–82, 105–21; MacDonagh, 'Irish Famine Emigration to the United States', 358–9, 362; Nolan, *Ourselves Alone*, 55–72; Miller, *Emigrants and Exiles*, 413–24; Brendan M. Walsh, 'Marriage Rates and Population Pressure: Ireland, 1871 and 1911', *The Economic History Review*, XXIII (April 1970), 162; Fitzpatrick, *Irish Emigration*, 5, 38–40; Guinnane, *Vanishing Irish*, 4, 22–3.

21. Miller, *Emigrants and Exiles*, 426, 556–68; Schrier, *Ireland and the American Migration*, 84–91; Guinnane, *Vanishing Irish*, 107.

22. Blessing, 'Irish', 528; Schrier, *Ireland and the American Migration*, 5; Thomas N. Brown, *Irish-American Nationalism, 1870–1890* (Philadelphia, 1966), 18.

23. Although Manhattan and Brooklyn did not become one city until 1898, the figures for both cities in 1890 have been combined here. Blessing, 'Irish', 531; Blessing, 'Irish Emigration to the United States', 22–4; Morton D. Winsberg, 'Irish Settlement in the United States, 1850–1990', *Éire-Ireland*, 20 (Spring 1985), 7–12; Carl Wittke, *The Irish in America* (1956; New York, 1970), 23–4; David Noel Doyle,

Irish-Americans, Native Rights, And National Empires: The Structure, Divisions, and Attitudes of the Catholic Minority in the Decade of Expansion (New York, 1976), 59; Steven P. Erie, *Rainbow's End: Irish Americans and the Dilemmas of Urban Machine Politics, 1840–1985* (Berkeley, CA, 1988), 25–6.

24. Blessing, 'Irish Emigration to the United States', 24.

25. Blessing, 'Irish', 530 (quote); Winsberg, 'Irish Settlement in the United States', 12; David Brundage, 'Denver's New Departure: Irish Nationalism and the Labor Movement in the Gilded Age', *Southwest Economy and Society*, 5 (Winter 1981), 10–23; David Brundage, *The Making of Western Radicalism: Denver's Organized Workers, 1878–1905* (Urbana, IL, 1994); David M. Emmons, *The Butte Irish: Class and Ethnicity in an American Mining Town, 1875–1925* (Urbana, IL, 1959).

26. James Edmund Roohan, *American Catholics and the Social Question, 1865–1900* (New York, 1976), 209–12; James P. Shannon, *Catholic Colonization on the Western Frontier* (New Haven, CT, 1957), 25–31; 214–44.

27. Roohan, *American Catholics and the Social Question*, 212–22.

28. Shannon, *Catholic Colonization*, 157–67.

29. Shannon, *Catholic Colonization*, 157–67 (quote 165), 264.

30. Blessing, 'Irish Emigration to the United States', 21–2.

31. Florence E. Gibson, *The Attitudes of the New York Irish Toward State and National Affairs* (New York, 1951), 16; Robert A. Burchell, *The San Francisco Irish, 1848–1880* (Manchester, England, 1979), 3, 155–8; Richard Stivers, *The Hair of the Dog: Irish Drinking and American Stereotype* (University Park, PA, 1976), 180 (quote) and *passim*; Diner, *Erin's Daughters*, 107–17.

32. Maureen Fitzgerald, 'Charity, Poverty, and Child Welfare', *Harvard Divinity Bulletin*, 25 (1996), 12–15; Suellen Hoy, 'The Journey Out: The Recruitment and Emigration of Irish Religious Women to the United States, 1812–1914', *Journal of Women's History*, 6 and 7 (Winter/Spring 1995), 64–98.

33. Fitzgerald, 'Charity, Poverty, and Child Welfare', 15.

34. Fitzgerald, 'Charity, Poverty, and Child Welfare', 15–17.

35. Blessing, 'Irish', 539; William V. Shannon, *The American Irish* (New York, 1963), 40–1, 97–100; Wittke, *Irish in America*, 267; Iver Bernstein, *The New York City Draft Riots: Their Significance for American Society and Politics in the Age of the Civil War* (New York, 1990); Michael Gordon, *The Orange Riots: Irish Political Violence in New York City in 1870–1871* (Ithaca, NY, 1993); Kevin Kenny, *Making Sense of the Molly Maguires* (New York, 1998); Brown, *Irish-American Nationalism*.

36. Miller, *Emigrants and Exiles*, 533; Schrier, *Ireland and the American Migration*, 105–7; Jones, 'Scotch-Irish', 907.

37. On ethnic identity as a necessary precondition for assimilation, see Gary Gerstle, 'Liberty, Coercion, and the Making of Americans', *The Journal of American History*, 84 (September 1997), 539–44; and John Belchem, 'Nationalism, Republicanism and Exile: Irish Emigrants and the Revolutions of 1848', *Past and Present*, 146 (February 1995), 112.

38. Miller, *Emigrants and Exiles*, 88–90; Jones, 'Irish', 905; E.R.R. Green, 'The Irish American Business and Professions', in Doyle and Edwards, eds. *America and Ireland, 1776–1976*, 200–3.

39. Stephan Thernstrom, *Poverty and Progress: Social Mobility in a Nineteenth-Century City* (1964; New York, 1970); Stephan Thernstrom, *The Other Bostonians: Poverty and Progress in the American Metropolis, 1860–1970* (Cambridge, MA, 1973); Jo Ellen McNergney Vinyard, *The Irish on the Urban Frontier: Nineteenth-Century Detroit, 1850–80* (New York, 1976); Clyde Griffen, 'Making it in America: Social Mobility in Mid-Nineteenth Century Poughkeepsie', *New York History*, LI (October 1970), 479–99; Dale B. Light, 'The Role of Irish-American Organisations in Assimilation and Community Formation', in Drudy, ed. *The Irish in America* (Cambridge, England, 1985).

40. Doyle, *Irish-Americans, Native Rights, and National Empires*, 59–76; Dennis Clark, *The Irish in Philadelphia: Ten Generations of Urban Experience* (Philadelphia, 1973); Dennis Clark, 'Ethnic Enterprise and Urban Development', *Ethnicity*, 5 (June 1978), 108–18; Vinyard, *Irish on the Urban Frontier*; Brundage, 'Denver's New Departure', 12; Brundage, *Making of Western Labor Radicalism*, 45; Burchell, *San Francisco Irish*, 54–60.

41. Diner, *Erin's Daughters*, 33, 45–6; Nolan, *Ourselves Alone*, 74–9; Guinnane, however, astutely notes that the American Irish ought to be compared not to the American population generally, but to its urban component (among whom rates of marriage were much lower), in which case most of the disparities disappear (*Vanishing Irish*, 223–4).

42. Diner, *Erin's Daughters*; Nolan, *Ourselves Alone*.

43. Diner, *Erin's Daughters*, Chapter 4; Nolan, *Ourselves Alone*, 73–81; Blessing, 'Irish', 531–2.

44. Diner, *Erin's Daughters*, 89; Nolan, *Ourselves Alone*, 68, 78.

45. Diner, *Erin's Daughters*; Nolan, *Ourselves Alone*.

46. Diner, *Erin's Daughters*; Nolan, *Ourselves Alone*.

47. Sarah Deutsch, *Women and the City: Gender, Space, and Power in Boston, 1870–1940* (forthcoming, Oxford University Press, 2000; cited with the author's permission), Chapter 2, especially 5–23; cf. Diner *Erin's Daughters*, 116–17.

48. Diner, *Erin's Daughters*, 74–80.

49. Carole Turbin, *Working Women of Collar City: Gender, Class and Community in Troy, 1864–86* (Urbana, IL, 1992); Diner, *Erin's Daughters*, 72–83, 100–1; Nolan, *Ourselves Alone*, 84.

50. Kenny, *Making Sense of the Molly Maguires*; Blessing, 'Irish', 538; Michael Gordon, 'The Labor Boycott in New York City, 1880–1886', *Labor History*, 16 (1975), 195–9; Michael Gordon, 'Irish Immigrant Culture and the Labor Boycott in New York City, 1880–86', in Richard Ehrlich, ed. *Immigrants in Industrial America, 1850–1920* (Charlottesville, VA, 1977), 120; Joseph P. O'Grady, *How the Irish Became American* (New York, 1973), 62; David Montgomery, 'The Irish and the American Labor Movement', in Doyle and Edwards, eds. *America and Ireland, 1776–1976*, 211–17; Ira B. Cross, ed. *Frank Roney: An Autobiography* (1931; New York, 1976), vii–xxxi; Alexander Saxton, *The Indispensable Enemy: Labor and the Anti-Chinese Movement in California* (Berkeley, CA, 1971), 117–27; Wittke, *Irish in America*, 226; Bayor and Meagher, eds. *New York Irish*, 328.

51. Gordon, 'Labor Boycott in New York City'; Gordon, 'Irish Immigrant Culture and the Labor Boycott'.

52. Kenny, *Making Sense of the Molly Maguires*. On predecessors to the Molly Maguires in the antebellum United States, see Chapters 2 and 3 of the present work.

53. Roney, *Irish Rebel*; Saxton, *Indispensable Enemy*; Matthew Frye Jacobson, *Whiteness of a Different Color: European Immigrants and the Alchemy of Race* (Cambridge, MA, 1998), 158–61.

54. Andrew M. Greeley, *The Irish-Americans: The Road to Money and Power* (New York, 1981), 88 (quote).

55. Jones, 'Irish', 906 (quote); John Higham, *Strangers in the Land: Patterns of American Nativism, 1860–1925* (New York, 1965), 61–3, 80–7.

56. Jones, 'Irish', 906 (quote); Higham, *Strangers in the Land*, 61–3, 80–7.

57. Erie, *Rainbow's End*, 36.

58. Douglas V. Shaw, *The Making of an Immigrant City: Ethnic and Cultural Conflict in Jersey City, New Jersey, 1850–1877* (New York, 1976); Douglas V. Shaw, 'Political Leadership in the Industrial City: Irish Development and Nativist Response in Jersey City', in Richard Ehrlich, ed. *Immigrants in Industrial America, 1850–1920* (Charlottesville, VA, 1977); Erie, *Rainbow's End*, 35–8; David Quigley, 'Reconstructing Democracy: Politics and Ideas in New York City, 1865–80' (unpublished Ph.D. dissertation, New York University, 1997).

59. Blessing, 'Irish', 535; Erie, *Rainbow's End*, 2–3, 22, 27; George E. Reedy, *From the Ward to the White House: The Irish in American Politics* (New York, 1991), 67–76; Edward T. O'Donnell, *Henry George for Mayor! Irish Nationalists, Labor Radicalism, and Independent Politics in Gilded Age New York City* (forthcoming, Columbia University Press; cited by permission of author), 96–7. Pittsburgh and Philadelphia, unlike most cities, had Republican rather than Democratic machines.

60. Erie, *Rainbow's End*, 11, 27, 58–64; Brown, *Irish-American Nationalism*, 148–50; Reedy, *From the Ward to the White House*, 112–13; Peter Quinn, 'Introduction', William L. Riordan, ed. *Plunkitt of Tammany Hall: A Series of Very Plain Talks on Very Practical Politics* (New York, 1995); Edward M. Levine, *The Irish and Irish Politicians: A Study in Social and Cultural Alienation* (South Bend, Indiana, 1966), 36–7; O'Donnell, *Henry George for Mayor!*, 97–9.

61. Erie, *Rainbow's End*, 85–6; Quinn, 'Introduction', *Plunkitt of Tammany Hall*, vii–xx.

62. Riordan, ed. *Plunkitt of Tammany Hall*.

63. O'Grady, *How the Irish Became American*, 106–8; Kenneth Jackson, ed. *The Encyclopedia of New York City* (New Haven, CT, 1995), 300.

64. Reedy, *From the Ward to the White House*, 112–42; Quinn, 'Introduction', *Plunkitt of Tammany Hall*, xiii–xiv; Levine, *Irish and Irish Politicians*, 45.

65. Levine, *Irish and Irish Politicians*, 34–51.

66. Blessing, 'Irish', 534, 538; John Cogley, *Catholic America* (New York, 1973), 219–29, 242; Andrew M. Greeley, *The Catholic Experience* (New York, 1967), 152–80; Robert D. Cross, *The Emergence of Liberal Catholicism in America* (1958; Chicago, 1968), Chapter VI.

67. Jay P. Dolan, *The American Catholic Experience: A History From Colonial Times to the Present* (Garden City, NY, 1985), 211–19.

68. Dolan, *American Catholic Experience*, 221–33.

69. Miller, *Emigrants and Exiles*, 528–31; Greeley, *Catholic Experience*, 152–64, 175; Blessing, 'Irish', 538; Cross, *Emergence of Liberal Catholicism*, Chapter VI.

70. Miller, *Emigrants and Exiles*, 529–30; Greeley, *Catholic Experience*, 178–9; Blessing, 'Irish', 538; Cross, *Emergence of Liberal Catholicism*, 121–3.

71. Miller, *Emigrants and Exiles*, 528–30; Greeley, *Catholic Experience*, 197–8.
72. Cross, *Emergence of Liberal Catholicism*, 130–45; Dolan, *American Catholic Experience*, 270–93.
73. Dolan, *American Catholic Experience*, 270–4.
74. Cross, *Emergence of Liberal Catholicism*, 108–23; James Edmund Roohan, *American Catholics and the Social Question, 1865–1900* (New York, 1976), Chapters VIII, IX and X.
75. Cross, *Emergence of Liberal Catholicism*, 108–23; Dolan, *American Catholic Experience*, 332–5; Greeley, *Catholic Experience*, 196–7; Roohan, *American Catholics and the Social Question*, Chapters VIII, IX and X.
76. Dolan, *American Catholic Experience*, 297; Greeley, *Catholic Experience*, 188.
77. Dolan, *American Catholic Experience*, 297; Greeley, *Catholic Experience*, 189.
78. Dolan, *American Catholic Experience*, 298; Greeley, *Catholic Experience*, 190–2.
79. Dolan, *American Catholic Experience*, 312–16; John Tracy Ellis, *American Catholics and Intellectual Life* (1956; Chicago, 1969), 120–2; Greeley, *Catholic Experience*, Chapter VI.
80. Greeley, *Catholic Experience*, Chapter VI; Thomas T. McAvoy, *The Americanist Heresy in Roman Catholicism, 1895–1900* (South Bend, Indiana, 1963); Thomas T. McAvoy, *History of the Catholic Church in the United States* (South Bend, Indiana, 1969), 325–6, 333–5.
81. Brown, *Irish-American Nationalism*, 23 (quote), 38, 41 (quote); Miller, *Emigrants and Exiles*, 545; Victor A. Walsh, 'A Fanatic Heart': The Cause of Irish-American Nationalism in Pittsburgh During the Gilded Age', *Journal of Social History*, 15 (1981), 187, 199; Victor A. Walsh, 'Irish Nationalism and Land Reform: The Role of the Irish in America', in Drudy, ed. *Irish in America*, 257, 264.
82. Brown, *Irish-American Nationalism*, 65 ('fundamentally conservative' quote); Eric Foner, 'Class, Ethnicity, and Radicalism in the Gilded Age: The Land League and Irish-America', in Eric Foner, *Politics and Ideology in the Age of the Civil War* (New York, 1980), 195 (quote beginning 'views working-class life . . .'); Walsh, 'A Fanatic Heart', 186, 199.
83. Jackson, ed. *Encyclopedia of New York City*, 861; Brown, *Irish-American Nationalism*, xiv, 38–41, 65–73, 136; Foner, 'Class, Ethnicity, and Radicalism', 163–4; Walsh, 'Irish Nationalism and Land Reform', 253–5; Wittke, *Irish in America*, 150–60; Terry Golway, *Irish Rebel: John Devoy and America's Fight for Ireland's Freedom* (New York, 1998), Chapters 1, 3, 4, 7.
84. Golway, *Irish Rebel*; Jackson, ed. *Encyclopedia of New York City*, 330; Brown, *Irish-American Nationalism*, xiv (quote).
85. Golway, *Irish Rebel*, 100–6.
86. Brundage, 'Denver's New Departure', 11 (quote); Bayor and Meagher, eds. *New York Irish*, 323–34; Brown, *Irish-American Nationalism*, 40–57; Foner, 'Class, Ethnicity, and Radicalism', 157–61; O'Donnell, *Henry George for Mayor!*, 118–24.
87. Walsh, 'Irish Nationalism and Land Reform'; Foner, 'Class, Ethnicity, and Radicalism'.
88. Brown, *Irish-American Nationalism*, Chapter 5; Golway, *Irish Rebel*, Chapters 8, 9, 10; O'Donnell, *Henry George for Mayor!*, Chapter 4.
89. Brown, *Irish-American Nationalism*, Chapters 5 and 6.
90. Brown, *Irish-American Nationalism*, 103–4, 109–10; Foner, 'Class, Ethnicity, and Radicalism', 184–8.

91. Brown, *Irish-American Nationalism*, 118–19; Foner, 'Class, Ethnicity, and Radicalism', 189–94.

92. Foner, 'Class, Ethnicity, and Radicalism', 189–91.

93. Foner, 'Class, Ethnicity, and Radicalism', 189–94; Brown, *Irish-American Nationalism*, Chapters 6 and 7.

94. The definitive account is O'Donnell, *Henry George for Mayor!*, especially Chapters 4 through 7.

95. O'Donnell, *Henry George for Mayor!*, 143–7, Chapters 5–7; Foner, 'Class, Ethnicity, and Radicalism', 177–9, 184–8, 195–200; Walsh, 'Irish Nationalism and Land Reform', 263.

Chapter 5: Irish America, 1900–1940

1. The term 'American Irish' here refers to all Americans of Irish birth, plus those with one or more Irish-born parents.

2. Patrick J. Blessing, 'Irish', in Stephan Thernstrom, ed. *The Harvard Encyclopedia of American Ethnic Groups* (Cambridge, MA, 1980), 528, 540; Jones, 'Scotch-Irish', in Thernstrom, ed. *Harvard Encyclopedia of American Ethnic Groups*, 907; P.J. Drudy, 'Irish Population Change and Emigration Since Independence,' in P.J. Drudy ed. *The Irish in America: Emigration, Assimilation, Impact* (Cambridge, England, 1985), 66, 73–5.

3. Drudy, 'Irish Population Change', 73–5.

4. Drudy, 'Irish Population Change', 70–2; Robert E. Kennedy, *The Irish: Emigration, Marriage, and Fertility* (Berkeley, CA, 1973), 83.

5. Kennedy, *Emigration, Marriage, and Fertility*, Chapter 7.

6. Blessing, 'Irish', 528; Patrick J. Blessing, 'Irish Emigration to the United States, 1800–1920: An Overview', in Drudy, ed. *Irish in America*, 13; figures after 1930 are for Éire only. Measuring the ethnic group as first- and second-generation is fairly straightforward; beyond that, Americans often have multiple ethnic affiliations, though many continue to state a single preference, e.g. 'Irish-American' or 'Italian-American'. There are no agreed-upon criteria for inclusion or exclusion beyond the second generation.

7. Blessing, 'Irish Emigration to the United States', 21–4. The regional designations are those of the US Bureau of the Census, with the 'Central' region corresponding to the Midwest.

8. Blessing, 'Irish', 530–1; Blessing, 'Irish Emigration to the United States', 21–4; Carl Wittke, *The Irish in America* (1956; New York, 1970), 24.

9. On the period 1850–80 see, for example, Stephan Thernstrom, *Poverty and Progress: Social Mobility in a Nineteenth-Century City* (1964; New York, 1970); Jo Ellen McNergney Vinyard, *The Irish on the Urban Frontier: Nineteenth-Century Detroit, 1850–80* (New York, 1976).

10. David Noel Doyle, 'The Irish and American Labour, 1880–1920', *Saothar: Journal of the Irish Labour History Society*, 1 (1975), 43–4; David Noel Doyle, *Irish-Americans, Native Rights, and National Empires: The Structure, Divisions, and Attitudes of the Catholic Minority in the Decade of Expansion* (New York, 1976), 45–7; Blessing, 'Irish', 531. See note 1 for the definition of the term 'American Irish'.

11. Doyle, 'Irish and American Labour', 43–4.
12. Kerby A. Miller, 'Assimilation and Alienation: Irish Emigrants' Responses to Industrial America, 1871–1921', in Drudy, ed. *Irish in America*, 91–3; Kerby A. Miller, *Emigrants and Exiles: Ireland and the Irish Exodus to North America* (New York, 1985), 495–6, 499.
13. Miller, *Emigrants and Exiles*, 496, 500; Hasia Diner, *Erin's Daughters in America: Irish Immigrant Women in the Nineteenth Century* (Baltimore, MD, 1983), 97–8.
14. Judith Walzer Leavitt, *Typhoid Mary: Captive to the Public's Health* (Boston, 1996).
15. Leavitt, *Typhoid Mary*.
16. Doyle, 'Irish and American Labour', 44 (quote), 46–7.
17. Doyle, 'Irish and American Labour', 46–7.
18. R.F. Foster, *Modern Ireland, 1600–1972* (London, 1988), 437, 438; Ronald H. Bayor and Timothy J. Meagher, eds. *The New York Irish* (Baltimore, MD, 1996), 328.
19. David Montgomery, 'The Irish and the American Labor Movement', in David Noel Doyle and Owen Dudley Edwards, eds. *America and Ireland, 1776–1976: The American Identity and the Irish Connection* (Westport, CT, 1980), 206; Blessing, 'Irish', 538; Doyle, 'Irish and American Labour', 46–8; Dennis Clark, *The Irish in Philadelphia: Ten Generations of Urban Experience* (Philadelphia, PA, 1973), 146.
20. Montgomery, 'Irish and the American Labor Movement', 206; Blessing, 'Irish', 538; Doyle, 'Irish and American Labour', 46–8.
21. Blessing, 'Irish', 538; Janet Nolan, *Ourselves Alone: Women's Emigration from Ireland, 1885–1920* (Lexington, KY, 1989), 84.
22. David M. Emmons, *The Butte Irish: Class and Ethnicity in an American Mining Town, 1875–1925* (Chicago, 1989); David M. Emmons, 'Faction Fights: The Irish Worlds of Butte, Montana, 1875–1917', in Patrick O'Sullivan, ed. *The Irish World Wide. History, Heritage, Identity*. Vol. II. *The Irish in the New Communities* (Leicester, England, 1992).
23. Emmons, *The Butte Irish*; Emmons, 'Faction Fights', 95 (quote).
24. Blessing, 'Irish', 544; Miller, *Emigrants and Exiles*, 503.
25. See Chapter 4.
26. David Brundage, 'In Time of Peace Prepare for War': Key Themes in the Social Thought of New York's Irish Nationalists, 1890–1916', in Bayor and Meagher, eds. *New York Irish*, 321–2; Alan J. Ward, *Ireland and Anglo-American Relations, 1899–1921* (Toronto, 1969), 8–10.
27. Brundage, 'In Time of Peace Prepare for War', 326–30; Miller, *Emigrants and Exiles*, 541; Ward, *Ireland and Anglo-American Relations*, 12–20.
28. Brundage, 'In Time of Peace Prepare for War', 330–3; Miller, *Emigrants and Exiles*, 542; Ward, *Ireland and Anglo-American Relations*, 24–6; Terry Golway, *Irish Rebel: John Devoy and America's Fight for Ireland's Freedom* (New York, 1998), 180.
29. Blessing, 'Irish', 537.
30. Francis M. Carroll, 'America and Irish Political Independence', in Drudy, ed. *Irish in America*, 276–7 (quote 277); Joseph P. O'Grady, *How the Irish Became American* (New York, 1973), 122; Ward, *Ireland and Anglo-American Relations*, 26–8; Golway, *Irish Rebel*, Chapters 13, 14, 15.
31. Carroll, 'America and Irish Political Independence', 277–8.

32. Brundage, 'In Time of Peace Prepare for War', 321, 334; Miller, *Emigrants and Exiles*, 542–3; O'Grady, *How the Irish Became American*, 122; Ward, *Ireland and Anglo-American Relations*, 145–6; Golway, *Irish Rebel*, 219–20, 244–6.

33. John Patrick Buckley, *The New York Irish: Their View of American Foreign Policy, 1914–1921* (New York, 1976), Chapters IV and V; Carroll, 'America and Irish Political Independence', 281–3; Miller, *Emigrants and Exiles*, 543; O'Grady, *How the Irish Became American*, 126–34; Ward, *Ireland and Anglo-American Relations*, 167–83; Charles C. Tansill, *America and the Fight for Irish Freedom, 1866–1922* (New York, 1957), Chapter 7.

34. Jones, 'Scotch-Irish', 907.

35. Ward, *Ireland and Anglo-American Relations*, Chapter 10, 250; Carroll, 'America and Irish Political Independence', 283–4; Buckley, *New York Irish: Their View of Foreign Policy*, Chapter VI; Brundage, 'In Time of Peace Prepare for War', 321; Miller, *Emigrants and Exiles*, 543; Tansill, *America and the Fight for Irish Freedom*, Chapters 9, 10; Golway, *Irish Rebel*, especially Chapters 16, 17.

36. Andrew J. Wilson, *Irish America and the Ulster Conflict, 1968–1995* (Belfast, 1995), 14–15.

37. Andrew M. Greeley, 'The Success and Assimilation of Irish Protestants and Irish Catholics in the United States', *Sociology and Social Research*, 72 (July 1988), 231; Diner, *Erin's Daughters*, 107–8.

38. Richard Stivers, *The Hair of the Dog: Irish Drinking and American Stereotype* (University Park, PA, 1976), 10–11. The study evidently excluded Native Americans.

39. Stivers, *Hair of the Dog*, 125–30, 164–80.

40. Andrew M. Greeley, *The Irish-Americans: The Rise to Money and Power* (New York, 1981), 170–82; Stivers, *Hair of the Dog*.

41. Devoy is quoted in Golway, *Irish Rebel*, 185.

42. Blessing, 'Irish', 544; William V. Shannon, *The American Irish* (New York, 1963), 259–94.

43. Shannon, *American Irish*, 233–58. Quotes from *BUtterfield 8* and on 'pride and grievance' both from Peter Quinn, 'Introduction: An Interpretation of Silences', *Éire-Ireland*, 32 (Spring 1997), 5.

44. Blessing, 'Irish', 544.

45. John Tracy Ellis, *American Catholics and Intellectual Life* (1956; Chicago, 1969), 124. Church and government measures of the number of Catholics frequently differ.

46. Jay P. Dolan, *The American Catholic Experience: A History From Colonial Times to the Present* (Garden City, NY, 1985), 338–9.

47. Andrew M. Greeley, *The Catholic Experience* (New York, 1967), 223; Dolan, *American Catholic Experience*, 342.

48. Greeley, *Catholic Experience*, 224; Dolan, *American Catholic Experience*, 343.

49. Greeley, *Catholic Experience*, 225–6; Dolan, *American Catholic Experience*, 344–5; Ellis, *American Catholics and Intellectual Life*, 141–5.

50. Greeley, *Catholic Experience*, 226–34.

51. Greeley, *Catholic Experience*, 216–34; Alan Brinkley, *Voices of Protest: Huey Long, Father Coughlin, and the Great Depression* (New York, 1982), 130–2, 260.

52. Greeley, *Catholic Experience*, 235–44; Brinkley, *Voices of Protest*, 82–106, 128–33, 258–60, 265–73; Shannon, *American Irish*, 297–320. The 'Protocols of the Elders of

Zion', which claimed to reveal a conspiracy to establish a world Jewish dictatorship, was concocted by the Russian Secret Police in the early twentieth century.

53. Brinkley, *Voices of Protest*, 140–1, 199–200, 206–7, 267–73; Greeley, *Catholic Experience*, 243; John T. McGreevy, 'Thinking on One's Own: Catholicism in the American Intellectual Imagination, 1928–1960', *The Journal of American History*, 84 (June 1997), 110–11; Blessing, 'Irish', 542; John Cogley, *Catholic America* (New York, 1973), 89–90.

54. McGreevy, 'Thinking on One's Own', 97–116. As prominent intellectuals of the 1920s and 1930s whose liberalism included an anti-Catholic component, McGreevy mentions, among others, John Dewey, Walter Lippmann and Howard Mumford Jones.

55. Steven P. Erie, *Rainbow's End: Irish Americans and the Dilemmas of Urban Machine Politics, 1840–1985* (Berkeley, CA, 1988), 19–22.

56. Erie, *Rainbow's End*, 27–8; Thomas O'Connor, *The Boston Irish: A Political History* (Boston, 1995), xi.

57. Erie, *Rainbow's End*, 22, 68–70, 102–6; cf. the description of a day in the life of George Washington Plunkitt, in William L. Riordan, ed. *Plunkitt of Tammany Hall: A Series of Very Plain Talks on Very Practical Politics* (New York, 1995), 90–8.

58. Erie, *Rainbow's End*, 68–87; Blessing, 'Irish', 542.

59. Terry N. Clark, 'The Irish Ethnic Identity and the Spirit of Patronage', *Ethnicity*, 2 (1978) 305–59; Robert K. Merton, 'Latent Functions of the Machine', in Alexander Callow, comp., *American Urban History* (New York, 1969); Edward M. Levine, *The Irish and Irish Politicians: A Study in Social and Cultural Alienation* (South Bend, Indiana, 1966), 155–9.

60. Clark, 'Irish Ethnic Identity and the Spirit of Patronage'; Merton, 'Latent Functions of the Machine'.

61. Clark, 'Irish Ethnic Identity and the Spirit of Patronage'; Merton, 'Latent Functions of the Machine'.

62. Clark, 'Irish Ethnic Identity and the Spirit of Patronage'; Merton, 'Latent Functions of the Machine'.

63. Clark, 'Irish Ethnic Identity and the Spirit of Patronage'; Merton, 'Latent Functions of the Machine'; Erie, *Rainbow's End*, 5–8, 57–64, 87–90, 241–9; Levine, *Irish and Irish Politicians*, 155–9.

64. Clark, 'Irish Ethnic Identity and the Spirit of Patronage'; Merton, 'Latent Functions of the Machine'.

65. Levine, *Irish and Irish Politicians*, 167–85; Clark, 'Irish Ethnic Identity and the Spirit of Patronage'.

66. Erie, *Rainbow's End*, 28, 42, 70, 109–10; Shannon, *American Irish*, 201–32.

67. Shannon, *American Irish*, 205.

68. Shannon, *American Irish*, 207–14.

69. Shannon, *American Irish*, 217.

70. Shannon, *American Irish*, 220–31 (quote 231).

71. Erie, *Rainbow's End*, 105–9, 119–22.

72. Erie, *Rainbow's End*, 109–14.

73. Erie, *Rainbow's End*, 102–38.

74. Shannon, *American Irish*, 160–8; Kenneth T. Jackson, ed. *Encyclopedia of New York City* (New Haven, CT, 1995), 1079.

75. Shannon, *American Irish*, 168–81; Jackson, ed. *Encyclopedia of New York City*, 1079; Blesssing, 'Irish Emigration to the United States', 543.

76. Shannon, *American Irish*, 327–39.

Chapter 6: Irish America Since the Second World War

1. Patrick J. Blessing, 'Irish', in Stephan Thernstrom, ed. *The Harvard Encyclopedia of American Ethnic Groups* (Cambridge, MA, 1980), 528 (figures are for Éire only); Ronald H. Bayor and Timothy J. Meagher, eds. *The New York Irish* (Baltimore, MD, 1996), 420; P.J. Drudy, 'Irish Population Change and Emigration Since Independence', in P.J. Drudy, ed. *The Irish in America: Emigration, Assimilation, Impact* (Cambridge, England, 1985), 76–8.

2. Drudy, 'Irish Population Change', 65–8, 78; Linda Almeida Dowling, '"And They Still Haven't Found What They're Looking For": A Survey of the New Irish in New York City', in Patrick O'Sullivan, ed. *The Irish World Wide. History, Heritage, Identity*. Vol. I. *Patterns of Migration* (Leicester, England, 1992), 197. Ireland lost population in every inter-censal period between 1926 and 1961 except one (1946–51, when the population gain was a modest 5,000). On the 1980s and 1990s, see the final section of this chapter.

3. Bayor and Meagher, eds. *New York Irish*, 421; Mary Corcoran, 'Emigrants, Eirepreneurs, and Opportunists: A Social Profile of Recent Irish Immigration in New York City', in Bayor and Meagher, eds. *New York Irish*, 461–3; Dowling, '"And They Still Haven't Found What They're Looking For"',199–200.

4. Corcoran, 'Emigrants, Eirepreneurs, and Opportunists', 462–3, 475; Dowling, '"And They Still Haven't Found What They're Looking For"', 197–9; figures rounded up to the nearest hundred.

5. Corcoran, 'Emigrants, Eirepreneurs, and Opportunists', 463–8; Dowling, '"And They Still Haven't Found What They're Looking For"', 200–1.

6. *New York Times*, Sunday, 23 March 1997, 'Irish Eyes Turning Homeward As a Country's Moment Comes', by Warren Hoge, Section A, 1, 6; *Austin-American Statesman*, 28 June 1998, A1, A10–12.

7. *New York Times*, Sunday, 23 March 1997, 'Irish Eyes Turning Homeward As a Country's Moment Comes', by Warren Hoge, Section A, 1, 6; *New York Times*, 30 May 1997, 'Election Brings Second Look: Is Irish Economic "Tiger" a Kitten?' by James F. Clarity (*http://www.nytimes.com*, 30 May 1997); *New York Times*, 7 December 1998, 'As Most of Ireland Prospers, the Poor Lament a Deepening Social Chasm', by James F. Clarity (*http://www.nytimes.com*, 7 December 1998).

8. *New York Times*, Sunday, 23 March 1997, 'Irish Eyes Turning Homeward As a Country's Moment Comes', by Warren Hoge, Section A, 1, 6; *USA Today*, 16 March 1999, 'Flourishing Ireland calls its Children Home', by David J. Lynch, 13A.

9. Blessing, 'Irish', 528; Morton D. Winsberg, 'Irish Settlement in the United States, 1850–1980', *Éire-Ireland*, 20 (Spring 1985), 13; Bayor and Meagher, *New York Irish*, 421–2.

10. Winsberg, 'Irish Settlement in the United States', 7, 20.
11. Morton D. Winsberg, 'The Suburbanization of the Irish in Boston, Chicago and New York', *Éire-Ireland*, 21 (Fall 1986), 92; Blessing, 'Irish', 542. On suburbanization more generally, see Kenneth T. Jackson, *Crabgrass Frontier: The Suburbanization of the United States* (New York, 1985).
12. Blessing, 'Irish', 541. According to Blessing, the Irish were outperformed by American males of German, Jewish and English descent.
13. Blessing, 'Irish', 541; Stephan Thernstrom, *The Other Bostonians: Poverty and Progress in the American Metropolis, 1860–1970* (Cambridge, MA, 1973), 138–42.
14. Blessing, 'Irish', 528, 543–5.
15. Blessing, 'Irish', 541.
16. Corcoran, 'Emigrants, *Eirepreneurs*, and Opportunists', 467–75; Dowling, '"And They Still Haven't Found What They're Looking For"', 197, 200. See, also, Ray O'Hanlon, *The New Irish Americans* (Niwot, Colorado, 1998).
17. Corcoran, 'Emigrants, *Eirepreneurs*, and Opportunists', 469–75; Dowling, '"And They Still Haven't Found What They're Looking For"', 200–1.
18. Corcoran, 'Emigrants, *Eirepreneurs*, and Opportunists', 473; Dowling, '"And They Still Haven't Found What They're Looking For"', 200–1.
19. Corcoran, 'Emigrants, *Eirepreneurs*, and Opportunists', 475; Dowling, '"And They Still Haven't Found What They're Looking For"', 204.
20. Corcoran, 'Emigrants, *Eirepreneurs*, and Opportunists', 478.
21. Blessing, 'Irish', 541; Marvin K. Opler and Jerome L. Singer, 'Ethnic Differences in Behavior and Psychopathology: Italian and Irish', *International Journal of Social Psychiatry*, 2 (Summer 1956), 11–23; Marvin K. Opler, 'Cultural Differences in Mental Disorders: An Italian and Irish Contrast in the Schizophrenias', in Marvin K. Opler, ed. *Culture and Mental Health: Cross-Cultural Studies* (New York, 1959); Richard Stivers, *The Hair of the Dog: Irish Drinking and American Stereotype* (University Park, PA, 1976).
22. Charles Fanning, 'The Heart's Speech No Longer Stifled: New York Irish Writing Since the 1960s', in Bayor and Meagher, eds. *New York Irish*, 509–10; Blessing, 'Irish', 544.
23. Donald H. Akenson, 'An Agnostic View of the Historiography of the Irish Americans', *Labour/Le Travail*, 14 (Fall 1984), 123–59; Donald H. Akenson, 'Data: What is Known About the Irish in North America', in Oliver MacDonagh and William F. Mandle, eds. *Ireland and Irish-Australia: Studies in Cultural and Political History* (London, 1986); Donald H. Akenson, 'The Historiography of the Irish in the United States of America', in Patrick O'Sullivan, ed. *The Irish World Wide. History, Heritage, Identity*. Vol. II. *The Irish in the New Communities* (Leicester, England, 1992).
24. Akenson, 'Historiography of the Irish in the United States of America', 121; Andrew M. Greeley, 'The Success and Assimilation of Irish Protestants and Irish Catholics in the United States', *Sociology and Social Research*, 72 (July 1988), 229–36 ('affluent' quote, 231); Andrew M. Greeley, 'The American Irish: A Report from Great Ireland', *International Journal of Comparative Sociology*, XX (March–June 1979), 67–70; Andrew M. Greeley, *The Irish-Americans: The Rise to Money and Power* (New

York, 1981), 1–9, 111–20; Blessing, 'Irish', 542. The NORC poll, it should be noted, surveyed only 15,238 people, though Greeley extrapolates its findings freely to the Irish-American populations as a whole, both Catholic and Protestant. Nor does Greeley explain how he arrived at his figures and findings for Catholics and Protestants for earlier periods in the twentieth century. Finally, Greeley does not appear be taking account of the economic success of Asian Americans here; his statement should almost certainly read 'the most successful Caucasian Gentile group'.

25. Kenneth Jackson, ed. *The Encyclopedia of New York City* (New Haven, CT, 1995), 279, 860, 1101–2; John Cogley, *Catholic America* (New York, 1973), 222–41; Bayor and Meagher, eds. *New York Irish*, 429–30; Joseph P. O'Grady, *How the Irish Became American* (New York, 1973), 143; Blessing, 'Irish', 542.

26. Blessing, 'Irish', 542.

27. John T. McGreevy, 'Thinking on One's Own: Catholicism in the American Intellectual Imagination, 1928–1960', *The Journal of American History*, 84 (June 1997), 97, 117–19. Other intellectuals mentioned by McGreevy whose liberalism included an anti-Catholic element were Talcott Parsons, Sidney Hook and McGeorge Bundy.

28. McGreevy, 'Thinking on One's Own', 125–8 (quote 128); Jay P. Dolan, *The American Catholic Experience: A History From Colonial Times to the Present* (Garden City, NY, 1985), 125; John Tracy Ellis, *American Catholics and Intellectual Life* (1956; Chicago, 1969), 176–7.

29. Dolan, *American Catholic Experience*, 357–8, 381–2, 441–2.

30. Bayor and Meagher, eds. *New York Irish*, 433.

31. Bayor and Meagher, eds. *New York Irish*, 433.

32. Steven P. Erie, *Rainbow's End: Irish Americans and the Dilemmas of Urban Machine Politics, 1840–1985* (Berkeley, CA, 1988), 140–55.

33. Bayor and Meagher, eds. *New York Irish*, 4, 419; Thomas O'Connor, *The Boston Irish: A Political History* (Boston, 1995), xi. In Philadelphia, by contrast, where politics had long been controlled by a Republican rather than a Democratic machine, the Irish never secured control of the city, and the first Catholic mayor was not elected until 1962.

34. Edward M. Levine, *The Irish and Irish Politicians: A Study in Social and Cultural Alienation* (South Bend, Indiana, 1966), 120, 145–6.

35. Len O'Connor, *Clout: Mayor Daley and His City* (Chicago, 1975); Milton L. Rakove, *Don't Make No Waves — Don't Back No Losers: An Insider's Analysis of the Daley Machine* (Bloomington, IL, 1975), 44–5 (quote), 48–60.

36. Rakove, *Don't Make No Waves*, 62–74 (quote 63).

37. Erie, *Rainbow's End*, 151.

38. Erie, *Rainbow's End*, 152–68, 183–92.

39. Erie, *Rainbow's End*, 152–68, 183–92.

40. Terry N. Clark, 'The Irish Ethnic Identity and the Spirit of Patronage', *Ethnicity*, 2 (December 1975), 331.

41. Cogley, *Catholic America*, 113; Blessing, 'Irish', 543; Andrew M. Greeley, *The Catholic Experience* (New York, 1967), 243–4.

42. Blessing, 'Irish', 543; Arthur Schlesinger, Jr., *A Thousand Days: John F. Kennedy in the White House* (Boston, 1965), 12–13.

43. Schlesinger, *Thousand Days*, 6, 9.

44. Theodore White, *The Making of the President, 1960* (New York, 1961), 126–9, 285–9.

45. White, *Making of the President*, 311–14, 468–72; Greeley, *Catholic Experience*, 277–86; Thomas T. McAvoy, *History of the Catholic Church in the United States* (South Bend, Indiana, 1969), 458–9. Quotes from 'Remarks of Senator John F. Kennedy on Church and State, Delivered to the Greater Houston Ministerial Association, Houston, Texas, September 12, 1960', reproduced in White, *Making of the President*, 468–72.

46. On the transition of Irish Americans and other 'white ethnics' from 'Roosevelt Democrats' to 'Reagan Democrats' and Republicans, see Samuel G. Freedman, *The Inheritance: How Three Families and America Moved from Roosevelt to Reagan and Beyond* (New York, 1996).

47. Andrew J. Wilson, *Irish America and the Ulster Conflict, 1968–1995* (Belfast, 1995), 15; Jones, 'Scotch-Irish', 908.

48. Wilson, *Irish America and the Ulster Conflict*, 17–21, 40–1.

49. Jones, 'Scotch-Irish', 908. The concluding comment in this paragraph is based on my experience teaching Irish and Irish-American history to undergraduates in Texas.

50. Wilson, *Irish America and the Ulster Conflict*, 23–31.

51. Wilson, *Irish America and the Ulster Conflict*, 31–7.

52. Wilson, *Irish America and the Ulster Conflict*, 40–2.

53. Wilson, *Irish America and the Ulster Conflict*, 42–3.

54. Wilson, *Irish America and the Ulster Conflict*, 42–8, 70, 98–103.

55. Wilson, *Irish America and the Ulster Conflict*, 85–97, 116–19.

56. Wilson, *Irish America and the Ulster Conflict*, 131–2.

57. Wilson, *Irish America and the Ulster Conflict*, 168–94 (quote 194).

58. Wilson, *Irish America and the Ulster Conflict*, 198–213.

59. Freedman, *The Inheritance*, especially Part Three.

60. Wilson, *Irish America and the Ulster Conflict*, 198–213.

61. Wilson, *Irish America and the Ulster Conflict*, 213–14.

62. Wilson, *Irish America and the Ulster Conflict*, 205–7, 254–6, 260–2, 264–7.

63. Wilson, *Irish America and the Ulster Conflict*, 277–84.

64. Wilson, *Irish America and the Ulster Conflict*, 293–8.

INDEX

◆

Please remember that this is a library book,
and that it belongs only temporarily to each
person who uses it. Be considerate. Do
not write in this, or any, library book.